THE FAMILY

ALSO BY JEFF SHARLET

Killing the Buddha: A Heretic's Bible (with Peter Manseau)

THE FAMILY

The Secret Fundamentalism
at the Heart of American Power

JEFF SHARLET

HARPER

An Imprint of HarperCollins*Publishers*
www.harpercollins.com

HarperCollins books may be purchased for educational, business, or sales promotional use. For information, please write: Special Markets Department, HarperCollins Publishers, 10 East 53rd Street, New York, NY 10022.

FIRST EDITION

Designed by Ellen Cipriano

Library of Congress Cataloging-in-Publication Data is available upon request.

ISBN 978-0-06-055979-3

08 09 10 11 12 WBC/RRD 10 9 8 7 6 5 4 3 2 1

In memory of Nancy Goodlin Sharlet

CONTENTS

THE FAMILY

INTRODUCTION

THE AVANT-GARDE OF
AMERICAN FUNDAMENTALISM

THIS IS HOW THEY pray: a dozen clear-eyed, smooth-skinned "brothers" gather in a huddle, arms crossing arms over shoulders like the weave of a cable, leaning in on one another and swaying like the long grass up the hill from the house they share, a handsome, gray, two-story colonial that smells of new carpet, Pine-Sol, and aftershave. It is decorated with lithographs of foxhunters and pictures of Jesus, and, in the bunk room, a drawing of a "C–4" machine gun given to them by their six-year-old neighbor. The men who live there call the house Ivanwald. At the end of a tree-lined cul-de-sac in Arlington, Virginia, quiet but for the buzz of lawn mowers and kids playing tag in the park across the road, Ivanwald is one house among many, clustered like mushrooms, nearly two dozen households devoted, like these men, to the service of a personal Jesus, a Christ who directs their every action. The men tend every tulip in the cul-de-sac, trim every magnolia, seal every driveway smooth and black as boot leather. Assembled at the dining table or on their lawn or in the hallway or in the bunk room or on the basketball court, they also pray, each man's head bowed in humility and swollen with pride (secretly, he thinks) at being counted among this select corps for Christ, men to whom he will open his heart and whom he will remember when he returns to the world not born-again but remade, no longer an individual but part of the Lord's revolution, his will transformed into a weapon for what the young men call *spiritual war.*

"Jeff," says Bengt, one of the house leaders, "will you lead us in prayer?"

Surely, brother. I have lived with these men for close to a month, not as a Christian—a term they deride as too narrow for the world they are building in Jesus' honor—but as *a follower of Christ,* the phrase they use to emphasize what matters most to their savior. Not faith or kindness but obedience. I don't share their faith, in fact, but this does not concern them; I've obeyed, and that is enough. I have shared the brothers' meals and their work and their games. I've wrestled with them and showered with them and listened to their stories: I know which man resents his father's fortune and which man succumbed to the flesh of a woman not once but twice and which man dances so well he is afraid of being taken for gay. I know what it means to be *a brother,* which is to say I know what it means to be a soldier in the army of God. I have been numbered among them.

"Heavenly Father," I begin. Then, "O Lord," but I worry that doesn't sound intimate enough. I settle on "Dear Jesus." "Dear Jesus, just, please, Jesus, let us fight for Your name."

THIS IS A story about two great spheres of belief, religion and politics, and the ways in which they are bound together by the mythologies of America. America—not the legal entity of the United States but the idea with which Europe clothed a continent that it believed naked and wild—America has been infused with religion since the day in 1630 when the Puritan John Winthrop, preparing to cross the Atlantic to found the Massachusetts Bay Colony, declared the New World the *city upon a hill* spoken of by Jesus in the Gospel of Matthew. Three hundred and fifty-nine years later, Ronald Reagan, during the last days of his presidency, would see in Washington's traffic jams that same vision, like a double exposure: "a tall proud city, built on rocks stronger than oceans, wind-swept, God-blessed." In his farewell address he'd call it a *shining* city upon a hill. This is a story about that imaginary place, so real in the minds of those for whom religion, politics, and the mythologies of America are one singular story, and how that vision has shaped America's projection of power onto the rest of the world.

My "brothers" were members of a very peculiar group of believers, not representative of the majority of Christians but of an avant-garde of the social movement I call *American fundamentalism,* a movement that recasts theology in the language of empire. *Avant-garde* is a term usually reserved for innovators, artists who live strange and dangerous lives and translate their strange and dangerous thoughts into pictures or poetry or fantastical buildings. The term has a political ancestry as well: Lenin used it to describe the elite cadres he believed could spark a revolution. It is in this sense that the men to whom my brothers apprenticed themselves, a seventy-year-old self-described "invisible" network of followers of Christ in government, business, and the military, use the term avant-garde. They call themselves "the Family," or "The Fellowship," and they consider themselves a "core" of men responsible for changing the world. "Hitler, Lenin, and many others understood the power of a small core of people," instructs a document given to an inner circle, explaining the scope, if not the ideological particulars, of the ambition members of this avant-garde are to cultivate.[1] Or, as a former Ivanwald brother who'd used his Ivanwald connections to find a foothold in the insurance industry told my brothers and me during a seminar on "biblical capitalism," "Look at it like this: take a bunch of sticks, light each one of 'em on fire. Separate, they go out. Put 'em together, though, and light the bundle. *Now* you're ready to burn."

Hitler, to the Family, is no more real than Attila the Hun as drafted by business gurus who promise unstoppable "leadership" techniques drawn from history's killers; or for that matter Christ, himself, as rendered in a business best seller called *Jesus, CEO.* The Family's avant-garde is not composed of neo-Nazis, or crypto-Nazis, or fascists by any traditional definition; they are fundamentalists, and in this still-secular age, fundamentalism is a religion of both affluence and revolution.

"Fundamentalist" is itself a relatively recent and much-contested word, coined early in the last century by a conservative Baptist who wanted to clear away the confusion about what Christians, by his lights, were supposed to stand for.[2] What they stood for, in fact, *was* confusing. One of the biggest surprises to be found in "The Funda-mentals," a series of dense pamphlets published between 1910 and 1915, is the argument that evolution is reconcilable with a literal reading of scripture. Much has changed since then; such is the evolu-tion of American fundamentalism. Imagine it traveling a path twisted like that of a Möbius strip, the visual paradox made popular in M. C. Escher's optical illusions, from liberation to authoritarianism. Amer-ican fundamentalism's original sentiments were as radically demo-cratic in theory as they have become repressive in practice, its dream not that of Christian theocracy but of a return to the first century of Christ worship, before there was a thing called Christianity. The "age of miracles," when *church* was no more than a word for the great fellowship—the profound friendship—of believers, when Christ's testament really was new, revelation was unburdened by history, and believers were martyrs or martyrs-to-be, pure and beautiful.

Is fundamentalism too limited a word for such utopian dreams? Lately some scholars prefer "maximalism," a term meant to convey the movement's ambition to conform every aspect of society to God. In contemporary America—from the Cold War to the Iraq War, the period of the current incarnation's ascendancy—that means a cul-ture remade in the image of a Jesus strong but tender, a warrior who hates the carnage he must cause, a man-god ordinary men will follow as he conquers the world in order to conform it to his angry love. These are days of the sword, literally—wealthy members of the movement gift one another with real blades crafted to battle stan-dards, a fad inspired by a Christian best seller called *Wild at Heart: Discovering the Secret of a Man's Soul.* As jargon, then, maximalism isn't bad, but I think fundamentalism still strikes closest to the move-ment's desire for a story that never changes, a story to redeem all that seems random, a rock upon which history can rise.

I offer these explanations not as excuses for the consequences of American fundamentalism, an expansionist ideology of control bet-ter suited to empire than democracy, but to point to the defining tension of a creed that is both fearful and proud even as it proclaims itself joyous and humble. It is a martyr's faith in the hands of the powerful, its cross planted in the blood-soaked soil of manifest destiny. It is the strange and dangerous offspring of two intensely fertile sets of stories, "America" and "Christianity."

Before moving into Ivanwald, I spent several months on the road, researching God in America for an earlier book. My quarry soon became the gods of America: a pantheon. Not Vishnu or Buddha or the Goddess, though they reside here too, but a heaven crowded with the many different Christs believed in by Americans. There's a Jesus in Miami's Cuban churches, for instance, who seems to do nothing but wrestle Castro; a Jesus in Heartland, Kansas, who dances around a fire with witches who also consider themselves Christians; a Jesus in Manhattan who dresses in drag; a baby Jesus in New Mexico who pulls cow tails and heals the lame or simply the sad by giving them earth to eat; a muscle-bound Jesus in South Central L.A. emblazoned across the chest of a man with a gun in his hand; a Jesus in an Orlando megachurch who wants you to own a black Beamer.

So many Jesuses. And yet there has always been a certain order to America's Christs, a certain hierarchy. For centuries, the Christ of power was high church, distant, and well mannered. The austere, severe god of Cotton Mather, the Lord of the Ivy League and country club dinners. But from the beginning another Christ has been vying for control, the ecstatic Christ of the Great Awakeners, Jonathan Edwards and Charles Grandison Finney, the angry farmer god William Jennings Bryan saw crucified on a cross of gold, the sword-tongued, fire-eyed Revelation Jesus of a thousand street-corner ranters. A Christ of absolute devotion, not questions. A volatile, exuberant, American god, almost democratic, almost totalitarian. This wild Christ is not supplanting the old, upper-crust Jesus; rather, the followers of these two visions of the divine are finding common cause. The elite and the populist Jesuses are merging, becoming once again a Christ who thrives not so much as a deity or through a theology as what the historian Perry Miller called in *The New England Mind*, his 1939 classic account of Puritanism, a *mood*.

•   •   •

"You can't put a heart in a box," one of my Ivanwald brothers, a Senate aide named Gannon Sims, told me one night. He was trying to make me understand why political terminology, *left* and *right,* *liberal* and *conservative,* could not contain the movement's vision. We were sitting on Ivanwald's porch, listening to the crickets and watching a silvery moon over the Potomac River wink through the trees. Gannon, former student body president of Baylor University, twisted his class ring. He had blue eyes and blond hair and a voice like an angel born in Texas; he sang in a choir and wrote songs about Jesus and hoped one day to be a senator like the one he worked for, Don Nickles, then the second-ranking Republican. Gannon wanted power. Not for himself but for God. It wasn't up to him; Jesus would use him. "I don't try to explain," he told me. "I just get involved."

Gannon referred to Senator Nickles as a member of the Family, and he dropped names of others he called members with ease: Senator James Inhofe, Republican of Oklahoma, for instance, who'd traveled across Africa on the Family's behalf, insisting that the continent's leaders hear him out about his American Christ before any business could occur, and Representative Joe Pitts, Republican of Pennsylvania, a leader of the anti-abortion movement since the 1970s who often stopped by the Cedars, a Family retreat for political leaders. But such elected officials—means to an end—didn't really impress Gannon because in the end he hoped for, the kingdom of heaven on earth toward which both he and the congressmen in the Family were working wouldn't be a democracy.

"It won't?" I asked.

*"King-*dom," said Gannon.

I remembered something another brother, Pavel, had said. He was Czech. His father had been influential in the former communist regime and the post-Soviet one that followed, but now he was a businessman, which was why, Pavel told me, he had sent him to Ivanwald. "Contacts," he said, shrugging his shoulders. One time we had a visitor, a Venezuelan evangelist, who asked Pavel if he had come to Ivanwald to learn about the American way of life. Pavel smiled. He was very tall, and he had a head shaped like a lightbulb. Alone among the brothers he possessed what might be called a sense of irony. "This is not America," he replied.

But it is.

WHAT FOLLOWS, "AWAKENINGS," begins with my own, at Ivanwald. Not to the exclusive truth of Ivanwald's Christ but to what Charles W. Colson, the Watergate felon who was born again through the Family, called in his memoir, *Born Again*, "a veritable underground of Christ's men all through government." This so-called underground is not a conspiracy. Rather, it's a seventy-year-old movement of elite fundamentalism, bent not on salvation for all but on the cultivation of the powerful, "key men" chosen by God to direct the affairs of the nation. From Ivanwald I traveled backward, to American fundamentalism's forebears: Jonathan Edwards, there at the creation of the First Great Awakening in 1735, and Charles Grandison Finney, who awakened the nation again a century later.

Edwards, remembered mostly for one violent phrase—"We are sinners in the hands of an angry God"—gave to what would eventually become American fundamentalism not its fury but its "heart," a sentimental story shaped and softened ever since by elite believers. Finney, the great revivalist of the Second Great Awakening, provided to the growing evangelical movement the theatrical tools for rallying its masses. Edwards and Finney are ancestors of the two great strands of American fundamentalism, elite and populist. Populist fundamentalism takes as its battleground domestic politics, to be conquered and conformed to the will of God; elite fundamentalism sees its mission as the manipulation of politics in the rest of the world. Both populists and elites call their attempts to control the lives of others "evangelism."

Secular America recognizes radical religion only when it marches into the public square, bellowing its intentions. When Charles Finney built the nation's first megachurch 170 years ago—at Broadway and Worth, in lower Manhattan—he understood that making a spectacle of faith provided a foundation for power. More recently, Jerry Falwell and Pat Robertson translated the tent revivals of old into political networks, moral majorities, and Christian coalitions. But now, even that modernization has become shiny with age. Falwell is dead; Robertson is a farce. The secular media finds itself wondering—as it has periodically ever since the Scopes "monkey" trial of 1925—whether theocratic politics are gone for good from America.

Not likely. From Jonathan Edwards and the Revolutionary War that followed the First Great Awakening to the War on Terror, the theocratic strand has been woven into the American fabric, never quite dominant but always stronger and more enduring than those who imagine religion to be a personal, private affair realize.

Part Two, "Jesus Plus Nothing," brings the elite thread into the twentieth century through the story of the founder of the Family, a Norwegian immigrant named Abraham Vereide, and his successor, Doug Coe. Vereide counseled presidents and kings and was spiritual adviser to more senators and generals than Billy Graham has prayed with in all his days of bowing to power. And yet his story is unknown. He preferred it that way; God, thought Vereide, works through men who stay behind the scenes. In Vereide's day, the Family maintained a formal front organization, International Christian Leadership. In Coe's, it "submerged," following instructions he issued in 1966, an era of challenge to the kind of establishment power Vereide and Coe protected as God-ordained.

Why haven't we seen them and their work? The secular assumption since the Scopes trial has been that such beliefs are obsessions of the fringe. In their populist manifestations—prurient antipornography crusaders, rabid John Birchers, screaming foes of abortion wielding bloody fetuses like weapons—they often are. But there is another thread of American fundamentalism, invisible to secular observers, that ran through the post-Scopes politics of the twentieth century, concerned not so much with individual morality as with "Christian civilization," Washington, D.C., as its shining capital. It is this elite thread, the avant-garde of American fundamentalism, and the ways in which it has shaped the broad faith of a nation and the uneasy politics of empire, that is at the heart of my story.

Part Three, "The Popular Front," carries that story into the present. The current manifestation of fundamentalist power is only—only!—the latest revival of emotions stirred by Jonathan Edwards nearly three hundred years ago, the fear of an angry God, the love of a personal Jesus, and the ecstasy wrought by the Holy Ghost. That trinity of sentiments was bound together then by the belief that to the European conquerors of the New World was given the burden of spreading their light—their power—to all of humanity.

This is not a book about the Bible thumpers portrayed by Hollywood, pinched little hypocrites and broad-browed lunatics, representatives of that subset of American fundamentalism that declares itself a bitter nation within a nation. Rather, it's a story that begins on Ivanwald's suburban lawn, with a group of men gripping each other's shoulders in prayer. It is the story of how they got there, where they are going, and where the movement they joined came from; the story of an American fundamentalism, gentle and militant, conservative and revolutionary, that has been hiding in plain sight all along.

I.

AWAKENINGS

1.

IVANWALD

NOT LONG AFTER SEPTEMBER 11, 2001, a man I'll call Zeke[1] came to New York to survey the ruins of secularism. "To bear witness," he said. He believed Christ had called him.

He wandered the city, sparking up conversations with people he took to be Muslims—"Islamics," he called them—knocking on the doors of mosques by day and sliding past velvet ropes into sweaty clubs by night. He prayed with an imam (to Jesus) and may or may not have gone home with several women. He got as close as possible to Ground Zero, visited it often, talked to street preachers. His throat tingled with dust and ashes. When he slept, his nose bled. He woke one morning on a red pillow.

He went to bars where he sat and listened to the anger of men and women who did not understand, as he did, why they had been stricken. He stared at photographs and paintings of the Towers. The great steel arches on which they'd stood reminded him of Roman temples, and this made him sad. The city was fallen, not just literally but spiritually, as decadent and doomed as an ancient civilization. And yet Zeke wanted and believed he needed to know why New York was what it was, this city so hated by fundamentalists abroad and, he admitted after some wine, by fundamentalists—"Believers," he called them, and himself—at home.

At the time Zeke was living at Ivanwald. His brothers-in-Christ, the youngest eighteen, the oldest in their early thirties, were much like him: educated, athletic, born to affluence, successful or soon to be. Zeke and his brothers were fundamentalists, but not at all the kind I was familiar with. "We're not even Christian," he said. "We just follow Jesus."

I'd known Zeke on and off for twelve years. He's the older brother of a woman I dated in college. Zeke had studied philosophy and history and literature in the United States and in Europe, but he had long wanted to find something . . . better. His life had been a pilgrim's progress, and the path he'd taken a circuitous version of the route every fundamentalist travels: from confusion to clarity, from questions to answers, from a mysterious divine to a Jesus who's so familiar that he's like your best friend. A really good guy about whom Zeke could ask, What would Jesus do? and genuinely find the answer.

His whole life Zeke had been searching for a friend like that, someone whose words meant what they meant and nothing less or more. Zeke himself looks like such a man, tall, lean, and muscular, with a square jaw and wavy, dark blond hair. One of his grandfathers had served in the Eisenhower administration, the other in Kennedy's. His father, the family legend went, had once been considered a possible Republican contender for Congress. But instead of seeking office, his father had retreated to the Rocky Mountains, and Zeke, instead of attaining the social heights his pedigree seemed to predict, had spent his early twenties withdrawing into theological conundrums, until he peered out at a world of temptations like a wounded thing in a cave. He drank too much, fought men and raged at women, disappeared from time to time and came back from wherever he had gone quieter, angrier, sadder.

Then he met Jesus. He had long been a committed Christian, but this encounter was different. This Jesus did not demand orthodoxy. This Jesus gave him permission to stop struggling. So he did, and his pallor left him. He took a job in finance and he met a woman as bright as he was and much happier, and soon he was making money, in love, engaged. But the questions of his youth still bothered him. Again he drank too much, his eye wandered, his temper kindled. So, one day, at the suggestion of an older mentor, he ditched his job, put his fiancée on hold, and moved to Ivanwald, where, he was told, he'd meet yet another Jesus, the true one.

When he came up to New York, his sister asked if I would take him out to dinner. What, she wanted to know, was Zeke caught up in?

We met at a little Moroccan place in the East Village. Zeke arrived in bright white tennis shorts, spotless white sneakers, and white tube socks pulled taut on his calves. His concession to Manhattan style, he said, was his polo shirt, tucked in tight; it was black. He flirted with the waitress and she giggled, he talked to the people at the next table. Women across the room glanced his way; he gave them easy smiles. I'd never seen Zeke so charming. In my mind, I began to prepare a report for his sister: Good news! Jesus has finally turned Zeke around.

He said as much himself. He even apologized for arguments we'd had in the past. He acknowledged that he'd once enjoyed getting a rise out of me by talking about "Jewish bankers." (I was raised a Jew by my father, a Christian by my mother.) That was behind him now, he said. *Religion* was behind him. Ivanwald had cured him of the God problem. I'd love the place, he said. "We take Jesus out of his religious wrapping. We look at Him, at each other, without assumptions. We ask questions, and we answer them together. We become brothers."

I asked if he and his brothers prayed a great deal. No, he said, not much. Did they spend a lot of time in church? None—most churches were too crowded with rules and rituals. Did they study the Bible in great depth? Just a few minutes in the morning. What they did, he said, was work and play games. During the day they raked leaves and cleaned toilets, and during the late afternoon they played sports, all of which prepared them to serve Jesus. The work taught humility, he said, and the sports taught will; both were needed in Jesus' army.

"Wait a minute," I said. "Back up. What leaves? Whose toilets?"

"Politicians," he said. "Congressmen."

"You go to their houses?"

"Sometimes," Zeke answered. "But mostly they come to us."

I was trying to picture it—Trent Lott pulling up in a black Lincoln, a toilet badly in need of a scrub protruding from the trunk. But what Zeke meant was that he and his brothers raked and polished for politicians at a retreat called the Cedars, designed for their spiritual succor.

"Really?" I said. "Like who?"

"I can't really say," Zeke answered.

"Who runs it?"

"Nobody."

"Who pays?"

"People just give money." Then Zeke smiled. Enough questions. "You're better off seeing it for yourself."

"Is there an organization?" I asked.

"No," he said, chuckling at my incomprehension. "Just Jesus."

"So how do you join?"

"You don't," he said. He smiled again, such a broad grin. His teeth were as white as his sneakers. "You're recommended."

ZEKE RECOMMENDED ME to Ivanwald, and because I was curious and had recently quit a job to write a book about American religious communities, I decided to join for a while. I had no thought of investigative reporting; rather, my interest was personal. By the time I got there, I'd lived for short spells with "Cowboy Christians" in Texas, and with "Baba lovers," America's most benign cultists, in South Carolina, and in Kansas with hundreds of naked pagans. I thought Ivanwald would simply be one more bead on my agnostic rosary. I thought of the transformation Ivanwald had worked on Zeke, and I imagined it as a sort of spiritual spa where angry young men smoothed out their anxieties with new-agey masculine bonding. I thought it would be silly but relaxing. I didn't imagine that what I'd find there would lead me into the heart of American fundamentalism, that a spell among Zeke's Believers would propel me into dusty archives and the halls of power for the next several years. I had never thought of myself as a religious seeker, but at Ivanwald I became one. Since then, I've been searching, not for salvation, but for the meaning behind the words, the hints of power, that I found there.

Zeke was gone by the time I arrived. He had returned to finance, a path the brothers approved of, and to his fiancée, whom they did not—she was a graduate student and a free-spirited Scandinavian who loved to party. Jeff Connally, one of the Ivanwald house leaders who picked me up at Union Station in Washington one April evening, told me he thought Zeke might have made the wrong choice. Zeke's fiancée did not obey God. She was, he said, a "Jezebel." Jeff was a small, sharply handsome man with cloudy blue eyes above high cheekbones. When he said "Jezebel," he smiled.

Jeff had come with two other brothers: Gannon Sims, the Baylor grad, and Bengt Carlson, the other house leader, a twenty-four-year-old North Carolinian with spiky brown eyebrows. In the car, after a long silence, he said, "Well, I think you're probably the most misunderstood Ivanwalder ever."

"Yeah?" I said.

"I didn't really know how to explain you to the guys," Bengt went on. "So I just told him we got a new dude, he's from New York, he's a writer, he's Jewish, but he wants to know Jesus. And you know what they said?"

"No," I answered, my fingers curling around the door handle.

"*Bring him on!*" My three new brothers laughed, and Gannon's Volvo eased down tree-lined streets, each smaller and sleepier than the last, until we arrived at the gray colonial that was to be my new home. Bengt showed me my bunk and two drawers in a bureau and a cubbyhole in the bathroom for my toiletries. One by one, a dozen men drifted by in various states of undress, slapping me on the back or the ass or hugging me, calling me "brother." Someone was playing the soundtrack to *Hair*. One man crooned the words to "Fellatio," but then he said he was just kidding, and another switched out *Hair* for Neil Young's "Keep On Rockin' in the Free World." Pavel the Czech winked.

Ready for bed, the men introduced themselves. From Japan there was Yusuke, a management consultant studying Ivanwald in order to replicate it in Tokyo; from Ecuador, a former college soccer star named Raf, a Catholic who was open about his desire for business connections. From Atlanta there was thick-necked Beau and bespectacled Josh, best friends who'd put off their postcollege careers; from Oklahoma, Dave, a tall, redheaded young man with a wide, daffy smile on a head of uncommon proportions. "Our pumpkin on a beanpole," one of the brothers called him, a "gift" to our brotherhood from former representative Steve Largent, who Dave said had arranged with Dave's father for Dave to be sent to Ivanwald to cure him of a mild case of college liberalism.

Before the lights went out after midnight, they came together to pray for me, Jeff Connally's voice just above a whisper, asking God to "break" me. Dave, already broken, mumbled an *amen*.[2]

IVANWALD, WHICH SITS at the end of Twenty-fourth Street North in Arlington, was known only to its residents and to the members and friends of the Family. The Family is in its own words an "invisible" association, though it has always been organized around public men. Senator Sam Brownback (R., Kansas), chair of a weekly, off-the-record meeting of religious right groups called the Values Action Team (VAT), is an active member, as is Representative Joe Pitts (R., Pennsylvania), an avuncular would-be theocrat who chairs the House version of the VAT. Others referred to as members include senators Jim DeMint of South Carolina, chairman of the Senate Steering Committee (the powerful conservative caucus cofounded back in 1974 by another Family associate, the late senator Carl Curtis of Nebraska); Pete Domenici of New Mexico (a Catholic and relatively moderate Republican; it's Domenici's status as one of the Senate's old lions that the Family covets, not his doctrinal purity); Chuck Grassley (R., Iowa); James Inhofe (R., Oklahoma); Tom Coburn (R., Oklahoma); John Thune (R., South Dakota); Mike Enzi (R., Wyoming); and John Ensign, the conservative casino heir elected to the Senate from Nevada, a brightly tanned, hapless figure who uses his Family connections to graft holiness to his gambling-fortune name. "Faith-based Democrats" Bill Nelson of Florida and Mark Pryor of Arkansas, sincere believers drawn rightward by their understanding of Christ's teachings, are members, and Family stalwarts in the House include Representatives Frank Wolf (R., Virginia), Zach Wamp (R., Tennessee), and Mike McIntyre, a North Carolina Democrat who believes that the Ten Commandments are "the fundamental legal code for the laws of the United States" and thus ought to be on display in schools and courthouses.[3]

The Family's historic roll call is even more striking: the late senator Strom Thurmond (R., South Carolina), who produced "confidential" reports on legislation for the Family's leadership, presided for a time over the Family's weekly Senate meeting, and the Dixiecrat senators Herman Talmadge of Georgia and Absalom Willis Robertson of Virginia—Pat Robertson's father—served on the behind-the-scenes board of the organization. In 1974, a Family prayer group of Republican congressmen and former secretary of defense Melvin Laird helped convince President Gerald Ford that Richard Nixon deserved not just Christian forgiveness but also a legal pardon. That same year, Supreme Court Justice William Rehnquist led the Family's first weekly Bible study for federal judges.[4]

"I wish I could say more about it," Ronald Reagan publicly demurred back in 1985, "but it's working precisely because it is private."

"We desire to see a leadership led by God," reads a confidential mission statement. "Leaders of all levels of society who direct projects as they are led by the spirit." Another principle expanded upon is stealthiness; members are instructed to pursue political jujitsu by making use of secular leaders "in the work of advancing His kingdom," and to avoid whenever possible the label *Christian* itself, lest they alert enemies to that advance. Regular prayer groups, or "cells" as they're often called, have met in the Pentagon and at the Department of Defense, and the Family has traditionally fostered strong ties with businessmen in the oil and aerospace industries.

The Family's use of the term "cell" long predates the word's current association with terrorism. Its roots are in the Cold War, when leaders of the Family deliberately emulated the organizing techniques of communism. In 1948, a group of Senate staffers met to discuss ways that the Family's "cell and leadership groups" could recruit elites unwilling to participate in the "mass meeting approach" of populist fundamentalism. Two years later, the Family declared that with democracy inadequate to the fight against godlessness, such cells should function to produce political "atomic energy"; that is, deals and alliances that could not be achieved through the clumsy machinations of legislative debate would instead radiate quietly out of political cells. More recently, Senator Sam Brownback told me that the privacy of Family cells makes them *safe spaces* for men of power—an appropriation of another term borrowed from an enemy, feminism.[5] "In this closer relationship," a document for members reads, "God will give you more insight into your own geographical area and your sphere of influence." One's cell should become "an invisible 'believing group'" out of which "agreements reached in faith and in prayer around the person of Jesus Christ" lead to action that will appear to the world to be unrelated to any centralized organization.

In 1979, the former Nixon aide and Watergate felon Charles W. Colson—born again through the guidance of the Family and the ministry of a CEO of arms manufacturer Raytheon—estimated the Family's strength at 20,000, although the number of dedicated "associates" around the globe is much smaller (around 350 as of 2006). The Family maintains a closely guarded database of associates, members, and "key men," but it issues no cards, collects no official dues. Members are asked not to speak about the group or its activities.[6]

"The Movement," a member of the Family's inner circle once wrote to the group's chief South African operative, "is simply inexplicable to people who are not intimately acquainted with it." The Family's "political" initiatives, he continues, "have always been misunderstood by 'outsiders.' As a result of very bitter experiences, therefore, we have learned never to commit to paper any discussions or negotiations that are taking place. There is no such thing as a 'confidential' memorandum, and leakage always seems to occur. Thus, I would urge you not to put on paper *anything* relating to any of the work that you are doing . . . [unless] you know the recipient well enough to put at the top of the page *'PLEASE DESTROY AFTER READ-ING.'**

"If I told you who has participated and who participates until this day, you would not believe it," the Family's longtime leader, Doug Coe, said in a rare interview in 2001. "You'd say, 'You mean that scoundrel? That despot?'"[7]

A friendly, plainspoken Oregonian with dark, curly hair, a lazy smile, and the broad, thrown-back shoulders of a man who recognizes few superiors, Coe has worked for the Family since 1959 and been "First Brother" since founder Abraham Vereide was "promoted" to heaven in 1969. (Recently, a successor named Dick Foth, a longtime friend to John Ashcroft, assumed some of Coe's duties, but Coe remains the preeminent figure.) Coe denies possessing any authority, but Family members speak of him with a mixture of intimacy and awe. Doug Coe, they say—most people refer to him by his first and last name—is closer to Jesus than perhaps any other man alive, and thus privy to information the rest of us are too spiritually "immature" to understand. For instance, the necessity of secrecy. Doug Coe says it allows the scoundrels and the despots to turn their talents toward the service of Jesus—who, Doug Coe says, prefers power to piety—by shielding their work on His behalf from a hardhearted public, unwilling to believe in their good intentions. In a sermon posted online by a fundamentalist website, Coe compares this method to the mob's. "His Body"—the Body of Christ, that is, by which he means Christendom—"functions invisibly like the mafia. . . . They keep their organization invisible. Everything visible is transitory. Everything invisible is permanent and lasts forever. The more you can make your organization invisible, the more influence it will have."

For that very reason, the Family has operated under many guises, some active, some defunct: National Committee for Christian Leadership, International Christian Leadership, National Leadership

---

*In a fit of pique or stunning stupidity, the recipient immediately responded to inform the Family that he accepted the rebuke and had made multiple copies of it for the other South African operatives as well, one of which survives. James F. Bell to Ross Main, May 19, 1975. Folder 25, Box 254, Box 459, Billy Graham Center Archives. Main to Doug Coe, June 19, 1975. *Ibid.*

Council, the Fellowship Foundation, the International Foundation. The Fellowship Foundation alone has an annual budget of nearly $14 million. The bulk of it, $12 million, goes to "mentoring, counseling, and partnering with friends around the world," but that represents only a fraction of the network's finances. The Family does not pay big salaries; one man receives $121,000, while Doug Coe seems to live on almost nothing (his income fluctuates wildly according to the off-the-books support of "friends"), and none of the fourteen men on the board of directors (among them an oil executive, a defense contractor, and government officials past and present) receives a penny. But within the organization money moves in peculiar ways, "man-to-man" financial support that's off the books, a constant proliferation of new nonprofits big and small that submit to the Family's spiritual authority, money flowing up and down the quiet hierarchy. "I give or loan money to hundreds of people, or have my friends do so," says Coe.[8]

Each group connected to the Family raises funds independently. Ivanwald, for example, was financed in part by an entity called the Wilberforce Foundation. Major evangelical organizations such as Young Life and the Navigators have undertaken the support of Family operatives, and the Family has in turn helped launch Christian conservative powerhouses such as Chuck Colson's Prison Fellowship, a worldwide ministry that has declared "civil war" on secularism, and projects such as Community Bible Study, through which a failing Texas oilman named George W. Bush discovered faith in 1985.

The Family's only publicized gathering is the National Prayer Breakfast, which it established in 1953 and which, with congressional sponsorship, it continues to organize every February at the Washington, D.C., Hilton. Some 3,000 dignitaries, representing scores of nations and corporate interests, pay $425 each to attend. For most, the breakfast is just that, muffins and prayer, but some stay on for days of seminars organized around Christ's messages for particular industries. In years past, the Family organized such events for executives in oil, defense, insurance, and banking. The 2007 event drew, among others, a contingent of aid-hungry defense ministers from

Eastern Europe, Pakistan's famously corrupt Benazir Bhutto, and a Sudanese general linked to genocide in Darfur.

Here's how it can work: Dennis Bakke, former CEO of AES, the largest independent power producer in the world, and a Family insider, took the occasion of the 1997 Prayer Breakfast to invite Ugandan president Yoweri Museveni, the Family's "key man" in Africa, to a private dinner at a mansion, just up the block from the Family's Arlington headquarters. Bakke, the author of a popular business book titled *Joy at Work*, has long preached an ethic of social responsibility inspired by his evangelical faith and his free-market convictions: "I am trying to sell a way of life," he has said. "I am a cultural imperialist." That's a phrase he uses to be provocative; he believes that his Jesus is so universal that everyone wants Him. And, apparently, His business opportunities: Bakke was one of the pioneer thinkers of energy deregulation, the laissez-faire fever dream that culminated in the meltdown of Enron. But there was other, less-noticed fallout, such as the no-bid deal Bakke made with Museveni at the 1997 Prayer Breakfast for a $500-million dam close to the source of the White Nile—in waters considered sacred by Uganda's 2.5-million–strong Busoga minority. AES announced that the Busoga had agreed to "relocate" the spirits of their dead. They weren't the only ones opposed; first environmentalists (Museveni had one American arrested and deported) and then even other foreign investors revolted against a project that seemed like it might actually increase the price of power for the poor. Bakke didn't worry. "We don't go away," he declared. He dispatched a young man named Christian Wright, the son of one of the Prayer Breakfast's organizers, to be AES's in-country liaison to Museveni; Wright was later accused of authorizing at least $400,000 in bribes. He claimed his signature had been forged.[9]

"I'm sure a lot of people use the Fellowship as a way to network, a way to gain entrée to all sorts of people," says Michael Cromartie, an evangelical Washington think tanker who's critical of the Family's lack of transparency. "And entrée they do get."[10]

The president usually arrives an hour early, meets perhaps ten heads of state—usually from small nations, such as Albania, or

Ecuador, or Benin, that the United States uses as proxies in the United Nations—without publicity, and perhaps a dozen other useful guests chosen by the Family. "It totally circumvents the State Department and the usual vetting within the administration that such a meeting would require," an anonymous government informant told a sympathetic sociologist. "If Doug Coe can get you some face time with the President of the United States, then you will take his call and seek his friendship. That's power."[11]

The president always speaks last, usually to do no more than spread a dull glaze of civil religion over the proceedings. For years, the main address came from Billy Graham, but now it's often delivered by an outsider to Christian conservatism, such as Saudia Arabia's longtime ambassador to the United States, Prince Bandar, or Senator Joe Lieberman, or, as in 2006, Bono. "This is *really* weird," said the rock star.

"Anything can happen," according to an internal planning document, "the Koran could even be read, but JESUS is there! He is infiltrating the world."[12] Too bland most years to merit much press, the breakfast is regarded by the Family as merely a tool in a larger purpose: to recruit the powerful attendees into smaller, more frequent prayer meetings, where they can "meet Jesus man to man."

In the process of introducing powerful men to Jesus, the Family has managed to effect a number of behind-the-scenes acts of diplomacy. In 1978 it helped the Carter administration organize a worldwide call to prayer with Menachem Begin and Anwar Sadat. At the 1994 National Prayer Breakfast, Family leaders persuaded their South African client, the Zulu chief Mangosuthu Buthelezi, to stand down from the possibility of civil war with Nelson Mandela. But such benign acts appear to be the exception to the rule. During the 1960s, the Family forged relationships between the U.S. government and some of the most oppressive regimes in the world, arranging prayer networks in the U.S. Congress for the likes of General Costa e Silva, dictator of Brazil; General Suharto, dictator of Indonesia; and General Park Chung Hee, dictator of South Korea. "The Fellowship's reach into governments around the world," observes David Kuo, a former special assistant to the president in Bush's first term, "is almost impossible to overstate or even grasp."[13]

In 1983, Doug Coe and General John W. Vessey, chairman of the Joint Chiefs of Staff, informed the civilian ambassadors of the Central American nations that the Prayer Breakfast would be used to arrange "private sessions" for their generals with "responsible leaders" in the United States; the invitations would be sent from Republican senators Richard Lugar and Mark Hatfield, and Dixiecrat John Stennis, the Mississippi segregationist after whom an aircraft carrier is now named. The Family went on to build friendships between the Reagan administration and the Salvadoran general Carlos Eugenios Vides Casanova, found liable in 2002 by a Florida jury for the torture of thousands, and the Honduran general Gustavo Alvarez Martinez, who before his assassination was linked to both the CIA and death squads. El Salvador became one of the bloodiest battlegrounds of the Cold War; U.S. military aid to Honduras jumped from $4 million per year to $79 million.[14] In Africa, the Family greased the switch of U.S. patronage from one client state, Ethiopia, to another that they felt was more promising: Somalia. "We work with power where we can," Doug Coe explains, "build new power where we can't." Former secretary of state James Baker, a longtime participant in a prayer cell facilitated by Coe, recalls that when he visited Albania after the collapse of Eastern European communism, the Balkan nation's foreign minister met him on the tarmac with the words, "I greet you in the name of Doug Coe."[15]

Coe's status within Washington has been quantitatively calculated by D. Michael Lindsay, a Rice University sociologist who traded on his past work with evangelicals as a pollster—and his sympathetic perspective—to win interviews with 360 evangelical elites. "One in three mentioned Coe or the Fellowship as an important influence," he reports. "Indeed, there is no other organization like the Fellowship, especially among religious groups, in terms of its access or clout among the country's leadership."[16] At the 1990 National Prayer Breakfast, President George H. W. Bush praised Doug Coe for what he described as "quiet diplomacy, I wouldn't say secret diplomacy."

Bush was apparently ignorant of one of the nation's oldest laws, the Logan Act, which forbids private citizens to do just that lest foreign policy slip out of democratic control. Sometimes Coe's role *is* formal; in 2000, he met with Pakistan's top economic officials as a "special envoy" of Representative Joe Pitts, a key power broker for the region, and when he and Bush Senior hosted an off-the-record luncheon with Iraq's ambassador to the United States in the mid-1980s, he may also have been acting in some official capacity. Mostly, however, he travels around the world as a private citizen. He has prayed with dictators, golfed with presidents, and wrestled with an island king in the Pacific. He has visited nearly every world capital, often with congressmen at his side, "making friends" and inviting them back to the Cedars, the Family's headquarters, bought in 1978 with $1.5 million donated by (among others) Tom Phillips, then the CEO of arms manufacturer Raytheon, several oil executives, and Clement Stone, the man who financed the campaign to insert "under God," into the Pledge of Allegiance.[17]

Coe, who while I was at Ivanwald lived with his wife in an elegantly appointed carriage house on the mansion's grounds, considers the mansion a refuge for the persecuted and the afflicted: Supreme Court Justice Clarence Thomas retreated there when Anita Hill accused him of sexual harassment; Senator David Durenberger, a conservative Catholic, boarded there to escape marital problems that began with rumors of an affair and ended with Durenberger's pleading guilty to misuse of public funds; James Watt, Reagan's anti-environmental secretary of the interior, weathered the controversy surrounding his appointment in one of the Cedars' bedrooms.[18] A waterfall has been carved into the mansion's broad lawn, from which a bronze bald eagle watches over a forested hillside sloping down to the Potomac River. The mansion is white and pillared and surrounded by magnolias, and by red trees that do not so much tower above it as whisper. The Cedars is named for these trees, but Family members speak of it as a person. "The Cedars has a heart for the poor," they like to say.

By *poor* they mean not the thousands of literal poor living in

Washington's ghettos, but rather the poor *in spirit*: the senators, generals, and prime ministers who coast to the end of Twenty-fourth Street in Arlington in black limousines and town cars and hulking SUVs to meet one another, to meet Jesus, to pay homage to the god of the Cedars. There they forge relationships beyond the "din of the vox populi" and "throwaway religion" in favor of the truths of the Family. Declaring God's covenant with the Jews broken, the group's core members call themselves *the new chosen*.[19]

The brothers of Ivanwald were the Family's next generation, its high priests in training. Sometimes the brothers would ask me why I was there. They knew that I was "half Jewish," that I was a writer, and that I was from New York City, which most of them considered to be only slightly less wicked than Baghdad or Paris. I didn't lie to them. I told my brothers that I was there to meet Jesus, and I was: the Jesus of the Family, whose ways are secret. The brothers were certain that He had sent me to them for a reason, and perhaps they were right. What follows is my personal testimony, to the enduring power of this strange American god.

AT IVANWALD, MEN learn to be leaders by loving their leaders. "They're so busy loving us," a brother once explained to me, "but who's loving them?" We were. The brothers each paid four hundred dollars per month for room and board, but we were also the caretakers of the Cedars, cleaning its gutters, mowing its lawns, whacking weeds, blowing leaves, and sanding. And we were called to serve on Tuesday mornings, when the Cedars hosted a regular prayer breakfast typically presided over by Ed Meese. Meese is best remembered for his oddly prurient antiporn crusade as Ronald Reagan's ethically challenged attorney general; less-often recalled is his 1988 resignation following a special prosecutor's investigation of his intervention on behalf of an oil pipeline for Saddam Hussein. He remains a powerful Washington presence, a quick-witted man who presents himself as an old gumshoe, carrying messages back and forth between social and fiscal conservatives. In 2005 and 2006, he shepherded Supreme

Court justices John Roberts and Samuel Alito through their nomination processes; in 2007, he gave the religious Right's stamp of approval to Attorney General Michael Mukasey.[20] Each week at the
Cedars, his breakfast brought together a rotating group of ambassadors,
businessmen, and American politicians. Three of Ivanwald's brothers
also attended.

The morning I was invited, Charlene, the cook, scrambled up
eggs with blue tortillas, Italian sausage, peppers, and papaya. Three
women from Potomac Point, an "Ivanwald for young women" across
the road from the Cedars, came to serve. They wore red lipstick and
long skirts (makeup and "feminine" attire were required on duty)
and had, after several months of cleaning and serving in the Cedars
while the brothers worked outside, grown unimpressed by the high-
powered clientele. "Girls don't sit in on the breakfasts," one of them
told me, though she said that none of them minded because it was
"just politics," and the Bible generally reserves such doings for
men.[21]

The breakfast began with a prayer and a sprinkle of scripture
from Meese, who sat at the head of a long, dark oak table. Matthew
11:27: "No one knows the Son except the Father, and no one knows
the Father except the Son and those to whom the Son chooses to reveal him." That morning's chosen introduced themselves. They were
businessmen from Dallas and Oregon, a Chinese Christian dissident
leader, and two ambassadors, from Benin and Rwanda, who sat side
by side. Rwanda's representative, Dr. Richard Sezibera, was an intense man who refused to eat his eggs and melon. He drank cup after
cup of coffee, and his eyes were bloodshot. A man I didn't recognize,
whom Charlene identified as a former senator, suggested that nego-
tiators from Rwanda and Congo, trapped in a war that had killed
more than 2 million, should stop worrying about who will get the
diamonds and the oil and instead focus on who will get Jesus. "Power
sharing is not going to work unless we change their hearts," he said.

Sezibera stared, incredulous. Meese chuckled and opened his
mouth to speak, but Sezibera interrupted him. "It is not so simple,"
the Rwandan said, his voice flat and low. Meese smiled. Everyone in

the Family loves rebukes, and here was Rwanda rebuking them. The former senator nodded. Meese murmured, "Yes," stroking his maroon leather Bible, and the words "Thank you, Jesus" rippled in whispers around the table as I poured Sezibera another cup of coffee.

The brothers also on occasion sat in quietly on meetings at the Family's four-story, redbrick Washington townhouse, a former convent at 133 C Street SE, run by a Family affiliate called the C Street Foundation. Eight congressmen lived there, paying below-market rents.[22] The C Street House is registered as a church, which allows it to avoid taxes. There's a house mother and a TV the size of a small movie screen, usually tuned to sports, and a prayer calendar in the kitchen that tells residents which "demonic strongholds," such as Buddhism or Hinduism, they are to wage spiritual warfare against each day. Eight Christian college women do most of the serving, but we brothers were on occasion called to stand in for them, the better to find spiritual mentors.

The day I worked at C Street, half a dozen congressmen were trading stories over lunch about the power of prayer to "break through" just about anything: political opposition, personal pride, a dull policy briefing. They spoke of their devotions as if they were running backs moving the ball, chuckling over how prayer flummoxed the "other team." They didn't mean Democrats—a few *were* Democrats—but the godless "enemy," broadly defined. All credit to the coach, said one congressman, who was dabbing his lips with a red napkin that read "Let Me Call You SWEETHEART . . . I Can't Remember Your Name." Later that day, I ran into Doug Coe himself, who was tutoring Todd Tiahrt, a Republican representative from Kansas. Tiahrt is a short shot glass of a man, two parts flawless hair and one part teeth. He wanted to know the best way "for the Christian to win the race with the Muslim." The Muslim, he said, has too many babies, while Americans kill too many of theirs.

Coe agreed that too many Muslim babies could be a problem. But he was more concerned that Tiahrt's focus on labels like *Muslim* and *Christian* might get in the way of the congressman's prayers. "Religion" distracts people from Jesus, Coe said, and allows them to isolate

Christ's will from their work in the world. God's law and our laws should be identical "People separate it out," he warned Tiahrt. " 'Oh, okay, I got religion, that's private.' As if Jesus doesn't know anything about building highways or Social Security. We gotta take Jesus out of the religious wrapping."

"All right, how do we do that?" Tiahrt asked.

"A covenant," Doug Coe answered. The congressman half smiled, as if caught between confessing his ignorance and pretending he knew what Doug Coe was talking about. "Like the Mafia," Coe clarified. "Look at the strength of their bonds." He made a fist and held it before Tiahrt's face. Tiahrt nodded, squinting. "See, for them it's honor," Coe said. "For us, it's Jesus."

Doug Coe listed other men who had changed the world through the strength of the covenants they had forged with their "brothers": "Look at Hitler," he said. "Lenin, Ho Chi Minh, bin Laden." The Family possessed a weapon those leaders lacked: the "total Jesus" of a brotherhood in Christ.

"*That*'s what you get with a covenant," said Doug Coe. "Jesus plus nothing."[23]

THE REGIMEN AT Ivanwald was so precise it was relaxing: no swearing, no drinking, no sex, no self. Watch out for magazines and don't waste time on newspapers and never watch TV. Eat meat, study the Gospels, play basketball; God loves a man who can sink a three-pointer. *Pray to be broken.* "O Heavenly Father. Dear Jesus. Help me be humble. Let me do Your will." Every morning began with a prayer, some days with outsiders—a former Ivanwald brother, now a businessman, or another executive who used tales of high finance to illuminate our lessons from scripture, which he supplemented with xeroxed midrash from *Fortune*—and Fridays with the women of Potomac Point. But most days it was just us boys, bleary-eyed, gulping coffee and sugared cereal as Bengt and Jeff C. laid out lines of Holy Word across the table like strategy.

The dining room had once been a deck, but the boys had walled

it in and roofed it over and unrolled a red Persian carpet, transforming the space into a sort of monastic meeting hall, with two long tables end to end, ringed by a dozen chairs and two benches. The first
day I visited Ivanwald, Bengt cleared a space for me at the head of the
table and sat to my right. Beside him, Wayne slumped in his chair, his
eyes hidden by a cowboy hat. Across from him sat Beau, an Atlantan
with the build and athletic intensity of a wrestler, still wearing the
boxers and T-shirt he'd slept in. Bengt alone looked sharp, his hair
combed, golf shirt tucked tightly into pleated chinos.

Bengt asked Gannon to read our text for that morning, Psalm
139: "O Lord, you have searched me and you know me." The very
first line made Bengt smile; this was, in his view, an awesome thing
for God to have done.

Bengt's manners and naive charm preceded him in every encounter. He was kind to his brothers and excellent with small children,
tall and strong and competent with any tool, deadly whenever he got
hold of the ball—any ball; all sports seemed to Bengt just a step
more challenging than breathing. His eyes were deep and kind of
sad, but he liked to laugh, and when he did he sounded like a friendly
donkey, an Eyore for whom things were suddenly not so bad. When
you told him a story, he'd respond, "*Goll-y!*" just to be nice. When
genuinely surprised, he'd exclaim, "*Good ni-ight!*" Sometimes it was
hard to remember that he was a self-professed revolutionary. He
asked Gannon to keep reading, and then leaned back and listened.

"Where can I go from your Spirit? Where can I flee from your
presence? If I go up to the heavens, you are there; if I make my bed in
the depths, you are there."

Bengt raised a hand. "That's great, dude. Let's talk about that."
The room fell silent as Bengt stared into his Bible, running his finger
up and down the gilded edge of the page. "Guys," he said. "What—
how does that make you feel?"

"Known," said Gannon, almost in a whisper.

Bengt nodded. He was looking for something else, but he didn't
know where it was. "What does it make you think of?"

"Jesus?" said Beau.

Bengt stroked his chin. "Yeah . . . Let me read you a little more." He read in a monotone, accelerating as he went, as if he could persuade us through a sheer heap of words. "For you created my inmost being; you knit me together in my mother's womb," he concluded. His lips curled into a half smile. "Man! I mean, that's intense, right? 'In my mother's womb'—God's right in there with you." He grinned. "It's like," he said, "it's like, you *can't* run. Doesn't matter where you turn, 'cause Jesus is gonna be there, just waiting for you."

Beau's eyes cleared, and Gannon nodded. "Yeah, brother," Bengt said, an eyebrow arched. "Jesus is *smart*. He's gonna get you."

Gannon shook his head. "Oh, he's already got me."

"Me, too," Beau chimed. Then each man clasped his hands into one fist and pressed it against his forehead or his chin and prayed, eyes closed and Jesus all over his skin.

THE SWEETEST WORDS of devotion I heard at Ivanwald came from the one man there who thought Jesus had a message more complicated than "Obey." Riley was the son of a Republican businessman from Wisconsin, but he sounded like a Spaniard who'd learned his English in Sweden. He'd "spent time overseas," he explained, and the accent had just rubbed off. Nobody believed him—he was clearly the most pretentious follower of Jesus since Saul changed his name to Paul and declared himself a Christian—but nobody scorned him for his airs. Riley wore his dirty brown hair long and tied in a braided ponytail, and if it was cool outside he favored a Guatemalan-style poncho. He didn't share the views of the other brothers; in fact, he stayed only long enough to attend a demonstration in Washington against Plan Colombia, a nearly $5-billion military aid package for that country's right-wing regime and U.S. defense contractors that began in 1999.

The Saturday of the demonstration, Riley slipped out before dawn, and I woke up early to attend a three-hour prayer meeting at the Cedars with some elder brethren: a Republican political couple from Oregon, an old stalwart of the movement who had for many years presided over a Family retreat in Bermuda called Willowbank, and John Nakamura, a businessman who that year was volunteering as host of the Cedars. We met in a room appointed with statues of bald eagles and photos of friends of the Family: there was Richard Nixon, scowling over the sofa, and there was Jimmy Carter, the first openly evangelical chief executive, flashing his toothy smile in a frame on the coffee table.[24] We got on our knees and held hands, and together we prayed, some of us rocking, some of us approaching the gift of tongues, Jesus-Jesus-Jesus, praying with Nakamura's guidance for Dick Cheney's ailing heart and for Bush, "who has said he knows the Lord." Roy Cook, one of Doug Coe's oldest friends, prayed for Jesus to "turn the evil" in the hearts of journalists, who "tell stories that go against the work Jesus is doing at the Cedars." Then we began praying about the demonstration Riley was attending. We prayed that the "stratagems of evil and wickedness"—that'd be Riley—would be washed from the streets by God's rain.

That night the brothers had their weekly house meeting. There was serious business. While I'd been praying at the Cedars, Riley had been arrested at the demonstration. Released after several hours, he hunkered down on Ivanwald's floor cross-legged and unraveled a tale of crowds and cops, handcuffs, and what he believed to be gentle heroism. He'd ridden in a police van with an old man, impossibly frail, soaked from the rain. "I asked him if he knew Jesus," Riley said, "and this old man smiled. So I asked him why he had done this thing, let himself be put into jail, and do you know what he said?" The brothers did not. "He said, 'For me it is a form of prayer.'" After the police let Riley go, he took the metro to Arlington and walked to Ivanwald in a driving rain. "At first I was not happy. But then I thought about what that old man said, and the rain began to change, or maybe I did. As I walked home to you brothers, the rain felt like a baptism."

The brothers were quiet. Finally, Jeff C. spoke up from across the room. "Thank you, brother." Murmurs rippled around the circle. Nervous laughter followed. Beau said, "Riley, can we pray for you?" and Riley said yes. Beau then asked Riley if he would lead us in this prayer. He would. So we closed our eyes and prayed with Riley for the old man soaked to the bone and then for the police and for an end to Plan Colombia, at which point the men's prayers sputtered into confusion; wasn't military aid between one God-led government and another a good thing? The brothers were relieved when Riley announced he was going back to Wisconsin. He walked into the pouring rain with his backpack and his sleeping bag. It was a mile and a half to the station. Nobody offered him a ride.

After Riley left, the brothers stood up and started moving furniture. "Okay," Jeff C. said, clapping his hands. "You ready, brothers?" I looked around. My brothers were blank-faced or smirking, clearing a space on the floor. "Jeff," Jeff C. said to me, "Andrew"—the other new man, a balding Australian who said he'd come to Ivanwald at the recommendation of a conservative Australian politician named Bruce Baird—"you guys are going to arm wrestle. Think of it," he said, putting a finger on his chin and mocking a pose of thoughtfulness, "as a test of your manhood."

He instructed us to lie down on our bellies. We lay like snakes facing each other and rose up on torsos, gripping hands, awaiting the signal.

"Fumble!" someone shouted. "Fumble! Fumble!"

I twisted around to find out what they meant, but not in time—all I saw was a blur of T-shirts and legs flying at me, and then the first man hit, slapping me back to the floor and flattening my lungs into empty airbags. Then the second man landed, and the third, and someone shouted, "Get his arms!" Did they think I was a stratagem of wickedness? Had they decided that the evil in my journalist's heart could not be overcome even by Jesus? I swung my one free fist and felt it collide with a stomach that remained unmoved because it was being pressed down by the weight of two, three more men, each of them flailing away at my ribs. I felt my face redden and my ears fill with a roar, and if I'd had any breath left, I would have screamed. But then I heard the brothers laughing, and in between blows I felt hands slapping my ass and ruffling my hair, and I understood what was happening. This was scripture in action, the verses we all memorized together (failure to do so meant sleeping in the cold basement): Ecclesiastes

4:9, "Two are better than one"; Philippians 2:2, "fulfill ye my joy that ye be likeminded, having the same love, being of one accord, of one mind." The brothers were of one mind and thirteen bodies, crushing Christ into me, and there was nothing I could do but to give in to their love. They wanted to welcome me. To brotherhood, to Jesus, to the Family. I gasped. A man near the bottom of the pile on top of me squeaked. "I can't breathe," someone above me whispered. One more man fell on top of us, jumping from the couch onto the tower. The Australian, who'd somehow escaped full fumble, gave it a push. It tumbled, I was free, and Jeff C. offered me his hand. Ecclesiastes 4:10: "If one falls down, his friend can help him up."

"Congratulations, brother," he said. "You're one of us."

A FEW WEEKS into my stay, David Coe, Doug's son, dropped by Ivanwald. My brothers and I assembled in the living room, where David had draped his tall frame over a burgundy leather recliner like a frat boy, one leg hanging over a padded arm.

"You guys," David said, "are here to learn how to rule the world." He was in his late forties, with dark, gray-flecked hair, an olive complexion, teeth like a slab of white marble, dark eyes so big they didn't need to move to take in the room. We sat around him in a rough circle, on couches and chairs, as the afternoon light slanted through the wooden blinds onto a wall adorned with a giant tapestry of the Last Supper. Rafael, a wealthy Ecuadoran, had a hard time with English, and he didn't understand what David had said. He stared, lips parted in puzzlement. David seemed to like that. He stared back, holding Raf's gaze like it was a pretty thing he'd found on the ground. "You have very intense eyes," David said.

"Thank you," Raf mumbled.

"Hey," David said, "let's talk about the Old Testament." His voice was like a river that's smooth on the surface but swirling beneath. "Who"—he paused—"would you say are its good guys?"

"Noah," suggested Ruggi, a shaggy-haired guy from Kentucky with a silver loop on the upper ridge of his right ear.

"Moses," offered Josh, a lean man from Atlanta more interested in serving Jesus than his father's small empire of shower door manufacturing.

"David," Beau volunteered.

"King David," David Coe said. "That's a good one. David. Hey. What would you say made King David a good guy?" He giggled, not from nervousness but from barely containable delight.

"Faith?" Beau said. "His faith was so strong?"

"Yeah." David nodded as if he hadn't heard that before. "Hey, you know what's interesting about King David?" From the blank stares of the others, I could see that they did not. Many didn't even carry a full Bible, preferring a slim volume of New Testament Gospels and Epistles and Old Testament Psalms, respected but seldom read. Others had the whole book, but the gold gilt on the pages of the first two-thirds remained undisturbed. "King David," David Coe went on, "liked to do really, really bad things." He chuckled. "Here's this guy who slept with another man's wife—Bathsheba, right?—and then basically murdered her husband. And this guy is one of our heroes." David shook his head. "I mean, Jiminy Christmas, God likes this guy! What," he said, "is *that* all about?"

"Is it because he tried?" asked Bengt. "He wanted to do the right thing?" Bengt knew the Bible, Old Testament and New, better than any of the others, but he offered his answer with a question mark on the end. Bengt was dutiful in checking his worst sin, his fierce pride, and he frequently turned his certainties into questions.

"That's nice, Bengt," David said. "But it isn't the answer. Anyone else?"

"Because he was chosen," I said. For the first time David looked my way.

"Yes," he said, smiling. "Chosen. Interesting set of rules, isn't it?" He turned to Beau. "Beau, let's say I hear you raped three little girls. And now here you are at Ivanwald. What would I think of you, Beau?"

Beau, given to bellowing Ivanwald's daily call to sports like a bull elephant, shrank into the cushions. "Probably that I'm pretty bad?"

"No, Beau." David's voice was kind. "I wouldn't." He drew Beau back into the circle with a stare that seemed to have its own gravitational pull. Beau nodded, brow furrowed, as if in the presence of something profound. "Because," David continued, "I'm not here to judge you. That's not my job. I'm here for only one thing. Do you know what that is?"

Understanding blossomed in Beau's eyes. "Jesus?" he said. David smiled and winked. "Hey," he said. "Did you guys see *Toy Story?*" Half the room had. "Remember how there was a toy cowboy, Woody? And then the boy who owns Woody gets a new toy, a spaceman? Only the toy spaceman thinks he's real. Thinks he's a real spaceman, and he's got to figure out what he's doing on this strange planet. So what does Woody say to him? He says, 'You're just a toy.'" David sat quietly, waiting for us to absorb this. "Just a toy. We're not really spacemen. We're just toys. Created for God. For His pleasure, nothing else. Just a toy. Period."

He walked to the National Geographic map of the world mounted on the wall. "You guys know about Genghis Khan?" he asked. "Genghis was a man with a vision. He conquered"—David stood on the couch under the map, tracing, with his hand, half the northern hemisphere—"nearly everything. He devastated nearly everything. His enemies? He beheaded them." David swiped a finger across his throat. "Dop, dop, dop, dop."

Genghis Khan's genius, David went on, lay in his understanding that there could be only one king. When Genghis entered a defeated city, he would call in the local headman. Conversion to the Khan's cause was not an option, as Genghis was uninterested in halfhearted deputies. Instead, said David, Genghis would have the man stuffed into a crate, and over the crate's surface would be spread a tablecloth, on which a wonderful meal would be arrayed.

"And then, while the man suffocated, Genghis ate, and he didn't even hear the man's screams." David stood on the couch, a finger in the air. "Do you know what that means?"

To their credit, my brothers did not. Perhaps on account of my earlier insight, David turned to me. "I think so," I said. "Out with the old, in with the new."

Yes, he nodded. "Christ's parable of the wineskins. You can't pour new into old." One day, he continued, some monks from Europe show up in Genghis Khan's court. Genghis welcomes them in the name of God. Says that in truth, they worship the same great Lord. Then why, the monks ask, must he conquer the world? "I don't ask," says Genghis. "I submit."

David returned to his chair. "We elect our leaders," he said. "Jesus elects his."

He reached over and squeezed the arm of Pavel. "Isn't that great?" David said. "That's the way everything in life happens. If you're a person known to be around Jesus, you can go and do anything. And that's who you guys are. When you leave here, you're not only going to know the value of Jesus, you're going to know the people who rule the world. It's about vision. Get your vision straight, then relate. Talk to the people who rule the world, and help *them* obey. Obey Him. If I obey Him myself, I help others do the same. You know why? Because I become a warning. *We* become a warning. We warn everybody that the future king is coming. Not just of this country or that but of the world." Then he pointed at the map, toward the Khan's vast, reclaimable empire.

THAT NIGHT, I slipped out of the house at close to eleven, padded around the pool of light cast by the streetlamp, and began making my way up the grassy hill of the park across the road. I had my cell phone with me, and behind the big oak tree at the top I hoped I could call a friend undetected. David Coe's lesson had been more than I could take without a dose of ordinary conversation, the kind that doesn't involve "warnings" and decapitations. But halfway up the slope a voice shot through the dark and hit me like a hardball: "Halt! Who goes there?"

Ten yards to my right stood Jeff C., lit by a pale yellow full moon.

"Secret orders, man," I said. "Going to have to kill you." The joke was as lame as Jeff C.'s, and neither of us laughed. I walked slowly in his direction, debating whether I should tell him I was out there for meditation or for exercise. Phone calls—contact with the outside world—was allowed but discouraged for new brothers. A late-night run, I decided. Endurance was something the brothers respected, endurance and strength and coordination, honing your body with exercise just as you hone your soul with prayer. Cardiovascular health was especially important if you wanted to have a heart for spiritual war.

But that night, Jeff C. had a heart for contemplation. "Look at the old fort," he said, gesturing down the hill at Ivanwald. "Guys come here and get *changed*. I think of all the guys that have gone through here over the years, and I wonder, How many of 'em come back? How many of 'em end up staying at the mansion?"

Along with Bengt, Jeff C. was a house leader, but if you asked him what he did for a living, he would cock his head, half smile, crinkle his sapphire-blue eyes like a natural-born southern lawyer— which is what his father was—and say, "Well, I work for the revolution." He'd studied rhetoric at Chapel Hill, and he loved making declarations that begged a conversation mainly because he'd laced them with subtle, nagging aggression.

"Maybe you'll come back to the Cedars one day," he said. He squeezed my shoulder. "C'mon, brother," he said, his fingers digging in and guiding me down the hill. "You can make your calls tomorrow."

The next morning, Jeff C. and I were up early, lacing our sneakers for a run down by the river. Sitting on the porch, he asked me why my Bible was a King James. I said I liked the passion of the language. "Yeah," Jeff C. said—he always agreed with everything, at first. Then he looked up from his sneakers as if something had just occurred to him. "You know, I'm not sure it's about passion."

"No?" I said.

"No, I think it's about Jesus."

"Not the Old Testament," I said.

"Well," said Jeff C., "you take Psalms, for example, every one of them, the way to read it is like it's just another piece of Jesus." He stared at me, half smiling, head cocked.

"Which part," I asked, "would you say is in Psalm 137?" Jeff C.'s lip twitched, his eyes shifted. "You know," I said, " 'O Daughter of Babylon'?" He arched his left eyebrow. " 'O Daughter of Babylon,' " I recited, " 'who art to be destroyed, happy shall he be that rewardeth thee as thou hast served us, happy shall he be that taketh and dasheth thy little ones against the stones.' Which part of Jesus is that?"

Jeff C. smiled fully and nodded. "Brother," he said, clapping a hand on my knee. "I'm not sure. But I'm pretty sure He'll let you know when it's time." Then he stood up and ran, waving over his shoulder as he went. He knew he was too fast for me.

WE WERE AT Ivanwald, a Family associate named Terry instructed, to study "the fundamentals, as opposed to the fancy plays," by which he meant "discipline," as opposed to "sissy stuff," an authoritarian faith, not a questioning one. Terry—golf-shirted and twitchy, drumming his fingers on our dining room table—was one of the many middle-aged men in the cul-de-sac who seemed to have no other job than to dispense wisdom. We should pray to be "nothing." We were there to "soften our hearts to authority." Democracy, we were told, was "rebelliousness." We instituted a rule that every man must wipe the toilet bowl after he pisses, not for cleanliness but to crush his "inner rebel."

Jeff C. crushed his by abstaining from "shady" R-rated movies, lest they provoke lusty dreams. He was a beautiful man, but he was indifferent to the effect he had on the opposite sex. The Potomac Point girls brought him cookies; the wives of the Family's older men asked him to visit. One night, when the guys went on a swing-dancing date with the Potomac Pointers, more worldly women flocked to Jeff C., begging to be dipped and twirled. The feeling was not mutual. "I just don't like girls as much as guys," he told me one day while we painted a new coat of "Gettysburg Gray" onto Ivanwald. He was speaking not of sex or of romance but of brotherhood. "I like"—he paused, his brush suspended midstroke—"*competence.*"

He wasn't gay. He wasn't, technically, anything. He was twenty-

five, but he was a virgin. He had kissed a girl once, and the experience had not moved his heart like Jesus did every day. He asked me
once what sex with a woman was like, "emotionally," but before I
could even think of how to answer, he silenced me. Sex for him was
pure and nonexistent in the natural order of things, a myth, elusive
and sweet. Jeff C. didn't need to sully it with details for it to be
true.

He ran nearly every day, often alone, down by the Potomac. On
the basketball court anger sometimes overcame him: "*Shoot* the ball!"
he would snap at Rogelio, a shy eighteen-year-old from Paraguay, one
of several internationals and the youngest brother. But later Jeff C.
would turn his lapse into a lesson, citing scripture, a verse we were
to memorize or else be banished, by Jeff C. himself, to a night in the
basement. Ephesians, chapter 4, verses 26–27: "In your anger do not
sin: Do not let the sun go down while you are still angry, and do not
give the devil a foothold."

Jeff C.'s pride surfaced in unexpected ways. Once, together in
the kitchen after lunch, I mentioned that I'd seen the Reverend Al
Green perform, up in Massachusetts, no less. This bothered Jeff C.
He was a southerner and I was not, and he did not like this news of
Yankee privilege. Also, he was certain I considered him racist, because that's what he believed all New Yorkers thought about all
North Carolinians. He wanted me to know that as a southern white
man, he was blacker than me. "I got an Alabama blacksnake in my
pants," he said. He was not just black, he was a black *man*. "Brother,
you're nothing but a white boy."

"Agreed," I said, hoping to calm him down.

But he could not be soothed. He left the room and returned with
a box and put in a CD and cranked up Al Green. He started to
groove. His hands balled into fists, his blue eyes wide. He began singing, a honey falsetto. "Here I a-a-m . . ." He grabbed his crotch and
shook his head like a rag, wrenched his shirt up and ran his hand over
his hard stomach, going deeper and deeper into Green. Then he
froze, dropped back to his ordinary voice as if he was narrating. "In
college, I used to work in this pizza parlor," he said. "It was a buncha,

I dunno, *junkies*. Heroin." He grinned. "But, man, they *loved* Al Green. We had a poster of him. He was, he was—man! Shirtless, leather pants. *Low* leather pants." Jeff C. tugged his waistband down. "Hips cocked." He slid across the floor and grabbed my waist so tight I could feel his pulse beating. Then he moonwalked away and snapped his knees together with his feet spread wide, hands in the air, testifying, baring his smooth, flat torso.

THE SPIRITUAL BONDS among Family members were, Doug Coe reminded us, expressions of *love,* though he used the term not merely to connote affection. Love in the Family was the love that "conquers," the love that "consumes." It was the love of competition, the love that "breaks a man down"; the love without which one was "a nothing," "a minus," "a zero." But with it one was a "plus," a "warrior," a man. The love, a Family elder once explained to me, that Jesus himself proclaimed when he said, "I came not to bring peace but a sword. For I am come to set a man at variance against his father, and the daughter against her mother." The senior brother who quoted Christ's sword at me did not mean anything so blunt as an actual blade but rather the divisiveness of a faith that scorns earthly affections that come between Jesus and his soldiers. The word *heart* was similarly unmoored in the Family's vocabulary, made weirdly functional, an expression of a quality or skill. A leader, for instance, was said to have a "heart for the Lord"; a man lower down in rank might have a "heart for His Word," a "heart for laborers" (not the working class but missionaries), or, like my brothers and me, the men-in-training, a "heart for spiritual war."

Spiritual war was a struggle to be fought everywhere, at all times. Through witnessing and activism and proselytizing and the passage of laws—or, rather, the "discovery" of laws already written for us by God—and, most of all, through prayer. The brothers prayed after sports and before every meal, over Froot Loops in the morning and steaks at night. At the beginning of each workday, or before we went out on a "date"—chastely accompanying a group of Potomac

Point sisters to a suitable movie, or an evening of swing dancing—we prayed. Our prayers were contradictions: We prayed because God was "awesome," because we were "nothing," and because the only thing we were good for was His praise. But we also prayed because we wanted things, like, say, a BMW, or divine guidance for our leaders, or a sunny day on which to paint the house. "Prayer," Andrew the Australian told me, "is everything you need." A gentle sentiment, at first blush, seemingly uncontroversial. But consider what Andrew did *not* think one needed: *"rights,"* a word I put in quote marks because he did. "Rights," the Family taught, are the product of an arrogant mind—an infringement on God's sovereignty.

The more I learned about the Family, the more difficulty I had in classifying its theology. It is Protestant, to be sure, though there are Catholic members. Its leadership regards with disdain not only the mainline denominations, but also evangelicals they consider "lukewarm." And yet they distance themselves from the bullying of televangelists and moral scolds as well, in part because of theological differences (Jesus, they believe, instructs them to cultivate the powerful regardless of their doctrinal purity) and in part based on style (the Family believes in a subtler evangelism). "They take the same approach to religion that Ronald Reagan took to economics," says a Senate staffer named Neil MacBride, a political liberal with conservative evangelical convictions that put him at odds with the Family's unorthodox fundamentalism. "Reach the elite, and the blessings will trickle down to the underlings."

Based on the almost-ecumenical face it presents at the National Prayer Breakfast—that of a Jesus to whom the Family welcomes non-Christians to pray—the Family might be considered *neo-evangelical.* Neo-evangelicals distance themselves from populist fundamentalism, which they consider a "folk"—read: white trash—religion, given to unseemly displays of emotion and tied too closely to cultural traditions. Whereas populist fundamentalists are strident and hectoring, neo-evangelicals pride themselves on flexibility. Unlike many *premillennialists* who, awaiting Christ's imminent return, merely do their best to stay out of trouble and to keep their eyes shut in prayer, neo-evangelicals are willing to engage the world in the hope that they can neaten things up in time for His arrival. They hew to Calvin's belief that worldly power can help shape a holy community, but they resist any kind of ethics or man-made morality, which they dismiss as *legalism* and consider almost a sin in itself.

But at Ivanwald, or in a prayer cell at the Cedars, or in conversations with world leaders, the Family's beliefs appear closer to a more marginal set of theologies sometimes gathered under the umbrella term of *dominionism,* characterized for me by William Martin, a religious historian at Rice University and Billy Graham's official biographer, as the "intellectual heart of the Christian Right." Dominionist theologies hold the Bible to be a guide to every decision, high and low, from whom God wants you to marry to whether God thinks you should buy a new lawn mower. Unlike neo-evangelicals, who concern themselves chiefly with getting good with Jesus, dominionists want to reconstruct early Christian society, which they believe was ruled by God alone. They view themselves as the new chosen and claim a Christian doctrine of covenantalism, meaning covenants not only between God and humanity but at every level of society, replacing the rule of law and its secular contracts. Since these covenants are signed, as it were, in the Blood of the Lamb, they are written in ink invisible to nonbelievers.

ONE NIGHT I asked Josh Drexler, a brother from Atlanta who was hoping to do mission work overseas, if I could look at some materials the Family had given him. "Man, I'd love to share them with you," he said, and retrieved from his bureau drawer two folders full of documents. While my brothers slept, I sat at the end of Ivanwald's long, oak dining table and copied passages from them into my notebook.

In a document titled "Our Common Agreement as a Core Group," members of the Family are instructed to form a *core group,* or a *cell,* which is defined as "a publicly invisible but privately identifiable group of companions." The cell has "veto rights" over each member's life, and everyone pledges to monitor the others for deviations from Christ's will. A document called "Thoughts on a Core Group" explains that "Communists use cells as their basic structure. The mafia operates like this, and the basic unit of the Marine Corps is the four man squad. Hitler, Lenin, and many others understood the power of a small core of people."

Jesus, continues the document, does not relate to all souls equally. "He had levels of relationships much like concentric rings." The masses were the outermost fringe; next were the hundreds who saw Jesus after he rose from the dead, and then came a ring of seventy, and so on until one reached the "inner circle." "It's quite obvious," the document concludes, "that he revealed more of himself to these." Later, I'd learn that the Family had drawn up blueprints for an underground chapel-cum-bunker beneath the Cedars, its altar designed on this concentric model of access to Christ's love. At its heart would stand Doug Coe, said by the brothers to be as close to Jesus as the disciple John. That's why Coe could walk into any politician's office, went their thinking; Jesus held the doors to power open.

Another document sets forth self-examination questions:

"4. Do I give only verbal assent to the policies of the Family or am I a partner in seeking the mind of the Lord?" The Family is aware that politicians and businessmen use it for strictly worldly ends, but it constantly pushes even its most cynical members toward sincerity. The Family does not ask them to stop seeking power or raking in profits; rather, it wants them to believe that they do so not for their own gain but for God's.

"7. Do I agree with and practice the financial precepts of the Family?" These precepts do not require one to tithe to good works. Rather, the Family's two major financial principles concern appearances. To practice the precepts of the Family, one must declare one's own fortune—great or small—wholly a gift from Jesus. It's not yours, even if it is; you're not really rich, even if you are. This allows Family members to be like Jesus himself by giving freely to other Family members without regard for formality—a process that has the added advantage of being off the books.

"13. Am I willing to work without human recognition?" The Family's commitment to secrecy—they call it privacy—demands a sort of political ascetism that they think of as humility. It is nothing of the sort; the Family renounces public accountability, not power.

Long-term goals are best summarized in a document called "Youth Corps Vision." Another Family project, Youth Corps distributes pleasant brochures featuring endorsements from political leaders—among them Tsutomu Hata, a former prime minister of Japan, former secretary of state James Baker, and Yoweri Museveni, president of Uganda—and full of enthusiastic rhetoric about helping young people to learn the principles of leadership. The name Jesus is never mentioned.

But "Youth Corps Vision," which is intended only for members of the Family ("it's kinda secret," Josh cautioned me), is more direct.

The Vision is to mobilize thousands of young people worldwide— committed to the principles, precepts, and person of Jesus Christ . . .

> A group of highly dedicated *individuals who are united together* having a total commitment to use their lives to daily seek to mature into people who talk like Jesus, act like Jesus, think like Jesus. This group will have the responsibility to:
> —see that the commitment and action is maintained to the overall vision;
> —see that the finest and best invisible organization is developed and maintained at all levels of the work;
> —even though the structure is hidden, see that the Family atmosphere is maintained, so that all people can feel a part of the Family.

Youth Corps, whose programs are often centered around Ivanwald-style houses, prepares the best of its recruits for positions of power in business and government abroad. Its programs are in operation in Russia, Ukraine, Romania, India, Pakistan, Uganda, Nepal, Bhutan, Ecuador, Honduras, Peru, and other countries. The goal: "Two hundred national and international world leaders bound together relationally by a mutual love for God and the family."

FROM TIME TO time, Bengt would walk down to the Cedars or next door to the house of Lee Rooker, a Department of Education official, or hop onto his bike or into his Volkswagen and drive over to—the brothers didn't know where he went, just that he was missing. No one worried. They all knew Bengt was having leadership lessons. Bengt had been tapped to become a future father of the Family. Sometimes, though, he seemed skeptical about his patrimony.

One day not long after I'd arrived, Bengt and I drove into Washington to pick up a new brother at the bus station. I'd spent the day chipping and sanding green paint, and because there'd been no mask most of the time, I was still coughing up paint dust. "You'll get used to it," Bengt said.

"It's fine," I said. "This is what I'm here for."

Bengt laughed. "Paint in your nose?"

"The work," I said. "It's a kind of prayer, right?"

Bengt glanced over at me. "Can be," he said.

I pressed the point. "You do the work every day until it's like praying. Isn't that the idea?"

"It is," Bengt said. "But you have to be careful. Even work can distract you." We stopped at a red light. "Sometimes," Bengt said. "Lately. Lately, I've been feeling like I've been losing the vision. Work is just work. Not because I don't like it. Because I like it so much. I like what I've learned to do. I can let my head fill up with this whole world of details until there's no room for God. I know He's in there, but I'm not paying Him the attention He's due."

"What do you do then? Do you pray?"

"I've had my more nihilistic moments." He paused, and we drove in silence, cruising through downtown D.C.'s deserted nighttime streets. Bengt turned right onto Rhode Island Avenue. "Yeah," he said. "I pray. But sometimes it's like putting pieces together. Trying to get this thing to work like it's supposed to."

"Which is . . . ?"

"I have enjoyed," Bengt said, "in the past anyway, the complete absence of doubt."

We pulled up to the bus depot, a squat, pale brick of a building tucked behind Union Station. We were a few minutes early, and we talked. Bus station hustlers drifted toward the car but kept their distance; addicts who couldn't even stand watched us through cloudy eyes.

"That's what prayer is?" I asked. "Absence?"

Bengt paused. "Yeah, I think it is."

Bengt stared at a fat woman in a red halter top; she was slapping a skinny drunk on the shoulder. When his Redskins cap fell off, he looked as if he might cry.

"You go in," Bengt said. "I'll wait here."

Most of the brothers didn't know it, but Bengt was thinking of going to graduate school. He had chosen a university close enough to commute to from Ivanwald, and a course of study in the classics that would complement his understanding of Jesus and provide him with an advanced degree that could prove useful on a political résumé. Two weeks into my stay, he began working on his application. After dinner every night, he'd disappear into the little office beside his upstairs bunk room to write his essay on the house's one computer. At breakfast Jeff C. would ask him how it was going, and he'd plow his fingers through his hair and sigh. Handing out work assignments for the day, he'd repeat himself needlessly.

One sweltering afternoon, he gave up writing and decided to chop down two magnolia trees in the front yard. All of Ivanwald's neighbors agreed that they were a shady, symmetrical adornment of what, without them, would look like a parking lot, but Bengt couldn't be stopped: the trees had to go. They had to die, and they had to be killed by his hand. With a long-blade Stihl chewing up magnolia, green leather muffs protecting his ears, his eyes hidden by goggles, Bengt relaxed for the first time in days. It took just a few hours to reduce the trees to a stack of five-foot lengths of branch. He put a booted foot on the pile and pressed, listening to the wood crack, and he smiled. "I just love getting a job done," he said.

"Bengt," I said later that night, "I may be able to help with your essay." Bengt looked confused. "Before I came here," I said, "that sort of thing was my job." Bengt smiled, clapped me on the shoulder— he'd just found the tool he needed.

A few days later, he gave me the essay. After I'd done some editing, we sat down in the office one night after dinner to talk it over. The room was barely big enough for the two of us; we sat with our legs crossed in opposite directions so as not to knock knees. "All right, dude," Bengt said. "Lay it on me. I'm ready." He leaned forward to peek at the pages. When he saw the amount of ink I'd added, he guffawed, slapped his knee, frowned, crossed his arms over his chest. "I can take it, boy," he said.

And he could; we marched through the text line by line, dissecting run-ons and shuffling clauses and chain-sawing irrelevant phrases. When we were done with the line-edit, we began moving whole sections, crafting from Bengt's collage of his life a chronological intellectual autobiography. *My formal education has been a progression from confusion and despair to hope,* the essay began. Its story hewed to the familiar fundamentalist arc of lost and found: every man and woman a sinner, fallen but nonetheless redeemed. And yet Bengt's sins were not of the flesh but of the mind. In college he had abandoned his boyhood ambition of becoming a doctor to study philosophy: Nietzsche, Kierkegaard, Hegel. Raised in the faith, he saw his ideas about God crumble before the disciplined rage of the philosophers. "I cut and ran," he told me. To Africa, where by day he worked on ships and in clinics, and by night read Dostoyevsky and the Bible, its darkest and most seductive passages: Lamentations, Job, the Song of Songs. These authors were alike, his essay observed. *They wrote about [suffering] like a companion.*

I looked up. "A double," I said, remembering Dostoyevsky's alter egos.

Bengt nodded. "You know how you can stare at something for a long time and not see it the way it really is? That's what scripture had been to me." Through Dostoyevsky he began to see the Old Testament for what it is: relentless in its horror, its God a fire, a whirlwind, a plague. Even worse is its Man: a rapist, a murderer, a wretched thief, a fool.

"But," said Bengt, "that's not how it ends."

Bengt meant Jesus. I thought of the end of *The Brothers Karamazov*: the saintly Alyosha, leading a pack of boys away from a funeral to feast on pancakes, everyone clapping hands and proclaiming eternal brotherhood. In Africa, Bengt had seen people who were diseased, starving, trapped by war, but who seemed nonetheless to experience joy. Bengt recalled listening to a group of starving men play the drums. "Doubt," he said, "is just a prelude to joy."

I had heard this before from mainstream Christians, but I suspected Bengt meant it differently. A line in Dostoyevsky's *The Possessed* reminded me of him: Shatov, a nationalist, asks Stavrogin, the coldhearted radical whom he had revered, "Wasn't it you who said that even if it was proved to you mathematically that the Truth was outside Christ, you would prefer to remain with Christ outside the Truth?"

"Exactly," Bengt said. In Africa he had seen the trappings of Christianity fall away. All that remained was Christ. "You can't argue with absolute power," Bengt said.

I put the essay down. Bengt nudged it back into my hands. "I want to know what you think of my ending." He had written about a passage from the Gospel of John in which John, with two travelers, encounters Jesus on the road. John hints at Christ's importance, so the two men travel with him. "Then Jesus turns around and asks the two men one question," Bengt had written. " 'What do you want?' he asks." The question, Bengt thought, might mean, "Why are you following me?" or "What is it that you are doing?" But Bengt had decided that what Christ was asking was "What do you desire?"

The word was important to him. "That's what it's about," he said. "*Desire.*" The way he said the word made it sound almost angry. He shifted in his chair. "Think about it: 'What do you desire?' "

"God?"

"Yes."

"That's the answer?" I asked.

"He's the question," was Bengt's retort. Downstairs, most of the men had gone to sleep; from the living room we could hear someone quietly picking a guitar.

"Bengt," I said, "I don't understand."

"You know," he said, "I don't either. That's what I've kind of come to realize. The thing is, I don't need to. I can just trust in the Lord for my directions. He'll tell me what I need to know."

"A voice?" I said, surprised.

"A prayer," he answered. The voice he heard was his own, his prayers, transformed by his inverted theology into revelation. What he wanted was what God wanted.

"Absence?" I said, realizing that what he'd meant by the absence of doubt was the absence of self-awareness, the absence of an understanding of his thoughts as distinct from God's and thus always subject to—doubt. But I did not say this. Instead, I just repeated myself. "Absence," I said, without a question mark.

"Totally, brother."

He half smiled, satisfied with this alchemy of logic by which doubt became the essence of a dogma. God was just what Bengt desired Him to be, even as Bengt was, in the face of God, "nothing." Not for aesthetics alone, I realized, did Bengt and the Family reject the label *Christian*. Their faith and their practice seemed closer to a perverted sort of Buddhism, their Christ everywhere and nowhere at once, His commands phrased as questions, His will as palpable as one's own desires. And what the Family desired, from Abraham Vereide to Doug Coe to Bengt, was power, worldly power, with which Christ's kingdom could be built, cell by cell.

WHENEVER A SUFFICIENTLY large crop of God's soldiers was bunked up at Ivanwald, Doug Coe made a point of stopping by for dinner. The brothers viewed his visit as far more important than that of any senator or prime minister. The night he joined us, he wore a crisply pressed golf shirt and dark slacks, and his skin was well tanned. He brought a guest with him, an Albanian politician whose pale face and ill-fitting gray suit made Doug Coe seem all the more radiant. In his early seventies, Coe could have passed for fifty: His hair was dark, his cheeks taut. His smile was like a lantern.

"He hates the limelight," Gannon had warned me. "It's not about him, it's about Jesus, so he doesn't like people to know who he is." But he knows who you are. When I reintroduced myself that night, he cut me short. "I remember you," he said, and moved on to the next man.

"Where," Coe asked Rogelio, "are you from, in Paraguay?"

"Asunción," he said.

Doug Coe smiled. "I've visited there many times." He chewed for a while. "Asunción. A Latin leader was assassinated there twenty years ago. A Nicaraguan. Does anybody know who it was?"

I waited for someone to speak, but no one did. "Somoza," I said. The dictator overthrown by the Sandinistas.

"Somoza," Coe said, his eyes sweeping back to me. "An interesting man. I liked to visit him. A very bad man, behind his machine guns." He smiled like he was going to laugh, but instead he moved his fork to his mouth. "And yet," he said, a bite poised at the tip of his tongue, "he had a heart for the poor." There was another long silence.

"Do you ever think about prayer?" he asked, but it wasn't a question. Coe was preparing a parable.

There was a man he knew, he said, who didn't really believe in prayer. So Doug Coe made him a bet. If this man would choose something and pray for it every day for forty-five days, he wagered God would make it so. It didn't matter whether the man believed or whether he was a Christian. All that mattered was the fact of prayer. Every day. Forty-five days. He couldn't lose, Coe told the man. If Jesus didn't answer his prayers, Coe would pay him $500.

"What should I pray for?" the man asked.

"What do you think God would like you to pray for?" Doug Coe asked him.

"I don't know," said the man. "How about Africa?"

"Good," said Coe. "Pick a country."

"Uganda," the man said, because it was the only one he could remember.

"Fine," Coe told him. "Every day, for forty-five days, pray for Uganda. 'God, please help Uganda. God, please help Uganda.'"

On the thirty-second day, Coe told us, this man met a woman from Uganda. She worked with orphans. Come visit, she told the man, and so he did, that very weekend. And when he came home, he raised $1 million in donated medicine for the orphans. "So you see," Doug Coe told him, "God answered your prayers. You owe me five hundred dollars."

There was more. After the man had returned to the United States, the president of Uganda called the man at his home and said, "I am making a new government. Will you help me make some decisions?"

"So," Doug Coe told us, "my friend said to the president, 'Why don't you come and pray with me in America? I have a good group of friends—senators, congressmen—who I like to pray with, and they'd like to pray with you.' And that president came to the Cedars, and he met Jesus. And his name is Yoweri Museveni, and he is now the president of all the presidents in Africa. And he is a good friend of the Family."

"That's awesome," Beau said.

Coe had told this story many times before, I'd learn; it now appears recycled in evangelical sermons around the world, a bit of fundamentalist folklore. It's false. Doug's friend was not just an ordinary businessman but a well-connected former Ford administration official named Bob Hunter. He may have made a bet with Coe, but his trip was hardly as casual as Coe suggested; I later found two memos totaling eighteen pages that Hunter had submitted to Coe, "A Trip to East Africa—Fall 1986," and "Re: Organizing the Invisible," detailing his meetings with Ugandan and Kenyan government officials (many of whom he already knew) and the possibility of recruiting each for the Family. Central to Hunter's mission was representing the interests of American political figures—Republican senator Chuck Grassley and Reagan's assistant secretary of state for Africa, Chester A. Crocker, among them—who might influence newly independent Uganda away from Africa's Left.[25] The following year, Museveni met with Ronald Reagan at the White House; he's served as an American proxy ever since. Once heralded as a democratic reformer, Museveni rules Uganda to this day, having suspended term limits, intimidated the press, and installed the kind of corrupt but stable regime Washington prefers in struggling nations.

"Yes," Coe told us, "it's good to have friends. Do you know what a difference a friend can make? A friend you can agree with?" He smiled. "Two or three agree, and they pray? They can do anything. *Agree. Agreement.* What's that mean?" Doug looked at me. "You're a writer. What does that mean?"

I remembered Paul's letter to the Philippians, which we had begun to memorize. *Fulfill ye my joy, that ye be likeminded.*

"Unity," I said. "*Agreement* means unity."

Doug Coe didn't smile. "Yes," he said. "*Total* unity. Two, or three, become one. Do you know," he asked, "that there's another word for that?"

No one spoke.

"It's called a *covenant*. Two, or three, agree? They can do anything. A covenant is . . . powerful. Can you think of anyone who made a covenant with his friends?"

We all knew the answer to this, having heard his name invoked numerous times in this context. Andrew from Australia, sitting beside Coe, cleared his throat: "Hitler."

"Yes," Doug Coe said. "Yes, Hitler made a covenant. The Mafia makes a covenant. It is such a very powerful thing. Two, or three, agree." He took another bite from his plate, planted his fork on its tines. "Well, guys," he said, "I gotta go."

As Doug Coe left, my brothers' hearts were beating hard: for the poor, for a covenant. "Awesome," Bengt said. We stood to clear our dishes.

ON ONE OF my last nights at Ivanwald, the neighborhood boys asked my brothers and me to play flashlight tag. There were six boys, ranging in age from maybe seven to eleven, all junior members of the Family. It was balmy, and the streetlight glittered against the blacktop, and hiding places beckoned from behind trees and in bushes. One of the boys began counting. My brothers, big and small, scattered. I lay flat on a hillside. From there I could track movement in the shadows and smell the mint leaves planted in the garden. A figure approached. I sprang up and ran, down the sidewalk and up through the garden, over a wall that my pursuer, a small boy, could hardly climb. But once he was over, he kept charging. Just as I was about to vanish into the trees, his flashlight caught me. "Jeff-I-see-you, you're It!" the boy cried. I stopped and turned. He kept the beam on me. I heard the slap of his sneakers as he ran across the driveway. "Okay, dude," he whispered. He clicked off the flashlight. Now I could see him. Little Stevie, whose drawing of a machine gun we'd posted in our bunk room. He handed the flashlight to me, spun around, started to run. Then he stopped and looked over his shoulder. "You're It now," he whispered and disappeared into the dark.

2.

EXPERIMENTAL RELIGION

. . . the election will obtain, and the rest will be blinded.

—JONATHAN EDWARDS, "SINNERS IN
THE HANDS OF AN ANGRY GOD"

L ITTLE STEVIE WAS RIGHT: As soon as I left Ivanwald, I became It. That is, I've been chasing the story I first encountered there ever since, trying to fit the religious practice I found in that Arlington cul-de-sac onto a spectrum of belief where it seems to have no place. It was at once as ordinary as a game of golf and stranger than anything I'd seen in years of reporting from the margins of faith. Maybe it was nothing but country club fundamentalism, worth little more attention than Rotary or the Freemasons. But experienced from within, the Family was as perfectly absurd and—granted its own logic—as perfectly rational as the Catholic dirt eaters of Chimayo, New Mexico, who consider the dusty soil in one small spot in the mountains capable of curing any ailment; or Shinji Shumeikai, an international sect of religious aesthetes who believe that by building modernist architectural masterpieces in remote places they're restoring the planet's balance, literally. But such convictions are self-contained, interested mostly in internal purity. Indeed, the more eccentric the religion, the more sharply its followers tend to define themselves against the rest of society.

And yet, despite the Family's theological oddities—its concentric rings of secrecy, its fascination with megalomaniacs from Mao to Hitler, its conviction that being one of God's chosen provides divine diplomatic immunity—it is anything but separate from the world. It so neatly harmonizes with the political shape of worldly things, in fact, that it's nearly indistinguishable from secular conceptions of social order. It's "invisible" not because it's hiding, but because it's not. Dismissed as "civil religion" by observers who know it only by the National Prayer Breakfast's annual broadcast on C-Span, the Family's long-term project of a worldwide government under God is more ambitious than Al Qaeda's dream of a Sunni empire. Had I not stumbled into its heart, I would never have seen it. Since I had, I began to ask basic questions. Was the Family's vision simply a pious veneer on business as usual? Do its networks actually influence the world the rest of us live in? Is it an aberration in American religion, or the result of a long evolution?

This last is a very different question from the one usually asked about radical religion: "What do the believers want?" An understandable concern, but one that obscures the true shape of fundamentalism. Those of us not engaged in "spiritual war" attempt to contain fundamentalism by reducing its ambitions to a program, an agenda: the abolition of abortion, homosexuality, or maybe sex in general. If the fundamentalists ever won, we tell ourselves, we would all be forced to live like Puritans, or worse—the Taliban. Fundamentalism, we conclude, is therefore un-American and doomed to wither on our democratic soil.

But faith, radical or tepid, gentle or authoritarian, is always more complicated and enduring than a caricature. The Family has grown and taken root directly at the center of American democracy, intertwining with the world as it is. "Business as usual" is the Family's business. The elite fundamentalism of the Family doesn't lead us back to Plymouth Rock, much less to the Taliban's Kabul. The Family's faith is not that of a walled-off community but of an empire; not one to come but one that already stretches around the globe, the soft empire of American dollars and, more subtly, American gods. If we want to understand this fundamentalism, we must ask not what it wants to do but what it has done: how it has run parallel to and at times flowed into the main currents of history. We must solve the equation presented by Doug Coe: Jesus plus nothing. $J+0=X$. To solve for X, the role of elite fundamentalism, we'll need to consider our variables: *American Jesuses,* plural, and *nothing. Nothing,* in this equation, stands for a great deal. All that fundamentalism has abandoned, the story it does not tell: the history of where it came from and how it came to live so close to the center of American power.

THE PLAINEST EXPRESSION of the relationship between the theology of Jesus plus nothing and the mundane world of secular democracy may be found in the words of George W. Bush. Bush is not a member of the Family, although his faith was shaped in a Bible study in Midland, Texas, organized by a group the Family started in the late 1970s for the very purpose of bringing influential men into personal relationships with each other and with a particular concept of Jesus. In 1989, Doug Coe, addressing a private gathering of evangelical leaders in Colorado Springs, assured them that Bush Senior—a secular sort whom they'd backed with reservations—was a Family relation, if perhaps a distant one. Moreover, he'd surrounded himself with godly men such as James Baker and Jack Kemp and, yes, even Dan Quayle, all associates of the Family. Most promising of all, said Coe, was Bush Junior, a good influence on his father.[1] Twelve years later the younger Bush ran for president. At a 1999 debate in Des Moines, Iowa, the moderator asked the then-candidate to identify his favorite philosopher. His opponents had already named John Locke and Thomas Jefferson, but Bush said Jesus, because Jesus had changed his heart. A murmur of surprise rippled through the crowd. The moderator asked Bush to say more, implicit in his question the problem of how *heart* reconciles with the traditional province of philosophy, *mind*. Bush answered as if the audience was not in the room. "Well, if they don't know, it's going to be hard to explain."

Pundits scoffed, but Bush's response proved brilliant, a flare in the night for fundamentalist America—the equivalent of Ronald Reagan's

flirty 1980 remark to a convention of the National Religious Broadcast-
ers, "You can't endorse me, but I can endorse you." And Bush's words
meant more than those of Reagan, who seemed merely to promise political favors. Bush avowed a strength of belief that must be felt to be fully
understood, a faith outside the tidy terminology of liberal religion. You
must be in the Word to get this powerful feeling. *Well, if they don't know,
it's going to be hard to explain.* It's beyond rational definitions. It's an idea
that denies ideas, a fixed intellectual position that rejects the primacy of
intellect and the significance of "positions." Jesus plus nothing.

As a statement of philosophy, Bush's first answer—*because He
changed my heart*—insists on timelessness (Jesus in the present tense),
spacelessness (Jesus in Texas, in Des Moines, in Bush's body), and
selflessness, though this last not in the sense of a modesty of spirit that
might lead one to help others, but rather in that of an inward gaze
that is simultaneously narcissistic and blind to the particulars of the
self it sees there, able only to perceive a heart remade by God. There's a
word for this wide-eyed stare: *piety.* We are all familiar with the figures of the pious church lady and the sanctimonious school marm, and
yet such characters fail to embody the meaning of *piety* as it has existed
for hundreds of years in Christianity and took root in America, first
through the Puritans and then, in the fashion in which it lives on today, in the 1730s, in Northampton, Massachusetts, summoned from
the hearts of men, women, and children by the words of Jonathan
Edwards, the author of the Great Awakening.

Edwards's legacy lies not in the Republic built on the Enlightenment ideas of Locke and Jeffersonian skepticism, but in the fact that
more than two centuries later, that nation remains one of the most religious on Earth, much of it devoted to a vision of Christendom that
originated with him. That this vision was at its inception theocratic is
barely worth mentioning; among the elites of Edwards's day, theocracy
was simply the "Calvinist scheme" which their forebears had come to
the New World to pursue. That the United States is, as much as ever, a
Christian nation, is a more controversial claim. "Historians of the
United States," notes George Marsden, Edwards's most perceptive biographer, "have been prone to give much more attention to Benjamin

Franklin than to Edwards as a progenitor of modern America." That oversight explains why most of American history cannot account for the country's ongoing religious fervor. Although American fundamentalism has lately attempted to claim Franklin as a forebear—a collection titled *American Destiny: God's Role in America* trumpets three apparently pious utterances of Franklin's out of context and without mentioning his equal enthusiasm for the sensual life and a Christless deism—the legacy of Franklin's ideas remains staunchly secular. But the nation does not. Christ thrives in America not so much as an idea or a deity as a mood: a feeling, a conviction, a sentimental commitment to manifest destiny on a personal level, with national implications.

When I left Ivanwald, one of the senior men, a former chief counsel to Republican senator Don Nickles, told me I was making a terrible mistake. "You may not be able to come back," he said. He left it unclear whether that would be my choice or the Family's, but I think I know now what he meant. If I left, prematurely in his eyes, I would literally no longer be within the mood. The ideas I'd encountered there might travel with me (as they have, in a manner the Family didn't anticipate), but the mood could not. After I left, I went to the Billy Graham Center Archives at Wheaton College, where the Family had deposited more than 600 boxes of documents, and I sifted through these seventy years of its history in search of explicit theology, an explanation for what I'd encountered. There were snatches of argument, passages of theory, references and allusions which I have since spent several years pursuing. But most of all there was the mood. Oftentimes, in letters to one another, Family men wrote of it as a "spirit" that spread like a disease, a "contagion," they called it. Men would come from around the world to spend time with Doug Coe, or his predecessor, Abraham Vereide, to "catch the spirit of the work." Sometimes they'd talk politics; sometimes they'd make business deals. But more often they simply basked together in the glory of "the work." One did not "learn" anything; one found it in one's own heart.

There is little taste for history among Family members, and the disarray of the 600 boxes it shipped off to the Billy Graham Center suggests that nobody has ever been interested in looking backward. Not to

1935, when the Family began as a businessmen's antilabor alliance in Seattle, and certainly not farther back, to the roots of "the work." Those origins lie not in the New Testament, which is ultimately little more than a fabric from which the Family constructs contemporary realities, but in the dream of a Christian nation, "awakened," as it was by Jonathan Edwards in 1735, by a piety infused with enthusiasm and—an element overlooked by most historians of the Great Awakening—an adoration of power, divine and worldly, the intangible foundation of American empire. The love of power—world-changing power, messianic power—is not an American invention; but our civil religion, the belief that such a love can coexist peacefully with both God and democracy, is.

Biographers of Edwards note the unlikely marriage within his thought of the rigors of John Calvin—who argued that God cares so little for good deeds or bad that he saves whom he will and damns the rest of us—with the revelations of the Enlightenment, Locke's political ideas and the scientific discoveries of Isaac Newton. But Edwards was no mere synthesizer. His preaching and writing helped spark a fire of religiosity that swept the colonies and leaped back across the ocean to the heart of the British Empire. Edwards rationalized religion; set it on a course of wildfire evangelism; and built a web of ideas in which the radicalism of the American Revolution would be entangled with a spiritual authoritarianism, an idea of God that did not so much emphasize *might* rather than *love* as equate the two. Edwards's Jesus was personal, intimate, dedicated, like the Family, to the slow breaking of souls.

Of all insects, no one is more wonderful than the spider, especially with respect to their sagacity and admirable way of working.

—JONATHAN EDWARDS, "OF INSECTS," IN HIS PRIVATE JOURNAL, 1716[2]

EDWARDS'S GENIUS WAS to describe his God not through declaration but through observation. He wrote like a naturalist, of flowers and insects and cloud formations, all of creation bursting with revelation. "And scarce any thing," he confessed, "among all the works of nature, was so sweet to me as thunder and lightning." Edwards "felt God" at the first appearance of a thunderstorm: "I would fix myself in order to view the clouds, and see the lightnings play, and hear the majestic and awful voice of God's thunders."

He was tall and slender, his face long and his features delicate, his skin pale. He spoke in a soft, lovely voice, and he liked to sing aloud during storms, his lyrics the raw form of the prose he would later commit to writing. He began every day at four, because Christ rose early, too, just three days after his crucifixion. Then he prayed, secret prayers. Later, his wife, Sarah, would join him in his study, and they would pray together in that light that rises before the sun, the same blue light one finds at the heart of a flame.

He ate very little. He often studied for a dozen hours or more, time passed "not in perusing or treasuring up the thoughts of others," wrote his nephew, but in wrestling with data from his own congregation, tested against ideas transmitted directly from God. "New Light," the believers at the time called the religion of Jonathan Edwards. As a young man, he studied the *Opticks* of Newton, wrote papers about rainbows and twinkling stars, and took delight in science's discovery that the color of things in this world is not inherent but merely a matter of perception. He loved to look at flowers; he thought often of how they would soon die. Fruit trees proved yet more revealing. "That of so vast and innumerable a multitude of blossoms that appear on a tree, so few come to ripe fruit." So was it, he concluded, with "the mass of mankind."

He wrote of "true religion" as not of outward forms but of inward emotion. He called this quality *affection* and rated it more highly than the thoughts and deeds of great men. He wrote about people with whom powerful men had never concerned themselves.

One such was a woman named Abigail Hutchinson, whose last days Edwards presented as a case study of conversion in the long essay that first brought him trans-Atlantic fame. Edwards had the good fortune to publish *A Faithful Narrative of the Surprising Work of God in the Conversion of Many Hundred Souls* in 1736, just as developments in the technology and economics of publishing were giving rise to that modern genre known as "current events." Lengthy works might be made widely available so quickly that narratives that had once been "history" now became part of an ongoing conversation. He hoped that his careful case study of revival, played out in the microcosm of one sick young woman's ravaged body, would forge out of religion a new natural science. He had experimented on himself toward this end for years, recording day by day, sometimes hour by hour, the most trivial workings of God and Satan within his own mind and body. He monitored what he ate and how it affected his prayers, noted how many hours he slept and whether fatigue served as a good tool with which to break his will. But his experiments, before 1735, remained unreplicated, unverified. The Awakening of Abigail Hutchinson afforded him a guinea pig on whom to test the efficacy of devotion, the science of mind, the subjugation of heart to power.

ABIGAIL HUTCHINSON WAS a sickly, unmarried young woman who worked in a shop. She lived with her parents, people known for intelligence and sobriety, who were neither wealthy nor very poor. Their house was smoky, dark, and cold. They measured time by the sun and the sound of churchbells.

Before her conversion, Abigail was "still, quiet, reserved." She was gentle. There was, Edwards observed—with approval—nothing fanciful about her. She was very thin.

The spark that lit the spiritual fire which was to consume her came not from scripture nor from Edwards's pulpit but from the news of another woman's conversion, a young and popular and no doubt pretty girl, "one of the greatest company-keepers in the whole town," Edwards described her, granted a "new heart" by God, "truly broken and sanctified." The formerly loose woman's popularity grew as the men who once had courted her gathered round to hear the sweet young thing testify. One Monday in the spring of 1735, as the ice on the Connecticut River crackled and boomed and melted back into cold black water, Abigail's brother, a converted man, decided to speak with Abigail about "the necessity of being in good earnest in seeking regenerating grace." Abigail fumed. Why did she need to be told the necessity of being in "good earnest," a quality now attributed to a woman who went walking with men in the dark? Abigail was in good earnest. Why did she not experience the grace—the joy—now said to be visited upon a harlot?

Abigail decided to search for the answer in scripture, starting from page one. She read about Eve, who took the devil's fruit in her mouth; Ham, who looked at his naked father and laughed; Lot's daughters, who raped their father. God ran javelins through those whose love was wrong, incinerated those whose gifts were not worthy, broke infants beneath the hooves of horses ridden by infidels. No one was spared. After three days of reading, Abigail was too terrified to continue. Before, she had listened to the Reverend Edwards's sermons— nearly all variations on a theme, *damnation*, delivered in tones, Harriet Beecher Stowe would later imagine, "calm and tender"—but she had not heard. Now she *saw*: she was wicked, born wicked right from the start, cursed as Eve. She had murmured against God. "Her very flesh," Edwards recorded, "trembled for fear."

She shuddered when she recalled the doctors she'd consulted. Why had she believed her body deserved anything more than what God had given?

What had God given?

Hunger. A craving for food. At the same time an inability to consume. A slow strangling. The war of flesh, of belly, of the throat that closes, of the tongue that feels food's texture, sweet and savory. Suffering was the gift of the divine.

The next day she skipped ahead to Jesus, the New Testament, "to see if she could not find some relief there for her distressed soul." By Saturday, she could no longer read. "Her eyes were so dim," observed Edwards, "that she could not know the letters." She had been pious all her life, but now she knew that her devotions had availed her of nothing in Christ's eyes. She went to her good older brother. The Bible had become like a weapon turned against her, a knife held to her throat. It had revealed her to herself as filthy, defiled by sin; she was nothing, deserved nothing.

The next morning, Sabbath-day, she was too sick to get out of bed. But she needed to hear the Reverend Edwards. No, her family said, and restrained her; so he came to her. Around thirteen hundred people lived in Northampton then, and no man was better known. His grandfather, Solomon Stoddard, had built the congregation to which he ministered, and, in many ways, had built the town. Its residents called him "the pope of the Connecticut Valley." Edwards inherited the mantle, if not the full authority. Whereas Stoddard had memorized his sermons the better to perform them, Edwards gripped the pulpit and read softly, his pale face proof to his congregation of his sincerity. At times, they felt they could almost see through him.

Before the Awakening, he had wasted no time on chatter and had not often visited his flock in their homes. But in 1735, as revival burned through the town, he began making rounds, taking notes, asking questions, and shy Abigail became an object of great fascination to him. He visited her in her home, she visited him in his. Something great was happening in the valley; the fear of God had never been more palpable. Travelers spent a night and left transformed, carrying with them the spores of revival; stories would return to Northampton of spiritual fires lit across New England. In Boston, they called it hysteria; Edwards believed that Northampton's far remove secured it from dangerous ideas. To the west of the mountain lay wilderness. To the east, church steeples scraped the underbelly of clouds like thorns. Before Edwards's ascension to the pulpit, Northampton had reveled in its frontier freedom. It was a tobacco town, the giant green leaves aged until brown and hung like bodies in barns the sides of which opened like gills. Ale was more commonly drunk than water.

And then, revival—compared to its fervor, drunkenness must have seemed dull. God was wilder and more terrifying than the woodlands to the west, and also gentler, like late day winter sun turning the snow fields golden.

Edwards exalted. In revival, the ecstasy of the thunderstorm was wed at last to the theology he had crafted in his years of studying scripture, science, and the work of spiders. Come in, come in, he'd say to the young men and women who knocked on his door. Men would scream and weep on his knee; women's faces would flush, and they'd lay down before him. Such enthusiasm thrilled him, but it also frightened him. He knew about the tricks of the mind and the lies of the heart. Few said as much, but everyone knew: this could be Satan.

Cotton Mather, a rival of Edwards's grandfather, would have frowned and barred his door to the young revivalists. Edwards the pastor surely considered doing the same. But Edwards the scientist consoled, encouraged, and most of all, recorded. Page after page of data: "Some have had such a sense of the displeasure of God, and the great danger they were in of damnation, that they could not sleep at nights," he wrote, "and many have said that when they have laid down, the thoughts of sleeping in such a condition have been frightful to them; they have scarcely been free from terror while asleep, and they have awakened with fear. . . ."

Such was Abigail. A sweet soul who had never before given offense to anyone, she had grown violent of spirit in her despair. Edwards sympathized with her anguish. As a younger man he, too, had often wondered if he could anticipate heaven, his fear greatest when he felt closest, could almost smell the milk and honey. He likened souls such as his and Abigail's, those that paused on the cusp of salvation, to "trees in winter, like seed in the spring suppressed under a hard clod of earth."

This was how she blossomed: After three days of scripture reading and three days of terror, she awoke on a Monday morning before dawn. Her mind felt like a windless pond, clear and flat and still, reflecting the heavens. And then words filled her, language flowing in like water. "The words of the Lord are pure words, health to the soul, and marrow to the bones." And: "It is a pleasant thing for the eyes to behold the sun." A light so bright . . .

Abigail exclaimed to her good older brother, I have seen! As she had suffered in terror for three days, so "she had a repetition of the same discoveries of Christ three mornings together." Each time before dawn. Each dark morning, her frail body cold beneath layers of quilts, the sky blue-black in the window, her skin sallow and wed too closely to the bone, the light came—"brighter and brighter."

Her cheeks, no doubt pale like Edwards's, would have reddened, her eyes, huge in her emaciated skull, opened wide and shone like dark lanterns. She bloomed. She became a visible saint of the Lord. She asked her brother to help her to the homes of unconverted neighbors, that they might, she said, "see and know more of God." He was shining in her glassy eyes. She wanted to go right away! House by house! Now! Now! She wanted to be a warning.

Death became her obsession; Edwards did not discourage her. Together they spoke of her body, its submission to the divine. Her sister tried to feed her. She could swallow nothing. I have been "swallowed by God," she told her minister. He must have shivered; he had often thought of salvation in those very words.

Did Edwards lust for Abigail? He was not an unsensual man. He was a writer of love poems for his wife, Sarah, said to be the most beautiful woman along the Connecticut River, and father of ten children. He'd confessed to running elaborate mathematical problems through his mind to resist temptation. And yet despite the devices with which he meant to defend his purity, the thought of Abigail penetrated his mind. "Once, when she came to me," he wrote, "she was like a little child, and expressed a great desire to be instructed, telling me that she longed very often to come to me for instruction, and wanted to live at my house, that I might tell her what was her duty."

Did Abigail long for more than the pastoral care? She was not so ambitionless as she had once seemed. She wanted, most of all, to be seen, and the more she spoke of dying, rapturously, the more he saw her; indeed, seemed to stare at her, even wrote about her. "I am willing to live, and quite willing to die," she told him, "quite willing to be sick, and quite willing to be well." Anything for God.

She stopped drinking water. Her sister cried; Abigail smiled. "O sister, this is for my good!" Her sister could not understand. "It is best," explained Abigail, "that things should be as God would have them."

Her brother read to her from the Book of Job, pausing as he came upon a passage about worms feeding on a dead body. *No, go on.* "It was sweet to her," Edwards mused, "to think of *her* being in such circumstances."

Her eyes sank into her skull, her nostrils collapsed. Her hair became brittle. For three days she lay dying. Young men and women came to her bed and leaned in close to her dry lips to hear her. "God is my friend!" she'd whisper. Over and over. *God is my friend!*

He had finally made her a woman. "Her flesh," wrote Edwards near the end, "seemed to be dried upon her bones." On Friday noon, June 27, 1735, her "weak clog" of a body submitted to Christ's desire. She was, at last, beautiful in the eyes of God, and of Jonathan Edwards.

YEARS AFTER THE revival, not long before his church purged him in 1750, Edwards wrote a reevaluation of what he had wrought—in essence, an appeal to reason, one that laid the foundation for the hybrid of science and faith that would become the cornerstone of fundamentalism: "As that is called experimental philosophy, which brings opinions and notions to the test of fact," Edwards formulated, "so is that properly called experimental religion"—not in the sense of innovation, but of the science of sainthood—"which brings religious affections and intentions, to the like test."

Such tests were for the most part exercises of the mind. For example, Edwards was fascinated by atomic power. Not nuclear, of course, but what he perceived as the indivisibility of atoms, about which he had learned from Newton. The smallest of particles, he concluded, was also the most powerful, for it alone was possessed of the power of resistance; one could not break it down any further, surely proof of an animating force, a creator.

And then, Edwards surpassed Newton. In 1723, thinking of light and color, perhaps the green leaves of summer—which, Edwards had come to understand, were not really green, had no color at all—he leaped centuries ahead to imagine an indivisible atom divided, the power that binds it broken, an almost incomprehensible reversal of creation. That is, imagined the mind of God as he knew it removed from the green of the leaves, the blue of the sky, our bodies that are not our own. "Deprive the world of light and motion," he wrote, "and the case would stand thus with the world: There would be neither white nor black, neither blue nor brown, bright nor shaded, pellucid nor opaque, no noise or sound, neither heat nor cold, neither fluid nor wet nor dry, hard nor soft, nor solidity, nor extension, nor figure, nor magnitude, nor proportion; nor body, nor spirit. What then is become of the universe? Certainly, it exists nowhere but in the divine mind."

In Boston and London he was judged a genius or a fanatic. In the little towns around Northampton, people thought of him as either a new Moses, leading them to the Promised Land they had long believed the colonies to be, or vulgar Ahab—angry, obsessed, ignorant of the compromises one must make to get along. His own relations among the so-called River Gods of the valley—powerful merchants and more conventional preachers—rebuked him. He would not have survived in his pulpit as long as he did had he not been protected by a cousin, John Stoddard, another grandson of Solomon Stoddard. But whereas Edwards followed his grandfather to the pulpit, Stoddard followed his grandfather's example to power. The wealthiest landowner for miles, he made himself magistrate, representative to the assembly, and colonel of the militia. He was a feudal lord, and Edwards was the high priest of his benefactor's authority.

His religion was radical, available to all classes and even to slaves, an inspiration to the nascent sense of individual liberty that would become the American Revolution, but his politics were warlike and controlling. Empire struck him as an ideal vessel for the Gospel. He preached often against envy, but named as envy only that feeling which filled those of lesser wealth, or lesser land, or lesser status, who determined to band together to wrest power from above. Such less-privileged men gathered in taverns—Northampton had three—and instead of contemplating Christian harmony, conspired in "party spirit" to reshape not their souls but their fields. The wealthiest few of the valley owned at least a quarter of its arable ground.

Sin fermented in such taverns, charged Edwards, listing a catalog of crimes of the spirit that might just as easily come from the mouth of a fundamentalist today. He railed against the common man's propensity toward lawsuits, against young women who carried themselves like men and young men who dressed in an unmanly style. Pornography was another vice that preoccupied him. His downfall began when he rebuked a group of boys—converted Christians, no less—for stealing and reading midwives' manuals and applying their studies with hands-on investigations, the science of groping. The boys got off, so to speak, because they were wealthy, but another story surfaces when we consider that the boys in turn rebuked the reverend. Don't you point fingers, they said; we know where yours have been. Did you hold Abigail's hand as she lay dying?

The spring of Northampton's revival, Edwards spent much time counseling his uncle, Joseph Hawley, who under his nephew's tutelage began to see secrets within himself, and worse—the meaninglessness of self, of "Joseph Hawley." The hand of God dangled him over the pit by a spindly leg as if he was nothing but a spider. An angry God, yes, but what was worse—overlooked by historians who emphasize the wrath of Edwards's sermons—He was also a loving God. "Majesty and meekness joined together," wrote Edwards, ". . . an awful sweetness." Edwards cared little for the Calvinism of his forebears when put next to the vision of God he seemed to most favor, that of a giant mouth awaiting your submission—waiting to swallow you, Edwards would write in his diaries, to make you one with everything. Which is to say—nothing. Only your sense of *being* kept this from happening *now, now*. Not hellfire but the temptations of self—what later generations of evangelicals would rage against as *secular humanism*—birthed Joseph Hawley's despair.

Hawley stopped sleeping. He stayed up at night in the still of his home, "meditating on terror." In March, another man in a similar state slit his own throat, but he was in such a hysteria—a man of such weak character—that he botched the job and survived, blocked from entering hell as well as heaven. Joseph Hawley was not such a fool. He was a seller of guns and tobacco, a man of substance in Northampton.

But his nephew Jonathan revealed to him a deeper reality, in which substance itself became suspect. In May Edwards preached to the congregation as he might have spoken to Hawley in private settings: "You have seen the filthiness of toads . . ." *You,* declared Edwards with great and compelling certainty, are even lower. Next to the souls of the unchosen, even "putrefied flesh" smells sweet to God. Hawley, a man "of more than common understanding," took the lesson. Using what must have been a sharp blade—he also sold knives—he opened beneath his firm chin a bright red smile.

The pious and the melancholy, those who were saved and those were waiting, those who did not care at all—every sort of person came now to Jonathan Edwards, knocking on the pastor's door. *Can I come in? I heard something* . . . He knew what they'd heard. He'd been hearing it from them for days now, each testimony so much like the last that he must have forgotten who was giving voice to the words, man or woman, ancient or child, saying this: *I heard a strange voice in my mind; it seemed so compelling and right (like yours, Reverend Edwards).*

Edwards recorded the data. *Cut your own throat,* the voice without a body whispered into the ears of his flock. *Cut your own throat! Now! Now!*

He did not count the bodies of those who did so.

SALVATION WAS FOR Edwards a science, worthy of careful record keeping. The twin shadows of righteousness and purity—hatred and self-loathing—he dismissed as undeserving of the scrutiny of his amazing mind. Or did he? "Remember," he wrote to himself once, "to act according to Prov. 12:23, 'A prudent man concealeth knowledge.'" He did as much in his *Faithful Narrative,* weaving a web of logic and argument beneath the surface of a story that attracted a popular audience drawn by its portrait of sin and tragic account of redemption. In so doing, Edwards staked out a political position as well as a spiritual one, a subtly elitist conception of knowledge as a property to be possessed in different portions according to a divine hierarchy. The wise man of Christ knows that only to some does God give a calling, the power to draw closer to Him and understand His grand plan.

In 1750, Edwards's congregation purged him. Not for the blood that flowed from his revival, but simply as a result of the power he'd unleashed. To preserve the old Puritan order, Edwards had destroyed it; but he was ill prepared for what the new believers—fiercer in their faith than ever Puritans had been—would build from the ruins, not just in Northampton but across the colonies. Edwards's books enflamed men to burn other books on town commons, his tale of Abigail Hutchinson gave license to women to tear at their dresses on the cobblestoned streets of cities, screaming for contact with a God as intimate as Edwards's story. In Northampton, the believers turned against him not for the pain his religion drew forth but for shying away from the radicalism of the revolution he had inspired.

He went west—to an Indian mission in Stockbridge, a town even closer to the edge of British civilization than Northampton, itself a city considered by proper Bostonians still half-wild. Among the Mahican Indians he pondered the vicissitudes of the mood he had stoked, its brightness and its darkness, its hymnody and its screeching, the new birth it offered and the death's-head that grinned alike on the saved and the damned. He was a man given to the study of oneness. Perhaps he recognized that the heart full of feeling and the calculating mind full of knowing, like the thunder and lightnings he so adored, were simply two expressions of the same phenomenon, an American religion, one so well suited to the brutal demands of the building of a new Jerusalem—conquest; unrestrained capital; the rights of men and women to speak for themselves; and the rights of stronger men to command their submission for the greater cause— that it would still insist, two and a half centuries later, that all the world is a frontier, in dire need of revival, and a new chosen people.

3.

THE REVIVAL MACHINE

T HE MYTH PERSISTS," WROTE the historian Timothy L. Smith
several decades ago, "that revivalism is but a half-breed child of
the Protestant faith, born on the crude frontier, where Christianity
was taken captive by the wilderness."[1] Like all myths, it is almost
true. But the captive taken was wilderness itself, and the captor was
the American religion. Jonathan Edwards—and, later, Charles Grandison Finney—did not so much tame the wilderness of the American
mind as tap its secret power. Nearly a hundred years after Edwards
awakened Northampton, Finney would lead a series of revivals across
the Northeast and Britain that would win for his populist vision of
evangelicalism not the hundreds who were converted under Edwards,
but uncounted multitudes. In what was then the heart of Manhattan
he built the Broadway Tabernacle, the country's first megachurch. It
seated 2,500, and often close to twice that number crowded into the
sanctuary—a pillared theater in the round like a Roman stadium—
for Finney's orchestrations of scripture and sentiment, moralism and
sensation. Crowds fell like wheat before his beautiful, terrifying,
consoling voice. Most receptive to his message were the new little big
men of the nation, the petit bourgeoisie, physicians, inventors, entrepreneurs, self-made men and their wives, wealthier than the old Puritan aristocracy. "Under my preaching," Finney boasted of just one
of his many revivals in the new city of Rochester, "judges and lawyers
and educated men were converted by the scores."[2]

Andrew Jackson, elected in 1828, extended the vote to men

without property. Charles Grandison Finney, whose early career strangely mirrored Jackson's presidency, extended the passionate God of the frontier, the pious morality of hellfire and certainty, to the men and women who would lay the foundations of the Gilded Age. Here we find the origins of evangelicalism as we know it: the marriage of new money and "new life" that would stoke the furnaces of industrial empire. It was a different expression of democracy than Jackson's, but just as potent. And, overlooked by the successive generations of evangelicals and fundamentalists who study Finney's revivals to this day—Billy Graham insists that "no one can read [Finney] without being challenged by his passion for evangelism"[3]—we find also an intimacy, a love of secret feelings that Edwards would have understood and that we can recognize in the blend of masculinity and sentiment, muscle and tender self-regard, that suffuses fundamentalism even now.

ON THE AFTERNOON of October 7, 1821, after yet another church service that left him bored, Charles Grandison Finney decided to settle the question of God. "A splendid pagan of a man," in his grandson's description, he was, at twenty-nine, six-two, thick-chested, could wrestle any challenger to the ground.[4] Women thought him the most elegant dancer in Adams, a farming hamlet on the rough western edge of New York. His sandy hair was thin on top but given to a rakish curl, and his violet eyes were so bright they leap out even from black-and-white photographs, "intense, fixating, electrifying, madly prophetic eyes," wrote the historian Richard Hofstadter, "the most impressive eyes—except perhaps for John C. Calhoun's—in the portrait gallery of nineteenth-century America."[5]

Finney led the Presbyterian church choir, and he enjoyed discussing theology with his pastor, but until that October day in 1821, he'd had little use for and less belief in the Lord. Long set in the pride of his own intellect, he was past the usual age of such inquiries. As a young man he'd hoped to find a way to Yale, but instead he became a schoolteacher and now he was a lawyer, and many people believed that soon he'd be a politician, perhaps a senator one day. If that was to come to pass, he decided, he'd better get his inner life in order. That Sunday in October, he cleared his schedule for Monday and Tuesday and resolved to decide by Wednesday whether he was a man of God.

The truth was that religion had been creeping up on him. As a boy he had witnessed powerful Baptist preaching, the stomping, shouting, Holy Ghost power kind, but as a man he had remained immune to the revivals that swept the region so often that it would later be called the "Burned Over District" for the intensity of its spiritual fires.[6] Then, one day, he bought a Bible. For his law library, he said, and everyone believed him. Finney preferred it that way. He took to shutting his office door, clogging the keyhole with a rag lest anyone peep on him, and praying in whispers. When the Bible had been just one more big book among the tomes of law in his library, he'd read it openly. Now, it became a secret companion.

He had a reputation to uphold; his very name was in Adams the standard of Logic and Reason. "If religion is true," one man demanded of his wife, "why don't you convert Finney? If you Christians can convert Finney, I will believe in religion."

But no one could convert Finney. "I had not much regard for the opinions of others," he'd confessed. As he sought God from Sunday night through Monday and Tuesday, it seemed as if his heart grew harder. "I could not shed a tear; I could not pray." On Tuesday night, terror struck him. He thought he would die. "I knew that if I did, I should sink down to hell." He wanted to scream. He braced himself in bed and waited for dawn.

As soon as light broke, he dressed and hurried to his office, to return to the Bible that taunted him. The town was already awake. He nodded and smiled at farmers and ladies, quickening his pace to avoid unbearable conversation. And then, he froze. Stopped and stood dead still in the middle of the dirt road that was the town's main street. Creaky wagon wheels rolled left and right, their drivers cursing. Women may or may not have spoken to him. *Good day, Mr. Finney. Mr. Finney? Oh, dear. He doesn't hear. Quite unlike him!* Just how

long he stood still, he'd never be able to say. There was only one sentence among his thoughts, but it seemed to come from elsewhere,
spoken in vibrating, terrifying tones that did not correspond to the
seconds and sounds of the material world.

Will. You. Accept. It. Now. Today?

He bolted. Walking fast, smiling at passersby so they wouldn't
notice his distress, a cold, clammy feeling overtaking him. He aimed
himself for a piece of woods over a hill on the north side of the village, but he charted an indirect path, because he did not want anyone
to know where he was going. "I skulked along under the fence, til I
got so far out of sight that no one from the village could see me. I
then penetrated into the woods." He found himself a closet of trees,
fallen timber crisscrossing to create a mossy fort open to the sky. He
crawled in on a damp bed of pine needles and fire-red oak leaves and
knelt. There, he determined, he would *Accept It Now Today*, and if he
did not he would not return to the world. He waited for prayer. For
"relief." But he could find none. When he opened his mouth, he
heard only the rustle of leaves. He squeezed his eyes shut and groaned.
Somewhere close by, a twig snapped. Finney started, opened his
eyes, began to rise, blood flushing his cheeks. Had he been discovered? Openmouthed like a fish flopped down among the trees, the
knees of his lawyer's suit brown with dirt like those of a farmer? Had
they seen his knobby knuckles knitted together like those of a school-
boy? Would they laugh? Would God?

Then Finney broke. He screamed. "What!" he bellowed. What!
His voice lowered and quickened and heaved on a sea of gulping air
and grief and shame. "Such-a-degraded-sinner-as-I-am, on my knees,
confessing my sins to the great and holy God, and ashamed to have
any human being, and a sinner like myself know it, and find me on
my knees endeavoring to make my peace with my offended God!"

He went on for hours, tears streaming, his hands and his faith
brown with the dirt of the forest floor, his knees dark with mud, his
body aching, "releasing" all his shame, all his pride. He had found his
enemy at last. It was his own mind. God, he'd say, gave him promises
and revealed to him truths too precious for words. "They did not

seem so much to fall into my *intellect* as into my *heart*." The mind, he realized, was nothing but a tool.

Finney rose and began walking, stumbling like a drunken man back to town, his feet tangling, but his mind so quiet "it seemed *as if all nature listened.*" He'd left before breakfast. By the time he returned, his law partner, Benjamin Wright, had gone home, but, he'd later say, Jesus Christ himself stood in the office, "*face to face*," awaiting his deposition. Into the darkness came then the Holy Spirit. "*Like a wave of electricity*, going through and through me. Indeed it seemed to come in *waves*, and *waves of liquid love*." Finney roared out loud, his shame dissolved in his fear and ecstasy. "I shall *die* if these waves continue to pass over me." The waves kept rolling, and he dipped and bobbed in the spirit, the crests and the troughs of the ocean soaking one message into his bones, the idea-that-is-not-an-idea that he would take as his text for what would become the greatest revival since the days of Jonathan Edwards: before God, you are nothing.

FINNEY TITLED THE first postconversion chapter of his memoirs "I Begin My Work With Immediate Success." Not for him Jonathan Edwards's curiosity about the workings of the Holy Spirit he was so certain flowed through him like electric current. Finney's was the faith of the industrial age. Whereas Edwards wondered if religion might, like light itself, be subject to natural laws, Finney hit a switch and expected the power to flow. Likewise their political understanding of evangelism: Edwards studied Locke and anguished over the democratic contradictions of revival. Finney read the law books of Blackstone and took his Bible unfiltered and applied what he learned with equal-opportunity fervor. By Finney's reckoning, every citizen had the right—the obligation—to be as zealous as the man he called "President Edwards," in honor of Edwards's brief tenure as the head of Princeton University.

The night after Finney returned from his forest grotto a changed man, a member of the choir that old God-spurning Finney had led came to see him. The chorister found Finney in the dark. The lawyer's shoulders were shaking. His breath was loud and heaving. "What ails you?" the visitor asked. Finney wiped away his tears. "I am so happy that I cannot live," he answered.

But he did, into the dawn, at which point the Holy Spirit checked in on him. "Will you doubt? Will you doubt?" a voice demanded. Finney the lawyer knew the answer to that one. Same as a verdict, guilty or not guilty, black or white. "No! I *will not* doubt; I *cannot* doubt." Satisfied with Finney's reply, the Spirit "then cleared the subject up" in Finney's mind, the subject being the question of his conversion and whether he was saved. He was.

If such instant grace is a commonplace of American fundamentalism today, it was an oddity to be doubted in Finney's time. Saul had become Paul in a flash some eighteen hundred years previous, and there had been other miracles since, but not every country lawyer could call the voices in his head God's and be believed. Not until then, anyway; American Christendom was changing fast. Finney's epiphany contained in it the summation of two developing ideas of the times, ideas that would vastly expand Christ's jurisdiction over America in the minds of believers: the radical notion that to perceive the divine is to accept divine *authority*, without question; and the mechanistic understanding of faith as instantaneous for all who want it. Sign here, and you're a soldier in the army of God, ready for battle.

Finney sallied forth to his law office clad in his new spiritual armor and promptly began the war. Benjamin Wright passed by, and Finney threw off some remark. He did not pay enough attention to remember what it was, but such was the "efficacy" of his new religion that the remark he made pierced Wright "like a sword." Next came a client, ready to go to court on a civil matter. Finney shook his head. He could not even offer an apology. He was, he said, an "enlisted" man now. He quit his life's love, lawyering, on the spot and set about the cause of convicting souls. His method? Wander, argue, destroy. He was, if not the most educated man in the countryside, probably the brightest between Lake Erie and the Atlantic. Moreover he was a physical giant by the standards of the day, and his voice was deep, and there were those radiant eyes. Nobody could stand firm before his onslaught.

The first to fall was a young man in a shoemaker's shop, afflicted by modern ideas, *universalism,* the awkward faith of those not-quite-secular citizens who styled themselves sophisticated. "The young man saw in a moment that I had demolished his argument" and immediately fled. To safety? To reprieve from insistent evangelists? Impossible. Finney had shown him by force of logic the absolute certainty of God's total power. All that remained was for the man to conform his will. That was his only real choice: conform or be damned. Finney watched, pleased, as the broken universalist ran to the edge of town, hopped a fence, and made for the forest grotto. God would meet him in among the dark trees and fix his soul.

The grotto never failed. Finney's faith was, in comparison to that of Edwards, almost mechanical; it was industrial. In the weeks that followed, Finney sent a procession of townspeople tromping into the woods, there to repeat the form of his own intimate encounter. The story of his forest salvation was the secret weapon of his crusade, the mythic ammunition behind his "arguments" for the undeniable authority of God, more persuasive in his raw country town than the principles of Blackstone, spiritualized. Or rather, the two narratives worked in tandem, offering the citizens of pastoral Adams, New York—adrift in the great in-between of America, no longer wilderness and not yet settled—both savagery and civilization, a weeping, screaming, singing forest god and a straightforward, law-based, citizen-Christ for the democratizing nation.

Finney's law partner, Wright, a respectable man with connections to the coming political powers of the state, thought he could accept the latter without the former. Swept up in the townwide revival that followed in the wake of Finney's conversion, Wright determined to settle his accounts with the new Jesus. But "he thought that *he* had a *parlor* to pray in," and he would not go to the forest like Finney's other soldiers. Wright prayed in his parlor for days and nights. Jesus would not answer. He prayed out loud into the early morning. Jesus would not answer. Because Jesus had chosen a place shadowed by trees for their meeting. *I'm not proud!* Wright wept, but he could not receive the wave of Jesus-love of which Finney had spoken, the power without which he was certain he would die. He took from his pocket a small knife, weighed it in his hand, imagined its bite. Relief. He was not proud; he would prove it with blood.

But he *was* proud, and he threw the knife away, "as far as he could," said Finney, because Lawyer Wright knew he was too petty to resist temptation. For weeks he struggled. One night he collapsed in the muddy street, kneeling in puddles. See? I am not proud! But he was. He would not accept the Christ waiting for him among the trees.

"One afternoon I was sitting in our office," recalled Finney, when the shoemaker's universalist, now a "Christian," burst into the room. "Esquire Wright is converted!" he shouted. He had been up in the woods himself, there to pray, when he heard from a neighboring valley the echoes of shouting. He had climbed a hill for a view and spotted Wright in the distance. Wright was a fat man, heavy, not athletic like Finney, but there he was in the wild, marching and shouting. Like a soldier on watch, pivoting and turning, pivoting and turning, to and fro. He'd stop, wind back his arms like wings and clap "with his full strength and shout '*I will rejoice in the God of my salvation!*'"

As the man told the story, Finney heard shouting, looked up, and saw Lawyer Wright marching down the hill. The big man intercepted old Father Tucker on the edge of town and lifted him off the ground and squeezed him, dropped him, marched. Stopped, clapped, barked, "I've got it!" Wright fell to his knees before Finney and told him that he had been saved. He'd had a choice: suicide or the trees.

JONATHAN EDWARDS HAD been a scientist of religion, maybe a mad one. Finney—nothing if not sane, his language plain, "colloquial and Saxon"—became its promoter, its mass distributor, a pious variation on his better-remembered contemporary, Phineas Taylor Barnum. He favored raw emotion as his medium but practiced religion like a country lawyer, an American exhorter. "I came right forth from a law office to the pulpit, and talked to the people as I would have talked to the jury." Old churchmen shivered at his vulgar words. "Of course," he said of that crowd, "to them I was a speckled bird."

Theologians of that time and historians of ours parse Finney's words to discover whether he broke with Edwards or continued his tradition. They take a typical Finney proclamation such as this— "Knowing your duty, you have but one thing to do, PERFORM IT"—and consider it in light of debates over Calvinism and, if they're bold, the politics of Andrew Jackson. But they give little credence to the words Finney felt must be capitalized. *PERFORM IT.* Finney's was a faith of action, a fact commonly noted. He was an abolitionist, a temperance man. Less considered is the emphasis of the action that bridged the theological isms and the politics of the day: performance. The subtle delights and terrors of spectacle that link Finney's revivals to those of our present megachurch nation.[7]

For Edwards, revival had been a strange and wonderful phenomenon, a displacement of ordinary air by the immaterial body of the Holy Ghost. But it was delicate, revival, neither a force to be directed nor one that would abide exploitation. Its politics were implicit. For Finney, a self-taught preacher declaring a frontier Christ for the industrial age, revival was a machine made up of "new measures": "powerful preaching," a well-timed hymn, the "protracted meeting"—movements of the Spirit scheduled on a daily basis for weeks at a time. Its politics were as plain as the public confessions of sinners called to grease the gears of Finney's cleverest innovation, the *anxious bench,* the titillation of which P. T. Barnum would never rival.[8]

Finney was recently married when he conceived of the anxious bench, but not much drawn to his wife. He left her alone for most of the first six months of their marriage while he wandered from church to meetinghouse to schoolhouse to parlor in the little towns of western New York, preaching wherever he could find a pulpit or a room full of people. His reputation was growing, as the tall young man who spoke hellfire, who called sinners *blistered* and *skinned* and *broken down.* And what's more, called them by name. Not for Finney abstractions of theology and tics of old English that distanced the man in the pulpit from the men and women—mostly women—who filled the pews. Finney said "you." And he stared at you. And if he found out your name, he'd call *you* a sinner. It was thrilling.

One warm spring day, Finney walked three miles through a pine forest to a church in the town of Rutland. The first to arrive, he took a seat in the pews. He carried no sermon. A crowd began to gather, but nobody recognized him. In walked a woman, slender and lovely, "decidedly" so, graceful, wearing a bonnet adorned with plumes. "She came as it were sailing around, and up the broad aisle toward where I sat, mincing as she came." She sat right behind him. He could feel her close to him. He shifted his hips, threw an elbow over the back of his chair. Watched her watching him. Two beautiful creatures, a delight to behold. His violet eyes consumed her, "from her feet up to her bonnet and then down again. He was not secret in his glances.

She blushed. Hello, stranger.

His lips were thick and wide, set in a strange, calm smile, brown like his skin from the sun. But he did not look like a farmer. There were those Finney eyes, giant and glowing. When he opened his mouth, his voice was low, not tender.

"Don't you believe that God thinks you look pretty?"

What?

"Don't you think all the people will think you look so very nice?"

The blood must have drained from her cheeks.

His voice dropped lower. "Did you come here to divide the worship of God's house?"

This, Finney noted, made the pretty, proud thing "writhe."

"I followed her up in a voice so low that nobody else heard me, but I made her hear me distinctly."

Vanity, "insufferable vanity."

The woman was trembling, "her plumes were all in a shake." At last, Finney was ready to preach. He ascended to the pulpit and revealed himself as the man the congregation had been waiting for. The woman must have gasped; she began to shake.

He preached to a full house that followed him deep into the literal gospel. They saw what he had done to the woman and wanted him to slay them also, to convict them, to *crush* them. Such words were part of his new measures. Then—"I did what I do not know I had ever done before." He called on those who would be saved to rise from their seats and come to the front of the hall, there to stand exposed in their sin. Of course the woman rose, the first to respond. She fell out into the aisle. "Shrieked," remembered Finney.

Her squeal excited the crowd. They too surged forward, moaning and stumbling and screaming, eager to feel, as the shrieking woman had, the intensity of conversion. The machine was working, electrified by the anxious bench, Finney's most thrilling invention.

"THE *SPIRITUALITY* OF Christians does not lie in *secret Whispers*, or *audible Voices*," wrote an eighteenth-century New England divine who was firmly opposed to revivalism—its God-chosen men, its shouters and fainters and falling-down people.[9] True religion, he believed, did not depend on special revelations for the self-anointed nor the noisiness of a crowd shaking with Holy Ghost electricity.

Perhaps not. But power requires both, whispers and voices, the intimacy of the grove and the public outcry of the anxious bench. Finney's revival machine made use of both, and more important, made them interchangeable: private experience became public religion's badge of authenticity, and public religion's pulsing current gave to Finney's inner piety the intensity of a collective, a movement, a multitude. "The church," Finney would declare of the community of believers years after he'd left the upstate wilds, "was designed to make aggressive movements in every direction." Finney meant this politically—believers were "bound to exert their influence to secure a legislation that is in accordance with the law of God"—but also as a matter of performance.[10] "The church" was not bricks and mortar, nor even simply the sum of *Bible-Christians,* Finney's term for followers of his protofundamentalism. The church, to Finney, was the individual's encounter with Jesus in the wilderness, the mass contagion of the anxious bench; and it was the chemical reaction that occurred when the certainty of the former combined with the jolt of the latter to force the issue of Finney's American Christ onto the nation.

II.
JESUS PLUS NOTHING

4.

UNIT NUMBER ONE

The Idea, Part i

A FAMILIAR TABLEAU: A MAN on his knees before dawn, praying secret prayers for guidance. Only now it's the 1920s, and the heir to the title of First Revivalist is Billy Sunday, a former ballplayer who worked the stage as if he was covering second base and calling the game at the same time, dashing back and forth between velvet curtains, winding up for a big throw and hollering at the batter. *Sinner!* was Sunday's cry. He railed against reds and women's libbers and tippling bohemians. Christ he considered a man of action and then some. Jesus, he preached, was a boxer, a brawler, a two-fisted man's man who was also God. A twofer! Gone was the Jesus of Jonathan Edwards, austere and intellectual. And fading, too, was Finney's Christ, an idea of the divine that reflected Finney's own raw, native vision. Sunday preached a prosperity gospel—God loves the wealthy—and lived it as well. He was not a crook but a hustler, milking the masses with his holy-rolling vaudeville routines. Preoccupied with fame, he revived the nation again but left it largely unaltered. He did not advance the theocratic project, was not the next key man of American fundamentalism.

That honor goes to our man kneeling in the dim blue of predawn Seattle, murmuring prayers in a foreign tongue. The man is a Norwegian immigrant named Abraham Vereide, known to most as Abram, a preacher who has found in America the stature and respectability—by way of a prestigious pulpit—that eluded him in his native Norway. Still, something is beyond his grasp. He wants the peace he's certain God has promised him, yet suffering, in the abstract, distracts him. Abram is immune to despair by this point in his life, but it bothers him, and he wishes it wouldn't.

He is a big man—fit and square in the shoulders and in the jaw, his face broad, severe, and intensely handsome—and a bighearted man, too, and intelligent, but also simple, and glad to be so. He likes things to be in their places: God in His heavens, Abram by his Bible, men working where God puts them, all content with their calling. So it is clear something is wrong with the world: the poor. They are, it seems plain to him, out of place. Literally out of order. Something has gone wrong. God promised us we would be happy when we reached the Promised Land, and what, if not that, is America?

So what does God have in mind? Abram has not yet found an answer. He keeps praying.

This morning, 4:30 a.m., he prays alone but he is not alone. His son, Warren, is watching. He has newspapers to deliver. He moves quietly through the darkened house, pulling on socks and dungarees and tiptoeing down the back stairs so as not to wake his mother, so often ill, restricted to bed but never resting easy. Just before the last step, Warren hears a noise—a sudden intake of breath followed by an exhalation. Like laughter, only it's followed by a moan. Then Warren hears a voice coming from the kitchen. Perched on his step like a mouse, not making a sound, Warren listens to his father's deep murmur, still thick with the accent of the fjords. Abram's voice sounds strange—not the way it does when he speaks to Warren or Warren's mother or to the big men he counts as his friends. This morning he sounds as if he is talking to someone he loves and respects and of whom he is just a little bit afraid.

"Do you want me, Lord, to go as Thy Ambassador?"

Silence. Abram's shoulders seem to settle. Maybe he smiles. He has received instructions.

"It is done," Abram says, and Warren takes advantage of his father's moment of serenity to slip out into the early morning, leaving Abram alone with his God.[1]

ABRAM PRAYED LIKE this for years, and the years grew darker, the poor poorer, the world more broken, until one day in April of 1935 he received not just instructions for the day before him but a vision for the decades; God's hand moving His people in an entirely new direction. The revelation God gave him was simple: *To the big man went strength, to the little man went need. Only the big man was capable of mending the world.* But who would help the big man? Who would console him when he, as Abram did sometimes, wept in the early mornings? That the big men of society wept Abram never doubted. He thought that powerful people, so clearly blessed by God, must surely possess equally great reserves of compassion and love that they wished to shower down on the weak, if only someone would show them how.

Abram would show them how. This was his vision. His life thus far—in 1935, he was forty-nine, his once-dark brow gray like a North Pacific breaker—had followed an arc, he believed, but it had taken him a long time to see it. His ministry, he now realized, was not "among those who have had the bottom knocked out of life, its derelicts, its failures," as a friend would write years later, "but, ultimately, among those even more in need, who live dangerously in high places."

For nearly 2,000 years, Abram concluded, Christianity—that is, the religion, the rituals, the stuff of men with their weak, sinful minds—had bent all its energies toward the poor, the sick, the starving. The "down and out." Christianity gave them fishes when it could and hope when it had nothing else to offer. But what good had it done? What had been accomplished between Calvary and 1935?

Just look at Seattle, Abram's adopted hometown: nearly half the city was on relief, and the other half was dark-eyed, eyeing the blessings of the "top men" with envy, which is a blight on a man's soul. A rich man may have little hope of getting into heaven, but an envious man could turn to violence and lose all hope for this world or the next. Abram had to help such creatures, the derelicts, the failures. How? By helping those who could help them—the high and the mighty—that they might distribute the Lord's blessings to the little men, whose envy would be soothed, violence averted, disorder controlled.

Thereafter, Abram would spend his days arranging the spiritual affairs of the wealthy. It would be another decade—ten years spent cultivating not just Seattle's big men but those of the nation—before Abram would coin a phrase for his vision: the "new world order." By then, 1945, he'd moved to Washington, D.C., and he cut a different figure than he had as a preacher. He wore double-breasted suits with lapels like wings, polka-dotted bow ties, and wide-brimmed fedoras. He was often seen with his dark overcoat thrown over his shoulders like a cape. Other men considered him a spectacular dresser; those who knew him well considered his stylishness itself a minor miracle, since Abram was not wealthy. But God provided. As a young itinerant preacher, he'd traveled on horseback with a six-gun and a Bible, traveling from farmer to farmer. Now, he carried a silk handkerchief instead of a pistol, and he moved from rich man to rich man. He stayed in the best hotels and clubs—the Waldorf-Astoria in New York, the Union League in Chicago, Hotel Washington in the nation's capital—as the guest of friends, and he traveled over the years in the best cars (God led a rich man to give him the use of a twenty-thousand-dollar Duesenberg), on private planes, in Pullman cars especially reserved for his use.

When as a young preacher out West he had once faced a pressing debt of twenty-five dollars and had no hope of paying it, a woman unknown to him squeezed twenty-five dollars into his hand. She told him, he claimed, that she had been moved by God to give him cash; had set out for his church with five dollars; had been stopped by the Lord at the threshold and been given to understand that Abram required more of her; had plucked another twenty dollars from her purse; and had floated toward the beautiful preacher, her money— the equivalent today of hundreds of dollars—pressed, through no will of her own, from her hand to his.

His hands were enormous, his fingers long. His face was granite—
a straight, lipless line of a mouth and a jaw so square it could've been
used in a geometry class. His eyes, set deep and serious beneath long
dark lashes and craggy brows, looked like pale ice. They were the
eyes not of a seducer but a persuader, a gaze men more than women
remembered. "God gave him a majestic figure," his eldest son, Warren, would recall. Like all those entranced by his father, Warren believed that God had granted Abram his manly appearance for a
purpose: to win powerful men to his cause.

Abram would become an exponent of a religion for the elite—the
"up and out," as he called them—for the rest of his life. He termed
this trickle-down faith the Idea, and it was really the only idea he ever
had—the only one, he believed, God gave him. In one sense, it was
nothing more than a defense of the status quo. It neither challenged
power nor asked for anything from the powerful but their good intentions. In another, it was the most ambitious theocratic project of
the American century, "every Christian a leader, every leader a Christian," and this ruling class of Christ-committed men bound in a fellowship of the anointed, the chosen, key men in a voluntary
dictatorship of the divine.

From Seattle, Abram traveled the world with the Idea, winning to
its self-satisfied simplicity the allegiance of senators, ambassadors,
business executives, and generals. Every president beginning with
Eisenhower has attended the annual National Prayer Breakfast Abram
founded in 1953. He never achieved his dream—the United States is
no more a theocracy today than it was in Charles Finney's lifetime—but
in his pursuit of it he stood at the vanguard of an elite fundamentalism
that shaped the last half century of American and world politics in
ways only now becoming visible. Abram, observed two approving
evangelical writers in a 1975 study, *Washington: Christians in the Corridors of Power*, "personally influenced thousands of community, national,
and world leaders, who in turn influenced countless others, a remarkable chain reaction . . . Many of them have never heard of [Abram],
much less seen him. But his shadow is upon them."[2]

Shadow is indeed the word for Abram's legacy. In 2005, *Time* magazine labeled Abram's successor, Doug Coe, the *stealth persuader,* a term that might just as easily have fit his mentor. Abram's upper-crust faith was not a conspiracy, but it was not meant for the masses, either. Until recently, those masses—fundamentalist as well as secular—barely knew it existed.[3]

ABRAM HEARD HIS own peculiar God for the first time in Norway, one June morning in 1895 when as an eight-year-old boy he was taking his father's cattle to pasture in the high cold fields of the Norwegian village from which Abram's family took their surname. In later life, Abram would often insist that he had been born poor, but among the white houses and red barns of the one-thousand-year-old village of Vereide, his family's home—close to the church and surrounded by oak trees—was far from the humblest. The inlet near the village was narrow enough to resemble a river, and over it loomed two mountains, the peaks of which were perfect triangles of black and white, laced with snow even in June. In between stretched farmland, the future that awaited Abram if he remained. His father was a fore-man of sorts for land owned by the crown. But Abram was restless, a popular boy yet angry and given to fighting.

His mother had died shortly before the June day on which he first heard God's voice, and her last prayers had been for a calming of her boy's temper. That June morning, he took those prayers with him into the fields. As he closed the gate behind him, his grief combined with his anger into a cloud of guilt and regret, of longing for his mother and for the good son he believed he should have been. He couldn't bear himself: he ran. He abandoned the cows. He hid in a grove of elder trees, crying and shivering despite the sun that crept through the leaves. A brook burbled, and the air smelled of cow dung. He wanted to pray, but he didn't know how. He'd never paid attention to his mother's prayers. Then, into his mind came words: *Fear not, for I have redeemed thee and called thee by name, thou art mine.*

Abram would later say that at the time he had not yet read the Book of Isaiah, from which those words came. Perhaps he *had* read the verse, or heard it spoken by his mother, or maybe it was as he'd come to believe years later, in America: a supernatural call to the divine. Whichever the case, those words were the first intimations of what would become Abram's theology. They resolved the age-old question of theodicy—why does God let bad things happen to good people?—by ignoring the fact that they had happened at all. Rather than wrestle with grief and loss, as the best Christian thinking does so profoundly, Abram found in the grove the seeds of a faith that he'd thereafter use as a shield against even the awareness of pain, of doubt, of the danger of despair and the hard, precious hope won from that knowledge. This was the birth of Abram's "positive" Christianity: the censorship of suffering.

Ten years later, eighteen years old and educated to that point but with no prospects in Norway other than a life in the field, Abram left for America, the "land of the Bible unchained," as he dreamed of it. He arrived at Ellis Island after a stormy voyage, and very first thing a woman rushed up to him and said, "Welcome!" and pressed into his hands a New Testament. Abram thought her rude and wonderful, just like America. But her kindness added no advantage. Besides his new American Bible and a Norwegian copy, he had nothing. His clothes were homespun, stitched by his sisters; his shoes were goat-skin, from a goat he had slaughtered; his suitcase was a leather box of his own devising. He had only the name of a countryman who would help to seek out in Butte, Montana, a boomtown run like a fiefdom by giant Anaconda Copper, and just enough money to get there, a hard journey of fifteen days.

His connection turned out to be a man in a shack by the railroad, but the old hand knew what to do with a new Norwegian. "Let's go uptown and meet the boys," he said, and took Abram past a row of brothels punctuated by whore-lined alleys to a saloon. At the saloon Abram's guide sat him at a bar amid a gang of miners who sweated whiskey and copper, and all clinked glasses in his honor. He would not raise his glass. They called him a dumb greenhorn. He didn't care. They cursed him. He stood up, broad-shouldered and straight-backed, his icy blue eyes set in handsome features, ruddy but clear, a rebuke to the scars hard labor and whoring had written across his companions. He frowned upon them, the whiskey, the cleavage of women, the stink of the men, the rumble of the bar, the land of mammon unchained.

"You are in America now—do like Americans do," one man said.

That was exactly what Abram planned; he would do as the Americans of his imagination did. "No, thank you," he said, his voice controlled. "I never tasted liquor in my life, and I can get along without it."

Into the cold night under a sky filled with strange stars, he walked until he came to the cliffs that loom over Butte. He shivered and stared at the mines below, lit up for night shifts like glittering stones. There he wept, and then he shouted, to the God he had been certain he would find in America. And out of the darkness, he would say to the end of his days, he heard the voice of his Lord, speaking the clean English the immigrant would soon master. This time the words came from Proverbs: *There is yet a future and your hope shall not come to naught.*

"In America," he'd assured his worried father, "education is free, money is plentiful, and everyone has a chance." Instead, his first experience of the United States was the savage life of immigrants, men and women pressed into the hardest, most dangerous work. In the days that followed, he did such labor himself, knocking around the copper camps of Montana, a once-healthy farm boy eventually laid low by sickness and industrial poison, "copper-tinged water" that put him into a state of semiconsciousness that lasted for days, hallucinatory hours spent flat on his back in the shack by the railroad tracks, his gaunt body sweating away the butter and beef and herring on which he had grown strong in Norway. It was God's doing, he believed: "The European starch had to be washed out."

And it was. The boy from the village that bore his family name worked as a section hand, a floor mopper, and a hard laborer, beaten out of his wages again and again by crooked bosses who called him a "big-footed Norwegian"—feet, apparently, being the currency of bigotry with regard to Norsemen. On the Fourth of July 1905, Abram asked to be paid for work he had done as a painter in the town of Basin so he could buy some "American clothes" to celebrate the holiday. Stick it, said the boss. So Abram took the American option: "when I heard the train whistle, bound from Basin to Butte, I said goodbye." In Butte on that Fourth of July, Abram spent his last dime on a streetcar ride to a park on the edge of the city, where he found a grove of trees far from the American celebration. He had no money, no friends, no place to sleep. The city was too far behind for him to walk back, but that didn't matter: Abram wanted to die right there and be done. It was a moment like Finney's, only starker: Abram's suffering was in his belly as well as his soul. He sat in the shade of the trees beneath the high plains sun and waited for an answer. He'd brought all his possessions with him in a small bundle—the goat hide suitcase from home lost along the way—and from it he took out his New Testament and began to read through his tears. As his eyes scanned the now-familiar words, he sensed God Himself once again speaking: *Ye have not chosen me, but I chose you . . .* The Gospel of John, chapter 15, verse 16 . . . *Whatsoever you ask the Father in my name, he shall give it to you.*

Then—a sign, Abram thought—through the woods, came a man who found Abram wiping away his tears. The man had a beautiful smile. He opened his mouth to speak. Abram would later remember not so much the words as their sound: this messenger from God was a Norwegian. Not an angel but a former saloonkeeper who'd found Jesus before he'd found Abram. As if, Abram thought, God was lining up all his experiences in the New World to reveal a singular lesson. *Ye have not chosen me, but I chose you . . .* The Norwegian took Abram home to live with his family that Fourth of July, and through him Abram eventually found his way to a Methodist seminary, the free education he had boasted of to his father, and the hand in marriage of a well-off minister's daughter, the middle-class step up into American life Abram had been looking for. *Whatsoever you ask the Father in my name, he shall give it to you.*

The one word that does not appear in the notes on his life Abram prepared near the end of his life, when instead of sheepskin he wore silk and gabardine, when instead of miners and cowboys he preached to senators and presidents, is *power*. But in 1935, when Abram was just beginning to dream his real ministry, he wrote the word once, in the margin of a church program. It was at the bottom of a list of names of men he had recruited. Besides each was a responsibility: *organization, finances*. Beside his own name, he wrote *power*—and then crossed it out. If it must be said, it can't be had. Power, Abram realized as he moved through the high corner offices of businessmen and leaders, has nothing to do with forcing the devil behind you or making the company increase your wages. Power lies in things as they are. God had already chosen the powerful, his key men. There they are, Jesus whispered in Abram's ear; go and serve them.

Throughout the 1920s, Abram directed Seattle's division of Goodwill Industries. He didn't just open stores for used clothes; he organized 49,000 housewives into thirty-seven districts and set them to work salvaging goods for the poor. In 1932, Franklin Roosevelt, governor of New York, invited Abram to his office to discuss his organizing system. Later he'd come to see Russian red running throughout Roosevelt's New Deal, but at the time Abram was captivated by another man summoned to advise the governor, James Augustine Farrell, president of the United States Steel Corporation. Abram had met industry chiefs before then, but here was a titan. A tall, stern man of dark suits and high collars, Farrell had led U.S. Steel for decades, since not long after its creation as the biggest business enterprise in history, and he had a reputation as an industrial free thinker. The year before he'd rebuked a group of businessmen for treating workers like animals. Farrell looked on his employees more like children. Big business, he believed, ought to act as a big brother, and to that end he insisted that the age of competition had passed; captains of industry must be freed of antitrust legislation so that they might better council together for the good of the innocent and the poor.

Abram fixed his rapt attention on the "steel shogun," as the press of the time called the industrialist. "Mr. Farrell reviewed the history of America," he'd remember, "and pointed out that we have had nineteen depressions—five major ones—and that every one was caused by disobedience to divine laws." Farrell offered no evidence for his dismissal of economic factors, but he did have a solution on hand. "Now," Abram recorded his words, "I am a Roman Catholic and we don't go in much for revivals and such things, but I am sure as I am sitting here that if we don't get a thorough revival of genuine religion . . . with a return to prayer and the Bible"—an oddly Protestant aim—"we are headed for chaos." Farrell suggested that the time had come for the "leaders of industry" to take the reins not just of the economy but of the entire nation in order to restore it to a godly path.

Farrell, a former steelworker himself and thus living proof in his own mind that equal opportunity existed for all, was likely too modest to mention U.S. Steel's own efforts in this regard; most notably, its relief program for the Pennsylvania steeltown of Farrell, renamed just that year in honor of the great man himself. A desperate measure by a community of 30,000 utterly dependent on U.S. Steel and starving because of that fact. In Farrell, U.S. Steel fought the spiritual roots of its economic woes not through revival but by evicting from company housing those who were not part of the nation's godly heritage: foreign-born workers, black workers, and even the old white men who had built Farrell and now approached retirement and pensions. U.S. Steel replaced them all with young peons paid low wages. It was not a matter of getting the job done, since the mills were shuttered and there was no work to be done. U.S. Steel simply saw an opportunity for a correction.[3]

But then, so did the men and women whom companies such as U.S. Steel were liquidating. It's hard now, in the present United States, to imagine the fear that attended the Depression years, and harder still to remember the anger. Most forgotten of all is the optimism of ordinary people pushed to an edge over which they peered and saw not the abyss they had been told by their employers and their politicians awaited them, but—maybe, if they built it themselves—a future dramatically different from the past.

The 1930s were the hungry years, yes; but they were also radical, which is to say, visionary—an era of political imagination. American history has plunked Roosevelt at the left edge of the spectrum of our political life, but at the time Roosevelt was closer to the middle. To his right were fools and fascists; these were the days when one might respectably admire the methods of "Mr. Hitler" and wonder, in the pages of newspapers or on the floor of Congress, whether there might not be some part of his approach for Americans to copy. And to Roosevelt's left? There lies the missing history of America without which the rise of Abram's religion, the fundamentalism of the "up and out," the gospel of power for the powerful that soothes the consciences of fundamentalism's elite to this day, cannot be understood. The elite fundamentalist movement of which Abram would be a pioneer arose in response to a radical age. Abram's biographers say that for a brief moment in 1932, a Roosevelt aide charged with building a brain trust from which the future president's cabinet could be constructed promoted Abram to take charge of a social services portfolio on the strength of his Goodwill work, and began including him in meetings. "Abram was introduced to the inner workings of the economic and political forces of the nation," wrote Abram's friend and biographer Norman Grubb. There he saw "how serious was the danger of leftwing elements actually taking over the nation."

As far as Abram was concerned, they did. He had begun drawing up plans for government-backed religious revival as a cure for the nation, but FDR went the way of the New Deal. Roosevelt's name rarely appears in Abram's papers thereafter.

Nor, for that matter, does the name of anyone Abram thought beyond God's sphere of influence. Abram perfected a feel-good fundamentalism that was every bit as militant and aggressive as today's populist front but incapable of uttering a harsh word. It was country club fundamentalism, for men who believed in their own goodness and proved it to themselves and each other by commending Christ and the next fellow's fine effort at following His example. They followed the law of kindergarten: if you have nothing nice to say about someone, say nothing at all. Or put it in terms of abstraction, the preeningly polite language of upper-class religion: One might talk about a "Red Menace," but good Christians did not discuss what they deemed Roosevelt's communistic tendencies: One might bemoan moral decay, but it would not do to mention the name of a fellow business-man who kept ladies on the side. Only once, in the notes Abram gave his friend Grubb, did he come close to identifying an enemy: the no-torious "B."

Who is B? The Red Menace in the shape of a man, subversion personified, a zombie from Moscow.

That is, B belonged to a union. Which union? Hard to say. Two candidates present themselves, but neither fits Abram's description precisely. Rather, the mysterious B who inspired Abram to gather his decades of work and contacts and fundamentalist refinements into the Idea seems to be an amalgam of the two most powerful labor chiefs on the West Coast in 1935, and, indeed, perhaps the country: Dave Beck, the Teamster warlord of Seattle, and Harry Bridges, the Australian-born champion of longshoremen from San Diego to Van-couver.

The two men were a study in contrasts. Beck, with his "pink moon face and icy blue eyes," as the journalist John Gunther de-scribed him, a union leader so conservative he was "probably the most ardent exponent of capitalism in the Northwest," ran Seattle like a fiefdom with bully-boy squadrons of brass-knuckled goons and a mayor who actually boasted of being in Beck's pocket. Bridges, "a slight, lanky fellow," observed the radical writer Louis Adamic, "with a narrow, longish head, receding dark hair, a good straight brow, an aggressive hook nose, and a tense-lipped mouth," operated out of San Francisco but at only thirty-four years old had a rank-and-file follow-ing across the trades and industries up and down the coast. Beck wore double-breasted suits and painted ties and thought he looked pretty damn good in black and white on the front page of a paper. Bridges dressed like the longshoreman he was: black canvas Frisco Jeans with his iron cargo hook hanging from the back pocket, denim shirt, and a flat white cap. A shave, maybe, for a special occasion. He rarely spoke to reporters.[4]

Beck's integrity can best be summed up by the fact that years later—by then he was the boss of the whole union—when he was summoned to Washington to account for himself and his mysterious riches, he pled the Fifth, got drummed out of the Teamsters like a bad punch line, and Jimmy Hoffa took over. After Beck, even the Kennedy brothers thought Hoffa was good news.

Bridges? In 1934, the legend spread that the San Francisco ship owners sent an ex-prize fighter with $50,000 to try and buy him. Bridges met the boxer alone; considered putting the cash into the strike fund; but said no because he gleaned it was a trap. Had he taken the money, he would have been dead in two minutes, and his union brothers would have found an impossible wad of cash on his corpse, and that would have made for a very different story than the one that got around.

Abram knew Beck was a crook and probably knew Bridges was not, but he likely loathed them with equal intensity. Beck's muscle made a mockery of the government of God-led men Abram dreamed of for Seattle, and Bridges's pure-hearted radicalism must have seemed to Abram like a devil's parody of religious conviction.

" 'B'," wrote Abram of the conditions that sparked the Idea, "had a lot of folks up in arms against him, but most of them had now involved themselves in one way or another and didn't dare squeal. Some played the game and liked it, and others paid through the nose; but whether you were a businessman, a contractor, or a labor leader, you went along."

This "B" is almost definitely Beck; no businessman in America "went along" with Harry Bridges. And yet it was Beck, ironically, who inadvertently exposed big business of the 1930s for what it was: a racket with rewards reserved for the big men. In most parts of the country, that would be someone like James A. Farrell or Henry Ford, commanding Pinkertons and the police; in Seattle, it was Dave Beck, Teamster, who owned the law. That's why Abram hated him: Beck was living evidence that God's invisible hand blessed the ruthless as much as or more than those whom he considered the deserving.

But Abram had been living in San Francisco in 1934, leading prayer meetings for a group of business executives at the Pacific Union Club, and he had witnessed the power of Bridges up close, worse than anything he had seen during his years of preaching and organizing in Boston, New York, and Detroit. "It was the utter helplessness of the rank and file," wrote his friend Grubb, "under the political control of subversive forces in the saddle."

That's not Beck—his hit squads struck any union meeting that showed radical inclinations harder than the most brutal lumber baron could imagine. Abram wanted to convert communists; Beck wanted them beaten and dumped in the drink. No, the "subversive forces in the saddle" must have been Bridges, although Bridges was not subversive, he was a revolutionary. And in 1934 and '35, to Abram—indeed, to much of the world—it looked as if he might be successful.

BRIDGES WAS THE anti-Abram. Raised middle class and Roman-Catholic in Melbourne, Australia, he shipped out to sea when he was sixteen and got off the boat in America four years later. Abram had his faith, and Bridges had his. God hadn't spoken to him; a Wobbly had—a member of the Industrial Workers of the World. They aimed for one simple goal, paradise on Earth. They called it *One Big Union* and fought for it with the fine art of sabotage: Wobblies blasted steam into the pipes of refrigerated shipping containers, sabotaged blacktop so it cracked open, literally jammed wrenches into the works. They didn't steal from the rich and give to the poor; they *were* the poor, and they took. Most of all, though, they lingered and gabbed and winked at one another and then *quit*—they loved leaving work behind. "Hallelujah, I'm a bum again," went a favorite American Wobbly song. Abram had nightmares about such hymns, mistook their radicalized Tin Pan Alley humor for the ponderous phrasing of the European "Internationale."[5]

But the Wobblies weren't red; they were romantic, deliberately and desperately so, skeptical of power and organization and compromise, and constantly amused by themselves. Sabotage, after all, is a kind of joke—not just on the bosses but also on anyone who works, on the very idea of work. The God Wobblies believed in had made humanity not for hard labor but for pleasure. Why else did He give us legs on which to dance?

And yet the first noble truth of the Wobblies was suffering, a sure thing for as long as there was a ruling class with which to wage war. So Wobblies fought, but they fought for the paradise they felt in their bones and their bellies had been promised to them. A city upon a hill. What else was worth fighting for?

Their dream was ill defined, less an agenda than a story, about class warfare and the spoils that would one day go to the victors. They didn't have politics, they had a parable.

Wobblies whispered in young Bridges's ears as God had spoken to Abram in the elder trees. But Bridges was of a more independent turn of mind. He liked the Wobbly story about the One Big Union still to come, and took it as his own, but he didn't believe workers would win squat without organization. That idea he took from the communists, though he wasn't a communist, either. Like Abram, he loved to be around people and yet was a loner, kept his own counsel, looked inward, and what he found there he told no one. But unlike Abram, there is no record of him crying but for the day he stood by the coffins of two men he had led out on strike. The police had shot them down. Bridges wept and said nothing.

What the two men shared were dreams. The Australian and the Norwegian were utopians in the American vein. Bridges thought the Promised Land awaited construction; Abram thought it was simply to be recovered. Bridges had read a bit of theory, Abram some theology, but both believed that they could bring forth the good life for all who would accept it without recourse to ideology. Bridges took the communists into his ranks but never entered theirs, Abram strolled along the fence of fascism but never hopped over. Neither man cared much about ideas; both believed in power. Bridges wanted to see it redistributed. Abram wanted to see it concentrated.

Like Abram, Bridges knocked around, first as a sailor, then as an oil rigger, and finally as part of a San Francisco steel gang, unloading heavy metal on the docks. Like Abram, he'd been beaten out of his wages. He got beaten every day, in fact, just like every other long-shoreman. The shipowners had multiple methods for keeping their workers in line. Once, the San Francisco dockers had been among the toughest union men in the country, but the company had broken them back in 1919, herding them into the "Blue Book," a company collective in which the CEO effectively served as union boss, negotiating with himself. The bosses thought they were being kind. So did Abram. To him, such arrangements seemed like the "reconciliation" promised by Christianity, the solution at last to the old problem of labor and capital. The laws of property obtained—was it not the company's right to hire and fire at will?—but were softened, in the minds of Blue Book believers, by the company's voluntary decision to treat its employees not as hostile contractors but as children. That made sense to Abram, who divided the world between big men and little men and preferred the company of the former.

By 1933, the "children," the workers, ate—that is, earned—only if they could survive the shape-up, the speed-up, and the straw boss. The shape-up began before dawn, in San Francisco, Portland, Seattle. Along the Embarcadero, the long curving cobblestoned street between the Bay City and its eighty-two piers, 4,000 men gathered in the fog and the dark, hoping to be picked for one of fifteen hundred jobs. They jostled for a place close to the front of the crowd and puffed themselves up to look thick and strong even if they hadn't eaten in days. They felt, more than one man would remember, like whores trying to look pretty. The picker—the pimp—was called the straw boss. If you wanted to be chosen, you promised him a part of your wages. And if he gave you a job, you might work for four hours or twenty-four. You might work with a gang or with a small crew, too few men for the task. That was the speed-up: the job didn't go faster; you did. Longshoremen were not a delicate breed, but they collapsed with exhaustion and some dropped dead, their heart muscles bursting. Say a word about what you saw around you, and you were gone. Silence was golden. For the company, that is. In 1933 it shaved a dime off wages, and the Blue Book "union" accepted the loss as the cost of harmony.

But a few men didn't, and that summer, emboldened by FDR's New Deal, they organized. By spring of 1934 they were talking strike. In May it sparked: first in Seattle, where longshoremen battled deputized vigilantes, took their riot clubs away from them, and sent five to the hospital; then in San Francisco, where police shot a twenty-year-old kid in the heart as he led a striker's charge just hours after joining the union. There was something almost quixotic in the first responses of the owners: in San Francisco, shippers trolled fraternity houses for the state's best young men, who considered a few days of heavy labor the duty of gentlemen, and the Berkeley football coach recruited three squads of big-shouldered boys from the Golden Bears to join down-on-their-luck white-collar workers on a floating barracks for strikebreakers, a ship called the *Diana Dollar*.

Abram followed a teeth-rattling roller coaster of news for months, as the papers reported one day a red tide rising and the next labor peace in the offing. Neither story was true. The army of strikers grew larger and larger, bakers and cooks and waiters and even the proud and conservative Teamsters swelling the dockers' ranks.

No peace was coming. "Riot Expected," declared the papers in one of their grimmer moods. The Chamber of Commerce drafted a declaration and put it on the front page of the *Chronicle*: "American principles" vs. "un-American radicalism." The chamber stood for "free labor," for the "American Plan," for the "right to work." Lose San Francisco, and Seattle and Portland would fall like dominoes. "The winning of the strike means the abandoning of control by private owners over their own property," declared the columnist Chapin Hall. "San Francisco is the real seat of war and right nobly is she standing up to the firing line."

Seven hundred policemen in dark blue patrolled the waterfront on foot and in black cars and on high chestnut horses. Twice that number and more picketed or searched for strikebreakers. The middle class began contemplating last-minute vacations. The wives of the wealthy bunkered up at the Union Club, where Abram led prayer meetings for businessmen. As the blue tear gas sent tendrils up the hill, they must have felt frustrated by his optimistic lessons in biblical capitalism. Scripture has much to say about honest dealing and even more about handling the heathen, but not once does it mention organized labor. Kenneth Kingsbury, the president of the Standard Oil of California (and later a member of Abram's movement), peered out of the club's windows one day and saw pickets peering back; he panicked. A sign of the apocalypse, Kingsbury instructed a federal man to write his employers in Washington, was that Kenneth Kingsbury could not leave the club to hail a cab.

On July 3, the Industrial Association of San Francisco resolved to open the port by force. Mayor Angelo Rossi, a florist by trade, did not stop them. At 1:30 p.m. the steel doors of Pier 38 rolled up, and five trucks full of goods from the moribund ships in the harbor rolled out, police cruisers behind and alongside them. Driving the trucks were not ordinary strikebreakers but business executives, "key men," in Abram's vernacular. Young James A. Folger of Folger's Coffee took the lead. A crowd of 5,000 pickets watched without making a sound. The businessmen raced to a warehouse four blocks inland and unloaded: birdseed, coffee, and tires. They went back for more. The strikers looked on. No songs, no chants, no stones. Silent witness to the labor of businessmen. This was the story the papers told when Abram opened their pages on the Fourth of July 1935, his twentieth anniversary in "the land of the Bible unchained."

Did Folger and his 700 bodyguards in blue think, for just a moment, that peace was at hand? A police captain with gold braid gleaming on his shoulder, riding on the running board of a police cruiser with his revolver in the air, shouted, "The port is open!"— and gave the strikers the signal for which they had waited. They roared and attacked with cobblestones ripped from the street and bricks and stones, with clubs they tore from policemen's hands and with wooden shafts they hurled like spears. The police opened fire into the crowd.

And with that, the first fight was over—thousands melted into alleys, dragging the wounded with them. Blood pooled between the cobblestones. The air smelled acrid. At night the blue and green lights of helpless ships blinked from the bay and went unanswered.

The pool halls, the bars, the tattoo parlors, the brothels, were silent. Vice had been conquered, the Christian city on a hill defended from the barbarians.

There were not many picnics on the Fourth. A train burned and thirteen policemen's wives were given reason to curse the red bastards. The governor said troops were coming. The commanders of the Guard strategized.

"My men . . . will talk with bayonets," said their general.

This was not what Abram had dreamed of. Where were his key men, his top men, his up and out? Out of the city, hiding in the hills.

The next morning, the police went forward in waves, rows of Martians in khaki gas masks and black helmets, revolvers drawn. A few blocks from the water, on Rincon Hill, a knoll tall as a four-story building, a crowd of longshoremen gathered. From widemouthed riot guns police thumped out gas shells that sliced through dry brown grass and sparked it like tinder. Strikers scorched their fingers on the shells and hurled them back down the hill. Blue smoke from the gas, black and gray from the grass, an oily stink that pushed the armies away from one another. Up the knoll went the strikers. Policemen in ripped uniforms, blood dripping from facial wounds, squinted and aimed and unloaded revolvers and rifles. A striker crested and fell, shot like a turkey. A tear-gas salesman, deputized, cheered. The smoke stank of vomit and gunfire. Airplanes dipped and whined, dropping messages to police command. Horse hooves thudded; out of the blue smoke went the charge, horses snorting and shrieking.

The strikers were ready with slingshots: two poles stretching a car tire inner tube hurled a three-pound stone fast and hard 400 feet, or less should a policeman agree to catch it with his belly. Back down the hill went the horses.

Up went another charge, replied to with another volley. The police charged again, and this time they took a wall, but the men behind it had gone missing. So it went, charges and stone volleys and feints and men vanishing like quicksilver.

The police found them. They blocked off both ends of the street in front of the union hall. A plainclothesman drove into the crowd, stepped out of his car, and opened up with a shotgun held at the hip, and in front of the hall he brought down three men. One pulled himself up and looked at the crowd with blood in his mouth, blood in his eyes, and then his head dropped and his jaw cracked like an egg.

At least thirty-three more nursed gunshot wounds that night. They were laid in rows in the union hall or hidden in bedrooms by wives and mothers and brokenhearted fathers who boiled water and pried bullets out with thick fingers while their men screamed and the neighbors cried. Down on the docks a boat landed, and into the city marched soldiers, the first of 5,000. A sharp wind snapped the fog, the gas, the smoke up into the atmosphere, but the smell of violence lingered.

"I walked down Market that night," wrote the novelist Tillie Olsen, then twenty-one-year-old Tillie Lerner fresh from Nebraska, in one of her first pieces of published prose. "All life seemed blown out of the street; the few people hurrying by looked hunted, tense, expectant of anything. Cars moved past as if fleeing. And a light, indescribably green and ominous, was cast over everything, in great shifting shadows. And down the street the trucks rumbled. Drab colored, with boys sitting on them like corpses sitting and not moving, holding guns stiffly, staring with wide frightened eyes."[6]

That was what Abram didn't understand: the fear of death and the fear of sin, real sin, killing a brother or a sister. He was as delighted by the prospect of his death, whatever hour God should appoint for it, as Abigail Hutchinson had been. Compassionate in the abstract, he thought of the masses as just that, blocks to be arranged neatly. The troops that moved in on San Francisco that night had no feelings with which Abram would have been concerned; they were expressing the will of God, which to him was order. After the Strike of '34, Abram's allegiance would be forever given to the men who commanded soldiers, not the soldiers themselves. As for those defined as the enemy, they were not even human. Their grief never registered.

A few days later, men and women marched tens of thousands

strong five miles up Market Street behind two black-draped flatbed trucks. The trucks bore coffins and mountains of flowers, like canvases by Diego Rivera set in slow motion. A band played Beethoven. Nobody said a word. " 'Life,' the capitalist papers marveled," wrote Tillie Olsen, " 'Life stopped and stared.' "

It was incomparable drama, simultaneously staged and real. A ritual, yes, the procession of the plain folk, the march of the martyrs, a script older than Christendom. Bridges, surely aware of the moment's theatrical power, nonetheless choked up when his turn to speak came. Not a well-timed sob but wide-eyed, grief-stricken silence. He offered no inspiration. None was needed. The funeral was religion: not just solidarity, workers arm-in-arm, but communion, a coming together. The march up Market Street was the embodiment of faith, not as a metaphor but as a new fact in the American story. One Big Union on the move.

The strike went on, but the shippers were defeated by the time the coffins went into the ground. Their old beliefs could not compete. Management—capital—would require a new faith if it was to survive.

The Idea, Part 2

The strike of 1934 scared Abram into launching the movement that would become the vanguard of elite fundamentalism, and elite fundamentalism took as its first challenge the destruction of militant labor. *Destruction* was not the word Christians used, however. They called it *cooperation*.

The April after the strike, Harry Bridges traveled to Seattle to convene a meeting of a new federation of maritime workers, with "maritime" broadly defined to include pretty much anyone within driving distance of the ocean. For a brief moment that year, he came close to turning the old Wobbly dream of One Big Union into a political reality. But it wouldn't last. Indeed, the revived Wobbly dream began unraveling right there in Seattle, where Abram finally plucked up the theocratic strand and began pulling it taut into the twentieth century.

That April, Abram had been having dreams of his own, unpleasant ones. Subversives stalked his sleep, hammers and sickles danced like sugar plum fairies, a Soviet agent "of Swedish nationality" assigned to Seattle—probably the brawny and bellicose six-footer from the Seamen's Union whom Bridges had tapped to lead the maritime federation—roared his nightmare defiance of that which was godly. One night Abram could sleep no longer. He sat up in bed and resolved to wait for God. At 1:30 a.m., He appeared: a blinding light and a voice. Abram listened and took notes. "The plan had been unfolded and the green light given."[7]

A few hours later, Abram dressed and put on his coat and hurried to downtown Seattle for the morning rush, where he waited for God to bring him the means to put his plan into action. On a busy street corner, a local developer of means hailed him. "Hey, Vereide, glad to see you!"

The developer, a former major named Walter Douglass who still preferred to be addressed by his military title, cut straight to the matter on both men's minds: "Where is this country going to, anyway?"

"You ought to know," said Abram.

Indeed, the major did: "The bow-wows," he harrumphed, "and the worse of it is you fellows aren't doing anything about it."

"What do you mean?"

"Well," growled Douglass, "here you have your churches and services and merry-go-round of activities, but as far as any actual impact and strategy for turning the tide is concerned, you're not making a dent."

Abram could not have agreed more. While San Francisco had boiled, Abram had developed the prototype of the Idea, preaching a manly Christ to a group of business executives who had no time for hymnals and sob sisters and soup kitchens and the Jesus of long eyelashes beloved by old ladies. Jesus, for such men, "must be disentangled from church organization," Abram had discovered. In the 1930s, the meaning of that was plain: a rejection of the "Social Gospel" of good works for the poor in favor of an unhindered Christ defined by his muscles, a laissez-faire Jesus proclaimed not by spindly necked clergymen bleating from seminary, but by men like Major Douglass, officers who commanded troops who brought order to cities.

"You ought to get after fellows like me," Douglass told Abram. He was standing in just the right spot for chest puffing—behind him towered the city's Douglass Building.

These were the words Abram had been waiting for, in the place, he was certain, to which God had guided him. He revealed the plan God had given him just hours earlier that morning: the Idea. He kept secret the bright light, the voice, the automatic writing in the dark hours. Men like Major Douglass, men of affairs, would not understand. But Major Douglass got the Idea.

"We are where we are," Abram said—on the brink of anarchy, both men thought—"because of what we are." By that he meant sinful, only his concept of sin was not so much concerned with immorality as with "duty." "Top men" had a responsibility to do for God what lesser men couldn't. Their failure to take on this burden had led the nation to its terrible position. "Obedience," concluded Abram, is "the way to power." God wanted his chosen to rule—to "serve," as Abram liked to say. Were men such as Major Douglass ready to report for duty?

Douglass stared at the silver-haired preacher. A "piercing gaze," Abram recalled. "Vereide," he said, "if you will settle down in this city and do a job like that, I will back you."

Abram demanded specifics. Douglass delivered: a suite of offices in the building behind Abram and a check to get him started.

"That's tangible," said Abram.

Then they set off together to see William St. Clair, one of the wealthiest men in Seattle. There's a whiff of *The Wizard of Oz* in Abram's later retelling of this story, the major and the minister popping lightbulbs over their fedoras on the Seattle street corner and rushing on to the man who would bring it all together, but that is, apparently, what happened: St. Clair, president of Frederick Nelson, the biggest department store in the Northwest, cleared his office and insisted the two men sit down. "We told him the story," Abram remembered. "And he, too, looked searchingly at me and remarked, 'That's constructive.'"

St. Clair made a list of nineteen businessmen and invited them to breakfast at one of the city's finest hotels. St. Clair certainly didn't choose on the basis of Christian morality. Of the nineteen, only one was a churchgoer, and he pointed out at the first meeting that the other men there knew him mainly as a creature of cocktail lounges and poker tables. Among the nineteen sat a lumber baron, a gas executive, a railroad executive, a hardware magnate, a candy impresario, and two future mayors of Seattle. "Management and labor got together," Abram would later claim, but there were no union representatives at the meeting, where nineteen businessmen plus Abram agreed to use the "Bible as blueprint" with which to take back first the city, then the state, and perhaps the nation from the grip of godless organized labor.

Their first success soon followed. "One morning," remembered Abram, "a labor leader, who had been a disturbing factor in the community, was seen at the table." Abram never fails to provide full names and corporate titles for the management side of his equation, but his first convert from labor is known only as "Jimmy." Jimmy came back for more meetings, sitting quietly in the corner and listening as the businessmen testified to one another about the Bible's transforming power in their lives. So Abram took Jimmy aside and had a talk with him about his responsibilities. Jimmy had been a leader in the "big strike." There, at the breakfast table, sat many men in whom Jimmy's actions had provoked "bitter feelings." One man, in fact, had been burdened with leading the industrialists' committee that organized management's fight against the strike. Jimmy had now taken meals with this man but had done nothing to make amends. Jimmy remained "unreconciled."

The next week, before a group of executives that now numbered seventy-five, Jimmy rose and spoke for the first time. "You fellows know me." He nodded toward one businessman. "I picketed your plant." He looked toward another. "I closed your factory for months." He pointed to a third: "I hated you."

But with Abram's help, Jimmy had discovered "how absolutely honest" these men he had hated were. They were humble. They were sincere. In fact, Jimmy realized, if they could bring more business-men in on the Idea, "there would be no need for a labor union." This, understandably, had been a bit of a shock to Jimmy. He had gone to his knees in his home, he told the men, and begged God's forgiveness "for the spirit I had been manifesting." And now he was ready to ask their forgiveness. He had been a thorn in capital's flesh, he said, but he would prick no more.

Jimmy sat down. The room was silent. Then "the sturdy, rugged capitalist who had been chairman of the employer's committee in the big strike," Abram observed—this probably refers to the "Citizens Emergency Committee," headed by the aptly named John Prim[8]— stood at the head of the table and walked over to Jimmy without a word. Worker looked up at boss. Boss glared down at worker. The businessman let drop a heavy hand on Jimmy's shoulder.

"Jimmy," he said, "on this basis we go on together."

IN THE YEARS to come, Abram would tell polished versions of this story hundreds of times, in dozens of countries, to CEOs and sena-tors and dictators, a parable of "cooperation" between management and labor, the threat to Christ and capital subdued, order restored. That was where it began, he'd say: Jimmy the agitator confessing his sins before a room full of businessmen, God's chosen men. This was "Unit Number One" of what Abram called his "new world order."

Abram was a kind of artist, just discovering in 1935 that there were other men and women with powers like his, *feelings* like his—"American," he would say, "terrified," we might translate—with whom he could join forces. Together they would smooth the dream. They claimed their religion was very old, "first century Christianity," but in their hearts they understood that it was a new faith, a new politics. Its conservatism was not vestigial; what made it thrilling was that the new religion made conservatism forceful again. It was not just a veneer for capitalism, nor simply a vehicle for power. It was a different way of wielding power. It shrugged off old inhibitions. It scoffed at liberal restraints and ignored traditional conservative reservations. It was Rotary Club dada, surrealism for businessmen from Seattle. It was the Word made fresh for the industrial age, vital and strong.

Just like that of Edwards. Just like that of Finney. But Finney had been followed by Sunday, who'd made the Word muscular yet vulgar. In 1935, Abram breathed life into a faith for the elite, an American fundamentalism made up of both Edwards's "heart" religion and Finney's permanent revival. He would write to his comrades with exhilaration when he thought a "key man" was beginning to "catch" the Idea. The religion Abram rebelled against was a set of ethics, a rule book for women. He aspired instead to spread what he would come to call a *contagion,* passed from key man to key man, the avant-garde of American fundamentalism.

5.

THE *F* WORD

T HE DEFENDERS OF THE status quo," Henry Kissinger wrote in
his doctoral dissertation, published as *A World Betrayed* in 1957,
". . . tend to begin by treating revolutionary power as if its protesta-
tions were merely tactical." That this comment is sufficiently ambig-
uous to be worthy of the slippery career that followed it takes nothing
from the weight of its insight, and, more, its double meaning.
Kissinger himself provides a perfect illustration. Like most brilliant
political players, he became both a defender of the status quo and a
revolutionary, a champion of American hegemony where it already
existed and a clever tactician of revolution on behalf of that power
where it had not yet been achieved. The vast array of actors that com-
prise American fundamentalism do not include any single tactician of
Kissinger's caliber, and yet they have, as a movement, functioned in
just such a fashion, building on the foundation of American Protestantism's traditional power to strategize both its expansion and, in
true revolutionary fashion, its transformation.[1]

In one sense, the men Abram Vereide gathered for bacon and eggs
and Bible were defenders of the status quo. They sought not so much
spiritual sustenance as stability, an end to the Depression's hurdy-
gurdy years. Men, women, and children dwindled into thin and hopeless creatures, listless and dull-witted and red-eyed. Then would come
a strike or a street fight or a mob that had decided to take vegetables
from a moving train, or to march on city hall, and out came the bulls
like it was Pamplona. And there were words in the air, and a family

cold and huddled around a radio, heads bent toward the voice of a man such as Father Coughlin, the "radio priest" from Detroit, the Shrine of the Little Flower, preaching and ranting to more millions than the president himself some evenings. What did he want? He was no communist, that was for certain. He called *them* the "Red Fog." But he was no friend of things as they were, either. He was a furious man, his voice dulcet but his words full of hatred for the capitalists who had lined their silk pockets. Coughlin, as much as or more than the communists, seemed like he might call for blood one day, and soon.[2] It was against that threat, as much as communism, that Abram schemed.

Abram's men did not consider themselves blameless. But they believed their folly didn't lie in the economics of do-as-you-will that had brought the nation and the city to those days of breadlines and street battles. Their sin was slippage. They had enriched their coffers at the expense of their souls. Money was like power: Those who had it should not speak of it, concern themselves with it, acknowledge its existence as a factor. To do so was worse than bad manners; it was blasphemy, an attempt to refute God's ordering of economic affairs.

So they sought a return to that order. To reclaim it, they had to take steps they had never taken before. One of these was reading the Bible, a book that for most of them was long in the past, of interest only to grandmothers; now, they were determined to find in it a message for men such as themselves. They promised one another that they would study at least a chapter a day. Understanding was another matter. The churches had failed. They no longer taught truth but insisted on metaphor. The best pulpits were manned, if that word could be used, by foppish intellectuals who debated like Jews, sifting sentences like sand for grains of meaning. A useless endeavor. The ocean was crashing upon them. They needed rocks to stand on. They needed marching orders. "Men who did not want to be preached at" turned to one another for confirmation of their spiritual gleanings, "teachings practical in business, government, and social life," wrote Abram. "We discovered that, as the eye is made for light and the ear for sound, so the human personality is made for God. We discovered that sanity and normalcy are to be Christ-like."

That summer Abram took a core of Christ-committed leaders—a railroad man and a lumberman and a banker, a car dealer, a clothier, and a navy commander—on a retreat to the Canyon Creek Lodge, alongside a river amid the peaks of the Cascades. He gathered his troops around a tall stone hearth and led them in a "spiritual inventory," each man taking turns listing aloud that which troubled their city, their state, their corporation. Hunger, pride, whores, Harry Bridges, booze, degenerates, sloth, corruption, the Teamsters. Women with short hair. Communism in the colleges. Sailors, a dirty, immoral lot. Pessimism. Racy movies. The Soviet Union. The color red, in general, the "red tide," the "red menace," the "red-hued progeny" of Stalin. Also brown, for Brownshirts, a force so vital, so strong, so bursting with muscle—could America possibly compete with the fabulous rising of Italy, Germany, Austria? Round the room the men went, moaning their fears and their losses and their failures. They fell to their knees, old men's joints creaking, overwhelmed by the godlessness surrounding them, and, yes, they confessed, within them. "Utter helplessness," Abram recorded.

They had been reading the Bible for months, and most must have known its darkest corners, the truth of an angry God not as a bearded man in heaven shaking an ancient finger but more like the wilderness growling in the dark at the edge of the city. "He was like a bear waiting for me," warned Jeremiah, "like a lion in secret places." To them the thud of the billy club and the shriek of the gas canister were the sounds not of repression but of Christian civilization making its last stand. The tribes of labor were whooping. If history taught any lesson, it was that no Custer could save society from the coarse-clothed savages. "Subversive forces had taken over," observed Abram. "What could we do?"

It was at this moment on the edge of hysteria when a young lawyer named Arthur B. Langlie, kneeling among the big men, discovered his calling. A flat-faced, blue-eyed Scandinavian like Abram, Langlie was thirty-five years old that July, known equally for his wide smile and his zealous religion, a sharp-nosed teetotaling man who could work a party with just a glass of water in his hand.

He rose from his knees. "Men, it can be done," he said. "I am ready to let God use me."

Abram's brotherhood was ready to use him, too. On the spot one rich man said he would finance Langlie's crusade, and others followed with promises of time and connections. Langlie would be their key man. Abram's heart must have been pounding. This was what God had shown him. The brothers gripped hands in a circle before the fireplace and sang a song in the mountains for the city they meant to save.

> Faith of our fathers, living still
> In spite of dungeon, fire, and sword:
> Oh, how our hearts beat high with joy . . .

"There," Abram would declare, "was born a new regime." It was the beginning of the movement of elite fundamentalism that would, in the 1980s, come to be known as "the Family."

THAT MEETING ALSO marked a turning point in Langlie's long and successful political career. Langlie came to the prayer movement as a representative of a brotherhood of young businessmen across the state of Washington called the New Order of Cincinnatus. Twelve hundred strong, the Cincinnatans presented a "New Order" of moral and economic force in opposition to FDR's New Deal. Younger than Abram's establishment figures, the Order ran candidates for office under the banner of the ancient Roman general Cincinnatus, summoned from his farm five centuries before Christ to assume dictatorial power over a populace too exhausted by infighting to make decisions for itself.

When several of Langlie's Cincinnatans showed up at the city comptroller's office to register, they came flanked by men of the Order wearing identical white shirts, joining a rainbow of likeminded lovers of discipline and intimidation—not just Mussolini's Blackshirts and Hitler's Brownshirts but the Greenshirts of the

Romanian Legion of the Archangel Michael, the Blueshirts of Ireland, and, in America, the Silver Shirts, the initials of which, *SS*, deliberately chosen, justified the flamboyant color. The men of the Order gave themselves military ranks and considered adding a *sieg heil*–style salute to their public image, but decided that would be "*too* fascist." The Order's first "National Commander," an excitable former Republican operative, saw models for such qualities in the strong men across the Atlantic and the bureaucrats who made their governments run like Henry Ford's assembly lines. The Order craved efficiency. One of its first goals after its formation in 1933 was a Washington state constitutional convention at which local police forces would be eliminated and replaced with troopers trained at retooled state colleges.[3]

Langlie never officially joined the Order, but he became its chief candidate. The year of the big strike, the Order took control of Seattle's city council by invoking middle-class fears of a Wobbly insurrection. Poverty, it maintained, was part of the natural way of things. The Order had two solutions to economic malaise: slash taxes and attack vice. As councilman, Langlie purged the city's police department, which routinely ignored Sunday liquor sales, Chinese gambling halls, and the prostitution that prospered in a port city like Seattle. He then turned his ax toward the fire department (poor moral specimens) and public school teachers (indoctrinating the youth with godless notions). With his allies in the Order, he succeeded in passing a budget so brutal that the city's conservative Republican mayor, whose first act in office had been to literally lead a police charge against the previous year's strikers, vetoed it as contemptuous of human suffering. So Langlie decided to depose him. The Order's rise won attention as far away as Manhattan, where a titillated *New York Times* thrilled to the movement's youthful fervor.[4]

In Abram's telling, Langlie stood, pledged himself, and simply ascended to public office. Langlie had in fact taken his city council seat without the trouble of an election; his opponent, wary of a public fight with the Order, simply stepped down and appointed Langlie to replace him. But despite the Order's white-shirted military manner and

the financial backing of Abram's brotherhood, his first bid for the
mayoralty failed. The Democrat who'd been ousted in 1934, a flamboyantly corrupt opportunist named John Dore, charged Langlie with
running as the candidate of a "secret society." Dore wound up his
campaign with a ninety-minute speech denouncing Langlie as a fascist
so dangerous that his own almost-open corruption was preferable.
The city that had thrown Dore out in a special election only a year
before agreed with that diagnosis: Democrats, radicals, and even Republicans united to return the crook to power.

"The insincerity of [Dore] is almost unquestionable," the novelist
Mary McCarthy observed. Double-chinned Dore perched his spectacles on the end of his nose and reveled in his royal belly and, as a
sign of his high regard for the common man, occasionally went down
to the docks and passed out glasses of beer to incoming sailors. As far
as conservatives were concerned, he might as well have grown a mustache and changed his name to Stalin. But Mary McCarthy understood that the "Soviet of Washington," as one wag dubbed the state,
was more like a vaudeville routine than a government on the verge of
a worker's utopia. "The state of Washington is in ferment," she wrote
in The Nation; "it is wild, comic, theatrical, dishonest, disorganized,
hopeful; but it is not revolutionary."[5]

Dubbed "Labor's Mayor" by the conservative press, Dore was
really the right-wing Teamster chief Dave Beck's man. "Dave Beck
runs this town, and I tell you it's a good thing he does," Dore declared as he squared off with Langlie again in 1938, a bald confession
of fealty to bossism. The race garnered broad attention, "a mayoralty
election of national significance," in the words of the New York Times.[6]
At stake seemed to be the future of organized labor in the Northwest, which, as one of the labor movement's strongholds, was a
bellwether for the nation. Dore stood for Beck, and Beck stood for
the old, management-friendly craft unions of the American Federation of Labor. His opponent on the Left, Lieutenant Governor Vic
Meyers, championed the newborn Congress of Industrial Organizations, an alliance of more militant, pro-worker unions. And out in
right field stood Langlie, so far from friendly to any labor union that

even the rabidly right-wing *Los Angeles Times* tagged him as "ultra-conservative."[7]

Lieutenant Governor Meyers, the most well-liked man in the state, should have won. But for once the Left did itself in with a sense of humor. Meyers had entered public service in 1932 as a joke. A beaming, mustache-twirling master of ceremonies at the city's most fashionable nightclub, he'd campaigned at the head of an oompah band, wearing the uniform of a circus drum major. If elected, he'd promised, he'd put a pretty girl hostess on every streetcar.

Such was the state of the union in 1932—its disgust with the big business do-nothingism of Herbert Hoover—that Meyers and his trombone campaign marched into office on FDR's coattails. By 1938, though, after years of strikes and police violence, Meyers had grown serious about doing something for working people. Unfortunately, he still loved a good costume, and he campaigned dressed as Mahatma Gandhi. Even Harry Bridges, Meyers's chief backer, couldn't make the bandleader look like a serious candidate.

So Dore and Meyers canceled each other out, and between them slipped the winner, Arthur B. Langlie. The verdict was in: neither the AFL nor the CIO represented the future. "Good government," as Langlie called his platform of budget slashing and punishing moral rectitude, trumped labor. "Seattle Deals Radicals a Blow," declared the *Los Angeles Times*. "Whole Left Wing Beaten," amplified the *New York Times*.[8]

What did "good government" really mean? Langlie and his brotherhood promised an end to political corruption. (There's no evidence that Langlie ever even took a drink, much less a bribe.) The days of "honest graft" were over, at least for a while. But seen from another perspective—that of ordinary citizens without access to Langlie and Abram's elite network—Langlie didn't so much end corruption as legalize it. Langlie wasn't opposed to a government organized around the interests of the greedy; he just didn't want to have to break the law to serve them. His kind of good government meant deals for your friends but not envelopes full of cash. He didn't rule through fear or finesse but through prayer. If Abram and Langlie could help it, there would be no bullets, no bribes. Instead, there would be a circle of men listening to Jesus by listening to one another's remarkably similar views. It was the first fulfillment of Abram's dream of government by God.

And although no one could see it in 1938, the shape of the Langlie campaign—the New Order of Cincinnatus as his political commandos, Abram's God-picked elites, by then coming to be known as "the Fellowship," as his brain trust, and Abram's old network of housewives transformed into "prayer group" precincts for Langlie—was a bellwether indeed. Not of labor's future—that was already eroding—but of prayer breakfast politics in the Christian nation to come.

"WE WORK WITH power where we can, build new power where we can't." These words belong to Doug Coe, who seized the Fellowship's top spot in a succession struggle following Abram's death in 1969 and began transforming it into what I eventually encountered as the Family. His blunt formulation of the Fellowship's political theology is as much in play now as it was in 1969, and, indeed, in 1938, when Abram and his quiet gathering of businessmen staked Langlie to the beginning of his career. On the face of it, such words seem brutal, a foreshadowing of revolution—or *counterrevolution,* as conservatives like to say.

And yet Langlie-as-mayor, then governor, demonstrated the Fellowship's subtler ambitions. Theocratic by instinct and fascinated by fascism according to the fashion of the times, the Fellowship never molted into European-style authoritarianism. Its most radical goals were (and remain) long-term, its method—*the man-method,* Abram called it—painstaking, dependent not on mass conversion but on individual assimilation into polite fundamentalism. "The more impersonal our order becomes," observed Theodor Adorno in a study of 1930s fundamentalism, "the more important personality becomes as an ideology." Abram's man-method was a perfect illustration of this truth, but whereas Adorno, a refugee from Nazi Germany, saw this trend as leading only to populist demagogues, Abram recognized that "personality" in place of ideology could also preserve elite power in an age of mass movements. Good manners mattered to the immigrant preacher; the men he drew to him tended to be discreet, polished characters. They were fundamentalism's avant-garde, its most radical thinkers, but to all appearances they were creatures of the country club, golf course crusaders.

Langlie epitomized the breed. In 1935, at the Canyon Creek Lodge, he rose from his knees as a "God-led" politician, literally a theocrat, and he campaigned as a modern-day Cincinnatus. As governor, he attempted (and failed) to pass a law giving him the power to suspend the law—almost all of it—if he desired.

So Langlie accepted the constraints of democracy as he found them. He did what business asked: purged welfare rolls, abolished guaranteed wage laws, denounced Democrats as un-American. In 1942, he investigated the possibility of using martial law to suppress organized labor, but when his advisers told him it would be unconstitutional, he settled for ordinary strikebreaking.[9] He governed, in other words, as a right-wing Republican.

And yet the Fellowship was attracted to a kind of soft fascism. In 1932, Abram took as a Bible student Henry Ford. By then, the automaker was a wizened old leather strop of a man, wary of controversy. He had been the American publisher of the notoriously fraudulent *Protocols of the Elders of Zion*, an anti-Semitic fantasia concocted in czarist Russia to justify pogroms against Jews, and the author of *The International Jew*, a book many Nazis would later credit with awakening their Aryan anti-Semitism. During the previous decade, historians suspect, he'd illegally financed Adolf Hitler. But it was not just national socialism's bigotry that Ford supported, nor even mainly that. What Ford, inventor of the assembly line, loved above all was efficiency. Even his war of words against the Jews had been in the interests of standardization, the purging of "others" from the American scene. And yet, in 1932, Ford wanted certain details of his campaign for American purity to disappear. He wanted to sell cars to Jews. He was in need of a makeover, a quick bath in the Blood of the Lamb.

Ford's wife heard Abram speak in Detroit and insisted that he meet with her husband, no doubt guessing that Abram's theology of

biblical capitalism would sit well with the tycoon, an eccentric religious thinker who had been raised on populist American fundamentalism. Abram and Ford traded Bible verses through a series of meetings
in Ford's offices, and then Ford invited Abram to his home in Sud-
bury, Massachusetts. "They were together two days," records Abram's
biographer Grubb, "[Ford] unloading about spiritual, intellectual,
and business problems, and Abram seeking to give the answer for
himself and the nation." Abram thought Ford "befuddled," full of
half-baked religious notions gathered from partial readings of Hindu
texts and theosophy. "The question was," Abram thought, "How
could he be untangled?"

Their meetings continued in Michigan. Abram was drawn like a
moth to the great man's wealth—to the possibility that Ford might
put his tremendous worldly resources behind a campaign for government by God. But he was frustrated by Ford's failure to settle on one
simple fundamentalist explanation of life and the universe, until, at
their final meeting, Ford finally shouted, "Vereide, I've got it! I've got
it! I found the release that you spoke of. I've made my surrender. The
only thing that matters is God's will."

But Ford continued to see divine will best expressed in German
fascism. As Hitler's power grew, Ford became more comfortable
expressing his admiration. It was mutual; the Führer hung a portrait
of Ford behind his desk and told the industrialist, on a visit Ford paid
to Nazi Germany, that national socialism's accomplishments were
simply an implementation of Ford's vision.

That was a perspective that, unlike theosophy, gave Abram no
pause. Such was the nature of Abram's ecumenicism. For Jews he felt
nothing, one way or the other, but he would no more discriminate
against an anti-Semite than against a Presbyterian. He welcomed the
vigor anti-Semitism brought to his cause. After the war, another major American fascist sympathizer—Charles Lindbergh—would pre-
side for a brief period over a prayer cell modeled on Abram's original.
Lindbergh first came under FBI scrutiny, in fact, for his association
with a man who would become a stalwart of Abram's inner circle and
a member of the board of the Fellowship, by then incorporated as

International Christian Leadership. Merwin K. Hart was an "alleged promoter of the American Fascist movement," according to FBI files, and denounced publicly as a Nazi in all but name by Robert H. Jackson, the FDR-era attorney general who went on to serve as a justice of the Supreme Court and chief prosecutor at Nuremberg.

To Abram, Hart was a dapper habitué of New York's blue blood clubs, a crucial node in his network of top men. He was a recruiter; operating out of the Empire State Building, he organized business executives bent on breaking the spine of unionism into an organization called the National Economic Council, and from those ranks he selected men for the Fellowship whose devotion to the antilabor cause was religious in intensity. Hart was Abram through a glass, darkly: if Abram could not distinguish between men of power and men of morals, Hart could not tell the difference between communists and Jews, who through "deceit" and "trickery," he preached, threatened the "complete destruction" of the American way of life.[10]

Then there were the actual Nazis who would join Abram's prayer circles in the postwar years. But that story must wait until the next chapter. To understand Abram's weirdly ambivalent relationship with fascism—to understand the uneasy echoes of the last century's most hateful ideology in contemporary American fundamentalism—we must exhume an unlikely pair of "thinkers": Frank Buchman and Bruce Barton, two of the most influential hucksters of early twentieth-century America.

BUCHMANISM

In 1935, Frank Buchman was at the height of his powers, a small, well-nourished, and well-tailored man of no natural distinction, who found himself touring the world in the company of kings and queens and bright, young, rosy-cheeked lads from Oxford and Cambridge and Princeton. True, Buchman was banned from Princeton, where as a Lutheran minister he had stalked students he thought eligible for *soul surgery,* as he would come to call his variation on the born-again procedure; and Oxford University was contemplating legal measures to stop him from using its name for his movement. He was then calling his followers the "Oxford Group," having discarded "First Century Christian Fellowship"—a name Abram would later consider—as perhaps boastful, not to mention inaccurate when applied to Buchman's hundreds of thousands of twentieth-century devotees. "Oxford Group," though, was no more descriptive of the international circuit of confessional "house parties" for the well-to-do inspired by Buchman. He had not attended Oxford (or Cambridge, though he would claim the latter in his *Who's Who* biography). He was a graduate of modest Muhlenberg College in what was then Pennsylvania coal country.[11]

"Moral Re-Armament," coined by Buchman as Europe entered World War II, was the name that eventually stuck. Not quite an organization—there were no dues or membership rolls—but less democratic in spirit than a social movement, Moral Re-Armament deployed its military metaphors through Buchman's never-ending lecture tour, propaganda campaigns, and the spiritual warfare practiced by his disciples in service of an ideology "Not Left, Not Right, but Straight," in the words of one of Buchman's hagiographers.[12] Moral Re-Armament's aims were so broadly utopian as to be meaningless, but in practice it served distinctly conservative purposes: the preservation of caste. "There is tremendous power," preached Buchman, "in a minority guided by God."[13]

It is probably most accurate to name Buchman's innovation as did the papers of his day: Buchmanism. After all, it was Buchman's idea—later adapted and sharpened by Abram—that the mass evangelism practiced by men such as Charles Finney and Billy Sunday would never appeal to the "best people," those whom the liquor salesman's son from Pennsburg, Pennsylvania, had dreamed of cultivating for Christ since his first job, running a home for troubled boys in Philadelphia, had ended in abrupt dismissal.

The cause of Buchman's firing is murky, as is the precise nature of the charges leveled against him at Princeton. In the first case he seems to have paid too little attention to the children's needs, and in the second, too much to the undergraduates. In particular, the university's president resented Buchman's fascination with the sex lives of young Princetonians. Buchman estimated that between 85 and 90 percent of all sin is sexual, and thus to him it was natural to encourage young men to confess theirs in detail.[14] There is no evidence that he took advantage of the information. He had kissed a girl once when he was a boy, but thereafter lived as a sort of eunuch. In college his nickname was "Kate," and in the drama society he played mainly female roles. Many close to him thought it obvious that he inclined toward the best-looking men of the best universities, but in terms of Christian conservatism and the anxieties that plague it today, he was ahead of his time in the fury with which he denounced homosexuality as a threat to civilization. Moreover, he was an exceedingly careful student of the crisis: In a pamphlet titled *Remaking Men*, he observed, "there are many who wear suede shoes who are not homosexual, but in Europe and America the majority of homosexuals do." Also, Buchman declared, their favorite color is green.[15]

Buchman's own eyes were emerald, and capable of the most penetrating glances. His followers believed he knew their sins before they confessed them. He wore gold-rimmed spectacles and, though bald, was more than once described as "shampooed." He loved to be clean. Most striking about his appearance was his head; despite giant, pointed ears, it seemed several sizes too small for his round body. "Frank," as he insisted on being called, was the gnome of early twentieth-century elite fundamentalism.

In the early 1930s, he and Abram crossed paths. Buchman was in Ottawa to perform soul surgery on Canadian members of Parliament, and Abram, fresh from what would prove to be his short-lived salvation of Henry Ford (Ford would later require renewal by Buchman, for whom he built a retreat in Michigan), was lecturing in Canada on behalf of Goodwill Industries. The two met, and Abram suggested to Buchman that he come on with Goodwill as a chaplain, to infuse the organization with his "life-changing" evangelical fervor. Buchman answered by proposing a *Quiet Time*.[16]

Besides confession of sexual sin, Quiet Time was the core practice

of Buchmanism: a half-hour-long period of silence in which the believer waited for "Guidance" from God. Guidance was more than a
warm feeling. It came in the form of direct orders and touched on
every subject of concern, from the transcendent to the mundane.
"The real question," Buchman would preach, "is, 'Will God control
America?' The country must be 'governed by men under instructions
from God, as definitely given and understood as if they came by
wire.' "[17] Guidance meant not just spiritual direction but declaring
one's own decisions as divinely inspired. "We are not out to tell God,"
Buchman announced to an assembly of twenty-five thousand in 1936.
"We are out to let God tell us. And He will tell us."[18]

"What did God say to you?" Buchman asked Abram when their
Quiet Time was completed. Abram believed he had heard God's
voice several times in his life, and had even considered the possibility
that he might be a prophet, but he had not yet been exposed to the
idea that God spoke to men *regularly* and in detail. "He didn't say anything," Abram confessed, disappointed.

Well, Buchman replied, God *had* spoken to him. "God told me,
'Christianize what you have. You have something to share.' "

Blander words no Sunday school teacher ever spoke, but to
Abram they seemed like a revelation. God had told Buchman not to
join Goodwill, but that didn't matter. What was important was the
discovery that God should be consulted not just on broad spiritual
questions but on absolutely everything. This, Abram decided, was
what it meant to die to the self: to turn all responsibility over to
God. That such a transfer meant the abdication of any accountability
for one's actions, that it provided justification for any ambition, did
not occur to him.

Thereafter he transformed his daily prayer ritual into Buchmanite
Quiet Time. And, soon enough, God filled the silence with instructions: go forth, he said, and build cells for my cause like Buchman's.

The cell of spiritual warriors that elected Arthur Langlie was one
result. That cell of men listening to God during their Quiet Time
doubled itself, and the two became four, the four became eight. The
many cells for congressmen and generals and lowly government

clerks in the Washington, D.C., of the present are the offspring of that original mitosis, catalyzed by Buchman. But to call them Buchmanite wouldn't be quite right. When Buchman spoke of Christianity's "new illumination," "a new social order under the dictatorship of the Spirit of God" that would transform politics and eradicate the conflict of capital and labor, Abram took him literally.

Abram never actually attended a Buchman house party. Had he done so, he might have veered away from his new enthusiasm. The most successful events took place at one of the estates around the world that Buchman used as outreach stations. He had won the allegiance of a number of wealthy widows and heiresses and neglected wives of businessmen, and they regularly showered him with riches, including their great homes, to which Buchman would invite select groups for a day in the country. There would be tennis and golf and some praying, and then the group would gather for the party. A fire would be built, the lights dimmed, and Buchman or a trained confessor might begin with some minor transgression, a traffic ticket, a youthful prank. Another Buchman veteran might then up the ante. "Some lad might now turn evidence against a governess or an upstairs maid," observed a New Yorker writer in 1932. And from there it was on to the weaknesses that afflict not just college boys but also the grand dames who flocked to Buchman and the big men they dragged in their wake, all stumbling over one another in elaborate description of their private perversions, how they had been blinded to their purpose in life by sexual desire, and how "Guidance" had saved them. Around the circle they went, spurring one another on.

And yet Buchmanism was not purely narcissistic. Once one had been "changed," as Buchmanites called the experience of coming through soul surgery successfully, one was ready for political action. What sort of action? On this, Buchman was vague. Like Abram, he considered industrial strife an affront to God, to be solved by "changed" men among the captains of industry. Like Abram, he considered the sharp elbows of democracy an insult to the "dictatorship of the Holy Spirit." And it was from Buchman that Abram surely absorbed the idea of a leadership of "God-led" men organized into cells, consulting not the unchanged masses but the mandate of Jesus as He revealed Himself to them behind closed doors. Beyond that, though, Buchman rarely went. Even more than Abram, he so desired the company of powerful people that he was loath to align himself too closely with any one faction. But in 1936, in a sympathetic portrait published by the *New York World-Telegram*, Buchman named names.

"But think what it would mean to the world if Hitler surrendered to the control of God. Or Mussolini. Or any dictator. Through such a man, God could control a nation overnight and solve every last, bewildering problem." He seemed to think the process had already started: "I thank heaven for a man like Adolf Hitler, who built a front line of defence against the anti-Christ of Communism," he told the reporter.[19]

Buchman had just returned from the Olympic Games in Berlin, orchestrated by Joseph Goebbels as a visual symphony of black and red swastikas and eagles and the long, lean muscle of Aryan athleticism. Most of the world would remember the "Nazi Olympics" for the African American athlete Jesse Owens, but Goebbels's spectacle achieved its desired effect on Buchman, who left Berlin with a surging admiration for the vigor of the Third Reich. In particular, Heinrich Himmler, the chief of the Gestapo, had impressed him as a "great lad," a man whom he recommended to his followers in British government. The sentiment, to be fair, was not mutual. After World War II, Buchman's followers, eager to "wash out" their leader's past, would produce Gestapo documents condemning Buchmanism, though in terms not exactly reassuring: Himmler, it seems, saw Buchman's Moral Re-Armament as too close of a competitor to national socialism.

In 1936, flush with the excitement of Hitler's Olympics, Buchman gathered some American Oxford Group men at a house party at a Lenox, Massachusetts, estate. The Oxfordites sat on the floor in their tweeds as Buchman described the vision he brought back with him.

"Suppose we here were all God-controlled and we became the Cabinet," he said. Then he designated the *World-Telegram* reporter secretary of agriculture and pointed to a recent Princeton graduate (they came to him, since he could not go to them) to replace Cordell Hull, Roosevelt's secretary of state. Around the room he went, referring not to the talents of his followers but to their willingness to govern by Guidance.

"Then," he continued, "in a God-controlled nation, capital and labor would discuss their problems peacefully and reach God-controlled situations." The distribution of wealth would remain as it was, but the workers would be content to be led by employers who were not greedy but God-controlled. Echoing the words of U.S. Steel's James A. Farrell that had so inspired Abram in 1932, words which the Fellowship repeats to this day, Buchman declared, "Human problems aren't economic. They're moral, and they can't be solved by immoral measures."

In 1936, when men such as Henry Ford and Charles Lindbergh openly admired Hitler, it was still safe to name the style of government to which these words pointed. Human problems, Buchman told his little group that night in Lenox, require "a God-controlled democracy, or perhaps I should say a theocracy." Just as good, said Buchman, would be a "God-controlled Fascist dictatorship."

He paused. He let his emerald eyes glide over the young manhood of Buchmanism, sitting cross-legged on the floor before him as if he was a Greek philosopher. Frank smiled and adjusted the red rose in his boutonniere.

"THERE IS A book in the store windows in London and New York," Buchman told an assembly at the Metropolitan Opera House in November of 1935. "The title is *It Can't Happen Here*. Some of you who read the very important words of the Secretary of State, 'Our own country urgently needs a moral and spiritual awakening,' may have said the same thing, 'It can't happen here.' "

Buchman had taken the stage that evening to tell Manhattan's wealthiest that it could. "Think of nations changed," he told his audience, urging them to imagine soul surgery on a national scale, or something even grander: "God-controlled supernationalism."[20]

Buchman never was one for details. Had he bothered to pick up the book he considered too pessimistic, he would have discovered that the *It* of the volume's title was fascism. Five years earlier, the book's author, Sinclair Lewis, had become the first American to win the Nobel Prize for Literature, in recognition of novels such as *Babbit*, *Arrowsmith*, and *Elmer Gantry*. *It Can't Happen Here* wasn't Lewis's finest work, but it contained some of his scariest writing. Can't happen here? Lewis's novel contended that it already had, in countless little rooms across the country, at gatherings of Rotarians and the Daughters of the American Revolution, in hot-blooded church meetings and movie houses where gunfighters bestrode American dreams like Mussolinis in spurs. All that was wanting was the right key man to take up the sword and the cross and move into the oval office. In the novel, that man is Senator Buzz Windrip, a folksy southerner backed by a radio preacher called Bishop Peter Paul Prang and his "League of Forgotten Men."

The story opens with the "Ladies Night Dinner" of a small town Rotary Club, and Mrs. Adelaide Tarr Gimmitch, an expert on "Child Culture," lecturing a group of concerned citizens in eveningwear. Her sermon could have been lifted directly from Abram: "I tell you, my friends, the trouble with this whole country is that so many are *selfish!* Here's a hundred and twenty million people, with ninety-five per cent of 'em only thinking of *self,* instead of turning to and helping the responsible business men to bring back prosperity! All these corrupt and self-seeking labor unions! Money grubbers! Thinking only of how much wages they can extort out of their unfortunate employer, with all the responsibilities he has to bear!

"What this country needs is Discipline."

The novel's voice of reason is the local newspaper editor, one Doremus Jessup, into whose mouth Lewis packs a dense but brief account of the authoritarian strain in American history.

Why, there's no country in the world that can get more hysterical—yes, or more obsequious!—than America. Look how Huey Long became absolute monarch over Louisiana, and how the Right Honorable Mr. Senator Berzelius Windrip owns *his* State. Listen to Bishop Prang and Father Coughlin on the radio—divine oracles, to millions. Remember how casually most Americans have accepted Tammany grafting and Chicago gangs and the crookedness of so many of President Harding's appointees? Could Hitler's bunch, or Windrip's, be worse? Remember the Ku Klux Klan? Remember our war hysteria, when we called sauerkraut "Liberty cabbage" and somebody actually proposed calling German measles "Liberty measles"? And wartime censorship of honest papers? Bad as Russia! Remember our kissing the—well, the feet of Billy Sunday, the million-dollar evangelist . . . Remember when the hick legislators in certain states, in obedience to William Jennings Bryan, who learned his biology from his pious old grandma, set up shop as scientific experts and made the whole world laugh itself sick by forbidding the teaching of evolution? . . . Remember the Kentucky nightriders? Remember how trainloads of people have gone to enjoy lynchings? Not happen here? Prohibition—shooting down people just because they *might* be transporting liquor—no, that couldn't happen in *America!* Why, where in all history has there ever been a people so ripe for a dictatorship as ours![21]

And yet that fruit was never plucked. The United States did not then—and has not yet—succumbed to fascism. Nor, for that matter, does the contemporary Christian Right embrace even a modern strain of "national socialism." Many of the ingredients are there: militaristic patriotism, a blurry identification of church with state, a reverence for strong men, a tendency to locate such men at the top of corporate hierarchies, even a hated "other" (for American fundamentalists, Jews and Catholics gave way to communists, and now the populist front of the movement is divided over whom to demonize more, Muslims or gay people).

But other elements of European-style fascism never emerged in the United States. Despite the nation's near constant involvement in one war or another for the last sixty years, it has never adopted an ideology that explicitly celebrates violence. Nor do we have a significant secret police force. And it is Christianity itself that has prevented fundamentalists, America's most authoritarian demographic, from embracing the cult of personality around which fascist states are organized. No matter how much the movement may revere Ronald Reagan or George W. Bush or the next political savior to arise, such men must always accept second billing to Jesus—*The Man Nobody Knows*, in the words of Bruce Barton's 1925 best seller, perhaps the most influential forgotten book of the twentieth century.

Barton's publisher boasted that the book could be read in two hours, but most readers could bounce through it in half that time. Less a narrative than a collage of advertising copy, *The Man Nobody Knows* offered Christ on the cheap as "the most popular dinner guest in Jerusalem!"[22]

Exclamation points come by the bushel in Barton's work. "A failure!" the book opens—and here the exclamation point must be read as an incredulous question mark, a quotation of the supposed liberal view of Christ as "weak and puny," an effeminate sadsack who died on the cross because he could not do better. Barton responds with the greatest *Fortune* magazine story ever told: "He picked up twelve men from the bottom ranks of business and forged them into an organization that conquered the world."

Barton himself was such a man. Shaped like a shoe box, he had a flat-faced head atop a rectangle of a body but was handsome all the same in that lock-jawed manner that makes some men look like they were born to captain industry. Barton's name lives on as one fourth of the advertising giant Batten, Barton, Durstine, and Osborne, but his slim volume on Christ as the ultimate salesman exists now only as an academic curiosity, evidence to historians of the "secularization" of religion during the 1920s. Published in the same year as the Scopes monkey trial took place, *The Man Nobody Knows* has long looked to such observers like proof that the chief concern of secularism—business—had subsumed theology. Barton made Jesus into a management guru, and profit trumped prophet. Even in the era of a president who touts as his twin qualifications a business degree and his intimate relationship with Jesus, Fitzgerald's *Great Gatsby* and Lewis's *Babbitt* are celebrated as the definitive texts of that earlier age, the stories that shaped the later course of the nation.

And yet in the 1920s, *The Man Nobody Knows* outpaced them both. It was the book read on streetcars and the title punned on by admirers, the volume distributed in bulk at Christmas to friends and employees. So, too, its themes thrive now, far more so than Fitzgerald's despair or Lewis's contempt for capitalism. *Gatsby* and *Babbitt* may still be debated in high school English classrooms, but Barton's entrepreneur-Christ prospers on a broader scale, the "Master," as Barton called him, of best sellers such as *God Is My CEO: Following God's Principles in a Bottom-Line World*, and *Jesus CEO: Using Ancient Wisdom for Visionary Leadership,* and, most influentially, Rick Warren's spiritual time-management manual, *The Purpose-Driven Life*—more than 25 million copies sold since publication in 2002.

In Barton's own day, Frank Buchman declared *The Man Nobody Knows* one of the "three outstanding contributions to [his] life and work."[22] Abram did not record whether he, too, had read it, but he wouldn't have had to; Barton's business-faith had entered the bloodstream of American Christianity. Indeed, it's hard to imagine the rise of Abram's elite evangelicalism absent the precedent of "top man" religion set by *The Man Nobody Knows*. If the book espoused a literally fundamentalist Jesus—a Christ stripped clean of all that Barton considered feminizing cultural accretion—Barton was not, himself, a fundamentalist. He was less interested in the doctrinal battles of separatist religion than in the driving force of Christianity as the best means for national efficiency. In this sense, he followed the example set by one of his chief theological advisers, Harry Emerson Fosdick, even as he hewed to a morality and politics more akin to that of Billy Sunday.

In 1922, Fosdick had preached a sermon that drew the battle lines and became a manifesto of sorts for modernist Christians. "Shall the Fundamentalists Win?" attempted to prove that they couldn't. Ironically, it also established the political and theological vision that would allow more sophisticated fundamentalists such as Abram to build for the future.

"We must be able to think our modern life clear through in Christian terms, and to do that we also must be able to think our Christian faith clear through in modern terms," Fosdick preached from the pulpit of New York's First Presbyterian Church. Reminding his congregation of advances in science and, even more dangerously, biblical scholarship—the German "higher criticism" which held that the Bible could be better grasped with a knowledge of its historical context—he declared that "the new knowledge and the old faith [have] to be blended in a new combination."

Fosdick imagined that combination to be cosmopolitan and literary, shaped by a grasp of metaphor and a benign disdain for the literalists of years past. He had no concept of the other meanings future Christian conservatives would take from his call, shuffling the parts around not in the service of high-minded liberalism but of sophisticated, science-fueled fundamentalism. Fosdick's accommodationist vision of modernism illuminated the path for a traditionalist crusade in which later fundamentalists—influenced, not so indirectly, by Marx, whom some read with the idea of turning his ideas to conservative ends—realized that they could seize the means of cultural and political production. They could make better radio than the liberals, better propaganda, and most of all, they could shape and run and finance better politicians. Not just morally superior legislators but better *hacks*—men (and, eventually, women) who took from modernism only its rule book, not its goals, and bested its pure champions at the game they thought they'd invented.

Fosdick smoothed the way with his powerful denunciation of denominations, soon to become a bête noire of Christians who defined their faith by the "fact" of spiritual war, in which there are ultimately only two sides, theirs and the enemy's, Christ's and Satan's. "If," preached Fosdick, "during [World War I], when the nations were wrestling upon the very brink of hell and at times all seemed lost, you chanced to hear two men in an altercation about some minor matter of sectarian denominationalism, could you restrain your indignation? You said, 'What can we do with folks like this who, in the face of colossal issues, play with the twiddlywinks and peccadillos of religion?' "

Of course, those "twiddlywinks" are the intellectual marrow of Christianity and the convictions that prevent its more ancient precepts from merging too easily with modern politics. Barton, like Fosdick, saw no reason not to do so. Upon returning to the United States from a European tour in 1930, he wondered, "How can we develop the love of country, the respect for courts and law, the sense of national obligation, which Mussolini has recreated in the soul of Italy?"[23]

He praised Mussolini's "efficiency and progress" and Hitler's mastery of the adman's science, psychology, after another European visit in 1934. "Only strong magnetic men inspire great enthusiasm and build great organizations," he'd noted in *The Man Nobody Knows*. He wasn't defending the dictators' disregard for rights, he insisted, but he had to admire Hitler's anti-Semitic propaganda, so detailed in its documentation of Jewish influence in Germany that one could easily see why Hitler's rise "was not an unnatural thing to have happen."[24] Declaring himself of a "generous" frame of mind, he said that he preferred Roosevelt, whom he considered an antibusiness "dictator," to Hitler. Still, he seemed to see more similarity between them than difference. "Every new deal has to have some one to blame when all the promises do not come true. We blame the reactionaries; Hitler blames the Jews." Four years later, Barton entered Congress as a leading isolationist, opposed not only to war with the Axis powers but to aid to the Allies as well.

But Barton was not a fascist in the vein of Henry Ford (whom he quoted as an authority on Christian business in the *Man Nobody Knows*) or even fuzzy-brained Frank Buchman. He was an advertising man, an optimist. In an editorial for the *Wall Street Journal* titled "Hard Times," Barton quoted the *Journal*'s publisher on the necessity of poverty: "What is taking place on this earth is a great experiment in the development of human character. The Creator is not interested in money or markets, but in more enduring men . . . suffering develops them."[25]

That the subjects of this great experiment were not as interested in this development as were the captains of industry mildly puzzled Barton but did not bother him. He felt certain that they could be persuaded with a jingle and a catchy slogan, a "juster" peace.

Such newspeak represents the chummy self-satisfaction of a mind that mistakes the efficiency of short phrases for depth of meaning. In *The Man Nobody Knows* Barton tells the story of a newspaperman assigned to cover an unnamed great issue of the day in a single column. When the reporter protested that one column was not enough space, his editor told him to review the Book of Genesis—all of creation summed up in a tidy 600 words. Not for Barton the lingering work of theologians, who find in scripture at least as many questions as answers. Nor was he a man for the thickets of political theory, a limitation which, given his stated sympathies for strongmen, may have saved him from a more frightening path. *Mein Kampf?* That doorstopper weighed in at nearly 1,000 pages. Barton simply lacked the patience for fascism; Hitler was too deep for him.

But he also took one of fascism's central premises too seriously to embrace the ideology's violence. *Fascism,* the word itself derived from the Latin for a bundle of sticks bound together and thus unbreakable, promised unity. Barton wanted that: unity. As an advertising man, he believed it could be achieved through persuasion rather than force of arms. Moreover, he understood that the best way to sell a product was not fear alone but fear plus desire: to stoke the consumer's anxiety that he or she lacked something, and then to press some button in the brain that led to the conviction that acquiring it would lead to happiness. Consumption, not fascism, was the core of his Christianity.

FOR BARTON, AND later Abram, the something was Jesus, the ultimate "personality." To Barton, one nation under God meant a nation of consumers, their deepest needs and greatest wants in perfect accord with the products of BBD&O's clients, General Electric and General Motors and, in 1952, General Dwight D. Eisenhower. For Abram, unity meant the boss with his hand on Jimmy's shoulder,

Christ's masculine love flowing through his CEO key man and into the workingman's bones. Not fascism; in the future Barton and Abram helped forge, God's love would be hungered for and accepted gladly. There would be no secret police, no jackboots, no Buzz Windrip, no cult of personality.

Rather, a *Babbitt cult,* as one of Barton's Christian critics put it, a cult of many personalities, all of them more or less the same, vessels filled with His manliness, His will. The "man-method" that Abram shaped from Buchman's "Guidance" and Barton's big business theology, the freedom he dreamed of and preached for the next three decades, was that of obedience. In a 1942 pamphlet titled *Finding the Better Way,*[26] one of Abram's lieutenants described the Babbitt cult Abram had created and then replicated in San Francisco (led by a former secretary of the navy), Los Angeles (chaired by an oilman), and Philadelphia (started by Dr. Dan Poling, the squeaky-clean radio preacher who would also serve as frontman for the city's Republican machine), as well as Chicago, New York, Boston, and some sixty other cities.[27]

Washington, D.C. was one of them. That year, with the help of Senator Ralph Brewster of Maine—a calculating character, both a Yankee and a Klansman, Brewster evidently recognized Abram's more amiable Fellowship as the coming club for backroom dealing— Abram convinced dozens of congressmen to begin attending his weekly breakfast prayer meetings at the Hotel Willard. Abram himself was staying at the University Club, a clumsy old building next door to the Soviet embassy. His first meeting at the Willard took place in the midst of a blizzard in January 1942. Seventy-four men, most of them congressmen, gathered to hear addresses by Howard Coonley, the ultraright president of the National Association of Manufacturers—and Abram. "The big men and the real leaders in New York and Chicago look up to me in an embarrassing way," he wrote his wife, Mattie.

It was true. The president of Chevrolet requested an afternoon with Abram, and the president of Quaker Oats insisted on a morning meeting. In Chicago, he dined with steel magnates and railroad titans and Hughston McBain, the president of Marshall Field. In New York, Thomas Watson of IBM summoned a group of men to hear Abram speak at the Banker's Club, Coonley opened doors for Abram to discuss God and labor with the president of General Electric, and J. C. Penney, one of the financial backers of modern fundamentalism, took Abram to Marble Collegiate Church on Fifth Avenue to meet Norman Vincent Peale, the apostle of "positive thinking" and possibly the most deliberately banal man in American history. Abram soon joined Peale as one of "the Twelve," a council of Christian conservative leaders bent on working behind-the-scenes to rebrand fundamentalism in Peale's feel-good terminology.

In Washington, Abram was even more popular. "Congressman Busbey reported how respected, loved, and admired your husband was there and the contribution he had made to Congress," he wrote Mattie. In the evenings he summoned maids and busboys to his rooms for knee-cracking prayer sessions that stretched into the night. Black people, he liked to boast, loved him, and congressmen, he claimed, flocked to him. Within a year of his arrival, he could stroll freely into nearly any office in Washington. Senators Alexander Wiley of Wisconsin, Raymond Willis of Indiana, and H. Alexander Smith of New Jersey functioned as his lieutenants. Representative Walter Judd, a former medical missionary from Minnesota, later to become a red hunter nearly as cruel as McCarthy, became Abram's man on the House floor. David Lawrence, publisher of *U.S. News* (now *U.S. News and World Report*), the most influential media conservative in the country, joined the board of directors of Abram's newly formed National Committee for Christian Leadership. Lawrence was Jewish, but with Abram he prayed to Jesus as the only hope against communism—never mind that the Soviets were American allies at the time.

To further spread the Idea, Abram's *Finding the Better Way* explained that the Breakfast Groups—the basic unit of the Fellowship, from which some men would be recruited into cells—were nonpartisan, open to everyone. But those who chose to attend were of a distinct caste. According to the pamphlet, a "typical meeting" of the Seattle group consisted of prayers, "comments," and personal testimonies by top executives from an array of regional and national corporations. There was a man from J. C. Penney, and the president of Seattle Gas. The president of Frederick & Nelson, then the Northwest's largest department store—and its arbiter of upper-class tastes—offered "comments," as did an executive from the Chicago, Milwaukee, St. Paul & Pacific Railroad. The Democratic candidate for governor and the Republican candidate for the Senate made appearances, but the Republican got the better spot: the closing prayer, following Abram's summation. Clearly, "typical" meetings made for valuable campaign stops.

What of the pamphlet's promise that "representatives of both capital and labor find common ground" at such? Of seventeen speakers, only one spoke for labor, James Duncan (possibly the "Jimmy" of Abram's first sessions). An officer of the International Association of Machinists, Duncan helped drive a rift into the West Coast labor movement with his firm opposition to a popular rank-and-file initiative to allow African Americans to work for Boeing. His involvement with the bosses who made up the membership of the Seattle Breakfast Group provides a portrait of the labor leadership with which Abram's Fellowship felt it could stand on common ground: violent, reactionary, and thick with bigotry.

Abram himself never made an explicitly racist remark in his life, but he practiced a paternalism that amounted to a quiet declaration of his views on the matter. Some of Abram's closest allies would be Dixiecrats such as South Carolina's Strom Thurmond, who became a coleader with Abram of the senate's weekly prayer breakfast, and Mississippi senator John Stennis. At the left end of Abram's spectrum were men such as Representatives Brooks Hays of Arkansas and John Sparkman of Alabama, "moderates" who felt that slow and limited integration was an acceptable option, if not a necessity. Activism on its behalf bordered on treason.

Duncan evidently felt the same way, only more so. In 1941 at Boeing, Seattle's biggest employer, Local 751 of the Aero Mechanics Union voted to allow African Americans to join its membership, already 9,100 strong and sure to grow as the war demanded more planes. But the local's parent, Duncan's International Association of Machinists, claimed the union's constitution barred nonwhites, union democracy and the war effort be damned. The International accused the local's president of communism and replaced him in a coup with a red-baiter named Harry Bomber. To validate Bomber's unelected leadership, the International rented out Seattle's Civic Auditorium for a mass meeting of anti-red—and anti-black—workers. The city fathers, who by then comprised Abram's purest "God-led" political machine, approved; a few days before the meeting, the *Seattle Times* declared it "one of the most important in Seattle's labor history."[28]

Most of the members of the local didn't think so. Out of 9,100, only 2,000 attended, and just over half of those even bothered to vote on the International's slate of rigged issues. Even then, they cleared a man accused of communism of all charges. After the meeting, goons associated with the pro-business, anti-black slate delivered beatings to those they considered leaders of the pro-black faction. The victims filed charges. The district attorney, B. Gray Warner—a Fellowship man—took the case so seriously he declared its proper handling a matter of "national defense." That is, the victims were hindering national defense by complaining instead of buckling down to work. No cases went to trial.

By 1943, the progressives beaten, jailed, driven out of town, or cowed into submission, the Machinist leadership of which the Fellowship's Duncan was an officer produced an edition of their newsletter, *Aero Mechanic*, featuring a cartoon of a black man applying for a job at Boeing. "Stable Lizers," he says, in response to a question about airplane stabilizers. "Yas Suh! Ah sho knows 'bout dem." In an inset, we see a black man sweeping a stable.[29]

SUCH WAS THE underbelly of elite fundamentalism's labor-management "reconciliation"—the principles of Moral Re-Armament in practice, the fruits of Barton's business theology applied to the real world. In 1938, Barton ran for Congress. Like Abram, he believed economic depression to be a result of spiritual disobedience, though Barton preferred the term *distance*. The New Deal had moved us away from Jesus, he thought, by substituting man-made legislation for divine will, as revealed in the working of Christian businessmen unhindered by regulations. So in 1938 he won a seat in Congress by promising to "Repeal a Law a Day." Or, in the slang of today's fundamentalism: Let Go, and Let God.

The *Wall Street Journal* thought it a capital idea. "It is not that one congressman, more or less, especially a new one, can arrest the hitherto unstoppable juggernaut" of government, the paper editorialized, "but that [Barton's] election can well serve as a beacon to encourage other reasonable men, who have demonstrated their success in industry . . . to take action against the web of legislation in which the nation is currently struggling."[30]

Conventional wisdom holds that it was Ronald Reagan who began the real dismantling of the New Deal, but a closer examination of the legislative record reveals that the process began as early as 1943, in the midst of the war, when conservative southern Democrats teamed up with Republicans to pass the anti-union Smith-Connally Act, the first step in what would eventually become the repeal of most of labor's New Deal gains. In 1948, Representative Paul B. Dague, then one of Abram's disciples, wrote in a Fellowship newsletter that Abram's weekly meetings for congressmen had produced in them the "conviction that more of God's mandates and the teachings of the Nazarene must be written into current legislation." He did not offer examples. It is easy to guess, however, that he had in mind the previous year's Taft-Hartley Act, known by even conservative unions as the "slave labor law" for the ends to which it went to roll back the New Deal and replace strikes with employer-controlled "conciliation," a hallmark of Abram's vision for "industrial peace." The "teachings of the Nazarene" for such politicians amounted to deregulation, the removal of government intervention from matters they thought firmly taken in hand by Jesus and *His* chosen representatives. They were not libertarians; they were authoritarians.

"Our people as a whole have become the most highly organized in the world," declared Abram's *Better Way* pamphlet.

All the vital activities of industry, commerce, and government are carried on by corporations and other formal organizations. Such bodies are continually growing in size, and hence the top leadership is continually growing in power and influence.

We have entered an era when the masses of the people are dependent upon a rapidly diminishing number of leaders for the determination of their pattern of life and the definition of their ultimate goals. *It is the age of minority control.* [Emphasis mine.]

Lest anyone mistake Abram's meaning during wartime, the pamphlet went on to point to the Axis powers as examples of what could go wrong if "minority control" got into the wrong hands. The pamphlet had good things to say about Hitler's "youth work," but it had no use for Hitler's military adventurism, the crudest and ultimately most ineffective form of evangelism ever invented. But just as a minority "can wreck a nation," a "righteous 'remnant'" chosen by God can redeem it. "Men whose success shows them to have the ability to lead cannot evade the responsibility for delivering America from its present curse of spiritual indifference and moral decadence. These are the men whom others will follow."

Years later, at the height of American postwar affluence—the days when millions were questioning the wisdom of "following"—a German-Jewish refugee named Herbert Marcuse (writing not long after Kissinger paid his tribute to the subtleties of status quo power) would capture in his *One-Dimensional Man* the contradictions of Abram's Better Way, his celebration of strongmen and his fetish for conformity, his belief in providence and his reliance on behind-the-scenes planning, his love of liberty and his insistence on obedience.[31] After the years of fascist pageantry and war, wrote Marcuse in an essay titled "The New Forms of Control," comes the age of "comfortable, smooth, reasonable, democratic unfreedom."

6.

THE MINISTRY OF
PROPER ENLIGHTENMENT

He did not want to be one of those who now pretended that "they had always been against it," whereas in fact they had been very eager to do what they had been told to do. However, times change.

—HANNAH ARENDT, *EICHMANN IN JERUSALEM: A REPORT ON THE BANALITY OF EVIL* (1963)

MANFRED ZAPP, A NATIVE of Düsseldorf by way of Pretoria, merited a line in the news when he stepped from an ocean liner onto the docks of New York City on September 22, 1938, a warm, windy day at the edge of a South Atlantic hurricane. Just a few words in the *New York Times'* "Ocean Travelers" column, a list of travelers of note buried in the back of the paper. By the time he left the United States, his departure would win headlines.

Zapp quickly established himself, settling first at the Gladstone Hotel and later in a suite at the Waldorf-Astoria, surveying his options for office space before moving on to East Forty-sixth Street, just off Fifth Avenue, where a staff of ten soon joined him, Germans and German Americans, a dull-looking lot in whose company Zapp fairly gleamed.[1] He was thirty-five years old with Berlin behind him and the sea of Manhattan society before him, and when he spoke, the swells tittered or growled with approval for the Wagnerian vitality they imagined in his German-inflected Americanese. "I regard myself as having arrived in the place I always wanted to be," he exulted.[2] His chestnut hair was thinning and his cheeks swelled out into jowls, but big bones beneath and a strong cleft chin kept him handsome. He wore elegantly tailored pinstripes and shirts of slightly eccentric design. With the arch of a brow, he made smoking a pipe look more mysterious than old-fashioned. He was heir to a modest coal fortune, but he did not consider himself a businessman. He had earned an advanced degree, but he did not insist on being called "doctor," in the German fashion. He thought of himself as a journalist—"a respectable newspaperman!" he would spit at interrogators after he'd been captured.

Zapp had been given charge of the American offices of the Trans-ocean News Agency, ostensibly the creation of a group of unnamed German financiers. He had recently left a similiar post in South Africa. "It is of paramount importance," the German chargé d'affaires in Washington had written Zapp the month before his arrival, "that a crossing of wires with the work of the D.N.B."—Deutschland News Bureau—"be absolutely avoided." DNB was transparently the tool of the Nazi regime and thus under constant scrutiny. Transocean, as an allegedly independent agency, might operate more freely. "My task here in America is so big and so difficult," Zapp wrote the German ambassador to South Africa a month after he arrived, "that it demands all my energies."[3]

What was Zapp's task? During his American tenure, he flitted in black tie and tails from Fifth Avenue to Park Avenue enjoying the hospitality of rich men and beautiful women—the gossip columnist Walter Winchell wrote of Zapp's "madcap girlfriend," a big-spending society girl who seemed to consume at least as much of Zapp's attention as the news. He avoided as much as he could discussions of what he considered the tedium of politics. His friends knew he had dined with Cordell Hull, the secretary of state, and Roosevelt himself, and some must also have known that he had worked quietly—and illegally, if one must be technical—against the president's reelection. But one did not ask questions. He traveled, though no one was quite sure where he went off to. One moment he was hovering over the teletype in Manhattan; the next he was to be found in Havana, on the occasion of a meeting of foreign ministers. Some might have called him a Nazi agent, there to encourage Cuba's inclinations—a popular radio program, transmitted across the Caribbean, was called the The *Nazi Hour*—but Zapp could truthfully reply that he rarely stirred from the lobby of the Hotel Nacional, where he sat sipping cocktails, happy to buy drinks for any man—or, preferably, lady—who cared to chat with him.[4]

The fact was that Zapp was a man with little interest in political machinations. He thought of himself as an empirical man. He loved details and statistics—his idea of news ran toward almost artistic stacks of data and systemized summaries of man-in-the-street interviews—and he considered the conclusions he drew from them not ideological but factual. He was a commonsense man. Consider his rebuttal to a widely reported speech by Monsignor John A. Ryan, the "Right Reverend New Dealer" whose Catholic social justice writings inspired much of Roosevelt's program. "The German Reich," declared Zapp, irritated by the monsignor's partisan Catholicism, "with its new conception of the State, is in the last analysis nothing more than the national community itself."[5]

To Zapp, *totalitarianism*—the term he preferred to *fascism*—was, once pruned of its absurdities, a sensible and lovely idea. The torches and the "long knives," the death's-head and all that red-faced singing and table pounding, these activities Zapp did not care for. He actually preferred life in America, the canyons of Manhattan and the gin-lit balconies of the city's best people, conversations that did not begin and end with barking devotion. "Heil Hitler!" Zapp signed his letters with this invocation, and a portrait of the Führer hung in his office, but Zapp the journalist was too sensitive a recording device to enjoy all that arm snapping. If only Manhattan and Munich, Washington and Berlin, could be merged. It was a matter not of warfare but of harmony, democracy's bickering and bile giving way to the "new conception," in which power and will would be one.

Within a year, however, Zapp found cause to resist returning to that fine new system. After a series of unsolved murders and perplexing explosions and intercepted transmissions led the FBI to raid Nazi front organizations in Boston, Baltimore, Buffalo, Denver, New

Orleans, Philadelphia, Pittsburgh, and Zapp's spartan office off Fifth Avenue, where they found what they believed to be evidence of the orchestration of it all, Zapp began to reconsider his enthusiasm for Hitler's new order. He had failed the Führer. How would his will judge him? What power would be exerted in the Gestapo "beating rooms" that Transocean employees had once considered themselves privileged to tour?

The FBI seized him and his chief deputy and whisked them away to cold, bare rooms, on Ellis Island, no less, where not long before, the rabble of Europe had been processed into "mongrel" America, land of "degenerate democracy," as Roosevelt himself quoted Zapp in a speech denouncing Germany's "strategy of terror."[6]

This last phrase as applied to Zapp's pursuits was perhaps unfair. "We now know why Nazi sabotage efforts failed," the *Washington Post* would announce after the war. Zapp and his fellow Nazi spies had been too busy bickering.[7]

On one side were saboteurs of the "old line," men who planted little bombs disguised to look like chewing gum and set giant fires meant to be understood by Washington as arson, skulking and hulking figures who photographed munitions factories and murdered German American informants they suspected of disloyalty to their dishonest cause.

On the other were men such as Zapp. Along with a D.C.-based diplomat named Ulrich von Gienanth (whom he would rejoin after the war in Abram's prayer meetings), Zapp considered the coming conflict between the United States and the Reich one to be resolved through quiet conversation, between German gentlemen and American "industrialists and State Department men."

Von Gienanth, a muscular, sandy-haired man whose dull expression disguised a chilly intelligence, "seems to be a very agreeable fellow," Zapp wrote his brother, who had studied in Munich with the baron-to-be. Only second secretary in the embassy, von Gienanth maintained a frightening grip over his fellow diplomats. He was an undercover SS man, the ears and eyes of the "Reichsministry of Proper Enlightenment and Propaganda," charged with keeping watch over its secret American operations. He was, in short, the Gestapo chief in America. While Zapp worried about his legal prospects in the Indian Summer of 1940, von Gienanth was likely waiting for news of a major operation in New Jersey: the detonation of the Hercules gunpowder plant, an explosion that on September 12 killed forty-seven and sent shockwaves so strong that they snapped wind into the sails of boaters in far-off Long Island Sound.[8]

Von Gienanth did not approve of such gestures. So firmly did he oppose them as counterproductive, in fact, that he even attempted to denounce to Berlin the Nazi agents who perpetrated such deeds. Double agents or worse, his faction suggested, secret Jews bent on smearing the honor of the Reich.

Von Gienanth's initiatives were whimsical by comparison. Once, for instance, he paid a pilot to dump pro-Nazi antiwar fliers on the White House lawn. He devoted himself to changing Goebbels's gold into dollars, and those dollars into laundered "donations" to the America First Committee, where unwitting isolationists—Abram allies such as Senator Arthur Vandenberg and America First president Robert M. Hanes among them—stumped for recognition of the "fact" of Hitler's inevitability.

Like Zapp, von Gienanth considered himself a commonsense man.

And Zapp—Zapp simply reported the news and sold it on the wire. Or gave it away. To the papers of Argentina, Mexico, Brazil, and to the small-town editors of America's gullible heartland, Zapp offered Transocean reports for almost nothing. In some South American countries, 30 percent or more of foreign news—the enthusiastic welcome given conquering German forces, the Jewish cabal in Washington, the moral rot of the American people—was produced by or channeled through Zapp's offices. On the side, he compiled a report on Soviet-inspired "Polish atrocities" against the long-suffering German people and distributed it to thousands of leading Americans, the sort sympathetic to the plight of the persecuted Christian. Zapp's sympathetic nature would prove, after the war, to be as genuine as his distorted sense of history's victims.

Not long after Zapp's capture, the Gestapo seized two American reporters in Germany. The United States traded. With a Coast Guard plane keeping watch overhead, Zapp and von Gienanth sailed with several hundred other deported fascist agents aboard the USS *West Point*, bound for Lisbon.[9] When soldiers from the American 89th Division captured him again in April of 1945—an occasion for national headlines in the United States—he pled his failure on behalf of the Führer as his defense, as if his ultimate incompetence as a German spy in America before the war proved that he'd always been a secret enemy of Hitler's regime.

But Zapp had been heard plying his version of journalism throughout the war, broadcasting the "new conception" into Vichy France along with a bittersweet tune about his forsaken love, America—a land, he now lamented, thick with gangsters and Jews. A Democratic congressman from New York demanded that Zapp—along with "Little Alfie" Krupp, the "munitions king" captured that same week in his eight-hundred-room palace—be tried for war crimes immediately. Like Krupp—who actually was tried and convicted, but returned to high places by the occupation government—Zapp had a brighter future to look forward to.

The September 1951 issue of *Information Bulletin*, the magazine of the U.S. occupation government, marked Zapp's next appearance in the American press. By Zapp's standards, *Information Bulletin* was a publication of crass obviousness—an article in the previous edition was headlined "I Hate Communism"—but he must have appreciated the irony of a pictorial feature titled "German Newsmen Tour Army Bases." In a photo of twenty-two newsmen gathered around an American officer at an ordnance depot, Zapp can be seen just to the officer's right; he looks like he's rocking back on his heels. His tie is short, his pants ill fitting, and he's wearing shades—but he still smiles for the camera, an Aryan Zelig, born again into the Cold War.[10]

"THERE IS STILL a lot of misery in this part of the world," Zapp wrote Abram in 1949. "Every day between one thirty and two o'clock the radio is broadcasting the names of lost persons." What did Zapp do about it? Nothing. "I say to myself," Zapp wrote, "carpe diem, enjoy your life."

Over the next seven years, Zapp would write Abram tens of thousands of words, the musings of a man speaking for a nation he believed to be the war's true victim. By far the most prolific of what would grow to be Abram's deep pool of German correspondents, Zapp was also the most cogent in his description of Germany's suffering, and the most plain in his statement of the bargain he believed Germany still had the power to strike with America: its loyalty in a united front against communism—aka "materialism," radicalism, and that old byword, *degeneracy*—in exchange for desperately needed American dollars.

Abram was hardly alone in thinking this unwritten contract mutually beneficial. Such was the deal struck by Harry Truman, the Marshall Plan the Faustian trade of food for faith made at the hinge between wars, the one just ended and the Cold War which would stretch across the next five decades. But in 1949, nobody believed it would last that long. "Now," Zapp wrote Abram as North Korean troops massed along the Thirty-eighth Parallel in 1950, "everybody sees clearly that a great war between USA and Soviet Russia cannot be avoided."

Zapp understood as well as any Cold Warrior that the battle would be fought in faraway places. "Now it is Korea, tomorrow it might be Formosa, or China, or Indochina." One day, he feared, it would be Berlin. He was skeptical of America's chances. Had not the Wermacht slaughtered 20 million Slavs? And still they had come, the Red Army growing in numbers even as the ranks of its dead swelled to the size of a nation. Hitler could not stop them. German civilians thought the Americans would succeed where the Reich had failed. "Oh, the Russians can't do anything," Zapp summarized his man-on-the-street interviews. "Because as soon as a war starts the Americans will drop a chain of Atom bombs from the Baltic to the Black Sea and create a radioactive curtain right across Western Russia." But Zapp, who understood American propaganda and promises for what they were, knew better. "This optimistic opinion sounds to me like the whispering campaign Dr. Goebbels started at the end of the war, when he spoke of new decisive weapons, of which nobody knew anything."

Abram agreed. The "steel bath" of armaments alone would not protect them. Only the solution that had saved Seattle in 1935 would suffice. "The totalitarianism of God is the only answer," as one of the Cold War academics routinely trotted about by Abram had lectured a conference of diplomats in 1948. The gathering was the work of Donald C. Stone, director of administration for the Marshall Plan, a man who hardly seemed a likely candidate for fundamentalist crusades. Stone was a blue-blooded bureaucrat inspired by noblesse oblige, one of the many authors of Europe's reconstruction who never made headlines. But in the postwar era he had come to believe that the West stood for Christ-like perfection while communism was "hate" incarnate. Stone's ambition for the Marshall Plan was to conform the Western bloc "politically, economically, psychologically, and spiritually," to a "global offensive" of ideas. The idea, for Stone, was God. "My main use," he told Abram, "is to try to get the Christian Spirit into [the Marshall Plan]. I have worked at that constantly. It is vital."[11] In 1948, the newly formed National Security Council had issued a secret menu of covert actions to be pursued with Marshall Plan funds, with the only restriction being plausible deniability: "propaganda, economic warfare; preventive direct action, including sabotage, anti-sabotage, demolition, and evacuation measures; subversion against hostile states, including assistance to underground resistance movements, guerillas, and refugee liberation groups; and support of indigenous anti-communist elements in threatened countries of the free world."[12] The most important battlegrounds, Stone concluded, were the souls of the undecided, who must either give their absolute loyalty or be destroyed.

Stone, Zapp, Abram. Just three small men in the Cold War, they might be said to stand in for the three branches of America's ideological army. Establishment Cold Warriors of Stone's ilk dominate the history books. Zapp, the ally with an ugly past, is his dark shadow. But Abram and the influence of his fellow fundamentalists would remain invisible for decades, their influence unmarked by media and academic establishments. The role played by fundamentalists in refashioning the world's greatest fascist power into a democracy would go unnoticed. So, too, would the role of fascism—or, rather, that of fascism's ghost—in shaping the newly internationalist ambition of evangelical conservatives in the postwar era.

Between the Cold War establishment and the religious fervor of Abram and his allies, organizations that came of age in the postwar era—the National Association of Evangelicals, Campus Crusade, the Billy Graham Crusade, Youth For Christ, the Navigators, and many more—one finds the unexplained presence of men such as Zapp, adaptable men always ready to serve the powers that be. From American Christendom, Zapp and his ilk took the cloak of redemption, *cheap grace,* in the words of Dietrich Bonhoeffer, one of their most famous victims. To it, they offered something harder to define. This is an investigation of that transmission; the last message from the Ministry of Proper Enlightenment; the story of American fundamentalism's German connection.

ON CHRISTMAS DAY, 1945, one of Abram's men wrote him a letter about the world waiting to be made. "Well, Abram, D-Day is at hand." The letter writer, a member of one of Abram's cells called the "Lindbergh Group"—possibly that of Charles Lindbergh—referred not to the actual D-Day, eighteen months past, but to the battle for what Abram would soon take to calling the "new world order."

"We must move *now,*" wrote Abram's correspondent. "You have been raised up for a job like this."

And yet the following spring God and Abram's appendix laid him low, nearly killing him in the midst of a speaking tour of the Midwest. Lying on an operating table in Minneapolis, about to go under, he listened with unfrightened curiosity to the worldly disinterest of his doctors, one of whom thought the sixty-one-year-old silver-haired man would momentarily "shake hands with St. Peter." He may have. After the operation, Abram would say that he had spent his time hovering up near the ceiling of his hospital room, looking down at his body. Then

Jesus came and bobbed along next to him, floating on the stale currents of hospital air. This was not a dream, Abram would insist, but direct communication. Together they discussed flesh and "personality." The body, they concluded, is no more than "our means of contact with the physical world." Abram and the Jesus of his hallucination had reinvented the Gnostic heresy, the belief that bodies possess no essence of humanity, that flesh is meat, the suffering of which matters little or not at all. Such convictions have very worldly ramifications when wielded by the powerful—those in positions to make decisions about the suffering of others. Abram, of course, didn't think about that.[13]

Abram's mystical experience marked a transformation in his mission. Gone were any vestiges of the Social Gospel, any old-fashioned Christian notions of feeding the poor—food, that is, not scripture—as a matter of first concern. The Cold War and spiritual war would be one in his eyes, but this battle would be ideological, fought for hearts and minds, those of the leaders who could set terms for the unknowing masses. Thereafter Abram's religion, the faith of the fundamentalist elite, would be global in scope, with Washington, D.C., "the world's Christian capital." Fundamentalism could no longer simply defend its own ground; it must, as Finney had done, conquer new territory.

In 1947, an evangelical theologian named Carl F. H. Henry would publish a startling book titled *The Uneasy Conscience of Modern Fundamentalism*, since interpreted as a reconciliation of fundamentalism with the postwar world, a eulogy for William Jennings Bryan and Billy Sunday and the Bible thumpers of old that allowed fundamentalism to bury its dead and move on to an easier relationship with society at large. And yet *The Uneasy Conscience* still "breathes with fire," an editor of *Christianity Today* (the flagship evangelical magazine Henry started) wrote just a few years ago, "rejecting the failed theology of liberalism, discredited by the devastation of two wars."[14]

That one could view the ruins of Europe and the dead of Auschwitz, Bergen-Belsen, Dachau—or, for that matter, Dresden or Hamburg or Hiroshima—and conclude in 1947, or today, that *liberalism* was the problem, that Locke's tradition of tolerance had led to the slaughter, that what the world needed more of was the gospel of no compromise, was, whatever else we might make of it morally or historically, a bold assertion. It was American fundamentalism coming into its own, fulfilling the evangelical promise it claimed to uphold, no longer defending itself against modernity's encroachments so much as expanding into modernity's sphere. Henry's call for "positive engagement" with politics laid the foundation for a *popular front,* to borrow a term from the American Left of the previous decade: an ideological army of common cause, with "Christianity" the battle cry rallying the troops well beyond the confines of fundamentalism.

"I believe honestly," Harry Truman had announced at war's end, "that Almighty God intends us to assume the leadership which he intended us to assume in 1920, and which we refused." Truman was a hard-nosed liberal who borrowed heavily from American fundamentalism even as he held it at a distance. It took him another two years to fully blend the two in his 1947 "Truman Doctrine"—a mandate for massive military aid around the world—on behalf of a Greek government riddled with fascist collaborators, fighting a civil war against the very same mountain partisans—communists, indeed—who had been the chief resisters against the Germans.

Before the war, Truman had been such a devotee of Buchmanism that he had attempted (unsuccessfully) to corner FDR into an implicit endorsement of the Moral Re-Armament guru. In 1947, Senator Absalom Willis Robertson, a fiercely conservative Democrat from Virginia (and Pat Robertson's father) met with Truman to invite him to expand his sphere of piety to the Fellowship's meetings. Robertson would tell Donald Stone that Truman seemed excited by the idea, but nothing came of it. By then, Truman was officially distancing himself from MRA lest he be tainted by its prewar enthusiasm for fascism. It seems more likely that it was Truman's hardheadedness that influenced the Fellowship rather than the other way around, leading toward a more militant realpolitik than Abram, enamored of pomp and status, had yet imagined.[15]

Unlike Abram—who considered King Paul of Greece a messenger from God—Truman wasn't addled by royalty. The doctrine that began by making client states of Greece and Turkey, the old "imperial interests" as FDR had dismissed them, was too ambitious, too *abstract*, to be starstruck by Europe's quaint nobility. It was at best and at worst an ontological division of the world into heaven and hell, with the United States declared to be not only on the side of the angels but responsible for enforcing their dictums. "Worldwide Spiritual Offensive," Senator Frank Carlson would call this strategy at a twentieth-anniversary meeting of the prayer breakfast movement. He meant to summon the unified forces of politics and religion— power and will, as Manfred Zapp, a propagandist of a blunter regime, might have phrased the idea. "Moral Doctrine for Free World Global Planning," was how another Abram disciple, a Pentagon director of "information" named John C. Broger, would frame it in the barely secular terms of midcentury Cold War.[16]

Such was the language of the times: aggressive but vague. Five years before Carl F. H. Henry published his *Uneasy Conscience*, the denominational leaders of America's conservative Protestant factions had come together to form the National Association of Evangelicals. It was an alliance of orthodox fundamentalists, such as Bob Jones Sr., and "free enterprise" apostles, such as Abram's friend J. Elwin Wright. The NAE would fight "real dangers" threatening America, a category of menace sufficiently broad that it included both Roosevelt's "managerial revolution" and the separatist fury of fundamentalists too pure for politics. The NAE saw socialism and separatism as opposite ends of the spectrum of the beast known as *secularism,* which the NAE considered the unnatural division of believers and American power. "Personal legalisms"—this church doesn't approve of dancing, that one won't play cards—would thereafter be just that, personal, not to interfere with the war for a Christian nation. "Christ for America," proclaimed the NAE's president in his second annual address. Come on in, said the populist front, whether you speak in tongues and wave your hands on Sunday or sit on them and tsk, tsk at the sweat and tears of the holy rollers. Its fundamentalism was not theological; it was American. The totalitarianism of God, unlike that of man, welcomed all true believers.[17]

•   •   •

DURING THE WAR years, Abram had acquired a new patron, a young-ish widow named Marian Aymar Johnson, heiress to the fortunes of both her late stockbroker husband and of her old, Hudson River family. A lovely if empty-headed beauty raised between Newport, London, and Manhattan, she was a second cousin to FDR, but her isolationist politics were far to his right. Before the war, she'd been fond of Buch-manite house parties, hosting one herself at her Long Island estate—an event of sufficient gossip value to rate an article in *Time*. Tall and blue-eyed with a broad, open smile, after her husband died she resolved to develop greater gravitas. She gave up the life of a social butterfly for what she called Abram's "total Christianity." Her goal was the estab-lishment of "spiritual beach heads" from which to evangelize leaders. Only by accepting the same Christ, the "Supreme Leader" she had come to serve, could they save America from communism.[18] With her help, Abram bought a four-story mansion on Embassy Row in Wash-ington at 2324 Massachusetts Avenue. He hoped it would be a head-quarters for politicians and diplomats of all denominations, a place for businessmen visiting Washington (by this point, Abram's inner circle included the president of the National Association of Manufacturers) to share their concerns with brothers-in-Christ in spiritual, not material, terms. A "Christian Embassy."[19]

Abram kept offices on the third floor, and there was a reception hall, a library for small gatherings, a formal dining room, and a din-ing room for servants on the second floor. There were guest rooms above and drawing rooms suitable for *soul surgery*—a term Abram borrowed from Buchman—below. It quickly "became natural" for ambassadors "looking for a Christian approach and solution" to drop in for lunch, but Abram delighted even more in "drifters in from a pagan legalism"—what nonbelievers call *ethics*—who, sitting with Abram on the back porch during a summer meal, might catch the "contagion" of the Idea.

A magnificent garden in the back grew upon the green ridge of Rock Creek Park, the narrow gorge that separated the property from

the sculpted grounds of Dumbarton Oaks. It was there, in 1944—
the same year that Abram and his wife, Mattie, at last risen from her
sickbed in Seattle, moved to the Christian Embassy—that Roosevelt
and his advisers began planning the United Nations.[20] Abram at first
interpreted the United Nations as the result of divine intervention
leading the secular world toward international acknowledgment that
the truths of the world's religions were best summarized in the personality of Jesus. He turned his weekly congressional prayer meetings into lobbying sessions on the organization-to-be's behalf, and
his most conservative prayer disciples—especially the old arch-
isolationist Senator Arthur Vandenberg, converted to Cold War internationalism before World War II had even ended—helped quiet
American resistance to the endeavor.

History, not his Christ, would disappoint Abram. After the war
ended, after it dawned on him that the UN would not become an
international Christian congress, after the atom bombs fell, after
the Red Army boiled up to the edge of Western Europe and did not
stop so much as simmer, waiting, Abram was certain, for Stalin's
command, for Satan's whisper—after he had taken stock of the
war's victories and defeats, his anxieties and his enthusiasms grew
more warlike than the UN could accommodate. Communism no
longer meant the creed of insufficiently submissive workers; now it
was as great and grand as Lucifer's kingdom, an evil empire that had
launched "World War III," Abram decided. "Most of these communists are in fact rebels and should be treated as rebels," he said, waving the black flag of no mercy for those who disobeyed God—a
sentiment his followers in developing nations would later make real
by murdering hundreds of thousands of leftists. Abram's fundamentalism was polite only within the confines of Washington; projected
onto the world, it thrived on violence and raised up those most capable of it.

In 1946, Abram undertook a mission to scour the Allied prisons in Germany for men "of the predictable type" ready to turn
their allegiance from Hitler to Christ, and thus, in Abram's thinking,
America. In later years, Abram would say he had gone at the U.S.

State Department's request, and while it's true that the State Department did send Abram and provide any support he needed, it was Abram who initiated the trip, writing to Undersecretary of State Major John H. Hildring that the men of the Senate and House prayer groups had insisted that Abram carry "the Idea" to defeated Germany. Abram sailed on the *Queen Mary* in June, launched a prayer cell of Swiss bankers in Zurich, and flew from Frankfurt to Berlin on the private plane of General Joseph T. McNarney, commander in chief of the U.S. Forces of Occupation, to meet with General Lucius D. Clay, soon to take over from Eisenhower as military governor. Everywhere, he met with the "Christian forces of Germany"—those who saw Germany's suffering as penance for its embrace of the totalitarianism of a man rather than that of God. He found them all weeping, he wrote his wife, crying for their Führer, for the thousand-year Reich in the grave at age twelve, for the dead and the missing and the blank-eyed boys who had stumbled home in retreat from the Russians. In the West he wept with them; in East Berlin, he prayed with "secret cells" of Christians determined to overthrow communism. Even in the West, he believed, "atheistic devotees" of subversion—that is, those with strong anti-Nazi records, concentration camp survivors—had been elevated by an American military government blind to the threat posed by its eastern ally. "Nominal membership" in the Nazi Party was being held against good Christians with the necessary experience to govern. A coalition of leading German churchmen begged him to intervene, asking only that none but Christians be given authority.[21]

In Frankfurt Abram, with the churchmen and the pillars of the Third Reich to whom they introduced him, "the most intelligent, honest and reliable people of Germany," settled on a plan. They would provide Abram with a list of imprisoned men, "war criminals" according to the view of a certain un-Christian "element" among the Allies. Abram's friends in the military government and back home in Washington would certify them as "men not only to be released but to be used, according to their ability in the tremendous task of reconstruction." That September, U.S. secretary of state Jimmy Byrnes, under the advice of General Clay, delivered in Stuttgart a world-changing address, "Restatement of Policy on Germany." The burden of reparations would be lessened, Germany would be allowed to keep more of its industrial base, and the purge of National Socialism would soon come to an end: "It never was the intention of the American Government to deny to the German people the right to manage their own internal affairs as soon as they were able to do so in a democratic way."[22]

In Frankfurt, Abram claimed, God personally revealed to Abram a key man to quietly help manage the internal affairs of Germany's elite: Dr. Otto Fricke, an austere German churchman with an uncomfortable past. "You are God's man for this hour in Germany," Abram told him.[23] Had Abram asked about Fricke's role in Germany's previous hour, Fricke would have begged off explaining his activities during the Third Reich. As a radio preacher, he'd been recruited by Goebbels to propagandize, charged with explaining to the German people the decadence of jazz. "Terrible disharmonies," he warned. He presented as evidence of moral degeneracy the jazz standard "Dinah."[24]

> Dinah,
> Is there anyone finer
> In the state of Carolina?
> If there is and you know her,
> Show her!

History does not know if the recording Fricke played for a nation of secretly thrilled Aryans—the German love affair with jazz predated the nation's fetish for Hitlerian opera—was of Ethel Waters, Louis Armstrong, or a bare-chested, shimmying Josephine Baker.

Abram would not have asked.

He never asked.

• • •

IF WE ARE to understand the ease with which former Nazis and fascist sympathizers were born again as Christian Cold Warriors, we must consider for a moment the meaning of memory within the new religion—Christ at its center, no earthly Führer to serve—offered up by the Americans. And we must remember that this religion, a "spiritual Marshall Plan," as Wallace E. Haines, Abram's chief American representative in Europe, called it in a speech delivered at one of King Paul of Greece's palaces, was new not just to the former fascists who received it but to the Americans who gave it, transformed by the sight of suffering. Not of the Jews, invisible to Abram's men. Not of the Japanese—a missionary wrote Abram dozens of letters from the radioactive ruins, but he never received a reply. It was to Germany, the front line of the Cold War, that Abram's heart turned; Germany that raised for American fundamentalism the question of *theodicy*: if God is both good and all-powerful, why does he permit the suffering of innocents? That is a question with which all faiths must struggle—or learn to ignore.

Abram's German brethren chose the latter path. In Germany, after the war, sleep. Hunger and terrible labor, yes, months and then years of clearing rubble, bent-back human chains of men and women and children carting away pieces of the country in which they once lived brick by brick. But it was starving, red-eyed slumbering work, a dead sleep without dreams. No one could afford dreams. No one wanted history, the past translated by the night-mind into a landscape of guilt and shame. In Nuremberg, a little girl asked her mother where the Jews of "Jew Street" are. Hush. There are none, darling, there never were. In Frankfurt a group of American officers, concentration camp survivors, and the kind of Germans Abram considered "subversive" gathered in a small theater standing among ruins on a darkened side street and screened a twenty-minute film they were considering showing to the German people. More bodies, many more bodies, great piles of them, and gold, buckets of gold teeth, and then more bodies, joyful, cheering, marching Germans at torch-lit rallies, and a voice-over in German, "You remember, I was there, you were there . . ." The lights came up in the theater, and the Americans and the German subversives promised one another, "This we will show to every adult German. We will make attendance compulsory." The film played in every theater; but in the dark, Germany shut its eyes, literally, millions squeezing theirs shut until the short film was over and the main feature came up, a romance, a comedy, a subtitled Western. Anything but the German past.[25]

"At times," a German named Hans Kempe wrote Abram, "there are hours when I have to lie on the floor, as I can go no further." Kempe ran a camp for 500 German men displaced by the war, men to whom Abram in America was drawn. They were once so strong and now so broken. Kempe sent Abram stories: one man, a former government official—a Nazi official, but what does that mean anymore?—came to Kempe and told him he could no longer believe in a God who would allow Germany to suffer.

Their suffering was sweet. They had no fat and no meat, Kempe reported, but they'd gotten hold of sugar. That was their food. Kempe worked fourteen hours, eating sugar, and then collapsed. He lay on the floor, staring at the ceiling. There angels gathered. Angels and demons, "streams of grace" and a monster he called Hiob, sent by Satan to talk with him. Kempe rose. The men needed a mirror for shaving. This became his mission. He dispatched two to beg for one, and they returned with one and perhaps the men gathered round and stared at their reflections, Kempe staring at them staring. "Want, death, suffering, griefs and cares. Wherever I go, it is always the same." He lay on his floor, stared at his ceiling, waited for Hiob. He heard a storm coming. His men thought it had passed, but he knew it was coming. They were sleeping, and they must open their eyes, not to the past, which must be forgotten—put a mirror between yourself and history—but to the future. "Whoever does not already realize that we are at the midnight hour will awake too late," he wrote Abram. "The storm bells ring loudly."[26]

George Kennan heard them in Moscow. In 1946, the American diplomat padded through the embassy on a cold Russian winter night and sent his "Long Telegram" to Washington, "an eighteenth century Protestant sermon," he'd call it, a warning, a prophecy, a prescription, the language of diplomacy channeling the spirit of Edwards: we are as spiders, dangling over the abyss; the flames are rising. The Soviet Union was greater than the men in Washington imagine. They could not see what Kennan saw, could not imagine what he imagined, when he lay in his bed at night, staring at his ceiling. The storm bells rang loudly in his ears, and so he rang them for Washington. "Containment," he declared, a great clanging word. "Counterforce." The bell cracks. This, say the history books, was the beginning of the Cold War.[27]

But for Abram it had already started, and Kempe's demons and bells were simply confirmation of the crisis he believed had long been coming, the notorious "B" of his nightmares now writ large. For Abram the Cold War began the moment Germany's defeat was certain. By the time Kennan published the new creed of containment, under the pseudonym "X," the first great public statement of American strategy, the American vision for the coming decades, Abram had already been gathering his forces.

"The demand for this hour is for America to awake," declared one of his many manifestos, a 1945 agenda for a meeting of government officials Abram had organized. "Awake"—as if wartime mobilization had been nothing but a bleary-eyed prayer before morning coffee. "With faith in God and confidence in the Christian people of America, the undersigned, representing various national agencies, believe that the time has come when we should unite our forces in an effort to promote such an awakening." They would do so by establishing prayer cells first in every congressional district in the country and then overseas.[28] Germany, on the front lines, must awaken, not to its past, to its destiny. Even in 1945, when "destiny" was dust in the German rubble, Abram believed that Germany still had one. And Germany's destiny, he was certain, was in the hands of the Americans.

•   •   •

ONLY ONCE, EVER so delicately, would Abram raise the subject of Germany's recent unpleasantness. In 1948, Fricke wrote to Abram that he would be sending him a man named Gustav Adolf Gedat, a Lutheran pastor who had been a popular writer before World War II. Gedat was the honorary president of the German YMCA, an enthusiast for "boys' work," as it was called. He was a towering man, his shoulders sharp and so broad that his hairless head looked like a boiled egg made to stand on its narrow end between them. He believed as a matter of principle in big grins and bonhomie, but his face was made for sternness and his soul for discipline; the toothy, lipless grimace that emerges in photographs from his succession of chins calls to mind a malevolent giant in a nursery rhyme. At war's end, Gedat was a *staatsfiend,* declared an enemy of the Nazi regime, and on this basis he built a brilliant postwar career, not to mention a castle in the Black Forest for his boys' work, reconstructed with funds from American backers eager to support "good Germans."[29]

Maybe that's what Gedat had become. But even Abram, determined to believe in the goodness of all men granted status by Jesus, wondered otherwise. "We have had some negative reports," Abram wrote Fricke about Gedat in a letter marked "CONFIDENTIAL," "because of his former Nazi connections and publications." Abram did not care to know details one way or the other. Rather, he wanted to know if Gedat's past would interfere with his work for the organization Abram had by then rechristened the International Council for Christian Leadership.

"Dear Brother Vereide," responded Fricke, an unusually intimate greeting for the German pastor. He thanked Abram for arranging the attendance of John J. McCloy, the high commissioner of the American Military Occupation, at Fricke's most recent gathering of "really leading people." But, he went on, he could not tolerate such an inquisition. Gedat "did what we all tried to do in 1933 and '34," he wrote, "find a synthesis between the new party and Christianity." For this, other German churchmen, "willing to be the tools of Satan," had denounced Gedat as a Nazi. Fricke's "tools of Satan" would have included the martyr Dietrich Bonhoeffer had he survived, but such Christian resistance to Nazism meant nothing to Fricke. The truth, he argued, was that Gedat was a victim—of those unwilling to forget the past. "Even if Gedat had been a Nazi—which he has not been—and if he saw his failures, let us say only in 1945, and if he repented, would there not be the way of forgiveness from God and men?"

Is this a clue to the actual date of Gedat's repentance? In 1935, apparently still searching for synthesis, Gedat gave a speech in which he declared that "God ordered hunters to chase Jews to where God wants them." Two years previous, he had welcomed the new regime as the kind of full-strength disinfectant needed to rid Germany of "materialism," a concern that plagued him well into his postwar years. Gedat may have hoped that the Christian wing of National Socialism would triumph over its pagan mirror image.[30] When it did not—the two strands of fascism remained intertwined throughout Hitler's regime—Gedat turned against Hitler as a false prophet, a man bent on usurping Christ's rightful place at the head of the nation. Gedat took his totalitarianism seriously, could not stand to see it reduced in the personality of this uncouth little Austrian. He did not believe the problem with Jews was racial. It was biblical. He did not believe in a master race; he believed in a master class of key men from all nations. For this, Hitler banned him from speaking and even imprisoned him, and then "materialists" shadowed him with accusations. Yes, Gedat was a victim.

Would Abram join the materialists? Fricke wanted to know. Was Abram consumed by the "spirit of vengeance," the "spirit of Morgenthau," as Germans had taken to calling the tough policies of the Jewish American secretary of the treasury, the strongest advocate of denazification? Germans like Fricke struck a delicate balance with such implicit accusations. Allied justice equaled vengeance, they suggested, and vengeance was the stuff of the Old Testament. Putting their meaning more plainly would have been disastrous; even Abram would have recoiled, in 1948, from a German who blamed the Jews for his current troubles. Abram preferred the positive approach, the

New Testament, New World, American method: reinvention. He called it *reconciliation*. To argue for anything else, he'd insist—to demand justice—was un-Christian.

What did Morgenthau really want? No more than accountability. Not every German was a "willing executioner," as the historian Daniel Jonah Goldhagen puts it—indeed, many were themselves executed—but the Third Reich was not something imposed on an innocent German nation, as Abram and other American fundamentalists believed, but something it had brought about.

"It should be brought home to the Germans," declared a directive from the Joint Chiefs of Staff delivered to Eisenhower in April 1945, "that Germany's ruthless warfare and the fanatical Nazi resistance has destroyed the German economy and made chaos and suffering inevitable and that the Germans cannot escape responsibility for what they have brought upon themselves. Germany will not be occupied for the purpose of liberation but as a defeated enemy nation."[31]

This attitude, believed millions of Germans, was the true crime against humanity. They had said they were sorry; would the Americans behave like Bolsheviks and Slavs—purveyors of "Asiatic nihilism," as one of Fricke's political allies wrote Abram—and refuse to forgive? "The world is playing a very dangerous game with the German people," wrote Fricke, "if that repentance is not accepted."[32]

Abram replied immediately. The charges against Gedat had come from the liberal Federal Council of Churches. Not worth a dime. "I responded by pointing out how natural it would be for a man in Germany to look with hope to any aggressive leadership that could unite the forces against the Communistic infiltration . . . I am thrilled with the progress that is being made in Germany."[33]

GEDAT WAS AMONG the least tainted of the men that Abram and Fricke, and later Gedat himself, gathered into prayer cells to help forge the new West German state. But they *were* repentant men, this they testified to at every session. Repentant for what? It was hard to say. Every one of them claimed to have suffered during the war years. Men such as Hermann J. Abs, "Hitler's banker" and a vice president of Abram's International Christian Leadership (ICL), German division; Gustav Schmelz, a manufacturer of chemical weapons; Paul Rohrbach, the hypernationalist ideologue whose conflation of Germany with Christianity, and most of Europe with Germany, had inspired the Nazis to understand their war-hunger as divine; and General Hans Speidel, who had accepted the surrender of Paris on behalf of the Führer in 1940, insisted that he had never believed Hitler, had been forced into his arms by the Red Menace, had regretted the unfortunate alliance with such a vulgar fool, a disgrace to God's true plan for Germany. They had done nothing wrong; they, too, if one gave it some thought, were victims.

Perhaps some of them were. That is one of the many clever strategies of fascism: persecution belongs to the powerful, according to its rules, both to dole out and to claim as the honor due martyrs. Abram did not ask questions; he simply took out his washcloth and got busy with the blood of the lamb. He scrubbed his "new men" clean. Did it work? Abs, "Hitler's banker," became "Adenauer's banker," a key figure in the West German government's financial resurrection. Schmelz kept his factory. Rohrbach wrote on, authoring tributes to Abram's International Christian Leadership in the *Frankfurter Allgemeine*.

And Speidel? He was a special case, a coconspirator with Rommel in the attempted assassination of Hitler, the "July Plot" of 1944. There was something almost American about him; like Buchman, like Barton, he considered Hitler's racial policies a distraction from his really good ideas. For this ambivalence, the Allies rewarded him: he served as commander in chief of NATO ground forces from 1957 to 1963, when Charles de Gaulle, unpersuaded of his reconstruction, insisted on his ouster.[34]

Such men are only a few of those whom Abram helped, and by no means the worst. There were Zapp and von Gienanth, there were "little Nazis" Abram championed for U.S. intelligence positions, and there were big ones: Baron Konstantin von Neurath, Hitler's first foreign minister, and General Oswald Pohl, the last SS commander of the concentration camps, among them. For those beyond hope of blank-slate reinvention, Abram and his web of Christian cells pled medical mercy (von Neurath, sentenced to fifteen years for crimes against humanity, was released early in 1953; Abram took up his case upon learning from von Neurath's daughter that her father, classified as a "Major War Criminal," was receiving less than exemplary dental care in prison) or expediency (it was unjust, they felt, that Pohl, who while imprisoned by the Allies wrote a memoir called *Credo: My Way to God*—a Christ-besotted path that did not include acknowledging his role in mass murder—should be left wondering when he would be hanged).[35]

When occupation forces charged Abs with war crimes, he offered a novel defense. He did not deny what he had done for Hitler; he simply declared that he had done it for money, fascism be damned. He would gladly do as much for the Allies. And so he did, a task at which he so excelled that he would come to be known as the wizard of the "German Miracle." His past was forgotten—a phrase that must be written in passive voice in order to suggest the gentle elision of history in the postwar years, undertaken by those eager to see a conservative German state rise from the ashes, a sober son of Hitler's fatherland that would inherit the old man's hatred for one radicalism but not his love of another.

When, in 1982, the Simon Wiesenthal Center delivered to the public a massive case detailing Abs's crimes—among them the looting of the Third Reich's riches on behalf of Nazis fleeing to South America—Abs, not long retired from his spot at the helm of the Deutsche Bank, must have felt a sense of annoyed déjà vu. Would the world condemn his financial machinations for the glory of the Reich? Then it must also reject those on behalf of capitalism's easternmost bulwark in Europe, America's most crucial ally in the Cold War, the Federal Republic of Germany: a nation in which the past became the crass obsession of "materialists," those who preferred brute "memory" to more modern, more spiritual affairs.

"HUMILITY BEGETS POWER," Congressman Clyde Doyle of California preached at a prayer meeting convened by Abram to consider the problem of "reconciliation" as V-Day approached. Let us take the gentleman from California at his word. Let us suppose that the politicians Abram gathered to dedicate themselves to the "suffering" of the German people—men such as Senator Alexander Wiley, the Wisconsin Republican who'd declare even Kennan's muscular manifesto "panty-waist diplomacy"; Senator Homer Capehart, the Indianan who became the most vocal defender of former fascist "rights" after the war; Representative Walter Judd, the ex-missionary from Minnesota; and Representative O. K. Armstrong, a jolly Missourian who thrilled to the sound of Bavarian oompah bands—were true believers, humble and powerful and eager to be of service for their suffering brethren.[36]

Consider Capehart, a Hoosier who'd invented the mass-production jukebox. "The embodiment of Senator Snort with his vast paunch and triple chin, a large cigar fixed permanently in his round face, Senator Homer Earl Capehart was a cartoonist's dream," the *South Bend Tribune* would later eulogize him. Capehart was no Nazi; he was a Christian, a spiritual warrior, a red hunter, a vice president of Abram's organization, and a member of the Committee on Foreign Relations. Like Abram, Capehart only wanted to soothe the heartache of the most broken.[37] "The first issue" of the postwar situation, Capehart declared in a 1946 broadside against an unspecified "vicious clique" within the Truman administration, "has been and continues to be purely humanitarian." Capehart spoke of the "tragedy in Germany"—the rubble of Berlin, the empty stomachs of Hamburg— with such pathos that one might be forgiven for mistaking which side he had been on. Subsequent generations of neo-Nazis have done just that, endlessly recycling his speeches. "Those who have been responsible for this deliberate destruction of the German state"—he meant not the policies of the Reich itself but Morgenthau's short-lived plan

to "pastoralize" the fatherland into a second infancy—"and this criminal mass starvation of the German people have been so zealous in
their hatred that all other interests and concerns have been subordi-
nated to this one obsession of revenge."[38]

To Frankfurt and Berlin, Senator Snort and Abram and the Fellowship of the Senate dining room sent new suits, so that the Germans could dust themselves off and emerge from the rubble clothed
like gentlemen, and overcoats to protect them from the chill of a nation that burned what was left of its furniture to stay warm. What do
you need? Abram asked Fricke, promising to take up any matter in
the Senate dining room. "Though I hardly like to say it aloud," Fricke
wrote back, "shoes." So Abram gathered donations and sent shoes.

And he arranged passports, so that restricted Germans could
travel out of their country. In August 1947, he convened at Lake Geneva a council of nations to befriend the Germans, forgiving French-
men and Dutchmen and Czechs and Poles and Britons and a delegation
of Americans led by Senator Wiley, a member of the Foreign Relations Committee. "Choose two or three promising leaders," Abram
had advised Fricke for the German contingent. The Swiss minister of
finance would send the invitations, which the Germans should then
take to a certain American in the occupation government, who would
see to their arrangements for leaving Germany. At the head of the
table Abram placed Alfred Hirs, director general of the Bank of
Switzerland and a key figure in Abram's European calculations. Hirs
had credentials. His wife was a Bible teacher in Zurich, and his home
was a destination for traveling missionaries. The year previous he
himself had sought out Abram. A Youth for Christ missionary would
recall meeting Hirs at a "Christian businessmen's" convention in
Washington in 1946, at which Hirs had apparently complained of the
tepid temperature of the religiosity on display. Someone steered Hirs
to the Christian Embassy, where he found Abram and presumably
prayers of a more satisfying fervor.

Hirs was a man in need of consolation. He had come to Washington not to bask in American Christendom's good feelings but to fight
over the spoils of war, and it seemed, then, that he was losing. The

Americans were demanding that he reveal the secrets of Swiss bank-ing, and worse, that deposits be returned, not to Nazi depositors—suicides, Argentine exiles, men who would not ask for their money—but to Jews.

"Do you want to take 500 million Swiss francs of gold and ruin my bank?" he screamed at representatives of Morgenthau's Treasury Department. This sum—500 million Swiss francs in Hirs's bank alone, 1.25 billion dollars, money to be fought over for the rest of the century—no one in Washington had imagined that Hitler had ex-tracted such a rich vein from the bank accounts, jewel boxes, the jaws of Europe's Jews.

Back in Zurich, Hirs found more understanding friends. Nathan-iel Leverone, the vending-machine king of America, reported on what he learned in Zurich to American bankers and the National As-sociation of Manufacturers. The German guests spoke on the need for solidarity among men of free enterprise if the dollar was to stand as a bulwark against Stalin's tanks. Christ or communism was the choice they offered Leverone. By Christ, the German contingent meant to imply themselves.

And then there was Senator Wiley, a good friend for a man like Hirs to have. A Republican from Wisconsin, he was a pleasingly round-faced man of sixty-three years, dapper in a tux, and skilled in the use of a hawkish eye and a sly smile. He was, more than anything else, an opportunist: an isolationist before the war when indignant cries of dictatorship—FDR's, not Hitler's—could raise a man in the Republican Party, but an internationalist after it, when fighting com-munism won more votes than keeping our boys safe at home. He en-joyed a pulpit, and he didn't much care what faith it belonged to. "The Jews and the Arabs," he once declared, "should settle their dispute in the spirit of Christian charity." Such a faith had no trouble absorbing Hirs and the Germans, since Wiley was a deep believer in the moral relativism of anticommunism. During the war, he had been an advo-cate of the Jewish cause, calling for a Jewish "foreign legion" of exiles and Palestinian Jews. Afterward, Jewish gold was of no concern when weighted against the strength of the Red Army. That threat, real and imagined, drove Wiley to distraction. The Russians would rape the womanhood of Europa. In Korea Mao's Chinese would swarm like ants. In the union halls of Milwaukee honest Americans would turn like werewolves into godless monsters. Everywhere, he thought, communism was about to bubble out of its cauldron. He didn't want to just put a lid on it; he wanted to blow up the kitchen.

That had already been tried. Europe in 1947, the year of its coldest winter in decades, remained a rubble of roofless buildings and bridges into thin air. "At night," one German American returnee wrote in his journal, "you see ever so often the dim sky *through* the walls of a building: the filigree of chaos. Then it seems beautiful in a weird way and you forget that houses are good only when they protect people from rain and cold."[39] That thin line of indigo was a stronger barrier to hostilities than the "iron curtain" Winston Churchill had warned of.

Senator Wiley wanted total war. Take the men of Hitler's old panzer divisions, bless 'em under Christ, and point 'em toward Moscow. Abram's German point man, Otto Fricke, wasn't so bloodthirsty; he merely wanted twenty-five rearmed German divisions to slow the Russian invasion he saw coming. "What Do We Christians Think of Re-Armament?" was the theme of one of Fricke's cell meetings in 1950. They were conflicted, tempted to take "malicious joy that the 'Allies' are now forced to empty with spoons the bitter soup that has been served by the Russians." The judgments at Nuremberg had dishonored the Wermacht, and the dismantling had insulted and robbed Germany's great industrialists, Krupp and Weizäcker and Bosch—all well represented in Fricke's cells. By all rights they should stand down, refuse to rearm, let the Americans defend Christendom from the Slavs. But there it was: Christendom. They were Christian men, chosen not by a nation but by Jesus himself to lead their people into the "Order" God revealed to them in their prayers. "To accomplish these tasks," the Frankfurt cell concluded, "the state needs power and this powerfulness is indispensable for the sake of love."[40]

But the Russian blitzkrieg wasn't actually coming. The Soviet Union quickly realized its interests were best served in Western

Europe by parliamentary democracies, in which communists untainted by collaboration could seize power without a shot fired. Or so Stalin thought. Across the continent in those cold, hungry days, middle- and upper-class conservatives regained the power they'd lost to the fascist rabble. They were not, however, militarists, at least not of the operatic breed. The Germans did rearm under Chancellor Konrad Adenauer, the most pious politician in all of Europe, but much more than militarization, Germany threw itself into *making* the tools of Cold War. It was the nonpolitics of Krupp and Hirs, quiet men who knew how to hold on to money not properly theirs, that conquered Western Europe as Hitler never had.

"I am modernizing my factory," Baron Ulrich von Gienanth, Zapp's old Gestapo colleague, boasted to one of Abram's aides in 1952.[41] He had 800 workers in his employ, he went on, men organized according to Christian principles. And he was opening a new factory in Switzerland. His ICL brother-in-Christ, Baron von der Ropp, a "prophet" according to Abram, provided men such as von Gienanth with a new Christian management theory. Von der Ropp, before the war a Prussian propagandist for a "greater" Germany, was a Christian nationalist who had resented Hitler's cult of personality—a vulgar parody, he thought, of the Christian destiny for Germany proclaimed by Martin Luther. In a stroke of luck, he had been banned from public speaking just before the war's end, and on that thin moral basis reinvented himself, like Gedat, as an instructor of boys.[42]

Von der Ropp specialized in young working-class men, or "the Stirred," as he referred to those distracted by "social problems" from the masculine model of Jesus. On one hand, von der Ropp's religion was straightforward American fundamentalism, remarkable only for the thoroughness with which he transplanted it to German soil. But he also anticipated the middle-class fundamentalism of the American future, the point at which Abram's upper-class religion and the popular front would converge. A geologist by training, he preached that "too much science" would lead to "intellectual shallowness," a foreshadowing of the claims of today's fundamentalism, intellectually critical and anti-intellectual at the same time. He taught that the

poor, with their demands for government services—which he understood as a failure to trust that God would provide—were "the
adversaries of the church." But not through their own doing; rather,
absent some modicum of prosperity, they were too bitter to properly appreciate Christ's providence. This, in essence, was the faith
that would thrive in future decades, when both the cell group and
the megachurch became staples of evangelicalism, the microscope
and the telescope of American fundamentalism. It certainly did not
take hold in Germany; but it evidently made an impression on
Abram.

Perhaps, too, on von der Ropp's fellow aristocrat, Baron von
Gienanth. The two would have met often at Abram's private conven-
tions of Germans and Americans. The difference was that von der
Ropp, never a Nazi official, could travel and spread his ideas at
Abram's international meetings. Von Gienanth was bound to the Fatherland. This, he complained to Abram, was an impediment to reconstruction. He'd wanted to attend a conference in Atlantic City
with further ideas of expansion in mind. Would the American military really say that a man of his stature would blemish the boardwalk?
He was on a list of undesirables, he had learned from certain
connections—probably ICL men within the occupation. This would
be "understandable," he thought, if he had been a communist. "But I
don't see any sense in including people of my attitude"—ex-fascists
ready to make common cause with the United States.

Among the many testimonies von Gienanth collected on his own
behalf was a letter from an American diplomat's wife who insisted
the baron had not been a Nazi so much as an "idealist." Eventually,
von Gienanth had believed, "the good and conservative element of
the German people would gain control." Fascism had been like strong
medicine, unpleasant but necessary to what von Gienanth had always
believed would be the reestablishment of rule by elites like himself.
"In the coming years of reconstruction," his advocate wrote, "such
men will be needed who can be trusted."[43]

Abram contacted the Combined Travel Board that decided on
which former Nazis could be allowed to leave the country. The baron

was needed, Abram insisted. There were high Christian councils to be held in The Hague. "Expedite the necessary permit."

Should that argument prove inadequate, Abram hired von Gien-anth's wife, Karein, as a hostess on call for Americans traveling on Christian missions. She was an American citizen, though she'd spent the war with her SS officer husband. Now her American passport was being threatened. Abram saved it. That summer, he sent the baron and his wife a gift of sorts: a congressman from California, to be a guest on the baron's estate. The following winter Senator Frank Carlson visited. "As you know," Abram advised Karein, "he is one of the closest friends and advisors to Eisenhower."

A "serene confidence has filled me," she replied, "as to President Eisenhower's guidance by God." That summer, her husband flew with her to England, his passport evidently restored.

THE CASTLE OF the Teutonic Order sits on the eastern edge of a small island in Lake Constance, a Bavarian gem at the intersection of Germany, Austria, and Switzerland. Shaped like a fish, the waters are emerald, sapphire, and amber, depending on the time of day. The island itself, called Mainau, is even more dazzling, the "island of flowers," a botanical garden formed according to the whimsy of the Swedish princes who have lived within this fortress for generations. Since the nineteenth century they have been collecting blossoms and butterflies for their retreat, and, most of all, trees, giant redwoods and cedars from Lebanon and palms, more palm trees, surely, than in all the rest of Germany combined, gathered from around the globe.

The crest emblazoned on the castle is a bristle of swords and spears and gray flags that resembles a charging, heavy-tusked bull elephant with a purple crown between his great ears. But the castle itself, raised in 1746 on the ruins of older castles, celebrated as an ideal of the architectural style known as Southern Bavarian baroque, looks like a giant cake made of pale orange sorbet. Its walls are smooth and creamy, its windows like the ornamentation of sugar cookies. "You would have liked the surroundings," Abram's chief representative in Europe, Wallace Haines, wrote him in June 1951. Haines had just presided over an international meeting which Abram's health had prevented him from attending. Mainau, he gushed, was a "fairy island," and the conference, judging by his letter alone, might have been something out of a fairy tale: flowers sculpted into the shapes of strange creatures, great candle-lit halls, "divine services" in the chapel, ornate and glittering as a Faberge egg's interior.[44]

The first meeting at Castle Mainau had taken place in 1949, the same year the Allies allowed Germans to begin governing themselves again. The 1951 meeting was planned to mark what Abram considered the complete moral rehabilitation—in just two years—of Germany. Abram wanted the Americans to go to them, a grand contingent of senators and representatives. Gedat, now the unofficial leader of the German organization, was thrilled. But when word came that official duties in Paris prevented the American delegation from attending, he was furious. There was more bad news. Chancellor Adenauer, Gedat's keynote speaker, was called away to a crisis. And Abram himself, slowed down by more bad health, would not be there. His representatives could take notes.[45]

"For our God is a consuming fire"—Hebrews 12:29—was the conference's theme. What did this mean? "God is the God of power," said one of the first speakers. God is *not* the God of ethics, of morality; God is great, God made this order and chose its leaders. Prince Gottfried Hohenlohe opened the meeting on a Thursday evening. "God gave me my place in the world," he told 150 assembled worthies, a statement not of pride, in his mind, but of humility, a modesty shared by his audience, men and women now trained for several years, through weekly cell meetings, in Abram's religion of key men and destiny.

General Speidel was there, as was Rohrbach the propagandist: There were representatives from the major German banks and from Krupp and Bosch, and there was the president of Standard Oil's German division. There was at least one German cabinet member, parliamentarians, mayors, a dozen or more judges. A U-boat commander, famed for torpedoing ships off the coast of Virginia, cut a dashing figure. A gaggle of aristocrats, minor princes and princesses, barons and counts and margraves, were intimidated by some of the best minds of the old regime. There was the financial genius Hermann J. Abs, and a fascist editor who had once been a comrade of the radical theorist Walter Benjamin before throwing his lot in with the Nazis.

Wallace Haines spoke for Abram. He stayed up all night before his lecture, praying for the spirit that spoke aloud to his mentor. The Americans, God told him to say, were thrilled with the "eagerness" of the Germans to forget the war. The Americans came to the Germans humbled, he told them. Haines brought proof of their newfound wisdom: a letter of repentance for the sins of denazification signed by more than thirty congressmen including Wiley and Capehart and a young Richard Nixon.

On Saturday night, Theophile Wurm, the former Lutheran bishop of Württemberg, spoke in the White Hall, a confection of gold gilt dully shining by the light of candles. First there was music, cembalo and violin, "old music," reported one of Abram's Germans, a former Nazi propagandist named Margarete Gärtner. Blue darkness fell on the lake, and Bishop Wurm began to speak. All felt sacred, for here was a man of deep character. He'd been an early and enthusiastic supporter of national socialism, had helped purge the German church of dissenters, had drawn up lists of the weak, the deformed, the degenerate. This, as Fricke had said, was simply as they "all" had done. But Bishop Wurm was different; Bishop Wurm did not believe in killing. Not more than necessary, anyway. This watery conviction, he thought, made him a "resister." His identity at the end of the war, when the clock sprang back to zero in 1945, *stunde null,* the Germans called it, was his identity forever. He was the man who wrote Berlin a letter asking the Reich to spare some Jews. "Not from any predisposition for Jewry," he'd written, "whose immense influence on cultural, economic, and political life was recognized as fatal by Christians alone, at a time when almost the entire press was philosemitic." No, Bishop Wurm wrote, his version of truth to power, "the struggle against Jewry" was correct; but shouldn't the Reich first try to convert them?

In the White Hall Bishop Wurm stood before a great window,

the snow-covered Alps glowing purple in the dusk. A thunderstorm rolling in over the lake split the sky and boomed through the castle, setting the candles aquiver, silhouetting Wurm when lightning flashed. He spoke of the mechanization of man and the loss of faith in free enterprise, God's delicate weavings, the idea, the promise, that God helps those who submit totally. The lightning cracked, and Frau Gärtner, Bishop Wurm, the barons and the generals and the captains of industry submitted, totally. "We are children of fear," Prince Hohenlohe had proclaimed at the meeting's beginning, but that night, fortified by the spirit of Wurm and electrified by lightning glaring off the lake and over the mountains, their bellies full of warm stories and good wishes from around the world, the children of fear felt like children of God, and for this fine sensation, wrote Frau Gärtner and Wallace Haines and Gedat, they sent their thanks to Abram.

FOR YEARS, MANFRED Zapp had been Abram's harshest correspondent, constantly warning that the "man on the street" with whom he seemed to spend a great deal of time had had enough of America's empty promises. America had committed "mental cruelty," he charged, holding "so-called war criminals" in red coats—the uniforms of the Landsberg Prison—awaiting execution indefinitely.

Abram agreed, and sent to the occupation government letters signed by dozens of congressmen demanding action.

America prevented German industry from feeding the nation, Zapp argued.

Abram agreed, and intervened time and again on behalf of German factories. He saved as many as he could, though a steel foundry named for Herman Göring was beyond even his powers of redemption.

America had put leftists and trade unionists and Bolsheviks in power, Zapp complained.

Abram agreed. The cleansing of the American occupation government became an obsession, the subject of his meetings with the American high commissioner John J. McCloy and his weekly prayer meetings with congressmen.

"Idealists" were prevented from serving their people, said Zapp. The man on the street was losing faith in the American religion. "Freedom in their interpretation is the ideal for which we shall fight and die but the reality is nothing else but a beautiful word for services for Western powers . . . The word freedom is not taken seriously anymore."

Within a few years, nobody cared. The "Morgenthau Boys" were as much a part of the past as the history no German cared to speak of. "*Tabula rasa*," declared Konrad Adenauer when he took power as the Bonn Republic's first post-Hitler ruler.[46] Abram met with Adenauer on several occasions, but the "Old Man of Europe," a creature of the Weimar Republic's forgotten tradition of conservative reformers, never took to him; Adenauer was a Moral Re-Armament man, a great friend of Buchman's. But by then Buchmanism had diluted its fundamentalist flavor, had become 100 percent Cold War spirits, suitable for men and women of any faith who hated Bolshevism. More, Adenauer was too Roman Catholic to really embrace Abram's religion—even, one might say, too Christian. A former mayor of Cologne, he had been deposed as soon as the Nazis took power in 1933, and had spent most of the next twelve years gardening and reading theology. At the heart of European politics for two decades after the war, by inclination he was a monastic, his face disfigured by an accident in his youth, his old bones subject to chills that led him to wrap himself in blankets on long journeys. His Christian Democratic Union (CDU)—the German equivalent of the Republican Party— was ascetic in its devotion to purging Germany of leftist tendencies but liberal in its economy. Adenauer did not like to see his Germans go hungry.

Given Abram's influence in postwar Germany—if Adenauer kept his distance, many of his ministers did not—what kept the nation from falling into the orbit of American fundamentalism? Why did its Christian Democratic Union, Germany's most powerful party, not become part of a Christian bloc within the Western bloc, the foundation of an evangelical supranationalism beside which the strength of the contemporary movement would pale?

Part of the answer lies in its Christianity, essentially Catholic, and its Democracy, which was, with occasional hiccups, actually democratic, in the most pedestrian sense—that of dull bureaucratic order. More, it was a political party; in the United States fundamentalism grew during the 1950s and '60s by presenting itself as a greater force, to which men of either party could pay tribute in return for divine favors.

But most of all there was old, wrinkled Adenauer himself, more blatantly Christian in his pronouncements than any American politician could ever be, but also more cautious. *Keine Experimente,* "No Experiments," was an official campaign slogan. The "values and sense of justice of Western Christendom"[47] was the political plank on which he plodded forth, but it was the very lack of such a sense that made of Adenauer's Germany a secular nation. For it was a nation with no concept of sin. That had gone into the dustbin right along with history when Adenauer in his first act as chancellor dropped all charges against—*privileged* was the official term—nearly 800,000 minor Nazi officials, many of whom would become the functionaries of his blank-slate regime.

In place of the very real dangers of German romanticism, the bloodlust of Wagner, Adenauer offered modest family values. A depoliticized philosophy of inward-looking households, the moral conformism of proper Germans. The man-on-the-street in the era of Adenauer, lamented Zapp, nostalgic for the thunder of the "new conception" now past, wants only "his job, his food, his movie, and his sport."[48]

In the end, Abram and the Americans learned more from the Germans than the other way around. It was after the CDU turned *family* into cultural code that American fundamentalism found a way to make the term both modern and traditional, used to describe—and shape—the postwar suburban world as well as that of a mythical small-town past. Abram finally retired *normalcy,* the Harding-era neologism that for two decades had defined his mission, his Christ, and his politics. It was a notion to which postwar Americans studiously subscribed even as they celebrated the myth of themselves as rugged individuals, but *family* captured that paradox more neatly, a nation of cozy little kingdoms ruled by Father. And the new evangelical alliances, forged along the lines of spiritual war rather than the eradication of vices traditionally considered masculine—drinking, gambling—made sure that Father knew best about not only his little unit's material welfare but also its spiritual morale, once the province of Mother. "Men must reclaim the Bible from their wives," Abram's "prophet," Baron von der Ropp, taught the workers of the Ruhr, a succinct statement of the old nineteenth-century muscular Christianity that took on new meaning in the postwar era.

. And then there were the questions of sin and of history, inescapable in Europe and thus ignored. But sin and history presented more nuanced dilemmas to American fundamentalism. Not its prewar mild sympathy for fascism—the blood of D-Day had wiped that record clean as far as most Americans were concerned—but the drag the actual, awful past put on the movement's new global ambitions. What were they? Nearly the same as those of the nation's. For a muddled period after the war, the United States had pretended that it could shrink back to its prewar isolationist ways, but by 1947, with the Truman Doctrine and the Marshall Plan in place, it was firmly committed to the "new world order" hoped for by Abram and Senator Wiley and their bipartisan alliance of Christian internationalism.

"The United States has been assigned a destiny comparable to that of ancient Israel," Harold Ockenga, the president of the National Association of Evangelicals, had declared at its inception, reviving the old notion of manifest destiny and extending it around the globe.[49] But manifest destiny, the original westward thrust that erased a continent of Native souls, burns history like coal and knows no sin but that of its enemies. So, too, Abram's dream, in both its religious and secular manifestations. And in this regard, too, the Americans learned from the Germans, who understood that mythology makes of the past a parable, smooth and enigmatic, best understood by those who ask no questions.

7.

THE BLOB

THE MOST UNEXPECTED EARLY fruit of Abram's prayer breakfasts was *The Blob*, a 1958 B-movie about the creeping horrors of communism. "Indescribable . . . Indestructible! Nothing can stop it!" warned the tagline. *It* is mindless glop from outer space. The Blob absorbs the residents of a small town, growing bigger, grosser, and more ravenous until the townspeople discover they can defeat the Blob by freezing it—the Cold War writ small and literal. *The Blob* was the result of an unlikely collaboration between a screenwriter named Kate Phillips and an evangelical minister named Irvin "Shorty" Yeaworth. The two met at the 1957 Presidential Prayer Breakfast. Phillips, a former actress who'd appeared in forgotten films such as *Free, Blonde, and 21* and *Charlie Chan's Murder Cruise*, wasn't known for her faith. She attended the Prayer Breakfast as a guest of a friend from Islip, Long Island—probably Abram's patron, Marian Aymar Johnson, at whose Islip estate Abram did much of his planning.[1] Phillips was accustomed to Hollywood glamour, but she felt lost amid the crowd of congressmen and business titans gathered for breakfast in a ballroom of Washington's Mayflower Hotel. "All of a sudden," Phillips later told a fan, "a chap came out of the hotel and said that somebody had suggested he talk to me because I was a writer."

The chap was Yeaworth, a director of "Christian education" films looking to subliminally broadcast his message into the mainstream. Shorty had backing for a full-length science fiction flick. The catch was that it had to be "wholesome." And as if by providence, here was a screenwriter at a prayer breakfast. "I would like to have you be a part of the picture," Shorty declared, and a few days later he traveled up to Phillips's Long Island home to show off a two-pound coffee can full of the blob stuff that would come to serve as the Cold War's most ridiculous metaphor for communism.

If picturing the Red Army as a carnivorous mass of Jell-O was absurd, the symbolism fit the bigger concept of *Cold War,* an amorphous fight that absorbed ideological nuance as it grew bigger, grosser, and more ravenous for the hearts, minds, and economies of two dueling empires. Between the rebirth of fundamentalism in the 1930s and '40s and its emergence as a visible force during the Reagan years sits the historical blob of the Cold War, an era as bewildering to modern minds as any in American history. There is, to begin with, the question of whether the United States won this war or the Soviet Union lost it. A third school of thought wonders if both sides were losers. And then there is the more vexing question of just what we mean by *Cold War.*

To today's conservatives, it was a philosophical stance—better dead than red—that resulted in "our bloodless victory."[2] For liberals eager to reclaim a mantle of muscular progressivism, meanwhile, *Cold War* refers to an abstract strategy of *containment*—as if the Cold War didn't explode into dozens of "regional" conflicts strategized in Moscow and Washington, "civil wars," fought with the empires' weapons, that killed millions. Most memorably, the dead, American and otherwise, of Korea, Vietnam, Cambodia, and Laos, but also the forgotten losses of the Shah's Iran, Suharto's Indonesia, Mobutu's "Zaire," Pinochet's Chile, Papa Doc's Haiti, the United Fruit Company's Guatemala, and many more. One could draw up just as long a list to lay at the Kremlin's door or Beijing's, but it's our own sins that most require recollection, that fade to nostalgia in the sepia-toned memories of both liberals and conservatives.

Even those terms—*liberal* and *conservative*—befuddle us. Which was which, for instance, when Eisenhower ran against Adlai Stevenson in 1952 on a campaign promise of *decreasing* military spending, while Stevenson boasted that "the strange alchemy of time has somehow converted the Democrats into the truly conservative party of this country"?[3]

How do we categorize Cold Warriors such as Senator Mark Hatfield—a Republican from Oregon, vocal opponent of the Vietnam War, and staunch advocate of evangelical political power—versus his colleague to the north, Senator Henry "Scoop" Jackson of Washington, a "godless" Democrat whose relentless militarism inspired neoconservative protégés such as Richard Perle and Paul Wolfowitz, architects of the Iraq War?

That the ideological spectrum in America more closely resembles a Mobius strip, left and right twisting into one another, than it does a radio dial is a basic truth of political history. But what of religious history?[4] What of the role of Christianity, and particularly that branch of the faith dedicated to "fundamental" principles, whether they're those of Christ's sovereignty over all, or of America's divine destiny? How did American fundamentalism intertwine with the new internationalism to create the DNA of a Cold War in which one of the nation's most militant commanders in chief—I am thinking here of Kennedy, not Reagan—reduced the issue to one of a belief in God, "ours," versus the Soviets' lack thereof?

THE CHRISTIANITY OF American fundamentalism is a faith for futurists, the sort of people who delight in imagining what is to come next, even if it's awful. World War II had changed the steady plod of Christian futurism, quickened it. Christendom had at times raced toward apocalypse before, but never with such technology at its disposal—no rockets, no bombers, no nuclear missiles. The stakes were higher in the new era, the enemy stronger. Fundamentalism responded with great imagination, not just following the popular trend of spotting flying saucers and aliens among us, but driving it. The aliens among us were not green men from Mars; they were red, at least on the inside, and they could be your neighbors. On the outside, they looked just like good Christian Americans. Many of them were Christians, in fact, or so supposed the conservative mind. By the end of the decade, FBI chief J. Edgar Hoover would declare that communist stealth operatives, "schooled in atheistic perversity," had made Christian pulpits a main objective—and tool—of their propaganda. A "deadly radioactive cloud of Marxism-Leninism," he preached, was fogging America's liberal houses of worship.[5]

Hoover kept files on liberal churches; Abram kept friendlier files on Hoover, a man who seemed to naturally speak the language of holy cause-and-effect Abram had refined before the war. "The criminal is the product of spiritual starvation," Hoover was quoted in a pamphlet Abram saved, *The J. Edgar Hoover You Ought to Know*. The pamphlet's author was an ally of Abram's, Edward L. R. Elson, a mainline Presbyterian whose paranoia placed him at the far end of the religious spectrum. Elson joined another friend of Abram's, Charles Wesley Lowry, to create the Foundation for Religious Action in the Social and Civil Order, and Lowry, in turn, joined Abram in behind-the-scenes council of upper-crust Christian conservative leaders known as "the Twelve."

Before the war, such initiatives were the stuff of the fringe, disaffected Babbits, America Firsters. After the war, they were mainstream. In the 1950s, the soldiers of Christ didn't wear armor; they wore cufflinks. Consider this convention of Fellowship worthies, gathered in a hotel lobby for a group portrait. On the left is Abram in his customary double-breasted suit, lapels like bat wings, his silk kerchief neatly folded in his breast pocket and a slim leather Bible spread open in his right hand. To his right stands Billy Graham, his famous blue eyes glowering between his rock jaw and a wave of blond hair, almost good looking enough to play a gunfighter. And rising between them stands a fascinating character named Kenneth M. Crosby.

Crosby was literally our man in Havana, or at least one of them. He'd been a spy throughout Latin America during the war. Officially retired at its end, he took over Merrill Lynch's Cuban operation in 1946 and stayed until 1959, when Fidel Castro drove out the dictator Fulgencio Batista, reporting all the while back to U.S. intelligence, a happy double posting which also allowed him time to set up prayer cells for Abram. His "Havana Group" consisted of American embassy personnel, representatives from American banks and the United Fruit Company. Cuban sugar cartels boasted openly in the *Havana*

Post of the prayer cell's use as a lobbying tool, noting that one of the International Christian Leadership officers, Congressman Brooks Hays, returned home from a spiritual session in Cuba ready to fight for Cuban sugar in the House Foreign Affairs Committee. Crosby was even more loyal to the regime, serving as an intermediary between Batista's Palacio Presidencial and American businessmen in Havana and New Orleans.

At the time, even *Christianity Today* considered Fidel preferable to the profoundly corrupt Batista.[6] But to Crosby, Castro was "another Hitler." It was Crosby, briefing CIA director Allen Dulles, who laid one of the first bricks in the Cold War construction of the island nation as one of America's greatest enemies. These were the days of citizen soldiers, spooks and "psyops" commandos, and, for the first time in American history, preachers on the front lines. Front lines of what? "Total cold war," Eisenhower would call it, a battle not of bullets—although plenty of those would fly—but of ideas, many of which wouldn't.[7] Against communism's promise of "People's Democracy," for instance, Madison Avenue, at the behest of Eisenhower, coined "People's Capitalism," a catchphrase that somehow failed to inspire even the Americans who practiced it, much less Soviets supposed to be seduced by it.[8]

Preachers provided the ammo capitalism couldn't manufacture. "Your government," one of Abram's British protégés wrote, "is aware of the need of much greater propaganda to Russia and her satellites if we are to control the Communist menace." The Brit hoped to obtain Abram's help with a plan to smuggle New Testaments into the Eastern Bloc under diplomatic cover. The aim was "to place dynamite just where it is needed."[9] Bible smuggling boomed in the 1950s, but very few efforts to sneak Western wisdom into the Soviet bloc made as much impact on their intended targets as on the West itself, which reveled in its crusades. Some of the schemes were truly quixotic: the use of hot-air balloons to drop leaflets on Albania, for instance, an effort that probably did more to spread the American love of UFO-logy than the Cold War double-dogma of God and private property.[10] Such is one of the overlooked legacies of the Cold War: the weirding of American fundamentalism. Abram's was a space-age faith, thrilling to the vibrations of Eisenhower's "Atoms for Peace" and throbbing to the conviction that God would guide our missiles, if only we could conform our national will to His. That was the stated goal, repeated over and over: conformity. Conform or die. Nuclear annihilation, should it occur, would be the result of rebellion, the "effect of the tragic choice of disobedience."

Abram's religion was sleek and powerful, an aerodynamic update on the clumsy bombs dropped by fundamentalism's old angry ranters. Two of Abram's "field representatives," Dr. Bob Pierce and J. Edwin Orr—both to achieve fame of their own as major twentieth-century revivalists—coached young Billy Graham in the mores and manners of overseas operations and educated society. Harald Bredesen, another field representative who'd go on to build a powerful ministry of his own, performed a different service for a youthful Pat Robertson, teaching the senator's son a folksy appeal that would complement his political acumen. One Abram understudy, Dr. Elton Trueblood, made a career of packaging militant fundamentalism in the language of country club banal, churning out best sellers that conflated spiritual war with Cold War; he also drew a paycheck from the United States Information Agency, for which he headed up the Office of Religious Information. On his watch "spiritual roots"—Christian ones, that is—as the foundation of American democracy became government policy, channeled through private organizations so that the office's plans would not look like a "propaganda gimmick."

Abram's closest ally in the Senate, Frank Carlson, Republican of Kansas, coined the Fellowship's slogan, "Worldwide Spiritual Offensive." Carlson was a farmer from Cloud County, Kansas, who first made a national name for himself in 1936 when as a young congressman he double-crossed his patron, Governor Alf Landon, by ripping into the New Deal as a subversion of American principles. Landon had hoped to pitch his policies as a more moderate version of FDR's vision, and here was his protégé, declaring the sitting president un-American. Not that Landon had a prayer, anyway; he became the losingest presidential candidate in American history. But Carlson prospered. Over the next decade, he rebuilt the Landon machine under his own name. He took the governor's office in 1946, and when three years later one of Kansas's senators died in office, Carlson inserted as a placeholder a flunky who then dutifully stepped aside when Carlson was ready to return to Washington in 1950 as a member of the nation's most exclusive club.

In the early days of his career, Carlson cultivated a myth of himself as a modern-day Cincinnatus who entered politics only at the behest of a delegation of small businessmen that found him literally tilling his fields and begged him to help stop Dictator Roosevelt—the "destroyer of human rights and freedom," as Carlson called him. By then, Carlson was chairman of the Interstate Oil Compact and he had denounced not only the New Deal but also Hoover's business-friendly policies before it as an "insidious attack" on "free enterprise"—by which he meant government subsidies for Big Oil.[11]

And yet Carlson enjoyed a reputation as a moderate and even, in the surreal political landscape of the 1950s, a "liberal" Republican. His face was tanned and leathery, flanked by white wings of hair and almost-pointed ears, framed by arched eyebrows and a broad, lipless mouth, all of it centered on a nose the shape of a mushroom; he looked like a sunburned Bela Lugosi. It was hard to imagine this comically featured man as an ideologue in the mold of hammerhead Joe McCarthy of Wisconsin. Carlson was a backslapper, an arm gripper. A Baptist teetotaler himself, he presided over the end of "Dry Kansas" and joined two other Fellowship senators in raising funds for a Republican club in Washington that would feature the best cigars and the finest Scotch whiskey. He was a Republican wise man, "sagacious," according to the columnist Drew Pearson, "the 'No Deal' Dealer," in the words of another pundit. It was Carlson who in 1951 coined for his friend and fellow Kansan Ike the double-duty slogan of "No Deal." Eisenhower, then the electoral underdog even though he was the most popular man in America, meant that he wouldn't horse-trade with crooked local GOP organizations, most of which were in the back pocket of "Mr. Republican," Senator Robert Taft of Ohio, the presumed front-runner. But the slogan also implied a none-too-subtle rebuke to FDR's New Deal and

Truman's more conservative Fair Deal. *No Deal* meant more than the "rollback" of progressivism, as Carlson claimed, a conventional conservative assault on social welfare. By *No Deal,* Carlson and Eisenhower meant no politics. That is, they hoped to capitalize on Eisenhower's popularity as a victorious general, incorruptible in peacetime, to replay the Cincinnatus story on a national scale.

Carlson spread the rumor that he and a shadow cabinet of more senior senators led by Henry Cabot Lodge of Massachusetts were pushing Ike for the White House without Ike's permission. Eisenhower privately wondered, meanwhile, whether it would be legal to win the nominations of both political parties. It wasn't that Eisenhower transcended ideology—history has revealed him to be one of the most masterful politicians of the postwar era—but rather that he believed that he could best achieve his goals by pretending not to have any.

Eisenhower was the great literate of midcentury politics, the man who knew how to parse a moment, to respond to the masses as if they were all individuals, each unique in his sameness. Eisenhower was a PR man; he had learned on the battlefield the secrets of *psyops,* of psychological warfare. "Don't be afraid of that term," he advised the voters. He was a bridge player; he knew how to bluff and win. He bluffed the Republicans, in whose traditional ranks he did not properly belong, and the Democrats, who, having lost their chance to nominate him, dismissed him as an amateur. Eisenhower knew what Americans were looking for and he let them see it in him, a hero both grand and ordinary. "The sort of prince who could be ordered from a Sears Roebuck catalogue," as Saul Bellow described him.

In 1952, Carlson and a small group of like-minded Republicans put in their order, and Ike delivered. The ringleader was ostensibly Senator Lodge, but Carlson ran Ike's Washington campaign headquarters, and his sidekick and former senatorial substitute, Henry Darby, ran the nominal HQ on the second floor of the Jayhawk Hotel back in Topeka. Carlson's abandoned patron Alf Landon briefly tried to swing his state to Taft, but Carlson effectively smeared Taft—and Landon, his more moderate former mentor—as reactionaries nonetheless too soft for "total cold war." Carlson had laid the groundwork for his new middle-ground reputation the year before. And he did it with the help of Abram.

In April 1951, Abram enlisted ICL president Ed Cabaniss, a wealthy manufacturer, to round up some businessmen interested in the Idea who could help create an advisory prayer cell for every governor who wanted one, to be organized by Carlson. Cabaniss, a holdover from the pre–1950s Fellowship, was an Old Guard conservative. He had a V-shaped head, a tiny jaw, and a giant brow; he looked like a praying mantis, and his affect was that of one as well, slow and chilly. For his latest undertaking, Abram wanted more dynamic men. He specifically requested that two of the most effective red hunters in his circle be included: Howard Coonley, the former president of the National Association of Manufacturers who'd helped win him access to big business during the 1940s, and Merwin K. Hart, a wealthy member of his board of directors who recruited businessmen for the Fellowship through his pet project, the National Economic Council.

The council was little more than letterhead, a desk in the Empire State Building, and Hart himself, a goggle-eyed, tuxedoed blue blood with a fringe of hair around his narrow skull and more than a hint of fascism around his politics. "If you find any organization containing the word 'democracy,'" Hart declared, "it is probably directly or indirectly affiliated with the Communist Party." Hart wasn't kidding; effective in his deregulation crusades, he was never able to achieve one of his fondest ambitions, the disenfranchisement of the poor, whom he considered spiritually unfit for voting.

The war had made Hart toxic for a spell, since unlike Lindbergh, who'd abandoned his own fascist inclinations to fly for the United States, Hart never repented for his prewar fascist position. But the Cold War changed everything, Cabaniss wrote Abram. "It seems to me there is a growing proportion of the public, particularly in the political world, who are coming to a realization that Merwin Hart is not so far 'off the beam' in his thinking." The business world was coming around, too; Hart counted among the supporters of his National Economic Council's program of God and laissez-faire capitalism top men from Standard Oil, DuPont, and General Motors.

This theology of the dollar was not quite as cynical as it sounds. Abram was expanding his European operation into Greece's upper crust, an experience that was teaching him to refine the stealth evangelism he'd learned in Germany. First came capitalism; then came Christ. Capitalism, preached his friend Norman Grubb, was the wedge. "ICL," he commented to Abram, "is a bold attempt to reach a certain unreachable class with Christ, and is therefore not primarily concerned with presenting itself as sound in a 'fundamental' doctrinal basis; it is after fish who might refuse the bait if this fundamental doctrinal basis was flaunted in front of them."[12]

Hart, Coonley, and Cabaniss were to line up financial backers for the group (who, as it turned out, agreed to raise $100,000 for the project); Abram would explain the Idea; and the public face of the initiative would be two former governors who'd made the leap to the big leagues, Carlson and Senator Robert Kerr of Oklahoma. Kerr was a Democrat, thus blunting the growing concern within the Fellowship that it appeared to be simply a subsidiary of the Republican Party, and he was Carlson's kind of Democrat—"the chief of the wheelers-and-dealers," according to the journalist Milton Viorst, "a self-made millionaire who freely and publicly expressed the conviction that any man in the Senate who didn't use his position to make money was a sucker."

Like Carlson, Kerr was an oilman. Or, more precisely, oil's man. He knew a good investment when he saw one; he sent Abram a check for $500. Other senators fell in line: Robertson of Virginia contributed a fund-raising letter, Republican Ralph E. Flanders of Vermont gave $200 and the use of his name, and Pat McCarran of Nevada, McCarthy's Democratic mirror, wrote asking what would be most helpful—money or contacts (or both). That fall, the president of the ultraright William Volker Fund chipped in $500 from his own pocket. The Volker Fund had helped Friedrich von Hayek, until then an obscure Austrian economist, become a national celebrity in America by subsidizing editions of his *Road to Serfdom*. First published in the United States by the University of Chicago Press, the book appeared in shortened versions produced by *Reader's Digest* and *Look* magazine, which illustrated Hayek's argument that any attempt at "central planning" (including FDR-style government regulation of big business) would send a society down a "road to serfdom"—and mass murder along the lines of Hitler and Stalin—from which there was no return. Hayek's economic ideas were considerably more complex than the uses to which they were put, but as understood by the American public—and by Abram, who recoiled from *serfdom* even as he embraced what he happily termed *slavery* to God and his markets—they seemed to lend a scientific imprimatur to the Manichaean worldview of the country's most rabid red hunters. A decade later, the Volker Fund would hire Rousas John Rushdoony, a theologian who was to the far right of fundamentalism what Hayek was to economic conservatism; it was Rushdoony who helped marry the two with extensive writings on *theonomy,* a jargony term for what Abram's descendants would come to call *biblical capitalism.*

Both theonomy and biblical capitalism suggest an equal yoke between scripture and currency, but there can be little doubt about which was the driving force behind this new plan to surround governors with prayer warriors vetted by Abram and his friends in corporate America. And yet it was Carlson, who disliked even acknowledging the existence of dollars, who quietly climbed Abram's chain of command. The following spring, he took time off from Eisenhower's still-unofficial campaign to travel to The Hague, where Holland's Queen Wilhelmina anointed him as the new chair of International Council for Christian Leadership, the overseas division of Abram's ICL composed at that point mainly of Germans who didn't want to talk about their pasts and French businessmen just as eager to smooth over history in the service of profits. Three fellow GOP congressmen, all Abram disciples, accompanied Carlson. They flew on the public tab, and the trip occasioned sharp questions from the press. Why had the secretary of defense given the four use of a U.S. military plane for private travel? The ICLer's mission, said a spokesman for the secretary, was in "direct relationship to the national interest."[13]

At The Hague, Queen Wilhelmina, a strong monarch famous for bypassing Holland's parliamentary system,[14] presided over this American interest, and the inner circle of the Fellowship's trans-Atlantic organization elected Carlson their new chairman. Carlson looked like a stand-in, though, for the general running the Allied command in Paris. That seemed to be as Carlson wanted it; he was in Holland to recruit allies for an American campaign. Besides Abram, there were industrialists who'd line up behind Eisenhower, including the automobile titan Paul G. Hoffman, who'd become one of Ike's economic advisers; a pair of ultraright congressmen to shore up Ike's conservative flank; and, in addition to GOP heavies such as Senators Wiley and Flanders, a delegation of "Dixiecrats," Southern Democrats to the right of most Republicans. That summer, Carlson declared that Eisenhower would contest the traditionally solid-Democratic South, a quixotic quest that anticipated Nixon's "Southern Strategy" by more than a decade.

Far more troublesome to Eisenhower than the Democratic South, though, was a singular midwestern Republican, the de facto party boss, Senator Robert Taft of Ohio. To the uninitiated, Taft did not appear be a formidable obstacle. He was a dull speaker, unmemorable in appearance, indifferent to the public. But no politician could claim a more perfect pedigree: grandson of a secretary of war, son of a president, first in his class at Yale and Harvard Law. "The best mind in Washington," went a popular Democratic jab, "until he makes it up." And yet he played the part of a common man. Not like Roosevelt, who'd disingenuously claimed to be a farmer, but rather, in the name of an ill-defined middle class—in reality, the managerial class, small businessmen and second bananas who dreamed one day of being bosses themselves—that would become a template for conservative "populism" long after Taft's name was forgotten.

If Taft was hardly just another Rotarian-on-the-make, he truly was in every sense a provincial man, and proud of that fact. A son of Ohio beholden to neither the New England aristocracy nor the solid South, wary of Wall Street, contemptuous of Europe and its wars, he was a conservative at the last time in American life when such views connoted a kind of pacifism. His enemies murmured of fascist sympathies because he did not want to fight Hitler, but it was war itself that he loathed. When World War II ended and the Cold War began, he opposed it even more strongly, opposed the draft and opposed military spending and opposed what he feared, correctly, was the coming age of American empire, an era in which the United States would wage the wars the old colonial powers could no longer afford.

In 1952, Taft was known as the champion of the "Old Right," an anachronism in the day of the atom. He was the engineer of the New Deal's deconstruction, the author of the 1947 Taft-Hartley Act which spelled the end of labor's brief reign as the definitive power in American life. Taft-Hartley reduced labor to an "interest group"—eliminated the vision of solidarity as a force that gave people meaning. Maybe Taft dreamed that with labor rebound, the nation's economic life would return to its pre-Depression condition. But that world was as long gone as the fantasy of the United States as an island, immune from the troubles of other nations. A New Right, New Liberalism, New Middle were rising, shaped by the war and by Europe, by the hunger of an economy that had grown fat on weaponry, by the *idea* of totalitarianism. Total Cold War was coming. Ideology, technology, and—overlooked by the mandarin historians of the period—theology were converging.

Taft had the support of the old GOP local party operations, but he did not have God and he did not have Frank Carlson. He would not recruit public piety as a banner for his campaign. His lieutenants were not wily; they were hedgehogs, nudging Taft's Old Right views along, decrying the possibility of a "garrison state" as if the Cold War hadn't already led the United States to embrace a permanent military footing, spiritual warfare thinly secularized as "psyops" and arms races against a godless enemy. Such was the method of foxes. Carlson slinked from delegate to delegate behind the scenes, the " 'No Deal' dealer" smiling and speaking of spiritual things, one nation under God, unity, a general (not a politician!), never speaking ill of old "Mr. Republican" but promising patronage to those who'd abandon him. "The Kansan is clearly the man to see if you want an 'understanding,' " cooed an admiring reporter.[15]

At the Republican convention in Chicago, enough delegates "caressed by personal letters, wined & dined at party shindigs, promised a secure future by politicos," reached such "understandings" with the general's lieutenants and sold out their man to the new order.[16] To the populist Right, the activists who'd sent delegates to Chicago to stop Ike from entangling America in more of Europe's troubles, the convention took on "mythic proportions," a stab in the back of conservatism by Ike and his internationalists.[17] Carlson, as conservative as Taft, understood that anger—and how to turn it to his man's advantage. Jesus, Carlson believed, had been a "psyops" man like Ike, and Christ and the general both taught the same lesson: it was the spirit, not the material, that mattered. Emotions, not facts. Carlson and Eisenhower did not need to crush the anger in Taft's supporters; they only had to redirect it toward international communism.

After Eisenhower routed Adlai Stevenson—the electoral vote was 442 to 89, with Ike poaching four states of the Old Confederacy—Carlson set about ensuring Taft's loyalty to the new regime. His method, though, left some wondering about Eisenhower's loyalty to the broad middle ground he'd staked out in his campaign. First, Carlson brokered a breakfast between his man and Taft, at which Taft agreed to stand aside while Eisenhower waged Cold War abroad if the general would commit to a war on the New Deal at home. Taft had decided that if he could not be president, he would like to be majority leader; after all, he and Ike shared a distaste for organized labor, indifference to civil rights, and a firm conviction that capitalism constituted a natural law more certain than the physics of nuclear fission. The next afternoon, Carlson met with Taft after church and cut a deal. His—and, implicitly, Ike's—backing for Senate majority leader, a betrayal of promises already offered to Senator Styles Bridges of New Hampshire. "An amazing political feat," the columnist Drew Pearson wrote of the Taft revival. "Carlson sold the idea."[18]

The idea Carlson sold was the Idea: Abram's dream of a big tent conservatism, a political philosophy that denied the reality of the political and disdained "philosophy" as the province of eggheads. In a September 1952 mass mailing, Abram had directed his two-hundred-plus prayer cells across the nation to devote themselves to spreading "alertness to the right choice and vote in the November elections." God, he wrote, had spoken these words to him: "Your mission is to concentrate on a few men in leadership capacity." One of his new lieutenants, a Lithuanian named Karlis Leyasmeyer who claimed to have escaped a death sentence at the hands of the Soviets (with the help of the Nazis), added that such men could become a "sixth column," the secret counterweapon with which the establishment could fight communism. The sixth column would transcend politics. In a voter's guide prepared for the state of Washington by Abram's men—a tactic that would be repeated decades later by the Christian Coalition—God tapped both Democrats and Republicans. His slate, however, was of sufficient political conformity for a bipartisan coalition to raise charges of fascism. But the '*f*' word had lost its power. Most of Abram's candidates won. "Red" was the new brown, against which all Christian soldiers must fight together. One God, one nation, one ideology.

DURING THE WINTER following Eisenhower's election, the United States did not even have an ambassador in Moscow. It was in that particularly cold season that Abram—with the help of Carlson, Billy Graham, and Eisenhower himself—made his master move, following the president's inauguration with what would become an annual political ritual, the Presidential Prayer Breakfast (later to be renamed the National Prayer Breakfast). Not for Abram the clash of politics or even the intellectual battle of theology. His ambition for the breakfast—hosted by Conrad Hilton, presided over by Carlson, blessed by Graham, and sanctified by Ike's blandest speech yet—was that it serve as a chance to lop off the left end of the political spectrum and cauterize the wound. "Their differences," wrote the *Christian Herald* of the several hundred assembled politicians, Democrats and Republicans, "are fused into a striking similarity."

Billy Graham had been summoned to the Eisenhower campaign by Carlson. The senator had concluded that the young preacher would be an asset, especially given that some Democrats were actually floating the notion that it was Republicans who were soft on communism and cold toward Christ.[19] Although Graham himself was a registered Democrat, he had decided for Eisenhower before the general even announced, and had prayed on the matter with one of his supporters, an oil baron named Sid Richardson. (This period of Graham's career might be called his oil phase. In 1953, with backing from yet another oil baron, he would release a feature film called *Oiltown U.S.A.*, a tribute to the free market's ability to foster the virtuous exploitation of God-given resources.) Carlson called Graham to the Chicago GOP convention for an off-the-record meeting. "Carlson had sold Eisenhower on the idea that I could contribute a religious note to his campaign speeches," Graham would recall.

"Frankly," the preacher told the general, "I don't think the American people would be happy with a president who didn't belong to any church or even attend one." (In fact, there have been several.)

"As soon as the election is over," Eisenhower promised, "I'll join a church."

Graham wanted more. He'd been talking with Abram about a Presidential Prayer Breakfast, a parachurch ritual they hoped would settle the question once and for all of whether the United States was a Christian nation and the New Testament, not the Constitution, its ultimate authority. Abram had long dreamed of such an event, a public dedication of the governing class to the service of the Christian God, but no president previous to Eisenhower would cooperate. It was Graham, according to his own curiously immodest account, who made it happen. He arranged with Conrad Hilton (to whom he'd been introduced by Carlson) to sponsor the event, and he gave the main address—at most of the first fifteen annual breakfasts. But Carlson was Abram's pipeline to the White House, and Abram's invitation to the president-elect went through the No Deal Dealer. Ike declined. "He did not want to set a precedent," Graham recalled. But Graham intervened, and Ike called Carlson over to say that he would show, after all. There were debts to be paid. Eisenhower was the first twentieth-century Republican to come to power in part through an alliance of populist evangelicals (led by Graham) and of elite fundamentalism. Now Graham and Carlson wanted their return.[20]

"The only one thing," Ike warned Carlson, "let's not have any television or radio around." That suited the man to whom Carlson reported this news. Abram did not much care what the masses saw or did not see. He was playing to an audience of power; "up and out" went his spiritual broadcast. Eisenhower, meanwhile, was wary of advertising his foray into the no-man's-land between church and state. "You can tell the Cabinet I'll be there," Eisenhower instructed Carlson. "I suppose that's tantamount to telling them to come." Come, they did, and with the exception of those tapped for Abram's table, they found their own seating. There were no arrangements, Abram boasted; all were left to fend for themselves, "regardless of rank," just as in the Kingdom of God—supposing, that is, that such a kingdom were inhabited only by men of high rank, the powerful pretending at egalitarianism within the confines of the most exclusive breakfast club in the land.

There were 400 such men at the first Prayer Breakfast. It was 8:00 a.m., Thursday, February 5. The theme was "Government Under God." Abram wore his trademark bow tie. He was sixty-seven that year, and he would soon suffer a heart attack, and soon Stalin would die, and Kinsey would publish his report on *Sexual Behavior in the Human*, and *Fortune* magazine would crow over a "spiritual awakening" among top businessmen. At the Mayflower, Conrad Hilton hung above the dais a painting of Uncle Sam on his knees, "not beaten there by the hammer and sickle" but submitting America to Christ, a sentiment the Senate's chaplain admired. "There are signs," he observed of the painting-in-lieu of a cross, "that once again, as in the former days of the Nation's true glory, America is bending its knees."[21] Printed beneath Uncle Sam was a prayer of Hilton's own composition. Hilton was a Catholic, but he thrilled most to the religion of anticommunism. "Be swift to save us, dear God, before the darkness falls." There was no darkness in the Mayflower, only bacon. Abram presented Eisenhower's cabinet to God. "Save them from self-deception, conceit, and the folly of independence of Thee, oh God." Eisenhower mumbled up to the podium, the pulpit.

He said, "All free government is firmly founded in a deeply felt religious faith." And then, "As long as you feed me grits and sausage, everything will be all right." These were the twin doctrines of a prosperity doctrine.

"There is the sound," observed the Senate chaplain, swept away by the deep spirituality of these words, "of a *going* in the tops of the mulberry trees," a supernatural sound. He thought it might be Eisenhower's prayers, winging up to heaven like B–52s.

TWENTY YEARS LATER, Abram's successor, Doug Coe, would explain his predecessor's calm at the Presidential Prayer Breakfast: "It is only one-tenth of one percent of the iceberg," he'd say. "[It] doesn't give a true picture of what is going on."[22] The Fellowship's true work was always both great and small, an accumulation of symbolic gestures and actual legislation. Sentiment and policy cohered into a religiously motivated movement, mostly Republican but also Democratic, that absorbed politicians and ordinary businessmen into its mass so smoothly that the townspeople never noticed; never rallied to resist or to even question the growing blob of political fundamentalism. The Fellowship, wrote one of Abram's field representatives, "should be primarily an organism and not an organization."

"The idea of a Christian lobbyist program might well emanate through the Breakfast Groups," one of Abram's original Seattle brothers wrote him. It's worth noting that the "Christian" issues of the day were not pornography or abortion; they were surveillance and weapons, the perceived need for more of both. Abram's correspondent wanted "more unity on civil defense"—read, anticommunism—"and foreign policy." Abram wrote back to say that he'd already moved the Fellowship beyond anything so crass and limited as a lobby. In the 1960s, it began distributing confidential memos to involved members of Congress on its progress around the world. The memos stressed that "the group, as such, never takes any formal action, but individuals who participate in the group through their initiative have made possible the activities mentioned." The Fellowship was not a conspiracy; it was a catechism, its questions asked in the privacy of Abram's prayer cells and answered in the public arena.

In 1954, "Under God" was added to the Pledge of Allegiance, an initiative sponsored in the Senate by Homer Ferguson, a Republican

ICL board member, and financed by ICLer Clement Stone, and "In God We Trust" was added to the nation's currency by a bill sponsored by a Dixiecrat congressman named Charles E. Bennett, also a member of the Fellowship's inner circle.[23] Bennett, a self-styled ethics crusader, saw himself as a small-government man; God and the dollar would redeem the nation, if only Congress would unshackle them. "Congress can't remake the soul of America," he'd say, a notion he evidently thought justified his opposition to civil rights.[24] It was Bennett who prayed the opening prayers at Abram's second Presidential Prayer Breakfast that February, at which Supreme Court chief justice Earl Warren—then still a conservative—declared that separation of church and state was fine, so long as "men of religious faith" were in charge of a country he described as "a Christian land, governed by Christian principles."

That same year, Abram's old ally Alexander Wiley, now chair of the Senate Foreign Relations Committee as well as the upper house's weekly prayer meeting, decided to extend those principles southward. He declared a democratically elected government in Guatemala a front for communist invasion and quietly green-lighted U.S. participation in its overthrow, an action that culminated in a ticker-tape parade in New York City for the dictator installed in its place by America, and a banquet in his honor at Hilton's Waldorf-Astoria.[25]

And that year a Vietnamese Catholic named Ngo Dinh Diem, "directly and personally aided by God," by his own account, came to America to appeal to a nation in the grip of religious revival for its support in a fight against godless communism. A year later, Eisenhower obliged, installing Diem's Christian—and profoundly corrupt—regime over a Buddhist nation when the French lost their hold, the first great step toward the American war in Southeast Asia that Robert Taft had feared. Wiley, a former Taft-style conservative transformed by Abram's Christ and Ike's Cold War into a militant internationalist, was the president's point man in the Senate, bullying liberals and conservatives alike into backing "hard and fast military commitments" to South Vietnam, no questions asked.[26]

Nineteen fifty-four was also the year that several Fellowship brothers steered Joe McCarthy off the national stage. It was a matter of politics, not ideology; Tailgunner Joe—raw, red-nosed, thick-browed, uncouth, uncontrolled, *hungering* Joe—made anticommunism look low-class.

McCarthy's downfall and Ike's disdain for him have been chronicled at great length elsewhere. Less noticed was Eisenhower's careful use of McCarthy during his campaign. Carlson was the middleman. "I fully expect that Senator McCarthy will be speaking vigorously for the ticket," Carlson told the press in September 1952. McCarthy did so, lashing out at Ike's opponent, Adlai Stevenson, as surrounded by communist sympathizers. Weapon deployed. Mission accomplished. "Sen. Frank Carlson of Kansas," the press dutifully reported, "commented that the General did not owe anything to McCarthy for the speech, and was still a 'no deal man.'"[27] After the election, the press assumed that Carlson would be rewarded for his services with a cabinet post. Instead, Carlson stayed in the Senate of his own volition, where he chaired a seemingly obscure subcommittee on civil service employees. It was a job that allowed him to quietly purge government of far more "security risks"—most of them guilty of no more heinous a crime than loyalty to the New Deal—than McCarthy had ever dreamed of, thousands erased from the rolls through backroom bureaucratic maneuvers.

Carlson also served on the special committee appointed to consider McCarthy's censure after he went too far by slinging mud at other senators. But the man who first wrote the resolution to censure was Carlson's predecessor as president of the Fellowship, Senator Ralph E. Flanders of Vermont. Flanders was a genteel Republican, an engineer, an industrialist, a banker. His wife collected New England folk songs. Smooth-domed and whiskered, his spectacles slipping down his nose and his pipe in hand, he looked like a professor and was sometimes mistaken for a liberal. But his record was as right-wing as many of the Senate's more outspoken firebrands. In 1954, the year he moved to censure McCarthy, he revived an old fundamentalist favorite: an amendment to the Constitution that would have rewritten the United States' founding document to declare, "This nation devoutly recognizes the authority and law of Jesus

Christ." And yet, because of his resolution against raving McCarthy, he is remembered as a sane man in paranoid times, footnoted in histories of the Cold War as one who stood up for common sense.

Only the radical journalist I. F. Stone perceived otherwise. Flanders, he wrote in 1954, did not challenge McCarthy's paranoia but rather his effectiveness in its promulgation. "To doubt the power of the devil, to question the existence of witches," Stone wrote following Flanders's ostensibly heroic gesture, is

to read oneself out of respectable society, brand oneself a heretic, to incur suspicion of being oneself in league with the powers of evil. So all the fighters against McCarthyism are impelled to adopt its premises . . . The country is in a bad way indeed when as feeble and hysterical a speech [as Flanders'] is hailed as an attack on McCarthyism. Flanders talked of "a crisis in the age-long warfare between God and the Devil for the souls of men." He spoke of Italy "as ready to fall into Communist hands," of Britain "nibbling at the drugged bait of trade profits." There are passages of sheer fantasy, like this one: "Let us look to the South. In Latin America, there are . . . spreading infections of communism. Whole countries are being taken over."[28]

This last, singular point would soon be made true in Guatemala, albeit the result of a more genteel anticommunism expressed through a U.S. bombing campaign. Whereas McCarthy used anticommunism to promote himself, men such as Flanders and Carlson and Eisenhower believed it should be reserved for the construction of empire.

The ethos of Abram's "Worldwide Spiritual Offensive" ran parallel to and often infused American Cold War tactics. Secretary of Defense Charles E. Wilson—whose "New Look" policy of nuclear weapons and air power consolidated the "military-industrial complex" Eisenhower himself would lament at the end of his presidency—embraced Abram's Idea of strength through spiritual conformism, allowing prayer cells to proliferate within the Pentagon and signing off on a

Fellowship project called "Militant Liberty," developed by a fundamentalist propagandist on Abram's payroll named John C. Broger. Broger, also an ill-defined "consultant" on the Pentagon payroll, was promoted to the Department of Defense's Office of Information and Education, a post from which he'd control the Pentagon's propaganda on more than 1,000 military radio and television stations and in 2,000 newspapers for almost three decades. In 1958, Abram made him a vice president of the Fellowship, bringing Broger's propaganda to the elites even the Pentagon couldn't reach. "The seed," Broger would say, speaking of his fundamentalist faith, "was dropped thousands of times."[29]

A tall, jowled man, balding and mustachioed, a squinter, Broger learned how to propagandize as an American aide to Filipino guerrillas in World War II. In December 1945, he turned those talents toward the Gospel, incorporating the Far East Broadcasting Company to bring the Good News to Asia. In 1948, from a patch of Philippines jungle littered with the scraps of war, he first sang "All Hail the Power of Jesus' Name," live on KZAS, "Call of the Orient" radio. He built more stations, scouting them out himself from planes made of corrugated tin in which he'd fly over China, Vietnam, Cambodia. In 1950, Admiral Arthur W. Radford, a zealous Presbyterian, asked for a briefing; Broger would now get his chance to combine his passions for propaganda and evangelism.[30]

The year before, Radford had been caught circulating a secret memo tearing down Truman's defense secretary. That led to exile in Honolulu, where he met Broger. But in 1952, he caught President-Elect Eisenhower's attention with a plan for battle by proxy, a blueprint for decades of dirty wars. Let's use Chiang Kai-shek's troops in Korea, he told Ike on a walking tour of Iwo Jima. Ike liked the idea enough to go golfing with the admiral and introduce him to General Motors CEO Charlie Wilson, about to become Ike's defense secretary.[31] In 1953, with Wilson's sponsorship, Radford came in from the islands to become chairman of the Joint Chiefs of Staff, and a year later he brought Broger to join him. By then Broger was working for Abram. The admiral and the preacher bankrolled Broger's ideological crusade.

A statement of its goals can be found in the Fellowship's archives: the recruitment of "indoctrinated personnel who will form nucleus groups for the implementation of . . . the highest concepts of freedom, whether socially acceptable or not."[32] By *highest concepts of freedom,* Broger meant the American Jesus, a Christ of strict order; "Social Order," "Law and Order," "Economic Order," and "Religion" were among the main topics of indoctrination. But Broger's own sense of order was more than a little skewed, as evidenced when he came under scrutiny for a peculiar Pentagon scheme to recut a movie called *Operation Abolition,* itself already a dizzying collage of newsreels and film clips which, through a series of unconnected images, implied that Abram's old foe, the union organizer Harry Bridges, was behind a plot to violently assault the House Un-American Activities Committee. Broger wanted to make *Operation Abolition* into an even weirder movie, modeled on a theory of his that behind even Harry Bridges was yet another, more insidious enemy: Japanese communists bent on taking over the minds of American teenagers.[33]

Operation Abolition was a bust; even the most ardent red hunters found it kooky. But throughout much of the 1950s and '60s, Broger broadcasted his notions into the hearts and minds of millions of U.S. troops and an unknowable number of foreign nationals—"articulate natives," as Broger referred to his "targets." These would be either Christians or those who were willing to convert to the faith, located across Latin America, Africa, Asia, and the Middle East, "traditional cultures [that] have become unable to furnish an acceptable comprehension of existence."[34]

If *Operation Abolition* was aborted, Broger had better luck with his other film ventures. Early on, he managed to recruit more talented collaborators. Some of the most talented in America, in fact: the director John Ford, John Wayne, and Merian Cooper, the producer who paired Fred Astaire with Ginger Rogers.

Ford had worked as a spy during the war, photographing guerrilla warfare in occupied Europe; Cooper had fought Pancho Villa in Mexico and flown against Germany in World War I; and John Wayne was John Wayne.[35] In 1955, Broger flew to Hollywood for a series of daylong meetings with the moviemakers, and Ford asked for eighteen copies of the Militant Liberty program to distribute to his screen-writers. He also suggested that Broger insert Militant Liberty into the movie he was directing at the time, *The Wings of Eagles*, in which Wayne played a navy flier battling naive pacifists in Congress for funding. Broger obliged; thankfully, the movie has disappeared from film history.

As has Broger's most successful effort: the big-screen, epony-mous adaptation of Militant Liberty, financed by the Fellowship and shown not just to the military but to schools, church groups, and prayer cells across the country, and made available to all of Abram's disciples. Blunt in his beliefs—the Constitution, Broger once lec-tured in the Pentagon's "Protestant Pulpit" series, was "hewn and shaped to the spiritual concepts of biblical truths," a guarantee of "Christian freedoms"—he subscribed to Abram's philosophy when it came to the exercise of power. Each key man spreads the Idea through the means available to him: the Senate, the Pentagon, a radio tower in the Philippines. "Christian Action," as he and Abram called their activities, should be behind the scenes, in the air.

That ephemeral sense, along with the legacy of the Cold War to which it contributed some small portion of fear and misinformation, appears to be all that remains of *Militant Liberty*, the movie. A declas-sified Defense document tells us that it was in color and hints at its story. Broger was its hero, presenting Militant Liberty to an all-star panel of brass and political power that included Congressman Charles Bennett, Frank Carlson, and Abram.[36] Beyond that, nothing more. I have not been able to find a copy of the film; I have only the records of its existence in Abram's files, the press reports of the day, and that picture of Broger with Defense Secretary Charlie Wilson, accepting the "Spiritual Values" award at the Freedoms Foundation's headquar-ters in Valley Forge, Pennsylvania. Standing with them are Carlson and the two producers of the film, an assistant to Abram, and a hand-some, sandy-haired man, visibly proud to be counted among such august company: Irvin "Shorty" Yeaworth, just months away from the Prayer Breakfast at which *The Blob* will be born.

8.

VIETNAMIZATION

RIVALS

Saigon, 1966. At the Hotel Caravelle, the swankiest address in the city, a middle-aged missionary named Clifton J. Robinson slips out a page of hotel stationery to write a report on his conquests for Christ in Vietnam. Robinson is big and broad-chested, dark-browed, looks good in a suit, at the rooftop bar popular with reporters from NBC, CBS, and the *New York Times*, flashing a smile of absolute certainty. He's associate secretary general for the Fellowship in Southeast Asia. That means he's Abram's man. He's writing back to Abram's headquarters in Washington—although Abram, his beautiful voice gone soft and sleepy with age, spends most of his time in a retirement community called Leisure World. Robinson is writing to thank Senator Carlson, who's sent a string of letters of introduction to precede Robinson on his grand tour of the region's friendly regimes. In each country Robinson visits, the American ambassador stands ready to receive him and pass him along to local power brokers. Robinson feels as if Jesus himself is opening doors, a neatly trimmed savior in a linen suit. He knows, however, that the name of a U.S. senator on the Foreign Relations Committee, not Christ's, is the reason the diplomatic corps genuflects before him. A "capital" notion, thinks Robinson. "Invaluable 'inside' help they've been able to be to us," he scrawls beneath the Hotel Caravelle's logo.[1]

Among his most fruitful meetings was time spent with William H. Sullivan, U.S. ambassador to Laos. As chair of the State Department's Vietnam Working Group in 1963, Sullivan had been one of the architects of the war, a de facto "field marshal," according to General William Westmoreland.[2] Such a man was an unlikely source of inspiration for Robinson, who called himself a Quaker. But preaching Abram's Idea overseas had put him at odds with the Society of Friends. Like another lapsed Quaker, Richard Nixon, Robinson had no patience for pacifism. He saw himself as a man of action, a "jungle" missionary on the move. He spoke with the quick velvety voice of an old-time radio announcer and used it to dispense axioms and analogies about the need for key men in the Cold War, Bruce Barton jingles as interpreted by James Jesus Angleton, top man religion as geopolitical strategy. Sullivan provided fodder for Robinson's commando theology.

"He said the strategy of the VC was the same as International Christian Leadership's," gushed Robinson, "except applied physically and militarily." Robinson's vision of Worldwide Spiritual Offensive could not yet accommodate Ho Chi Minh's tactics, but Sullivan convinced him their enemy was a worthy one. "They spend hours, days, weeks, whatever time is necessary setting up for the LEADERS and then either by ambush, assassination, or other intrigue, they do away with *them*—not the *people*, the *leaders*. He said to kill 32 top level people"—as the Vietcong had done the previous month—"was tantamount to immobilizing thousands."

The lesson was that the Fellowship should understand itself as a guerrilla force on the spiritual battlefield. Specifically, Sullivan, who directed the CIA's "secret air war" in Laos and turned its Hmong minority into cannon fodder against the North Vietnamese, wanted the Fellowship to recruit Buddhist businessmen to collaboration by matching them with Jaycees under the guise of a " 'brotherhood of leadership'—or some such slogan." But Robinson also took Sullivan's words as an endorsement of Abram's key man strategy.

"The strength of the wolf is the pack," Abram reminded his disciples that year, retreating into parable as he advanced into his last days, "but the strength of the pack is the wolf."[3]

Evangelical steamrollers such as the Billy Graham Crusade might win millions, but the Fellowship could neutralize the enemy—"bold Satanic forces," as Abram described it, the Vietcong's "sweep of communism," America's "secular cyclone"—by conquering the select few souls of the strong. "Assassination" was just a figure of speech to Robinson; Abram wanted elites to "die to the self," to submit totally to Jesus of their own volition even as they held on tightly to the power that could advance His kingdom. Long after Abram's death—and Ho's total victory in Vietnam—the Fellowship would distribute a tract purporting to be "ten steps to commitment from a Viet Cong soldier."[4]

Robinson was writing not to Abram but to Doug Coe. Abram was technically retired, although he still maintained top spiritual authority in the Fellowship. The question of succession was one nobody discussed, but Robinson was surely thinking of it. He'd recently opened a wedge for the Idea in India by recruiting the nation's minister of defense productivity into a Christian prayer cell. Whether that led to the kind of results Abram would have called "tangible"—a relationship with a Fellowship-approved defense contractor, a commitment to pulling India's left-leaning government rightward—it at least provided the Fellowship with the kind of bragging rights that impressed American congressmen: the Fellowship had connections everywhere, even in non-Christian nations. Robinson may have imagined himself the man for Abram's job.[5] But three years earlier, he'd angered Abram when he wrote that Indians are "more adept than wet eels in squirming out" of responsibility. "I feel we need to let the Indians know the 'world' is our battlefield." With the stakes so high, they were "expendable."[6]

Abram agreed—except for the part about letting the Indians know their place in the Fellowship's hierarchy. As the Fellowship grew along the military trade routes of the Cold War, its "field representatives" learned to ape and polish the politics of flattery by which powerful nations make weak ones feel crucial to the cause. But Robinson was too hot for the Cold War Christ. He genuinely believed he was spreading old-time religion revamped for the space age, not a new empire in democratic disguise. "Is this ICL message a kind of Christian fringe benefit, a casual sophistication, a pink tea variety of discussion subject?" he demanded of the Fellowship. "Or is it a revolution?"

Writing for Abram, a third would-be heir named Richard Halverson responded sharply. 1. Stop challenging Abram's vision. 2. You don't understand Abram's vision, anyway. 3. Here's what it's really about: "A revolution can be anarchy, Clif, or it can be tyranny. It can be noisy and rambunctious and spectacular like a Fourth of July fireworks celebration, or it can be quiet and penetrating and thorough like salt, like benevolent subversion."[7]

That was the key—subversion. There was bad subversion, like that of the Vietcong, and good subversion, also like that of the Vietcong, only in the name of Jesus, a subtle practice of persuasion. Robinson took the lesson, committing himself to raising funds directly for the Indian work so that its costs wouldn't be on the Fellowship's books, and inviting in Fellowship speakers, such as a British member of Parliament named John Cordle, who lectured the Indians on "Corruption," a subject about which he knew more than he let on. He would later be exposed as one of Britain's most flamboyantly crooked politicians.

Another speaker was Halverson, who lectured to a five-man "core cell" of U.S. embassy personnel on "Infiltrating Secular Society with the Spirit of Christ."[8] It wasn't a matter of proclaiming the gospel boldly; it was a trick of getting the heathen to fight your battles for you.

ROBINSON FAILED IN his succession bid; as would Halverson. Robinson's mistake was to take the Fellowship's internationalism too literally—far off in Asia, he failed to court Abram's favor personally. When he swept in from the field, he'd regale rooms full of Fellowship men with his adventures, forgetting that his audiences were composed of politicians used to being the center of attention themselves. Robinson extended the Fellowship's reach across Asia at a time when American power most wanted behind-the-scenes men in the Far East, but never understood that he also needed to be a behind-the-scenes man in Washington, too. The details of Doug Coe's victory are murky—at the time, few suspected quiet Coe would be Abram's heir—but Coe, alone, seems to have understood that in an organization that denies being an organization, power goes to the man least visibly concerned with pomp and circumstance. And yet Robinson and Halverson still matter to the story of the Fellowship. In part because they remained significant players, representatives of American fundamentalism to government around the world. And in part because they illustrate the different streams feeding into Coe's vision. Robinson was the public man, the character you put in the front of the room to tell stories. Halverson was more complicated.

Halverson's story, like that of the Family's, began in 1935, when he got off a bus in Hollywood fresh from North Dakota, where he'd grown up with the unlikely ambition of being an actor. Blandly handsome by small-town standards, in Los Angeles he hardly looked like movie star material: his lips were too full, his cheeks too chubby, his eyes too deeply set. He wasn't bad looking, but he wasn't Clark Gable, either. His strength was a certain gee-whiz sincerity, an earnestness augmented by intelligence. Dick Halverson wasn't a good guy because he didn't know any better; he was a good guy because he'd calculated the angles and concluded that decency was his best bet in this world.[9]

Thereafter, he pursued it mightily. In later years, Halverson would help build up one of the world's largest relief agencies, World Vision, a Christian outfit that supplies food for the starving and medicine for the wounded and gospel tracts only to those who ask. Although it has long been plagued by accusations of serving as a CIA front, World Vision's verifiable record is admirable—the sort of Christian effort to which Abram paid lip service and nothing more. But Halverson also helped build the Fellowship into a network of truly international scope, introducing the American Christ to any number of nations. Halverson, in other words, was an imperialist of the old school, bringing light to the natives and clearing the way for other men to extract a dollar. He was no hypocrite. He believed with all his heart he was helping, and he never thought too deeply about whom. Halverson loved public speaking, and he was good at it, too, invited to preach in pulpits around the world. He wrote popular books and mailed out newsletters and presided over a conservative Presbyterian church outside of Washington that was popular with politicians. In 1981, Ronald Reagan would make him Senate chaplain, the pinnacle of his career.[10]

Coe, meanwhile, was all along studying Abram, learning the methods of self-effacing persuasion. And studying, too, other sources of authority, strong men of history whose biographies he consumed and distilled into the leadership lessons he dispensed to his disciples the same way he cited, always smiling, scripture verses intended to "break" the powerful men to whom he ministered, the jujitsu of an alpha male proclaiming his desire to serve. God's word, not his; so it was written.

Coe brought to the Fellowship a radically different spirit than Halverson's, a darker appeal. Raised in a small town, middle-class home in Oregon, he'd gone to college at Willamette in the state capital of Salem, where he majored in physics and got serious about God. He'd been something of an Elmer Gantry—a good-looking flirt, friendly with everyone, close to none—according to Roy Cook, his sidekick for the last six decades. It was Cook, then an unsmiling, bespectacled boy with a crooked pompadour, who led Coe to Jesus. What kind of Jesus? In a talk to a group of fundamentalist activists years later, Coe ticked off what he gave up for his new Lord: smoking, drinking, dancing, and most of his friends. At twenty, he married an eighteen-year-old girl named Jan. Soon they had the first of six children, all born before Coe reached his early thirties. And as the 1950s opened, that might have been all: a pulpit, maybe, in rural Oregon, a brood of children, a stern but conventional God.

But Coe had fallen under the "discipleship" of Dawson Trotman, the founder of a worldwide ministry called the Navigators. Daws was a square-jawed, wavy-haired, bear-hugging man, a cruder version of Abram. Like Abram, who called him a "very dear friend," Daws scorned old-school fundamentalists who considered themselves "separate" from the culture, and like Abram, he'd begun his ministry in the 1930s, in opposition to the economic liberalism of the New Deal. Both men had little use for denominational distinctions, but Daws, unlike Abram, didn't understand them to begin with. He hated ideas;

he loved "jokes." He installed a remote control for his doorbell beneath his dining room table so he could send underlings running to answer it over and over, and he planted firecrackers set to explode in umbrellas when they opened. He actually wore a squirting flower in his lapel. And yet he'd publicly rebuke staffers he thought were "playing games with God," and he could drive even the manly men with whom he surrounded himself to tears. In place of a traditional ministry, Daws offered a pared-down concept of "discipleship" by which an evangelist picks a target and sticks with him until his "disciple" submits totally to Jesus as the discipler teaches him, the theological equivalent of hazing. Daws wasn't stupid; he was a strategist who understood that fundamentalism was *too* intellectual for the men he wanted to reach, men like him—or, more often, men who wanted to be like him. He boiled it down to Jesus plus nothing. "Daws really had only one string on his guitar," wrote an admiring biographer, "and he plunked it often and loud."[11]

That brute simplicity was what Coe, newly born again, missing his old habits and his old friends, wanted to hear. He went on a retreat to Daws's headquarters in Colorado Springs, a gothic castle called Glen Eyrie, moated and inhabited by suits of armor and graced by very little sun; it was deep in a canyon, and the sky above it was narrow. There Coe prayed to Jesus for a way out of what seemed the small but overwhelming life of a father and a churchman. How can I do it, God? How can I finish school and provide for my family and make time for the Bible and pray every day? Coe thought his faith demanded the memorization of a rule book over a thousand pages long. He couldn't do it. He couldn't keep Nehemiah and Jeremiah and Esther straight. *You don't have to*, Jesus told him. What then? Coe asked. That was when Coe discovered, or decided, that all of Christianity, 2,000 years of faith and ideas and mistakes and miracles and arguments and signs and wonders, could be reduced to one word: *love*. And what did *love* mean? "Obey." That's what Jesus told him. "Obey, then teach."[12]

Coe taught. At Willamette, he led one of his professors, a young political scientist named Mark Hatfield, into evangelicalism. Hatfield, in turn, led a parade of students singing hymns to file his candidacy for the state legislature. Stories would later circulate that it was Hatfield who, when he moved up to the U.S. Senate, invited Coe to Washington, but it was the younger Coe who nudged Hatfield onto the national stage and Coe who went to the capital first. And yet, outside of evangelical circles, he made little impression as a college man; his picture appears in yearbooks only once, a gangly, unsmiling dark-haired boy with big features, posing with the golf team. An odd man out, wearing hunter's plaid, a townie among the preps. It was an image of modesty he'd use to advantage in the years to come as he pledged himself to older men in the Fellowship—Halverson, Robinson, Germany's Gus Gedat, and most of all Abram—and then supplanted them.

Coe is, in fact, a striking man in both appearance and personality, gifted with a force field of charisma far greater than the more conventional appeal of Halverson and Robinson, backslappers both. He is tall, with strong facial bones and dark skin; he has been mistaken for an American Indian more than once. He is both ugly and handsome, in the manner of Lincoln, his features oversized and his entire being dominated by his broad smile. He dresses in golf shirts—after Jesus, golf has always been his passion—or in suits that look like they had to be pinned together around him, as if he's some loping, natural creature not meant to be bound by jacket and tie. He speaks with slow-motion intensity, his words languid and separated by silences in which listeners can ponder their meanings. There is something about his voice, a resonant, solid sound like an old oak tree talking, that makes you want to listen even if you disagree with everything he's saying. His fascination with the leadership secrets of Hitler extends to the Führer's speaking style, made over in Coe's loose-limbed mannerisms. He emphasizes his points by making his right hand into a fist and shaking it, even as his left hand slips into his pocket, a mixture of ego and insecurity that suggests an inner conversation the speaker would like to keep private. It is perhaps a tribute to his magnetism that a small group of fringe fundamentalists have dedicated themselves to investigating the question of whether he is the anti-Christ, believed to be a charming fellow with international inclinations. Coe would not be insulted; almost nothing insults him.

After college, he moved so quickly into leadership, spiritually "discipling" not just other recent graduates but business executives, politicians, even senior pastors, that it's hard to believe he needed much mentoring from Daws or, eventually, Abram. He was a natural leader: amiable, casual, not intimidated by anyone and interested in everyone, or so it seemed to those at whom he directed his devotion. Like Abram, he did not demand theological orthodoxy of his recruits. "Doug *hates* church," one of his followers, a former aide to Hatfield, told me. (Coe considers church irrelevant to the real Jesus encountered in one's prayer cell.)[13]

One of his associates later noted that Coe's wife, Jan, deserved much of the credit for her husband's work; he'd rarely met a woman "so uncomplaining and one who stayed put and waited patiently." Not as much could be said for the evangelical enterprises Coe left behind when he went to Washington in 1959 to work for Abram. The communal homes he'd organized, early prototypes of Ivanwald, were in danger of collapse, their inhabitants lost without Coe's effortless authority; churches were splitting over Coe's new doctrine; worst of all, young wives were in revolt, acting out the fears of all those who believed that Alfred Kinsey's 1953 report, *Sexual Behavior in the Human Female*, would set in motion chain reactions of feminine hysteria. "I definitely believe Jewell . . . is demon possessed," one of the Oregon brothers wrote Coe. "In fact, I have talked with her (in Helen's presence) and the demon coursed through her." That wasn't all. "I have also come to believe that Jim's wife is in the same boat. In fact she said she was, but you would have to see and talk to them to appreciate this. The other night she went into a rage when Jim was just sitting on the davenport and tore his shirts off of him. Then she said she was out to get love and had solicited the devil's help. You can imagine Jim is having a tough time."[14]

Spiritual war had changed since the early days of the Fellowship. Whereas for Abram the fight manifested itself physically between godless strikers and the forces of law and order, for Coe it was more personal, a matter of marriages, a battle fought in bedrooms. Such was the changing tone of American fundamentalism, echoes of Jonathan Edwards's fascination with Abigail Hutchinson suddenly amplified as feminism emerged to challenge fundamentalism. Coe's correspondence with his demon-plagued friend, as with all his old Salem associates, was at once blandly pious and marked by a new militant mysticism. Coe regularly received news from Oregon of individual men, churches, whole companies tipping over from "lukewarm" Christianity into on-fire faith. "We are still facing some opposition," a Baptist pastor wrote Coe, and families were breaking off, but "in the main we are all divining the will of God."[15] Coe occasionally responded with advice, but more often he sent his friends form letters. The Salemites did not complain. "Mr. Douglas Coe, Big Wheel, City of the Wheels" one man addressed a letter in full earnestness.[16] They sent him checks, new suits, shoes in which they liked to think of him walking the halls of Congress and parliaments in distant lands. Coe's response would be a canned account of a meeting with "top men," who were being "used" by God to put him in touch with more top men. Senator X or Ambassador Y or Mr. Smith, president of ACME Products, was here, he'd respond. "Please pray he will understand the idea of saturating every community and every state with the gospel of Jesus Christ." There'd be a word about golf; he'd ask for their prayers; and then he'd sign off with scripture, a citation without explanation. "Amos 8:11–12," he closed one batch of letters, a passage that reads like a warning: *Behold, the days come, saith the Lord GOD, that I will send a famine in the land, not a famine of bread, nor a thirst for water, but of hearing the words of the LORD: And they shall wander from sea to sea, and from the north even to the east, they shall run to and fro and seek the word of the LORD, and shall not find it.*[17]

What did it mean? Coe did not explain. His admirers were left to wonder: Would *they* find it? Were they exempted from God's, from Coe's, judgment on a secular nation? Who among them would enter the circle of the saved, the elect, with Coe and his mysterious "top men" in Washington, in London, in Berlin, and in other more exotic cities Coe mentioned, Jakarta, Addis Ababa, Brasilia?

Shortly after Coe arrived in Washington, D.C., he wrote home to his parents to tell them of his immediate success; or, rather, that of

Jesus, working through him. "God has gone before us to prepare hearts," he wrote, noting that he followed in one of several private planes that had been put at his disposal.[18] One of his first conquests was Haiti, then just entering a long darkness of dictatorship that still reverberates today. Winning Catholic Haiti's acquiescence to U.S.-style Cold War evangelicalism had been a Fellowship ambition since 1955, when an Abram associate had declared it a "soft spot of communism" that would require the ministrations of "Magnificent Americans" preaching a new equation of Christ and free markets. "I have been expecting to hear that you are making this your personal prospect," joked one of Coe's Oregon friends, a man who claimed to have been led by the Lord into building a small trucking parts empire. It wasn't God, though, who the trucking boss thought would draw Coe to the island nation, one of the poorest in the world. "Am told they have wonderful golf courses."[19]

Coe counseled a Haitian senator and then Haiti's ambassador to the United States, easing both into commitments to a Christ-led nation, with the understanding that the Christ Coe preached led not toward the socialism that tempts any bitterly poor people but toward an economics of "key men" who would share their wealth as God instructed them. Senators Frank Carlson and Homer Capehart, both members of the Foreign Relations Committee, did the follow-up work, leading a Fellowship delegation of twelve businessmen to instruct the Haitian parliament in prayer cell politics. François "Papa Doc" Duvalier, who would declare himself not only president for life but also the nation's official "Maximum Chief of the Revolution" and "Electrifier of Souls"—he was the weirdest and most vicious dictator in the Western Hemisphere—impressed the senators with his spirituality.

Perhaps he told them, as he was fond of saying, that he literally personified Haiti, that he was a stand-in for God. A personality! That was the Fellowship's whole theology in a nutshell, so they didn't bother to ask questions about his Vodoun-driven militia, the Tonton Macoute assassins. Instead, they promised to twist arms in Washington on Papa Doc's behalf: foreign aid, exemptions on sugar tariffs. It wouldn't be a hard sell. The Cold Warriors in State, under Ike and every administration that followed, preferred Papa Doc's public proclamations of Christian brotherhood to a free black nation that might seek support from the Soviet Union.[20]

And so it went through the 1960s, Coe and Halverson and Robinson and dozens of lesser brothers traveling the world for the Fellowship, almost always finding their way through Christ's leading to the next hot spot in the Cold War. Not only did South Korea host a prayer breakfast, but its dictator, General Park Chung Hee, tried to use the Fellowship to channel illegal funding to congressional candidates of Nixon's selection. (Nixon's representative, a Fellowship man named John Niedicker, declined.) Coe and Carlson double-teamed Emperor Haile Selassie of Ethiopia, a strategic prize in the struggle between the United States and the Soviet Union. Selassie, who like Papa Doc considered himself an embodiment of the divine, depended on his Fellowship brethren to represent his interests in the United States.

Those interests were considerable. For two decades, the United States provided more aid to Ethiopia than to the entire rest of the continent. In return, the emperor granted the National Security Agency basing rights for the largest overseas intelligence facility in the world, a high-tech "listening post" from which the United States could keep tabs on the Middle East. He also deeded the Fellowship a prime parcel in downtown Addis Ababa from which to proselytize the rest of Africa. Just like dominoes, Coe wrote home to Salem.

Coe was as much of an elitist as Abram, but differently so. Aristocracy didn't impress him; more important, he never lied to himself about the virtues or lack thereof of the top men he was courting. Coe understood early on that he would be dealing with violent characters, and that didn't bother him. Indeed, it seemed to excite him. He dreamed of their power harnessed to the new American fundamentalism, a fascination with strength and influence given clearest voice in the words of one of his disciples, attempting to grasp Coe's vision. "I have had a great and thrilling experience reading the condensed version of *The Rise and Fall of the Third Reich*," a protégé wrote Coe, following up on reading advice Coe had given him. "Doug, what a lesson in vision and perspective! Nazism started with 7 guys around a table in the back of an old German Beer Hall. The world has been shaped so drastically by a few men who really want it such and so. How we need this same kind of stuff as a Hitler or a Lenin."[21]

Abram had thought as much, albeit phrased in stuffier terms. "An epochal opportunity is ours," one of his tracts had advertised to the new men of his congressional Fellowship back in 1942, "to control the future of America by the simple strategy of controlling the character and ideals of [a] relatively small minority of [college-age] men and women. Hitler long ago perceived this strategy, and established his elaborate system of . . . leadership training. The democracies have been asleep."[22] Indeed—asleep to the Hitler method of disciplining youth into a revolutionary cadre, a concept that absent the Führer's bloodlust would lead to Abram's later support for groups such as the Navigators and Campus Crusade. Neither was fascist any more than Coe actually subscribed to the philosophies of Hitler or Lenin. It was the myth of brotherhood that Coe thought such men exemplified, the "7 guys around a table" that would become a trademark of his teaching. That such a view bore little correspondence with history—both Hitler and Lenin brutally pitted their supporters against one another—was of no concern. What mattered was the model, the seven or the twelve, circles of access to a power defined by a personality at the center: Jesus. Contrasting American fundamentalism to secularism at a Fellowship meeting in 1962, Bill Bright, the Fellowship fellow traveler who founded Campus Crusade, one of the biggest popular fundamentalist groups in the world, put it succinctly: "We worship a person, they worship ideas."[23] That was American fundamentalism's Christ: a person, purged of the ideas that defined him, as if what mattered most about Jesus was the color of his eyes and the shape of his beard.

Coe understood the cult of personality better than Clif Robinson and Dick Halverson. He may even have understood it better than Abram, who, after all, was moved first and foremost by "the Idea." Not Coe. For Coe, it was Jesus plus nothing—a formula into which he could plug any values. It was a theology of total malleability, perfect for American expansion.

From the start of Coe's tenure, the Fellowship began turning away from its old European allies. The German Gus Gedat found Coe impetuous; Wallace Haines, Abram's longtime man in Paris, despaired of pleasing him. "I have retreated step by step before your desires," he wrote the new leader. Not *my* desires, Coe corrected him; God's. Haines accused Coe of tearing down the neat organization of European aristocrats and merchant-princes Abram had spent years building.

"Wallace," Coe replied. "I am not against structure. I am for structure. I just think it needs to be underground."

Other men "caught" Coe's vision of a decentralized web that would reach not just between Europe and the United States but around the world. "I regard the program . . . as being the most effective for promoting the basic ideology for which the United States stands," announced an enthusiastic supporter of Coe's new emphasis on nations Abram had ignored. He didn't define that ideology, but its broad outlines were known to all in the Fellowship. First and foremost, there was "free enterprise," unrestrained capitalism, property—the foundation, fundamentalists believed, of all other freedoms. Those freedoms were more undefined. The American ideology was as amorphous as its empire, defined not by borders but by influence, invisible threads, transcendent alliances. It was, to Coe, an empire of spirit, and Coe took Worldwide Spiritual Offensive to mean more than conferences in The Hague and prayer meetings in Bavarian castles; Jesus must rule every nation through the vessel of American power.

Robinson and Halverson also saw the importance of smaller countries, but it was Coe who dispensed with any concern at all for politics in the Fellowship's expansion; he would pray with anyone, and he would bless anyone, so long as they had the strength to submit their nation to God. That was his greatest virtue in Abram's eyes: he never complained, never insisted on honors, never questioned whether Jesus really cared most for men with power.

WHAT WAS IT they wanted? What drove Coe and his spiritual brothers to conflate the Gospel with the needs of a nation expanding into empire? Over "lamb chops and hash-browned potatoes and fried apples and fried tomatoes," reported the *Washington Post* in 1966, Billy Graham followed LBJ to the podium of the National Prayer Breakfast to preach the fury of Christ down on America's enemies in Vietnam. "I am come to send fire on the earth!" he quoted Christ. "Think not that I am come to send peace but a sword!" "There are those," Graham continued, "who have tried to reduce Christ to a genial and innocuous appeaser; but Jesus said, 'You are wrong—I have come as a firesetter and a sword-wielder.' "[24]

A firesetter—were they revolutionaries after all? Or did they fantasize a new Holy Roman Empire, recast in the terms of the twentieth century as an empire of influence, not territory? Maybe it was more trivial, pious posturing as cover for petty crimes.

Sometimes, at least, it was just that. In attendance for Graham's thundering warcry were two generals who devoted their free time to Fellowship work, crisscrossing the nation to lecture prayer cells and prayer breakfasts on the need for revival. One of them, General Harold K. Johnson, chief of staff of the army, ordered the other, General Carl Turner, to work with Coe, "quietly, and I repeat quietly," to give the army's "substantial" assistance to the production of the Prayer Breakfast. That in itself may have been a violation of the First Amendment's establishment clause, but it paled beside General Turner's real sideline: reselling mothballed army weapons to Third World gangs, a crime for which he was sentenced to prison in 1971 after General Johnson's attempt to help failed.

Is that all it was? A spiritual alibi for get-rich-quick schemes? A Fellowship tract titled *Studies for Public Men*, 10,000 of which were printed up by a Chevron Oil executive, claimed that such abuses are inevitable, but not attributable to the piety with which such men cloaked their misdeeds. When pious men committed crimes, went the thinking, godlessness was to blame—"secularism in its worst form!" In a section titled "Accountability," the tract explained why the Fellowship should not be held accountable for the actions of its individual members, the American generals, General Turner and General Johnson, the overseas divines on Coe and Carlson's government gravy train, Papa Doc and Emperor Selassie, General Park in Korea, General Suharto in Indonesia, General Medici in Brazil: "Persisting in the accusation of collective guilt finally immobilizes a society," advised the tract. Perhaps, but the Fellowship denied individual guilt as well, denied the very concept of guilt for the powerful. That was a legalistic notion, an encroachment on God's sovereignty as expressed in Romans 13: "The powers that be are ordained of God." Who was Coe to question them?

Romans, declared a Fellowship study guide for bankers, is "the Bible in miniature in a layman's words." The layman is Paul, formerly Saul, who on the road to Damascus saw the light and abandoned the law, for better and worse. "With the Jew in mind," declared the study guide, "not to mention the memory of his own experience, Paul shows that the purpose of the law was not to save but to reveal sin."[25] Elite fundamentalists, unlike the moralistic masses of popular crusades, did not care much about sin; they cared about salvation, a concept they understood in terms of nations, not souls, embodied by the rulers to whom God had given power, whether through ballots or bullets.

Senator Carlson, writing to President José Joaquín Trejos Fernández of Costa Rica in 1967, made that explicit. As a spiritual guide for the Catholic nation's National Prayer Breakfast, he wrote, the Fellowship was sending Representative William Jennings Bryan Dorn, a South Carolina Dixiecrat who advocated extending the Monroe Doctrine, by which the United States dominated Latin America, to the entire world. Romans 13, Carlson reminded the Latin American leader, lest he balk: "For there is no authority except from God, and those that exist have been instituted by God."[26]

In the decade that followed, Costa Rica, the region's most stable government, became increasingly a base for Fellowship operations and increasingly submissive to God's instituted authority. "The program to expand the activities of the Movement have been fulfilled according to schedule," the Fellowship's Costa Rican key man, a well-connected lawyer named Juan Edgar Picado, wrote Coe in 1976, assuring him that the leaders of both the nation's minority and majority parties had been absorbed into prayer cells. "We have achieved the objectives as programmed." Coe never sent Picado anything but prayer suggestions, but one of his assistants forwarded Henry Kissinger's plan for the protection of U.S. investments in the region, which Picado promptly made a matter for consideration in his men's prayers. Political brokers like Picado work in a loop of power. The more he did for the Fellowship, the more the Fellowship did for him, and the more powerful he became. "Through [a] private world Christian organization," reported a Costa Rican paper, "Picado [has] had the opportunity to meet in Washington with . . . Dwight Eisenhower, John Kennedy, Lyndon Johnson, Richard Nixon and Gerald Ford."[27]

"Why does God look for one man who will listen to Him?" asked the Fellowship's *Studies for Public Men*. "What effect can one man have in a group, community, city, nation, and world?" Good question. What effect, for instance, did General Suharto hope for when he turned his army loose on his own people, a half million civilians murdered as "communists" in a year? What effect did Coe hope for when in 1971, he helped Suharto organize his first Indonesian National Prayer Breakfast to celebrate the fifth anniversary of the March 11, 1966, decree by which he seized power and commenced slaughtering hundreds of thousands of his own people?

The simple answer would be that it was nothing but cynicism, war by other means, Cold War conquests for the American way. It was that, but it was also more. The prize was never Indonesia or Haiti or Costa Rica. The prize was the Promised Land. Not Israel—like Abram, Coe didn't seem to care about Zionism one way or the other. The Fellowship's Promised Land was as it had been for Jonathan Edwards: the New World. Edwards could hardly have been a nationalist before the American nation existed, but Coe was no nationalist, either. The Promised Land was America. Not a destination but a concept to be perfected and spread around the world. His Jerusalem, the New Jerusalem, was an idea, not a place. "My Jerusalem," one of Coe's men wrote to him from a businessmen's revival he'd sparked in Billings, Montana.[28] By that he meant the Kingdom of Heaven at home: first-century Christianity reconstructed, restored, resurrected on whatever ground you claimed as your own. To raise that ancient reality from the mythological depths—to seize hold of Christianity's platonic shadow—Coe's Fellowship adopted the strategy with which Edwards ended his days, the strategy with which, centuries later, a decade after Coe reinvented it, the new Christian Right would claim power in the public sphere. It was simple: Convert the weak. Encircle the strong.

Edwards dreamed of doing so by leading Native Americans to Christ, thus shaming the colonials into the piety even "savages" could attain. One day, hoped Edwards, Boston and New York and the Northampton that had driven him from his pulpit would wake up to discover a frontier of saintly natives. In the late 1970s, the Christian Right wedged its way into Washington not by massive national campaigns but through local elections, PTAs, town councils, precinct captains. One day the Republican Party woke up to discover its base was Christian, fundamentally inclined, Edwards's America achieved at last. The Fellowship's strategy was—is—similar, but on a global scale. To work, though, it must be a surprise. Secularism must be confronted with overwhelming numbers, a host of believers in every direction. Unexpected, unimaginable in this modern age.

Coe used the power of the American flag to win submission (if not fidelity) to the fundamentalist God of key men in little nations nobody cared about and big nations nobody understood. There was Somalia's Siad Barre, a self-styled "Koranic Marxist" for whose allegiance in the 1980s Coe won access to Reagan and a military aid budget nearly doubled in size. There was Jonas Savimbi, the brutal rebel of Angola cultivated by other key men from the United States and apartheid South Africa.[29] There was Brazil's General Costa e Silva, the Catholic dictator who acquiesced to a secret cell of Brazilian legislators organized by Coe and subsequently won the good graces of a far more powerful group of American congressmen, who helped pour a billion dollars in aid into Brazil's long dictatorship of the generals.[30] "I never invite them," Coe said in 2007 of his dictator friends. "They come to me. And I do what Jesus did: I don't turn my back to any one. You know, the Bible is full of mass murderers."[31]

Coe has always claimed he's not a nationalist, and it's true—unlike immigrant Abram, who cared most for America, Coe, Oregon-born, cares most for the American Christ, His power spread throughout the world even as the homeland is denied Him in the secular folly of church/state separation. One day, Coe believes—not yet—America (and Old Europe, too, the Germans and French and Italians who drifted from Christ once their prosperity was assured) will wake up and find itself surrounded by a hundred tiny God-led governments: Fiji, a "model for the nations" under a theocratic regime after 2001, a Family organizer boasted to me; and Uganda, made over as an experiment in faith-based initiatives by the Family's favorite African brother, the dictator Yoweri Museveni; and Mongolia, where Coe traveled in the late 1980s to plant the seeds for that country's postcommunist laissez-faire regime.

Nobody notices; nobody cares what happens in small places. This is what George H. W. Bush praised in 1992 as Coe's "quiet diplomacy."

In 1966, with the Christian Right just starting to emerge as a visible front for fundamentalism, Coe decided to go in the opposite direction. "The time has come," he instructed the Core, "to submerge." Thereafter, the Fellowship would avoid at all turns any appearance of an organization, even as Coe crafted ever more complex hierarchies behind-the-scenes. Business would be conducted on the letterhead of public men, who would testify that Fellowship initiatives were their own. Finances would be more "man-to-man," which is to say, off the books. The Fellowship was going underground.[32]

The decision was not so much conspiratorial, as it seemed to those among Abram's old-timers who responded with confusion, as ascetic, a humbling of powers. Or, rather, of power's visible expression. The Fellowship had long been protected from scrutiny by the fact of its membership's elite positions; not since the days of the muckrakers had the press really pressured the country's "top men" of affairs. The same principle that forbade photographers to picture FDR's shriveled legs prevented reporters from asking for details about the private devotions of public men. But such protections were withering. Assassination, the civil rights movement, and the Vietnam War demanded tougher questions, and it wasn't just the press that was asking them; ordinary citizens called for answers, marched for them, fought for them. Power—political, cultural—appeared to be democratizing beyond the scope of God's anointed leaders, just as it had during the 1930s, when Abram first conceived of his backroom brotherhood. The decision to "submerge," to make the Fellowship "invisible," was, then, merely a reaffirmation of Abram's founding principles, recast in response to a new populism, deepened, even, to suit the needs of Coe's new internationalism.

COE ANNOUNCED THE decision in a series of letters to the old guard of Abram's European leadership: Pierre Harmel, the foreign minister of Belgium; Edmond Michelet, a former hero of the French resistance who'd gradually sullied his reputation for integrity through a series of cabinet positions in General de Gaulle's government; and, in Europe's sphere if not its territory, Charles Malik, a Lebanese Christian. To anyone who is familiar with the United Nations' Universal Declaration of Human Rights, which Malik helped write, his name may be the most surprising of all those to emerge from the Fellowship's archives. Yet Malik had been party to Abram's schemes for almost two decades. In 1949, Abram and a retired U.S. admiral, C. S. Freeman, waged a secret diplomatic offensive against Israel. Christian Zionism as a feature of American fundamentalism was still decades away; Abram and Freeman—and their strongest ally in the United Nations, Malik—saw the Jewish state as an obstacle to the "gradual readjustment of political and economic control in the Near East in line with the divine plan as declared in the Bible," a plan they believed best served by U.S. power in Lebanon.[33] In Israel's place they proposed an ostensibly neutral international zone. Of course, to Abram, neutrality would only lead to Jesus, the "universal inevitable," as he called his God. The plan was a total failure but for one detail: Abram's acquisition of Malik's name for his letterhead, an impressive declaration of elite fundamentalism's international connections.

The connection seemed to seduce Malik. By the time Coe joined the Fellowship in 1959 and began pushing for the evangelization of

African, Asian, and Latin American leaders, Malik, then the president of the thirteenth session of the United Nations' General Assembly, had veered from his own sense of "universal human rights" to the
Fellowship's, declaring that Christians had a responsibility to eradicate "tribal and national deities" in Africa and Asia.[34] As Coe's influence in the Fellowship grew, so did Malik's intolerance. Christians,
he declared, "worship a person," while "they"—everyone else—
"worship an idea"—words that Campus Crusade's Bill Bright would
convert into mainstream American fundamentalism. Christians, Malik went on, worshipped Christ's "strength," and in the end, Malik
worshipped strength, indeed, becoming one of the founders of the
Lebanese Front, the right-wing alliance of Christian militias in Lebanon's long and awful civil war. Malik's old internationalist friends
may have been surprised, but it's hard to imagine that Coe was.
Through Malik's involvement with the group, his name became popular with mainstream American fundamentalists like Bright, happy
to add Malik's intellectual credentials to their case.

In 1963, Coe collected a group of other people's speeches he labeled "Thoughts on Prayer," as close to a statement of his beliefs as one
can find from his early years.[35] Malik's ideas were well represented,
just one clue that Coe's ideas about what prayer was for were international in scope, despite his own personal mysticism. "Thoughts on
Prayer" began with Senator Strom Thurmond railing against the 1962
Supreme Court decision *Engle v. Vitale*, which outlawed official school
prayer. Following Thurmond came the once moderate John Mackay,
president of the Princeton Theological Seminary, declaring that the
nations of the world could now be divided into three categories: the
secular (increasingly, Western Europe), the "demonic" (the Communist bloc), and the "covenantal," an echo of the old "City upon a hill"
thinking that understood the United States not so much as a country
as a holy mission. But pride of place in "Thoughts on Prayer" belonged
to a speech by Bill Bright, based on Malik's ideas and delivered to a
1962 Fellowship prayer breakfast for the governor of Arizona.

Bright, a candy maker before he launched Campus Crusade, was
not a charismatic man. He wore a pencil-thin black mustache that

made him look like a cartoon, and he was so stiff that next to him Pat Boone, his musical apostle, seemed like a genuine rocker. Bright's genius was organizational discipline. To the world, Campus Crusade was as simple as Bright's "Four Spiritual Laws," a dumbing-down of the gospel that made even his allies uneasy. Internally, Crusade organizers were required to adhere to a book-length set of rules for fundamentalists that ranged from evangelism techniques to what kind of socks to wear (argyle was forbidden) to the proper way to pick up girls.

Bright took the same approach to politics. He publicly declared that Campus Crusade had none, and since Crusade didn't donate money to candidates or lobby for specific legislation, the press accepted Bright's contention. Among friends, he told a different story. "The house is on fire," he raged to the Arizona governor's prayer breakfast, "and there is no time to fix the pictures." The "house" was America; the "pictures" were niceties of the Bill of Rights, such as the First Amendment's establishment clause separating church and state. Citing Malik, Bright declared that only Christians could save American government from communism. The time had come for America to embrace 2 Chronicles 6.

What did this mean? That was a question the businessmen and politicians assembled that spring day in Arizona must have asked, too, for in the collection of Bible verses bandied about by fundamentalists—as if scripture was *Bartlett's Quotations*—2 Chronicles 6 had little standing. It was Old Testament, and unlike the prophecies of Isaiah, it could not, by any stretch of the imagination, be said to foretell Christ. Instead, it promised a new political order. It's the story of Solomon's construction of a temple to be the heart of an Israelite nation, to house the mythic ark of the covenant, "the ark of your might," as Solomon called it, that would make his kingdom undefeatable in battle.

The Jewish temple was destroyed nearly 2,000 years ago, in 70 CE. The ark is now nothing but a story. Within Judaism, 2 Chronicles 6 is both history and mystery, scripture to be studied and pondered and parsed for ancient meanings. To Bright, though, guided by Malik, 2 Chronicles 6 was a blueprint for a new God-led nation.

Bright wanted to rebuild the temple, but in Washington, not Jerusalem. The prayer armies he dreamed would be unstoppable were
those of American fundamentalism. To the world, Bright's Campus
Crusade preached Bible studies for college kids, ice cream socials,
and even Christian dance parties. To the movement, he preached
spiritual war. Like Coe, he anticipated the coming Jesus wave, and
recognized that for the movement to be successful, it would need
men to work the deeper currents. Bright organized the masses; Coe
cultivated the elite. And Coe's most successful protégé, Charles W.
"Chuck" Colson, would soon do both, combining Bright's populist
style with Coe's political sophistication.

AT THE 1970 National Prayer Breakfast, a Washington lawyer named
James Bell led a seminar for college men who'd been selected by
their institutions' presidents.[36] The men were told only that they'd
be having breakfast with Richard Nixon, but in Washington, Fellowship brothers handed them from one instructor to the next, alternat-
ing fundamentalist theology with "private" lectures from politicians
and businessmen. Secretary of Defense Melvin Laird explained that
Christ had a special message for elites. The former student body
president of Stanford, just back from Vietnam, spoke of the dedication of the Viet Minh as a model for evangelizing Washington. Paul
Temple, a Standard Oil executive, explained how the Fellowship had
won him access to key men in General Francisco Franco's government in Spain. "Public events" had two purposes, said Bell: (1) to
declare to the world "the relevancy of God in the Establishment's
life"; (2) to recruit "the up and outer." The real work of the Fellowship that the college men had been chosen for took place in small
groups, where, away from publicity, men "attack the basic social
problems of America." Bell didn't list those problems, but he gave a
hint of his meaning: "All of us cry over our martinis about law and
order, but very few of us do a blooming thing about it."[37]

The Fellowship did. How? Not through proposing laws or cam-
paigning. Its politics were cultural, in the broadest sense; its method

the capture of leaders' souls, the eradication of their egos, the replacement of their will with Christ's. Their goals were not the rollback of the 1963 school prayer decision, or antiporn laws, or the "Christian Amendment," a perennial proposal to formally dedicate the nation to Christ. It was bigger, deliberately vague, and so long-term—think generations—that the Fellowship would never have to answer for its successes and failures. Coe made the strategy of deferral into Fellowship doctrine. The distant goal was "a leadership led by God," said Bell. "Period." Few men in the Fellowship expected to see it in their lifetimes. But the college boys could get in on it if they felt so called—by conscience or career. "If you want some doors opened . . . there are men in government, there are senators who literally find it their pleasure to give any kind of advice, assistance, or counsel."[38]

Three years later, Chuck Colson, destined to become one of the leading theorists of American fundamentalism, would discover as much as he faced the prospect of prison. Colson was no ordinary criminal. He was one of Richard Nixon's closest aides, the smartest, toughest man on his staff, Nixon's "hatchet man": responsible for Nixon's "enemies list," said to be the brains behind schemes to firebomb the Brookings Institution and hire Teamsters to beat up antiwar protesters. He was, the court would soon rule, a Watergate felon, the most powerful of the Nixon "dirty tricksters" to be sent to prison.

He wouldn't go alone, though; accompanying him would be the Jesus of the Fellowship, whom he'd discovered was a good friend, indeed. The Fellowship, he'd write in his 1976 memoir, *Born Again*, comprised a "veritable underground of Christ's men all through government."[39] Colson would later claim that it was news to him, but he was a man who understood the power of friends and the politics of religion.

A former marine from Massachusetts, a scholarship student at Brown, and a Harvard lawyer by dint of brain power and no silver spoons, Colson was (and is) a beefy, square-headed man with thick black square-shaped glasses. He's always had the jowls of a bulldog and a natural sneer like that of late-stage Elvis—the same bloated cockiness but without any sex appeal. His job for Nixon was not to look pretty but to cut deals with constituencies Republicans had either ignored or taken for granted. He brought in the working-class vote by playing to poor men's fears of hippies, feminists, black power, and, as always, the red tide. And he brought in the religious vote in a way no American politician had attempted to do until then: he arranged for Nixon to hold church services directly in the White House, "quasi-spiritual, quasi-political," he'd call them. Colson recognized the political power of religion years before he was born again, before he joined the Fellowship. He brought in a different religious leader every Sunday, a photo op every week that put Nixon's mug in the pastor's offices of the nation's most powerful churches. St. Dick of the Second Chance, the most enduring man on the American political scene. Billy Graham's best political buddy; a friendship, Colson understood, worth more in a changing America than the waning power of the old city machines that had stolen the White House from Nixon in 1960. The machines were rusting; their troops were moving to the suburbs; and the suburbs were getting religion. And Colson got them, because he understood what they wanted, visible access. Proof that they mattered. Image was everything, and they wanted pictures of themselves in the White House, a new visual narrative about the distribution of power in America.

There was something almost democratic about it. Only, Colson didn't let the multitudes in; he simply made room for the bosses, the men who ran the old machines and the new and improved ones. The unions, grinding into irrelevance, and the Jesus-engines, revving, revving, ready to bring the war home, indeed, and fight it with the discipline of the Viet Minh, the stealthiness of the Vietcong, and the revolutionary fervor of rock and roll. What Colson recognized was that in America the time for sermons was past. A new politics, raw and emotional, was being born (again), and Colson did what he could to make it work for the most overcooked, overcalculated president in history.

So, did this political fixer really not know about Abram and Coe and the dozens of congressmen networked in prayer cells before he

faced prison time? Was he unaware of the White House cell that met
weekly under Nixon's Federal Reserve chief, Arthur Burns, a Jew for
Jesus before anyone had heard of such a notion? Did he not know that
Gerald Ford, the House Republican leader, his soul saved by a
preacher named Billy Zeoli, had for years been in a prayer cell with
Melvin Laird, now Nixon's secretary of defense?

Well, he says so. White House correspondent Dan Rather found
fishy Colson's sudden discovery of prayer for himself as well as the
rubes. At a 1973 press conference, Rather demanded to know why,
after Colson had left the White House in disgrace, he continued to
pop in on a regular basis. For prayer meetings, answered an embarrassed press secretary. Come on, Rather replied, we all know what
goes on when politicians get together to talk about their souls. The
press secretary shrugged, Rather gave up, and Colson continued on
his amazing spiritual journey. Later that year, a syndicated columnist
discouraged further inquiries into Colson's "underground prayer
movement," lest the press undermine its ability to humbly arrange
for the redemption of "big" men: "they meet in each other's homes,
they meet at prayer breakfasts, they converse on the phone. . . .
They genuinely avoid publicity. In fact, they shun it."[40]

Colson wasn't the only Watergate conspirator to find solace in
the Fellowship as the indictments began. James W. McCord, the ex-
CIA man who served as "security director" of the Committee to Re-
Elect the President, CREEP (sentenced to two and a half to eight
years), received "spiritual undergirding" from Halverson; Egil "Bud"
Krogh, the chief of the "plumbers" (sentenced to six months), who
tried to silence Daniel Ellsberg, prayed with a Fellowship prayer cell
right before heading off to prison; and Jeb Magruder (sentenced to
four months to ten years), who blamed his participation in the plot
on the liberal ethics he'd been taught at Williams College by the Reverend William Sloane Coffin, joined a Fellowship cell just as he was
pleading guilty, albeit only to get "the best possible deal." But Colson
was the one who actually made something real of his new faith—
indeed, he transformed it.[41]

Colson's first contact with the Fellowship came through Tom

Phillips, the CEO of the missile manufacturer Raytheon. Back in private practice after leaving the White House under a black cloud, waiting to go to trial, Colson was pumping his Republican network hard for new clients. One such was the International Brotherhood of Teamsters under Frank "Fitz" Fitzsimmons, the mafia-friendly successor to Jimmy Hoffa and one of Nixon's staunchest allies. Nixon was no friend to working people, but with Colson's help, he managed to seduce right-wing union bosses by turning a blind eye toward their looting of their own treasuries (Nixon ordered the Justice Department to drop its investigations of the Teamsters after Fitz took over in 1971) in exchange for their muscle at the ballot box and in the streets, as when Colson asked the Teamsters to crack skulls at an antiwar rally. (From the Nixon tapes: "Haldeman: Colson's gonna . . . do it with the Teamsters. Nixon: They've got guys who'll go in and knock their heads off. Haldeman: Sure. Murderers . . . They're gonna beat the [expletive deleted] out of some of these people. And, uh, and hope they really hurt 'em.")

Fitz would remain a Colson client well into Colson's "born again" phase; the dissonance between his newfound piety and "friends" like Fitz angered liberal Christians, but it wasn't a problem for the Fellowship. When Phillips raised the subject of Jesus with Colson at Phillips's Massachusetts home one summer night in 1973, he didn't speak of accountability or Christian ethics; instead, he read Psalms to Colson and told him that Jesus, alone, could make the frightened dirty trickster feel whole again. Colson wept all the way home, filled with repentance for his godlessness but not for his crimes. He denies them to this day, despite having pled guilty. "Had I fought [the charges] I would have won," he boasts to fellow fundamentalists. "But, no, God had a *plan* for my life."[42]

Soon after Colson's fit of weeping, Coe paid him a visit in Washington. Colson had no idea who he was. Coe simply walked into Colson's law office, threw off his raincoat, draped himself sideways over a leather chair, and informed Colson that Phillips had been sharing his private, confessional letters about his growing religiosity with Coe. "I hope you don't mind," Coe said. Colson *did* mind, but "there was such kindness in his eyes my resistance began to melt." Coe reached across Colson's desk, held his hand, and asked him to pray. Thereafter, Colson was his brother, a member of the underground, eligible for advice, assistance, and counsel from all its members, not just Republicans but Democrats as well—especially a popular liberal senator from Iowa named Harold Hughes, well known for his opposition to the Vietnam War in general and Nixon very much in particular.

Hughes was a perfect frontman for Coe, sufficiently liberal that Coe could claim to have transcended politics, but also so kooky that his actions were easily manipulated. He was a former truck driver and a recovered alcoholic who turned to Jesus after spiritualism and ESP failed him. He was said to have the demeanor of an evangelist and the eyes of a mystic. In unpublished portions of his memoir, Hughes wrote that his encounters with UFOs were the source of his deep sense of perspective. That "perspective," combined with Hughes's faith—and, perhaps, the diminution of his career after a failed 1972 presidential bid—led Hughes to view Colson, under investigation for Watergate, as an underdog who needed his help. Hughes vowed to do all that he could to see that Colson got off lightly; a bout of on-their-knees prayer the two had undertaken had sufficiently redeemed Colson in Hughes's eyes. Hughes lobbied hard for his new "brother," as he called Colson, and even broke ranks with Democrats to keep Watergate pardons in the pipeline under Ford. Once Colson was in prison, Coe and Hughes worked hard for his early release. It worked; Colson ended up serving less than seven months of his one-to three-year sentence for his role in Watergate. It wasn't hard time. "If you think what you've done was done for the right reasons," he boasted shortly before he began his sentence, "then the consequences are easy to live with."[43]

In prison, Colson claims, he gave up politics for God. But in a June 11, 1974, letter defending his conversion to his parole board, Colson wrote, "That which I found I could not change or affect in a political or managerial way, I found could be changed by the force of a personal relationship that men develop in a common bond to Christ."[44] Doug Coe, in a letter to the board dated one day later, wrote that

Colson's freedom was necessary so that a group of Christian men could put him to work on a program for "reaching youth" in juvenile delinquent homes. Upon his release, the two men collaborated on what would become the model and inspiration for what may well be a generation or more of "faith-based" governmental activism.

The story of Prison Fellowship—the largest ministry for prisoners in the world, with 50,000 employees and volunteers dedicated to helping convicts become law abiders—has been recounted in short, inspirational bursts many times since Colson founded it with Coe's help and the Fellowship's money shortly after his own release from prison in 1975. So many times, in fact, that it's not a story anymore but a myth, a legend of how a brilliant but bad man got God in prison and came out a babe in Christ; of how the liberals and the cynics didn't believe Colson at first but soon saw the light. Say what you will about Prison Fellowship's fundamentalist Jesus, the story goes, but Colson's Christ *works*. He saves souls. And, more important, he transforms rapists, murderers, and thieves into docile "followers of Jesus." Even nonbelievers would rather ex-cons thump Bibles than their fellow senior citizens.

And yet Prison Fellowship—indeed, compassionate conservatism writ large—is implicitly political. Colson sees it as a bulwark against "moral decadence," he told me, and even as an almost governmental institution. "Government, theologically, has two major roles: to preserve order—we can only have freedom out of order—and to do justice, to restrain evil." The evil that most concerned Colson at the beginning of his Prison Fellowship days was black radicalism; today it's "Islamofascism," a word that in Colson's usage functions as a warning against secularism. "To the extent that we become a decadent society," he explained to me, "we feed Islamofascism." What disturbs Colson most, though, isn't "Islamofascism" or black power or any particular dissident faction; it's simply the concept of authority being challenged, Romans 13—a key text for Colson that only begins to outline the scope of theological and political power, he told me—disobeyed. Discipline and obedience, Colson writes in *Against the Night: Living in the New Dark Ages*, were the foundations of the Roman Empire, just as "biblical obedience" should be—must be—the cornerstone of "the West's" stand against the "new barbarians," whether they come in the form of Muslims or secular schoolteachers.

Colson's message breaks with the classic Christian concept of redemption through humility, argues Paul Apostolidis, a political scholar who has studied Colson's extensive archive of radio broadcasts. In its place, Colson offers a "fundamentalist logic according to which salvation is dispensed according to obedience—and, if necessary, outright humiliation—before authority." Colson fragments and then co-opts that which could otherwise be a potentially anarchic class of the disenfranchised. In keeping with the principles of evangelicalism, the same as those of compassionate conservatism, Prison Fellowship works on a one-by-one model, transforming adherents of "radical Islam" and other threats to the Republic—black power activists, white power supremacists, plain old thugs, prisoners who get an education—into an atomized class of isolated individuals, praying to be "broken" by God, to be "used" by His Son, to be "nothing" before the Holy Ghost.[45]

If this strikes men who've already been broken by the state as just one more humiliation, Colson reminds them that he offers the same counsel to CEOs and congressmen. Prisoners and senators, he tells convicts, are equal in God's eyes—a nice sentiment that neatly separates those who accept it from the realities of a world in which the power is in somebody else's hands. Had Colson directed his new pious energies at any other segment of society—had he tried to convert union members, for instance, or joined Bill Bright at Campus Crusade—he really might have been crucified. But Colson chose the lowest of the low, men and a few women on whom it has long been acceptable to experiment. Colson experimented, bludgeoning his way through bureaucracy with his political skills and his new Fellowship political allies to set up fundamentalist ministries in prisons around the country. A great story, according to conventional thinking. Colson must mean it; what could he have to gain from prisoners?

Colson knew the answer to that one. First there was a bestselling book, and then another one, and now there are literally dozens, books spinning out of Prison Fellowship every year. There was a movie, a comic book, and the secular press, which was not so secular after all when offered evidence of genuine jailhouse conversions. Even as the mainstream media fretted about the rising power of the new Moral Majority and the televangelists so bent on beaming their message, the mainstream media itself beamed Colson's message. What did Colson have to gain from the prisoners? The press didn't bother to ask, because it was the press that supplied him with his reward: more power than he'd ever had working for mean old Richard Nixon. "The kingdom of God will not arrive on Air Force One," he has declared, dismissive of his old obsession with party politics. What he meant by this, he told me, was that he had learned through fundamentalism to pursue pure power, not partisanship. Now, Colson boasts of his access to leaders around the world through Prison Fellowship, strongmen who would have looked at him as a diplomatic challenge in his White House days. Today, according to the elite evangelicals who responded to a survey by the sociologist D. Michael Lindsay, Colson has more political influence than James Dobson or Richard Land of the Southern Baptist Convention.[46] In a 1980 letter to Coe, Colson puts it as plainly as possible. He's describing a Fellowship cell in Bonn with which he had met at Coe's request. "It is a fabulous group of men. In fact, I've never met any group quite like it. I think we should arrange to use them as a model for leadership groups around the world. We'd better do it in a hurry, however, before they lead the next Nazi takeover out of Germany."[47]

And yet the Jesus at the heart of Prison Fellowship is not the commonplace Christ of mainstream evangelicalism, but a distinct entity growing out of Colson's political past and his subsequent philosophical passions. Colson's work is shot through with a cagey regard for Plato's "noble lie," by which the elite must govern masses who don't know what's good for them, and a reverence for "leadership" as a semimystical quality bequeathed to a small elect who already possess the kind of confidence others might call arrogance. The idealization of strength that manifests itself even in Colson's peculiar sense of humor is the foundation of Colson's faith. "We should look at our churches *exactly* the way you look at Marine Corps training for combat because that's what it *is!*" he instructs his followers. "That is how we are *preparing* today for the spiritual combat in which we live, and we should take it every bit as seriously as soldiers in the Marines preparing to go to war."[48] His first literary step as a follower of Christ was not the Bible but some of the more overlooked pages of C. S. Lewis, in which Lewis decries "men without chests." Colson preaches Lewis's "manly" Christ with the moral authority of a man who does, after all, dedicate his life to prisoners, and the political savvy of one who has been in the trenches of the culture wars since before the battle had a name. That combination allows Colson to escape the scrutiny afforded James Dobson or the Southern Baptist Convention.

It has also resulted in what might be best understood as a powerful new religious movement. *Faith-based initiatives, compassionate conservatism,* and *servant-leadership,* a term popular with evangelical politicians who insist that they consolidate power the better to help widows and orphans, can all be traced back to the model of Colson's Prison Fellowship, a radical revision of the "Social Gospel" of the early twentieth century. Evangelicals have always been at the forefront of aid work with the poor and the suffering, but they traditionally came from the left wing of the movement—the branch that seemed to die with William Jennings Bryan, the "Great Commoner," back in 1925. In the years that followed, evangelicals, and especially fundamentalists— elite and populist—disdained "good works," aid to the poor, as irrelevant to salvation. The only help the poor needed was Jesus. Colson thought so, too, but he understood that for people to accept the rule of Christ, they'd need some prep work. But it wasn't his idea; it was Coe's.

To understand where it came from, we must go back several years to 1968, the morning of April 4, when an assassin's bullet slammed into Martin Luther King Jr. while he stood on a motel balcony in Memphis. King was a Christian like Coe. Like Coe, he believed in the "beloved community," the Kingdom of God realized here on Earth, and like Coe, he was willing to work with those who didn't share his beliefs. But that is where the similarities end. Coe preaches a personal, private submission; King fought and died in public for collective liberation. Coe believes Jesus has a special message for the powerful; King believed God has a special message for everyone. Most important, in 1968, as Coe was constricting the already narrow vision of the Fellowship, King was doing as he had done his whole life: broadening his dream. King died just as he was raising his voice to speak out not only for racial justice but also for economic justice. He would pursue it not through private prayer cells but through public solidarity. And when James Earl Ray murdered him, millions of Americans expressed their solidarity with the dead not through polite mourning but through fury.

Following King's murder, the Fellowship's city on a hill, Washington, D.C., burned. More than 200 fires roared throughout the capital. White suburbanites in Arlington and Alexandria looked across the river and saw a sunrise at midnight, a terrifying new day dawning. Many white residents of the District had feared it for years. White flight from Washington began not with the civil rights movement but in the 1940s; it actually slowed down in the 1960s, but only because so many white people had already retreated to the suburbs. Even so, between 1960 and 1970, those suburbs grew in population by 61 percent, putting their numbers far higher than those of Washington proper, which remained static at around 800,000. In 1967, the city got its first black mayor since Reconstruction, the aptly named Walter Washington; but in 1968, twelve dead in the street after clashes between the people and the police (and then the National Guard), whole neighborhoods smoldering like they were part of Hanoi, the city seemed doomed.[49]

For Coe, this would not do. The Fellowship's Christian Embassy remained in the heart of the city. It had to be saved. Perhaps, too, Coe felt some modicum of guilt; even as he and his underlings courted the strongmen of Africa, he had paid almost no attention to African Americans. A letter to Coe during his early days in Washington suggests that his neglect was a conscious choice: "Are any of your [converts] Negroes," wrote a friend from Oregon, "or are you still discriminatory?"[50] Coe did not bother to answer. But in 1968, faced with what appeared to be revolution—Stokely Carmichael, dressed like a guerrilla commander to promote his book *Black Power: The Politics of Liberation in America*, told Howard University, "I've come to Washington to stay, baby . . . this is our town."—Coe turned the Fellowship's considerable resources toward those closest at hand, Washington's African Americans.[51]

Working with Halverson, a group of wealthy white businessmen, a black preacher named William Porter, and a former professor of Carmichael's, John Staggers, Coe oversaw the recruitment of "street dudes," black ex-cons, to become a paramilitary security force called the Black Buffers—the Fellowship's answer to black power. Like the Panthers, the Buffers patrolled inner-city streets. They even wore dashikis, bought in bulk on Coe's orders. But their African garb and their two-way radios were paid for by white businessmen, and Coe's counselors trained them to preach not black power but black capitalism. "They called us a spy group," remembers Reverend Porter, the first supervisor of the program, "because we'd find out what was happening"—in terms of black militance—"and shut it down if it happened."[52]

Drawing funds from the city government and the U.S. Labor Department (through the intervention of Fellowship brother Congressman Al Quie, who at the time was spearheading the GOP attack on federal aid for schools), the Buffers were supposed to be secular. They weren't. Everything they did—from running after-school martial arts classes for boys and "charm school" for girls, to monitoring street corners for militance, to violently enforcing discipline within their own ranks—was filtered through the fundamentalism of Jesus plus nothing.

"The biggest problem that blacks face in this country today happens to be the black man himself," Staggers would say. "Racial conflicts do exist in our country. Their solutions are not to be found in the passing of laws and other kinds of legislation, but only when man accepts God totally in his life."[53]

That was the idea the Buffers began with in 1968, the first seeds of what would become compassionate conservatism. The Buffers were a fundamentally right-wing organization—authoritarian, violent, and dedicated to the maintenance of established power—but they sometimes functioned like left-wing radicals, acting as literal buffers between black Washingtonians and the nearly all-white police force. About the police, they harbored no illusions. "If you ever have a confrontation with the police," Reverend Porter counseled the Buffers, "make sure there's five or six of you. Don't start nothing but defend yourself. He might kill one of you, but make sure you get him."

In the end, Coe got them. Not long after they were up and running, Coe installed a white staffer from the evangelical group Young Life in authority over the Buffers. Revered Porter realized that the Buffers were losing local control; the goal, he suspected, was to fold them into Young Life as a diversity program the almost all-white organization could boast about. He couldn't be sure; Coe surrounded his intentions with secrecy. Secrecy, in fact, was official policy. Coe and the white businessmen who financed the Buffers wanted tight control of the group, but they didn't want credit. Instead, they wanted to create the impression of spontaneous outbreaks of black submission (to Christ) instead of black power. They thought it might catch on. When it didn't, the financiers pulled the plug after not much more than a year, satisfied that order had at least been returned to Washington. Compassionate conservatism, beta version, was complete.

Staggers went to work for the Republican senator Richard Lugar. Coe began staking out suburban properties for the Fellowship, and in keeping with his new Ozzy and Harriet white-flight ethos, began calling it the Family. The Buffers drifted apart, and some went back to prison. Porter moved on to a pulpit in Maryland, although he kept attending Coe's inner-city prayer breakfasts until he finally grew tired of what he heard as Coe's broken-record message of "reconciliation" without substance. Porter was a theologically conservative Christian. He believed in prayer. But he also believed in power, and he quit the Fellowship—or the Family—when he realized that the men who ran it would never really share any with a brother who had nothing to trade, not even a whispered threat of revolution.

And Colson? He was just getting started. At the beginning, he seemed to enjoy boasting of his new Family connections, the smoothest political machine he'd ever encountered. But he soon learned the art of quiet diplomacy, Coe-style. He Vietnamized. In 1977, he appeared on Pat Robertson's *700 Club* program with his newest brother in Christ: Eldridge Cleaver, a founder of the Black Panthers. On the run in revolutionary Algeria, lost and far from home, Cleaver experienced a vision of Jesus that would have been immediately recognizable to the Family. "I was looking up at the moon," he'd later recount, "and I saw the man in the moon and it was my face." Then the face began to morph, becoming first one of Cleaver's strongman heroes, then another. From Cleaver himself to Castro to Mao to the strongest man of all, Jesus Christ, glowering down from the African night. Cleaver fell to his knees and wept, praying the Twenty-third Psalm, committed to memory as a child, and then the tears dried and Cleaver was ready at last to repent for black power—to surrender to American justice and the American Jesus.[54]

Cleaver, Colson told Pat Robertson, had joined a prayer cell with him, former senator Harold Hughes—by then working full time for the Family—and Tommy Tarrant, a former Klansman in prison for bombing a Jewish family. Cleaver, declared Colson, was reconciled.

In 1980, Cleaver, Panther no more, endorsed Ronald Reagan.

9.

J E S U S + 0 = X

Iₙ 2003, I PUBLISHED a portion of the account of Ivanwald with
which I begin this book in *Harper's* magazine. I might have left it at
that, were it not for a series of phone calls. In June of that year, I received an e-mail from a man named Greg Unumb, who wrote that
he'd read my article and wanted to talk to me. "I grew up with the
Coe family, went to school with their sons (that is, from elementary
school to through college), and was a part of the original group at
Ivanwald; however, I had a falling-out with them a number of years
ago." Greg thought I was correct in "some of [my] conclusions, but
certainly not on all of them." He wanted to offer me "insight."

Greg was finance manager for Pride Foramer's operation in oil-rich
Angola. Pride Foramer is a division of Pride International, which
drills in or off the coasts of more than thirty nations. The Pride Foramer division took care of business in five countries besides Angola:
Brazil, Indonesia, India, South Africa, and Ivory Coast. All six, as it
happens, have long been of special interest to the Family. But Greg
didn't want to talk about any of that. It was hard to tell what he did
want to talk about. When I reached him on the phone in Angola (ask
for "Mr. Greg," he wrote, "not Mr. Unumb"), he did not seem to recall any "falling-out." In fact, he was more interested in me. Such a
fascinating subject, he said—was I writing a book? Where did I live?
How much had I been paid for the article? How had I gotten in to Ivanwald? *Who recommended me?*

At the time, I lived on top of a hill in rural upstate New York. As

I talked to Greg, I sat in a lawn chair, looking out across miles of farmland, shooing bees away from my ankles. Ivanwald, the Family, its intrigues—beneath the bright summer sun, it all seemed hard to take seriously.

Greg wasn't the only one who got in touch. There was a corporate lawyer from Seattle, who claimed to have no connection to the Family but asked the same questions Greg had; I discovered that he had worked with several of the Family's visible fronts. End of conversation.

There were many devout Christians who contacted me. There was a Presbyterian pastor named Ben Daniel, a former member of the Family who'd quit after his first National Prayer Breakfast, where he was horrified to encounter the very same Central American death squad politicos he'd been reading about in the papers. There was an old, well-connected Republican lawyer named Clif Gosney, who on his visits to New York has introduced me to some of the city's most beautiful churches. After years of high-level service to the Family as a liaison to Chief Mangosuthu Buthelezi of the Zulu nation, he started drifting out in the early 1990s. When he asked Coe why almost no liberal Christian leaders were included in the National Prayer Breakfast, Coe raged at him, a rare instance of the sphinx's anger. Clif remembers hanging up the phone and realizing he'd just been purged.

When I went to Germany to speak on a panel about fundamentalism at the University of Potsdam, my German host told me that the U.S. embassy, a cosponsor of the lecture series, had refused to cover my expenses. I was, in the alleged words of Ambassador Dan Coats, a former Republican senator from Indiana, "an enemy of Jesus." If Coats really did say that, it didn't faze the German Christians with whom I shared a delicious meal that night.

And then there was Kate.* She wrote asking to have coffee with me because she was a fan. When a gorgeous blonde walked into the restaurant we'd agreed on and immediately said she *loved* my article,

---

* After she'd revealed her true purpose in contacting me, the woman I call "Kate" asked that I not identify her.

I thought, journalism has its rewards. But an hour into our conversation, I started making connections. She'd been living in Annapolis, Maryland, where the Family has a group of homes much like the compound in Arlington. She'd recently left a job at the National Security Agency. She'd been raised fundamentalist, but she'd left it behind; she wanted a relationship with Jesus untainted by tradition. So I asked her, "Do you know anyone in the Family?" Silence. I asked her again. For whatever reason—Christian conscience?—she confessed that she did know someone in the Family, David Coe. "He's like a father to me." In fact, she admitted, she'd been sent to spy on me.

We ended up talking for three more hours and drinking a lot of wine. I tried to persuade her that the Family was a secretive, undemocratic organization that aided and abetted dictators. She agreed, only she thought that was a good thing. She said the Family still loved me. I told her about some of the killers the Family had supported. She rallied by pointing out that we're all sinners, and thus shouldn't judge those whom God places in authority. "Jeff," she said, holding my eyes, twisting her wine stem between her fingers, "in your heart, have you ever lusted for a woman? Isn't that just as bad?"

So by the time Greg Unumb called, I wasn't too concerned about Family surveillance, which seemed to lead to nothing but good meals and bizarre come-ons. I answered Greg's questions as if he was the jittery one, the reporter looking over his shoulder. Relax, I wanted to say. Eventually, he did. For a moment, our conversation stalled.

Then he said, "You know, I used to run Ivanwald." And, he added, other Family houses just like it. That was a long time ago, before his oil career. He's since married a Frenchwoman, and he vacations in Sicily, and he goes to Washington only on business, the nature of which he said he'd rather not talk about. He remembered Ivanwald fondly, but now—"Generally, I don't see the Coes unless I run into them." He wouldn't explain why he'd broken off from them or why he continued to run into them.

But he still respects them. Their problem, he said, is one merely of "screening." They let "con artists" in. Scammers. People who raise money and disappear. People who "use an endorsement improperly." These are nothing but "relational problems."

All that other stuff, he said, just talk. Like the Hitler "stuff." "I heard those same illustrations used twenty years ago." The goal wasn't emulation but distillation. To look at "what they accomplished for evil, and turn it to good." I didn't say anything. I'd learned not to ask what a "good" genocide looked like.

He admitted that "sometimes, what they say is not what they do." And then there is the question of what they don't say. "What's secret is the top guys working with the leadership. It's not unlike a business. Business is a network. This is a Christian network, with a few people running it." Same deal as Pride International, he explained. There are people responsible for cities, and above them people responsible for regions, and above them people responsible for countries. And above them, there is Doug Coe.

"He's like [St.] Paul," Greg explained. He wanted me to understand Coe's famous $500 bet: that if a man prayed for something for forty days, he'd get it. Belief didn't matter. Jesus doesn't need your belief; he demands only your prayers, by which Greg seemed to mean obedience. Legend holds that Coe has never lost the bet. If you wager with him, he prays *for* you, so you can't lose. "He's confident enough in his relationship with Christ that he can ask for things," said Greg. And he'll get them. "Doug talks to Jesus man-to-man."

"Jeff," Greg said, "I advise you to explore that process. The process of becoming *intimate* with God." I was a smart guy. I could *do it*. For a lot of men, that relationship with God, it was nothing but personal. For a few, though, it meant something greater. "There are two types of people at Ivanwald. Sharp guys, with leadership potential, and problem kids. The sharp ones use Ivanwald to build their network. If they do become successful, there's an emphasis on maintaining contact.

"That," he said, "is how Doug uses Ivanwald."

By now I was out of my lawn chair and pacing with the phone in hand. Was I actually being recruited *back* to Ivanwald? It seemed impossible. But I didn't know how else to interpret it. Greg thought

I might have "leadership potential," might be someone Doug Coe could "use."

For what?

"The leadership work is secretive," Greg said. "It has to be. There is the problem of separation of church and state. And you can get so much more accomplished in secret." He boasted of the Family's behind-the-scenes negotiations with Israel, of Yasir Arafat's visit to the Cedars—an off-the-record event that had taken place long after Greg claimed to have broken with the Family. "Or Suharto," he said. The fact that Suharto had murdered 500,000 of his countrymen, as I'd written, was news to him. But so what? "Say he did kill a half million people. Let me ask you this: did he kill them before or during his relationship with Doug?"

Suharto's killing started before he knew Coe. In fact, it was the killing that caught the Family's attention. Since I'd left Ivanwald, I'd been doing some research on Indonesia; I thought that in the Family's relationship with a Muslim dictator there might be a clue to solving the problem of Jesus plus nothing. This is what I found out.

In September of 1965, a communist-led rebellion attempted to topple the aging hero of Indonesian independence, Sukarno, by then withered into an incompetent dictator. It fell to young General Suharto to beat back the rebellion, which he did easily, and to prevent a recurrence. This he accomplished by leading a nationwide slaughter of communists. "Communist" schoolchildren, babies, entire villages. When it was done, Suharto was untouchable—especially with his newfound friends, the Americans. LBJ, dominoes on the mind, was willing to cut deals with any devil God gave him if it meant he could move at least one Southeast Asian nation permanently out of the communist column.

American fundamentalists were even more enthusiastic about the Muslim dictator. In 1968, Abram declared Suharto's coup a "spiritual revolution," and Indonesia under his rule an especially promising nation, hope for the future in Abram's last years.[1] The CIA would

246 | JEFF SHARLET

eventually admit that the Indonesian massacre was "one of the worst mass murders in the 20th century." But that wasn't the mood at the dawn of Suharto's reign, as Clif Robinson, the Family's chief Asian representative, discovered in 1966, when he visited the American ambassador to Indonesia, Marshall Green. "The emergency," as Robinson called it, made demands on the ambassador's time, but the two men spent an afternoon together. Robinson wasn't able to see the Indonesian diplomat who'd originally introduced him to Jakarta politics though. He was in prison, one of 750,000 Indonesians jailed or sent to concentration camps for political crimes.

Robinson didn't try to intervene on behalf of his friend. But then, the ambassador would hardly have been the man to ask for help. In 1990, Green acknowledged the long-suspected fact that the American embassy had been busy at that time compiling for Suharto what one of Green's aides called a "shooting list": the names of thousands of leftist political opponents, from leaders identified by the CIA to village-level activists, the kind of data only local observers—conservative missionaries, classically—could provide. "We had a lot more information about [them] than the Indonesians themselves," Green boasted. Green and his aides followed the results of their gift closely, checking off names as Suharto's men killed or imprisoned them. "No one cared, so long as they were communists, that they were butchered," said one of Green's aides. Another, acknowledging that the list had left "a lot of blood" on American hands, argued, "But that's not all bad. There's a time when you have to strike hard at a decisive moment."[2]

One such moment occurred for Suharto in December 1975, when Portugal relinquished its claims to the tiny island nation of East Timor. It declared independence; nine days later Suharto's army invaded, on the pretext that its neighbor was communist. Two hundred thousand people—nearly a third of the island's population—were killed during the long occupation, to which the United States gave its blessing. Gerald Ford, the only president to have been a member of an actual prayer cell (when he was in Congress, with Representatives John Rhodes, Al Quie, and Melvin Laird, a cell that reconvened in 1974 to pray with Ford about pardoning Nixon),[3] told Suharto, "We will understand and will not press you on the issue. We understand the problem and the intentions you have." Kissinger, with Ford in Jakarta, added, "It is important that whatever you do succeeds quickly [because] the use of U.S.-made arms could create problems." Suharto did not succeed quickly—the killing continued for decades—but he never lacked for champions in the U.S. Congress, which saw to it that American dollars kept his regime in bullets until he was driven out in 1998.

The massacre of Indonesia preceded Suharto's friendship with the Family, but the slaughter and slow strangulation of East Timor coincided with it. A document in the Family's archives titled "Important Dates in Indonesian History" notes that in March 1966, the Communist Party was banned and Campus Crusade arrived in April. Suharto wasn't a Christian, but he knew that where missionaries go, investors follow. He also wanted to use God—any God—to pacify the population. In 1967, Congressman Ben Reifel sent a memo to other Fellowship members in Congress noting that a special message from Suharto calling on Indonesians to "seek God, discover His laws, and obey them" was broadcast at the same time as a Fellowship prayer session in the Indonesian parliament for non-Christian politicians. The Fellowship never asked Indonesians to renounce Islam, only to meet around "the person of Jesus"—considered a prophet in Islam—in private, under the guidance of the Fellowship's American brothers.

By 1969, the Fellowship claimed as its man in Jakarta Suharto's minister of social affairs, who presided over a group of more than fifty Muslims and Christians in parliament. Another Fellowship associate, Darius Marpaung—he'd later claim that God spoke through him when he told a massive rally that the time had come to "purge the communists," an event that helped spark the massacre—led a similar group in Indonesia's Christian community.[4] "President Suharto is most interested and would like to increase his contact through this medium with the other men of the world," wrote Coe's first follower, Senator Mark Hatfield, in a memo to Nixon that year. "He has indicated he would like to meet with the Senate [prayer] group if and when he comes to the United States."[5]

In the fall of 1970, Suharto did both. Coe often boasted that nobody but congressmen, himself, and maybe a special guest attended such meetings, but this time Secretary of Defense Melvin Laird and Admiral Thomas H. Moorer, chairman of the Joint Chiefs of Staff, joined the Indonesian dictator.[6] In October 1970, Coe wrote to the U.S. ambassador to Chile, Edward Korry. Suharto had just become the first Muslim to join the Fellowship's off-the-record Senate prayer group for a meeting "similar to the one we had with Haile Selassie," the emperor of Ethiopia. Korry was too busy to celebrate; October 1970 was the month his plot to overthrow Chile's democratically elected president, Salvador Allende, came to a botched end, opening the door to the more murderous scheme that brought General Augusto Pinochet to power three years later.[7] ("The sun is just now beginning to shine again," the Family's key man in Chile, the head of a right-wing civilian faction called the "Officialists," wrote Coe, promising to tell him the "real story" of Pinochet's coup in person.)

In 1971, Coe entertained a small gathering at the Fellowship House with stories from his most recent round of visits to international brothers, "men whom God has touched in an unusual way." Among them was General Nguyen Van Thieu, the president of South Vietnam, who arranged for Coe to tour the war zone in the personal plane of his top military commander; the foreign minister of Cambodia, "most eager to carry on our concept"; and Suharto. In Clif Robinson's telling, "Doug and I were escorted up the steps of the palace, no attempt to make any secret of it, and the president there so warmly welcomed us and the first thing he said as I walked into the room was to express his appreciation for what had been done, and to say that the *momentum* that we have seen started in this must not be allowed to slacken . . . Along toward the end, one of the men suggested it would be good if we had prayer together. And Darius Marpaung and Colonel Sombolem were present with us. And Darius Marpaung suggested that the businessman who was there would lead us in a prayer. And I think I have seldom been in a meeting where the prayer was so God-inspired."[8]

Coe and Robinson weren't the only representatives of the Fellowship to seek such inspiration with Suharto. In 1970, a memo to Fellowship congressmen from Senator B. Everett Jordan, a North Carolina Dixiecrat, reported that Howard Hardesty, the executive vice president of Continental Oil, listed as a key man in the Fellowship's confidential directory, had traveled to Indonesia to spend a day with the Fellowship prayer cells and join Suharto for dinner.[9] The following year, Senator Jordan himself traveled to Jakarta on the Family's behalf, where a special prayer breakfast meeting of forty parliamentary and military leaders was assembled for him by the vice president of Pertamina, the state oil and gas company that functioned like a family business for Suharto. Such corporate/state/church chumminess was hardly limited to dictatorial regimes. Jordan may well have traveled to the meeting on an airplane provided that year for congressional members of the Family by Harold McClure of McClure Oil, and the year previous, he'd boasted in a memo to congressional Family members, oil executives and foreign diplomats had used the National Prayer Breakfast in Washington to meet for "confidential" prayers.[10]

By 1972, some of Abram's old hands were concerned about the moral vacuum the Family now called home. Elgin Groseclose, the American economist who'd helped the Shah run Iran in the 1940s, worried that Muslims who saw through the facade of the "brotherhood of man" would ask, "Down what road am I being taken?" And, perhaps, decide to take Americans for a ride instead. "This has been one of the aspects of the . . . movement that has long troubled me," concluded Groseclose. "Where does politics end and religion begin?"[11]

Poor Groseclose. He could not grasp *power*. Suharto got it. "We are sharing the deepest experiences of our lives together," Clif Robinson wrote of his brother the dictator. "It was at this point when I was with President Suharto of Indonesia that he said, 'In this way we are converted, we convert ourselves—No one converts us!'"[12]

In the spring of 1975, Bruce Sundberg, a Family missionary to the Filipino government of the dictator Ferdinand Marcos, began planning with Marcos's chief financial backer for a summit in Jakarta. Included would be Marcos, Suharto, and General Park, the South Korean dictator. Sundberg called it "The Jakarta Idea," the "Idea" to be pondered the same one that had come to Abram forty years earlier in Seattle. That it had not evolved since 1935 was, to the men of the Family, proof of its eternal truth: the Idea that God's method is the "man-method," that God chooses His key men according to His concerns, not ours. That conviction enabled Coe to ignore Elgin Groseclose's concern about foreign nationals using them for their connections. People didn't use people, according to the Idea. People didn't *do* anything. Rather, they were used by God, and their only two choices were to struggle against the inevitable, or to allow God to pull their strings. Was Suharto using them? Only if God wanted him to. Everything the Family did for Suharto—the connections, the prayers, the blessings—they did for God.

On December 6, 1975, Gerald Ford blessed Suharto's invasion of East Timor. Twelve hours after Ford left Jakarta, Suharto's forces, armed almost entirely with American weapons, attacked East Timor's population of 650,000 on the premise that the island nation was planning a communist assault on Indonesia, a nation of 140 million people.

Here are the words of the last broadcast from East Timor's national Radio Dili, in the nation's capital: "Women and children are being shot in the streets. We are all going to be killed, I repeat, we are all going to be killed. This is an appeal for international help. Please help us . . ."

THE CONSERVATIVE ESTIMATE of Suharto's death toll, in East Timor and Indonesia proper, is 602,000, but most scholars of Indonesia believe it is two or even three times greater, ranking Suharto next to the Cambodian madman Pol Pot as one of the worst mass murderers of the twentieth century. What role the Family played, or did not play—which of their "deepest experiences" they shared—in the long occupation of East Timor that followed the invasion, a period during which it was transformed into "islands of prisons hidden with islands," I can't say. The Family restricted its archives before I could follow the story into the next decade. All I know is that in 2002 my Ivanwald brothers proudly proclaimed that one of Suharto's successors, President Megawati, had bent her knee to the Jesus of the Cedars.

I shared some of Suharto's story with Greg. I wanted to make some kind of connection. Not of politics to religion but between us, "man-to-man," as the Family likes to say. I knew almost nothing about him, but his tone reminded me of Bengt Carlson, one of his successors as leader of Ivanwald, and that made me think that like Bengt, Greg was probably a decent sort absorbed into a movement the awful shape of which he simply didn't see. It wasn't that I wanted to school him. I wanted him to know that I got it. That I understood good intentions and where they could lead. That I appreciated that diplomacy requires doing business with bad men. That I knew there had been honorable Cold Warriors—my father, a Sovietologist who advised the CIA near the end of Eastern European communism, was one of them—who believed that the threat of the Soviet Union justified terrible alliances.

But what I wanted him to say—and I admit it, I wanted him to answer for Coe, for Carlson, for the whole goddamn bunch, because, after all, here he was, apparently asking me to *join* them—was that making Suharto a brother, at least, had been a mistake. Why hadn't Coe risked his access, risked the Family's friendships in big oil, risked even his certainty about the biblically sanctioned authority of whichever strongman ends up in charge, to tell Suharto—after a prayer, maybe—to stop killing his own people? To hold him accountable, as the Family likes to say. For if the Family had not done so—if they had, in fact, greased Suharto's economic machine, voted for weapons, praised him to the world as a champion of freedom—they were accomplices. Brothers in blood, yes, but not that of the lamb.

Greg preferred to look on the bright side. "If not for Doug," he said, "maybe Suharto would have killed a million."

GREG'S MATH WAS the calculus used by Stalin when he said that a single death is a tragedy, but a million is no more than a statistic. Stalin, monster that he was, spoke not of flesh-and-blood murder but of politics by narrative, the stories to which even a dictator must resort if he is to wield the power he takes by the gun. As a human being, Stalin may have been worse than worthless, but as a fabulator, he was astute. A single death does make a better story. Suharto's victims—602,000, 1.2 million, or 1.8 million—may never find a place in literature. But they deserve a place in history, and to win them that, one small problem must be solved here in America, that of Jesus plus nothing, the logic of faith that allows American politicians to contribute to the nightmares of other nations, and the rest of us to vote for them.

Jesus plus nothing. Phrased like that, as Coe puts it, it doesn't sound like a problem at all. One who preaches Jesus plus nothing claims to be in possession of pure Godhead. Not Jesus plus the history of his believers and what they've done in His name, or Jesus plus the culture through which we view Him now, or Jesus plus the best efforts of the minds God, presumably, gave us, or Jesus plus humanity itself. Not Jesus plus scripture, since scripture, after all, contains a great deal besides Jesus. No burning bush, no voice in the whirlwind, no Daniel, no lions. Coe and his inner circle do believe in the trinity; a Washington fundamentalist activist told me, "but they'll give the Father and the Holy Ghost the weekend off. Because they clutter the conversation. Jesus is so easily presented."[13]

And what is it about Jesus that Coe presents? Not the teachings of Christ; simply the fact of His being, "the Person of Christ," as Coe called it in a four-part lecture series he presented to a conference of evangelical leaders in January 1989, recorded on two videotapes lent to me by an evangelical scholar distressed by Coe's peculiar concept of God. The lectures took place at the Glen Eyrie Castle in Colorado

Springs, the Navigators headquarters at which Coe first conceived of Jesus plus nothing. With a great stone hearth lit by two murky yellow lanterns behind him, Coe, in a dark suit and tie, his black hair slicked across his skull, doesn't drive toward his points; he ambles up to them. He tells a story about touring forty-two small nations in the Pacific with a member of Reagan's National Security Council, an Australian politician, and some American businessmen. On the tarmac of each country's airport, they pray for a key man, a power broker, and then they go off to meet a top man, the one with the power.

What am I supposed to say to them? asks the Australian.

"We wanna be your friend," says Coe.

Okay, says the Australian, but how?

"Tell 'em, 'By learning to love God, together, centered around Jesus Christ.' "

The Australian, who used to work in the foreign ministry, doesn't think he can say that. He'll sound crazy. He'll sound stupid. So Coe makes him a bet: if it doesn't work after two countries, they'll go back to Australia and play golf. But there's to be no golf in his near future, because on every little island they visit, Yap and Truk and Palau, this delegation of First World power finds prime ministers, presidents, parliamentarians, strangely receptive to their message. The NSC man, David Locke, a veteran of a similar trip with Coe, described it once. "It reminded me of the story in World War II, where the British sent an OSS type into Borneo . . . And this guy parachuted out of the sky and they had never seen anything like this so they looked on him as—he had blonde hair and white skin and he was a white god who had come out of the sky to mobilize them. Obviously his side was going to win so they had no trouble aligning themselves. Well, from the point of view of a lot of these little island countries, we were something akin to that."[14]

"All through these last forty years," Coe continues, "I've had the privilege of traveling to countries, I've been in China, in Vietnam with the Vietnamese, the Vietcong, Communists in Panama, Communists in Russia, the Red Guard in China, Nazis in Germany."

(Coe's first visit to Germany was in 1959. Did he know more about the past of Abram's key men in Germany than they liked to acknowledge?) "And you know, I discovered that the same things that they make people give vows to keep, are the same things that Jesus said . . . The only thing that was changed was the goal, the only thing that changed was the purpose. In essence, it was all the things that Jesus taught in private to the disciples. I began to realize why they were so successful in human terms."

Coe cites one of his favorite scripture verses, Matthew 18:20, "When two or three are gathered together in my name, there I am in the midst of them." "Hitler, Goebbels, and Himmler were three men. Think of the immense power these three men had, these nobodies from nowhere. Actually, emotional and mental problems. Prisoners. From the street. But they bound themselves together in an agreement, and they died together. Two years before they moved into Poland, these three men had a study done, systematically a plan drawn out and put on paper to annihilate the entire Polish population and destroy by numbers every single house"—he bangs the podium, dop, dop, dop—"and every single building in Warsaw and then to start on the rest of Poland."

It worked, Coe says; they killed 6½ million "Polish people." (The actual sum was closer to 5½ million, 3 million of whom were Polish Jews. But that, as Stalin would say, is just a statistic).

"These three men by their decision alone." What he's trying to explain, Coe says, is the power of friendship: between a man and Christ, between brothers in Christ. Once, he says, a friend who'd been France's foreign minister during its war with Vietnam told him he should try to meet Ho Chi Minh. " 'Even though he was our enemy, he was amazing.' He said, '[Ho] knows what it means, to be brothers.' " What does it mean to be brothers? It means, Coe learns when he finally meets one of Ho's, a foreign minister Coe says he happened to bump into in Mauritania, to be willing to—happy to— die for your cause.

It's late; the room is gloomy; Coe's brothers and sisters are sitting on hard chairs. He needs to make it very clear for them.

"These enemies of ours," he says, "they have taken the very words of Jesus Christ and used them for themselves." What words is Coe talking about? The ones about "social order."

"That's all that matters." The social order: "Jesus says, 'You have to put me before other people, and you have to put me before yourself.' Hitler, that was the demand of the Nazi Party." Coe slaps the podium, and the Führer creeps into his mannerisms: "You have to put the Nazi Party and its objectives in front of your own life and ahead of other people!" Now he's Coe again. "I've seen pictures of young men in the Red Guard of China," he says. "A table laid out like a butcher table, they would bring in this young man's mother and father, lay her on the table with a basket on the end, he would take an axe and cut her head off." Now he's Mao, punctuating his words by slapping his pulpit: "They have to put the purposes of the Red Guard ahead of the mother-father-brother-sister—their own life!"

He pauses, makes the fist. "That was a covenant. A pledge. That was what Jesus said." Now he's Jesus: "If you do not put *me*, before your father"—bang—"your mother"—bang—"your brother"—bang—"your sister"—bang—"you cannot be my disciple." Now as Coe: "If you're gonna have any movement that moves men and movements, that's"—he clenches his fist again at the end of the phrase—"you have to have that kind of commitment. Jesus knew that. *That's* the way the social order is run."

In America, Coe says, "Today. In this country. This very day"—that vision of social order is lost.

The next morning, Coe explains to the crowd how it can be regained. Remember, he says, he is talking about love. A necessary reminder, perhaps, since he continues to use Hitler and Lenin, and, today, Stalin, to illustrate the shape of the love he pursues. Why such monsters? Why not speak of the church? Coe removes a pair of eyeglasses from a pocket, but instead of putting them on, he twirls them on one finger. "There is nothing in the Bible about the Christian church. That isn't the name of it. The name of it is the body." The Body of Christ, of which all believers are cells. "His body functions invisibly." Coe draws an analogy to a tree. All you see are the leaves;

"you don't know what's going on underground." But look at the churches, he says, with all their pomp and circumstance, all their titles, every full-time church worker stuck in a hierarchy. It depresses people, Coe explains, when they can see who their master is. A movement that is visible is weak, vulnerable. It's an organization, not love. But the Body of Christ—"The Family," Coe says—"we are bound by the strongest power in the world"—*love,* I think, but I've lost hold of the connections—"and the whole world is afraid of it."

Let's return to our problem. Let J stand for *Jesus*. $J+0=X$. Is X a body of cells, or a social order, or a vision? Yes. All three. $X = a$ *vision*. The vision isn't the Sermon on the Mount; it's not the beatitudes; it's so simple it hurts (remember the Red Guard's axe): the vision is total loyalty. Loyalty to what? To the idea of loyalty. It's another M. C. Escher drawing, the one of a hand drawing the hand that is drawing itself. The Communist Party, plus Jesus. The Nazi Party, plus Jesus. The Red Guard, plus Jesus. What is the common denominator? Jesus? Or power? Jesus plus nothing equals power, "invisible" power, the long, slow, building power of a few brothers and sisters. $J+0=P$. We have our formula. Now let's run the equation for the twenty-first century. $J+0=P$ divided by the many permutations of the Family's present, its latest incarnation.

10.

INTERESTING BLOOD

THE REVEREND ROB SCHENCK, the founder of a ministry called Faith and Action in the Nation's Capital—a knockoff of the Family, the theological equivalent of fake Gucci—is one of the most unusual fundamentalist activists in Washington. He has the glad, plastic face and quick wit of a Borscht Belt comedian and the big brown eyes of a pitbull puppy. There's an echo of Brooklyn in his voice, which he amplified on my behalf. We had two things in common, we discovered when we met one day for sauerbraten at Schenck's favorite restaurant: a fascination with Jonathan Edwards and Charles Finney, and the fact that we're both "half-Jews," born of gentile mothers and Jewish fathers. "Makes for very interesting blood!" said Schenck. This realization was an occasion for Schenck to dust off his Yinglish, the mix of Yiddish and English usually reserved for bar mitzvahs, funerals, and *Fiddler on the Roof* revivals. It was probably the only time Jonathan Edwards has been described as a *luftmensch* and Finney as a schmoozer. (Between us, MOT, we agreed that Billy Graham is a theological *schlimazel*.) Schenck was that rarest of creatures: an ironic true believer.

Where I'd made sense of my half-Jew, half-Christian self by writing about those without doubts or divisions, Schenck, seventeen years old at the tail end of the hippie "Jesus People" movement in the early 1970s, decided to become one. With his twin brother, Paul, in tow, he began attending late-night stoner prayer-and-gospel guitar sessions. But that wasn't enough. It's a strange truth of American fundamentalism that several of its public ideologues—Marvin Olasky, the former communist who converted and coined the phrase *compassionate conservatism*, and Howard Phillips, a Yiddish-speaker who converted and recruited Jerry Falwell to create a "Moral Majority," and Jay Sekulow, the converted legal genius behind many of the movement's courtroom victories—came up in the deradicalized world of postwar American Jewry. It's as if, casting about for the political passion of their immigrant fathers and mothers, they settled on Christian fundamentalism as the closest approximation of that vanished world, its socialist unions and communist cells.

Schenck took it further than most: he helped organize Operation Rescue, the militant anti-abortion crusade that specialized in grotesque protests—the twin Schencks waved aborted fetuses like flags—and "direct action," such as a full-throated prayer vigil outside the home of a Buffalo abortion provider, Dr. Barnett Slepian, in 1997. A year later, an Operation Rescue volunteer named James Kopp shot Slepian to death. "My brother and I felt very badly about the shooting," Schenck told a reporter.[1]

It was true—by then Schenck had realized that there was a quicker path to power. He had begun praying in Washington with a rising star in the Senate from Missouri, John Ashcroft. He took to riding what he called the "vertical chapel"—the elevators of congressional office buildings—hoping to bump into more catches like Ashcroft. Instead, he kept running into members of the Family, on their way to meetings not just with fundamentalist fellow travelers such as Ashcroft but the entire spectrum of the political elite. "The mystique of the Fellowship," Schenck observed, "has allowed it to gain entrée into almost impossible places in the capital."

Schenck found a donor to buy him a town house across from the Supreme Court, where he began practicing a Coe-style ministry to judiciary staffers. In 2000, he prayed with Justice Antonin Scalia a day after the Supreme Court decision that made Bush president, and since 2001, Schenck has been able to penetrate the White House with ease, counseling staffers on their spiritual responsibilities. He does the same for congressmen in the quiet garden behind his town house, and fundamentalist activists from the provinces make Schenck's HQ a regular stop on their pilgrimages to power. But he's still, by his own admission, third tier. He remains an outsider with inside connections.

As such, he has become a sharp study of how the power he wants actually flows. In the first rank of fundamentalist influence, there are the old lions: James Dobson and Focus on the Family; Pat Robertson, batty but too rich to ignore; Chuck Colson, the "scholar in residence" in the house of fundamentalism. "Then you have the B list," which is comprised of dozens of mid-sized organizations with big membership rolls but little name recognition outside activist circles: American Values, led by Gary Bauer, a former top Reagan aide who worked with the Family in the 1980s; and the Traditional Values Coalition, led by Louis P. Sheldon, a longtime Family ally who uses their C Street House for "faith-based diplomacy" in the fight against what he calls the "Marxist/Leftist/Homosexual/Islamic coalition"—a clumsy coinage that marks him as too crass for the Family's inner circle.

"Where does the Family fit on this scale?" I asked.

Off the charts, said Schenck. Not more powerful; differently powerful. The big Christian lobbying groups push and shout; the Family simply surrounds politicians with prayer cells. They don't try to convert anyone. They don't ask for anything. They're as patient as a glacier. "It works. It works extremely well. Inside the beltway, if you're going to enjoy the platform of the National Prayer Breakfast—I mean, *really* enjoy it, not be invited courteously to show up, if you're going to have the force of that thing behind you, Coe's approval is a big deal. It's the kosher seal."

Coe doesn't demand doctrinal loyalty, only a willingness to do business behind the scenes, and liberals are free to join him in the back room. Testifying before Congress about global warming in 2007, Al Gore came under angry assault from Senator James Inhofe, a longtime member of the Family. Gore blunted the attack by invoking their "mutual friend, Doug Coe," with whom, he suggested, he and Inhofe ought to meet away from the cameras. "You know what

I think of when I think of Doug Coe?" Schenck asked, his voice thick with admiration and laced with envy. "I think literally of the guy in the smoky back room, you can't even see his face. He sits in the corner, and you see the cigar, and you see the flame, and you hear his voice—but you never see his face. He's that shadowy figure. Nobody ever sees him. At the Prayer Breakfast, he's never on the dais, but he puts the whole thing together. Nobody speaks from that podium, including the president, without Doug's nod of approval. It's a delicate play: He brings everyone together."

For instance, says Schenck, Senators Sam Brownback and Hillary Clinton, partners in prayer at Coe's weekly Senate Prayer Breakfast. The Family is dedicated to spiritual war, not the intramural combat of party politics, Schenck explained. Coe doesn't have a systematic theology, he has a vision of power. Not just to come, but as it exists. "They're into living with what is," said Schenck. "But you don't want to alienate them, you don't want to antagonize them. You need them as your friends. Even Hillary will need them. They keep a sort of cultural homeostasis in Washington. Washington right now is a town where if you're going to be powerful, you need religion. That's just the way it's done."

SAM

The senator looks taller than he is, looks broader than he is. He is slight, but you notice the narrow cut of his suits, the weightlessness of the man, only after you have been with him for a while. His face is wide and flat and smooth across the cheekbones. His skin is Washington-pale but thick, like leather, etched by windburn and sun from years of working on his father's farm in Parker, Kansas (population 281 and falling). You can hear it in his voice: slow, distant but warm, almost a baritone, spoken out of the left side of his mouth in half sentences with very few hard consonants. It sounds like the voice of someone who has learned how to wait for rain.

As a freshman in the House, part of the Republican revolution of

1994, he spoke with approval of his supporters' feelings about Congress: "blow it up," they demanded. He refused at first to sign the "Contract With America," Newt Gingrich's right-wing manifesto, not because it was too radical but because it wasn't fast enough. Don't just reform government, he insisted; erase it. He wanted to start by abolishing the departments of Education, Energy, Commerce, and the IRS. He wanted to do these things, he said, for the poor. He topped the *National Review*'s list of rising stars. Less than two years later, he was a senator. He grabbed his seat out from under Bob Dole's anointed successor.

He calls himself a "faith-journey man." He considers human rights his forte. He has been to Darfur and Iraq. He welcomes "pro-American" refugees. (Those who don't speak English, he has said, "would not work well in Kansas.") He worries a great deal about sexual slavery. He'd like to censor violent videos, but he's steadfast against making gay bashing a hate crime. "Religious freedom" is a top priority, and it may require force. He has suggested Iran, Syria, Saudi Arabia, and Sudan as military targets, and proposed sending troops to the Philippines, where rebels killed two American missionaries. "There's probably a higher level of Christians [being persecuted] during the last ten, twenty years than . . . throughout human history," he told Chuck Colson's radio program. He takes solace from scripture. "Blessed are those who are persecuted because of righteousness," reads Matthew 5:10, "for theirs is the kingdom of heaven." He believes he can feel it when people are praying for him.

BROWNBACK'S STAFF OFTEN seem puzzled by the intensity of his religion. They worry when the only thing he eats for lunch is a wafer, the Body of Christ, at the noontime mass he tries to attend daily since his conversion to Catholicism. On weekends he gets up early so he could catch a mass before meeting his family at Topeka Bible, the city's biggest evangelical church. He calls this routine a "great mixture of the feeding." One Sunday morning I joined him. His preferred seat was in the back row of the balcony. A guest preacher from Promise Keepers, a revival of nineteenth-century "muscular Christianity," had arranged for two men to perform a melodrama about golf and fatherhood. The senator chuckled when he was supposed to, sang every song, nodded seriously when the preacher warned against "Judaizers" who would "poison" the New Testament.

After the service, Brownback introduced me to a white-haired man with a yellow Viking mustache. "This is the man who wrote 'Dust in the Wind,'" the senator announced proudly. It was Kerry Livgren, of the band Kansas, born again. Brownback likes to take Livgren on fact-finding missions. He wants to take him to Israel, because he thinks songwriters are very spiritual, and he thinks Jews are also very spiritual. "Carry on, my wayward son . . . ," the senator warbled, trying to remember the words to the other big hit by Kansas.

When he ran for the House, Brownback was a Methodist, simple and proper. When he ran for the Senate, he was an evangelical, filled with Holy Ghost power. Now he's a Catholic, baptized not in a church but in the "Catholic Information Center," a chapel tucked in between lobbyists' offices on K Street in Washington, run by Opus Dei, a secretive lay order founded by a saint who saw in Generalissimo Franco, the late dictator of Spain, an ideal of worldly power. Brownback prefers Mother Teresa. He studies Torah with an orthodox rabbi. "Deep," says the rabbi. His daughter once told him that different churches have different aromas, and that there is a scent for everyone. Brownback wants to huff them all. "I am a seeker," he told me, an understatement of grand proportion. Brownback's faith is complicated, like American fundamentalism in the twenty-first century. The movement's two great strands—the populist, pulpit-pounding tradition of its masses and the mannered evasions of its elite—are coming together, intertwining to become the mutant DNA of men such as Sam Brownback, the next generation of spiritual warriors.

"Politics is a false god," Brownback once wrote. What he meant, he explained to me, is that God doesn't require brilliant leaders, erudite lawmakers. All he wants is those who submit. It's as simple as the love between father and child. Love, not the sharp-edged coexistence made possible by tolerance, is the fundamentalist covenant with America. Love, not the never-ending arguments of democracy.

WHEN BROWNBACK WAS growing up, he was more concerned with the weight of his hogs than the wages of sin. His parents still live in the dusty white one-story farmhouse in which he was raised, on a dirt road outside of Parker. Brownback likes to say that he fights for traditional family values, but his father, Bob, was more concerned with the price of grain, and his mother, Nancy, had no qualms about having a gay friend. Back then, moral values were simple. "Your word was your word. Don't cheat," his mother told me. "I can't think of anything else." Her son played football ("quarterback" she said, "never very good") and was elected class president and "Mr. Spirit." Like most kids in Parker, he just wanted to be a farmer. But that life was already gone by the time he graduated from high school. If he couldn't be a farmer, Brownback decided, he'd be a politician. In 1975, he went off to Kansas State University. There he joined a chapter of the Navigators, a fundamentalist ministry for young men and women founded by Doug Coe's first mentor, Dawson Trotman. The summer before his senior year, Brownback worked in Washington as an intern for Bob Dole. "The Prayer Breakfast folks had rented a sorority house for the summer, for people who were working on the Hill. I made contact." That was Brownback's first introduction to the Family, and to Coe. That fall, Brownback returned to K State with a new sense of the potential synergy between politics and religion.

In 1983, Brownback was fresh out of law school and considering a career in politics. He searched through Kansas history for a role model and settled on the forgotten Republican senator Frank Carlson. "He stood at the center of power when the U.S. had no peer," Brownback remembers thinking. In 1968, the last year of Carlson's Senate career—long before the term *culture war* was invented—he wrote an article for *U.S. News* calling for a "man to stand" against what Brownback now terms *decadence*. Brownback wondered, Could

I be the one? Carlson was still alive, so Brownback drove out to Concordia, Kansas, and as the light died one summer evening he sat on Carlson's porch, listening to stories. Tales from the Senate, legends of spiritual war, Carlson's now-ancient Worldwide Spiritual Offensive. Brownback thought he'd found a mentor. "He became a model to me."

In the years that followed, he stayed in touch with Carlson, and the Family stayed in touch with him, but Coe didn't invite Brownback to join a prayer cell until he went to Washington as a congressman in 1994. "I had been working with them for a number of years, so when I went into Congress I knew I wanted to get back into that," he says. The group was all Republican and all male. Conversation tended toward the personal. Or, according to the old feminist maxim, the personal as political. "Personal transformation will inevitably have cultural and ultimately, political implications," Brownback has said. He still meets with the prayer cell every Tuesday evening. The rules forbid Brownback to reveal the names of his fellow members, but those in the cell likely include some of the men with whom he lived in the Family's C Street House for congressmen: Representative Zach Wamp of Tennessee, former representative Steve Largent of Oklahoma, and Senator Tom Coburn of Oklahoma, then a representative and a medical doctor who took the personal as political to new depths when he shanghaied Hill staffers into a basement office for a slide show of genitals mutilated by sexually transmitted diseases, a warning against sex outside of marriage that Coburn underlined by advocating the death penalty for abortion providers.

Coe must have seemed like a voice of reason next to Brownback's new friends. He pointed out scripture verses to the congressman, mailed him poems, gave him books to study. In a nation under Jesus plus nothing, Coe explained, Brownback would ultimately have to answer to only one authority. Everything—sex and taxes, war and the price of oil—would be decided upon not according to democracy or the church or even, strictly speaking, scripture. In a prayer cell, Christ speaks directly to his anointed. "Typically," Brownback explained, "one person grows desirous of pursuing an action"—a piece of legislation, a diplomatic strategy—"and the others pull in behind."

In 1999, Brownback teamed up with two other Family associates—former senator Don Nickles and the late senator Strom Thurmond—to demand a criminal investigation of Americans United for Separation of Church and State. In 2005, Senator Coburn joined Brownback in stumping for the Houses of Worship Act, to allow tax-exempt churches to endorse politicians. Brownback's most influential effort is as chair of the Senate Values Action Team, a caucus that gathers on Tuesdays, before his Family cell meeting. Everything that is said is strictly off the record, and even the groups themselves are forbidden from discussing the proceedings. It's a little "cloak-and-dagger," says Brownback's press secretary. The VAT, as it's called, is a war council, and the enemy, says one participant, is "secularism."

The Senate VAT grew out of a House version chaired by Representative Joe Pitts, a burly, white-haired conservative from Pennsylvania Amish country who's a regular at the Family's Arlington mansion. The VAT was then-Representative Tom DeLay's creation, but as far back as 1980, Pitts had been one of the regional activists who'd helped push a relatively new concern for evangelicals—abortion—to its place at the center of American politics. In 2002, Brownback, whose concern with what he refers to as a "holocaust" against a womb-bound nation of fetal citizens, was the logical man for the job of leading the VAT's Senate version. The VAT demands a bridge builder's sensibility, the ability to convince fundamentalism's popular front, which demanded its creation, that it's taken seriously by more elite conservatives.

The VAT unifies their message and arms congressional staffers with the data and language they need to pass legislation. Working almost entirely in secret, the group has directed the fights against gay marriage and for school vouchers, against hate-crime legislation and for "abstinence only" sex education, against diplomacy with North Korea, and for war with Iran. The VAT is like a closed circuit between elite and popular fundamentalism, with Brownback at the switch.

Every Wednesday at noon, he trots upstairs from his office to a radio studio maintained by the Republican leadership to rally support from Christian America for the VAT's agenda. One participant in the broadcast, Salem Radio Network News, reaches more than 1,500 Christian stations nationwide, and Dobson's Focus on the Family offers access to an audience of 1.5 million. During the broadcast I sat in on, Brownback explained that with the help of the VAT he hoped to defeat a measure that would stiffen penalties for violent attacks on gays and lesbians. Members of the VAT mobilized their flocks: An e-mail sent out by the Family Research Council warned that the hate-crime bill would lead, inexorably, to the criminalization of Christ. When it comes to "impacting policy," Tony Perkins, president of the Family Research Council, told me, "day to day, the VAT is instrumental."

The VAT's efforts often go beyond strictly spiritual matters, rallying fundamentalism's popular front around laissez-faire policies—tax cuts, deregulation—in line with elite fundamentalism's long-standing dream of not just a nation but an economy under God. At its best, that makes for a paternalistic capitalism where bosses placed in authority by God, according to Romans 13, treat their employees with respect and compassion, to which the employees respond with devotion, leading to big profits, high wages, and smiles in every cubicle. More often—well, the world we live in *is* the "more often," an economy in which employers treat their employees as commodities and employees respond with fear and boredom. Only the big profits are the same.

In 1999, Brownback worked with Pitts to pass the Silk Road Strategy Act, designed, Brownback told me, to block the growth of Islam in Central Asian nations, essentially buying their oil and natural gas resources for American corporations through lucrative trade deals, granted with little concern for the abysmal human rights records of the region's dictatorships. Brownback also sits on the board of trustees of the U.S. Azerbaijan Chamber of Commerce, an organization created by the Azeri government with funds from eight oil

companies, including Exxon, Mobil, and Chevron. Current and former members include Henry Kissinger, Dick Cheney, Iraq War ar-
chitect Richard Perle—a neoconservative trinity too cynical for
prayer cells—and two of Brownback's Family brothers: Pitts and
former attorney general Ed Meese. One of the Silk Road Act's provi-
sions, which Brownback fought for, lifted U.S. sanctions on Azerbaijan, imposed in response to the Azeri blockade against neighboring
Armenia. Azerbaijan is 94 percent Muslim; Armenia is predomi-
nantly Christian. Brownback apparently issues indulgences where oil
is concerned.

Brownback's biggest financial backer is Koch Industries—the
largest privately held company in the United States, with extensive
oil and gas interests around the world. "The Koch folks," as they're
known around the senator's office, are headquartered in Wichita, but
the company is one of the worst polluters across the country. In
2000, the company was slapped with the largest environmental civil
penalty in U.S. history for illegally discharging 3 million gallons of
crude oil in six states. That same year, Koch was indicted for lying
about its emissions of benzene, a chemical linked to leukemia, and
dodged criminal charges in return for a $20 million settlement with
the federal government, an inexplicably cheap price to pay. Brownback has received nearly $121,000 from Koch and its employees.
During his neck-and-neck race in 1996, a shell company called Triad
Management provided $410,000 for last-minute advertising on
Brownback's behalf. A Senate investigative committee later determined that the money came from the two brothers who run Koch
Industries.

With Brownback, it's nearly impossible to draw the line between the interests of his corporate backers and his own moral passions. Everyone applauds his fight to keep the murder of hundreds
of thousands of Sudanese refugees prioritized in U.S. foreign policy. And by standing up to the regime in Sudan, he's also sending a
warning to China, which has been willing to overlook the Sudanese
government's murderous campaign in exchange for access to the

country's oil. Of course, Koch Industries might be interested in that, too.

Is that all there is to Brownback? Cash in an envelope? No—there is not even that. A Kansas businessman who calls Brownback his friend and has known him for years told me that the de facto price of doing business with the senator—the cost of admission for a single meeting—was, last he checked, $2,000. In that, Brownback is unexceptional. Many congressmen expect just as much from those who want face time. It's not illegal, just slimy. The difference with Brownback, said the businessman, is that he never touches the money. The businessman is used to putting a check directly into the hands of the politician whose help he needs. But whenever he visited Brownback's offices, a staffer always quietly intervened, relieving the businessman of the check beyond the senator's sight lines. "Sam," the businessman told me, "doesn't talk money."

One afternoon, I met Brownback in his corner office to talk Bible. On his desk, there was a New Testament open to the Gospel of John. I sat on a sofa beneath a portrait of Mother Teresa. There was also a painting of a little blond girl in a field of sunflowers. "What can I help you with?" Brownback asked, smiling. Two scripture passages, I said. Leviticus 20:13, and Romans 1, the proof texts on which most Christian conservatives base their opposition to homosexuality. Brownback frowned. He wasn't aware of the passages. His hatred of homosexuality derived not from an engagement with scripture—which academic Bible scholars say is not actually clear on the matter—but on what he considered direct revelation. "It's pretty clear," he said, his fingers folded into a temple beneath his chin, "what we know in our hearts." Brownback calls this knowledge "natural law." To legislate against it or any other practice his heart tells him is sin is not theocratic, it's "natural."

"There's a sacredness to it," he said. He meant heterosexuality. "You look at the social impact the countries that have engaged in homosexual marriage." He shook his head in sorrow, thinking of Sweden. "You'll know 'em by their fruits." He paused, and an awkward silence filled the room. We both knew he was citing scripture—

Matthew 7:16—but he'd just declared gay Swedes "fruits." He regretted that. Hate the sinner, love the sin, Brownback believes. In the Family, he'd learned to love everybody.

Although Brownback's 2002 Catholic conversion was through Opus Dei, an ultra-orthodox order that, like the Family, specializes in cultivating the rich and powerful, the source of much of his religious and political thinking is Chuck Colson. "When I came to the Senate," Brownback remembers, "I sought him out. I had been listening to his thoughts for years, and wanted to get to know him some." The admiration was mutual. Colson spotted Brownback's potential not long after Brownback joined a Family prayer cell. At the time, Colson was holding classes on "biblical worldview" for leaders on Capitol Hill. Colson taught that abortion is a "threshold" issue, a wedge with which to introduce fundamentalism into every question. Brownback, who'd been quietly pro-choice before he went to Washington, recognized the political utility of the anti-abortion fight and developed what is now a genuine hatred for the very idea that a woman's body is her own. It is not, he learned from Colson; it belongs to God, just like that of a man, a line of reasoning by which Colson claims that his fundamentalist faith is more egalitarian than feminism, an analysis he extends beyond the womb into an implicit critique of democracy itself. The two men began coordinating their efforts: Colson provided the philosophy, and Brownback translated it into legislative action.

For all his talk of moral values, much of Brownback's real work as a senator revolves around the same kind of "quiet diplomacy" practiced by his forebears in the Family, the art of backroom dealing perfected by Senator Frank Carlson. Liberals dismiss him as a prudish hayseed from Kansas, but to do so is to underestimate both the man and the place. Brownback, like Carlson before him, is yet another wheeler-dealer from the plains, possessed of a savvy in international affairs that is faith-based and rooted in the cornfields of Kansas.

In 2002, Brownback followed his pastor onto the stage of Topeka Bible—the minister had just told a joke about Muslim terrorists and virgins—to talk about a recent trip to Israel and Jordan. Jordan, Brownback explained, matters not just spiritually but strategically. The "person of Jesus" is a key diplomatic tool in winning its coopera-tion with the United States. Brownback said he'd met with King Abdullah about starting a fellowship group, a fellowship group around the person of Jesus. It wasn't a casual suggestion. Brownback gave Abdullah the name and number of a Christian brother with whom he wanted the king to meet. Before Brownback left Jordan, Abdullah let him know that he'd made contact with the senator's man and agreed to "fellowship" with him on a regular basis. "His father, King Hus-sein," mused Brownback, "was really quite interested in Jesus, and attended the National Prayer Breakfast several times." Since then, so has Abdullah. In 2005, he came to the prayer breakfast to conduct diplomacy, so he said, with American evangelicals.

Brownback doesn't demand that everyone believe in his God—only that they bow down before Him. The senator is part holy warrior, party holy fool. The faith he wields in the public square is blunt and heavy, brass knuckles of the spirit. But his intentions are only to set people free. He is utterly sincere in his belief that his particular idea of God is as universal as his faith in the free market. The religion of his heart is that of the woman whose story led him deep into his unearthly devotion, Mother Teresa; it is a kiss for the dying. He sees no tension between his intolerance and tenderness. Indeed, their successful recon-ciliation in his political self is the miracle, the cold fusion, at the heart of the new fundamentalism, of Hallmark and hellfire. "I have seen him weep," says Colson, his own voice thick with admiration. There can be no higher praise for a man of power who proclaims his own humility.

THE FIRST DAY I met Brownback, I was to bear witness to him among his interns at a luncheon in the Senate dining room. But when his press secretary and I arrived, there were no interns. Brownback saw me, though, and led me into the Senate dining room, where the maître d' seated the three of us at a table set for eight. Brownback began speaking about his faith. Only, he called it his cancer. This wasn't a metaphor; it was a melanoma on his side he discovered in 1995. Brownback's green-black eyes opened wide. He took his jacket off. His shoulders slumped. He began to talk about "solitude," about "meditation," about the dark night of the soul.

Once, he said, he was a bad man, just any other politician, in it for himself. And then came cancer, like a message from heaven. Only at first it brought not certainty but doubt. Brownback found himself wondering, What does anything mean?

For a short spell in his youth, Brownback was a radio broadcaster. It's easy to imagine his voice on the radio dial, deep in the darkness on a Kansas highway, not preaching so much as whispering to itself across the airwaves, creating a cocoon around the listener. The Senate dining room faded into silence. I saw Hillary Clinton, but I couldn't hear her. I saw John McCain slapping backs, but he seemed very far away. The powerful and the ugly swam past us like fish in the ocean, and Brownback kept talking, completely lost in the strangely serene recollection of his former fear. The doctors scooped out a piece of his flesh, a minor procedure, but in his mind, he had lost hold of everything. He asked himself, "What have I done with my life?" The answer seemed to be nothing.

"I went in search of things," he said. "I went in search of things that are eternal," he murmured.

One night, he got up while his family was sleeping. "I remember going over my résumé." Sitting in his silent house, in the middle of the night, a scar beneath his ribs where death had, for the time being, been carved out of his body, he looked down at that piece of paper and thought, "This must be who I am." And then he thought, "What is this paper?" And then, "It's not going to last."

Brownback turned, held my gaze. "So," he said, "I burned it."

He paused. He was waiting to see if I understood. He had cleansed himself with fire. He had made himself pure.

"I'm a child of the living God," he said.

I nodded.

"You are, too," he said.

He pursed his lips as he searched the other tables. "Look." He pointed to a man across the room, a Democratic senator from Minnesota. "He's a liberal." But you know what else he is? "A beautiful child of the living God." He continued. Ted Kennedy? "A beautiful child of the living God." Hillary? Yes. Even Hillary. Especially Hillary.

Once, Brownback said, he hated Hillary Clinton. Hated her so much it hurt him. But he reached in and scooped that hate out like a cancer. Now, he loved her. She, too, is a beautiful child of the living God.

HILLARY

Hillary may well be God's beautiful child, but she's not a member of Coe's Family. Rather, I'd been told at Ivanwald, she's a "friend," less elect then a member, but more chosen than the rest of us. A fellow traveler but not a sister. Her goals are not their goals; but when on occasion they coincide, Hillary and the Family can work together. Such collaborations, as much as the endeavors of true believers such as Brownback, are a measure of the mainstreaming of American fundamentalism. The theology of Jesus plus nothing is totalitarian in scope, but diplomatic in practice. It doesn't conquer; it "infects," as Abram used to preach. Within the body politic, it doesn't confront ideas, it coexists with them, its cells multiplying by absorbing enemies rather than destroying them. It's not cancerous, it's loving. In place of conflict, love. In place of debate, love. In place of tolerance, love. In place of democracy, loudmouthed, simmering mad and crazy hopeful democracy—love, all-encompassing.

In her memoir *Living History*, Hillary describes her first encounter with the Family. It was at a lunch organized on her behalf in February 1993 at the Cedars, "an estate on the Potomac that serves as the headquarters for the National Prayer Breakfast and the prayer groups it has spawned around the world. Doug Coe, the longtime National Prayer Breakfast organizer, is a unique presence in Washington: a genuinely loving spiritual mentor and guide to anyone, regardless of party or faith, who wants to deepen his or her relationship with God."[2] Or with the kind of politically useful friends one might not make otherwise. For the eight years she lived in the White House, Clinton met regularly with a gathering of political ladies who lunch: wives of powerful men from both parties, women who put aside political differences to seek—for themselves, for their husbands' careers—an even greater power. Among Clinton's prayer partners were Susan Baker, the wife of Bush consigliere James and a board member of James Dobson's Focus on the Family; Joanne Kemp, the wife of conservative icon Jack, responsible for introducing the political theology of fundamentalist guru Francis Schaeffer to Washington; Eileen Bakke, an activist for charter schools based on "character" and the wife of Dennis Bakke, then the CEO of AES, one of the world's largest power companies; and Grace Nelson, the wife of Senator Bill Nelson, a conservative Florida Democrat. The women sent her daily scripture verses to study, and Baker, the wife of one of the Republican Party's most cutthroat strategists, provided Hillary with spiritual counsel during "political storms."

Hillary's Godtalk is more sincere than it sounds, grounded in the influence of a Methodist minister named Don Jones whom she met when he was a twenty-eight-year-old youth pastor in Park Ridge, Illinois. Jones continues to counsel Hillary to this day. He calls the theological worldview behind her politics a third way, a reaction against both old-fashioned separatist fundamentalism and the New Deal's labor-based liberalism. He describes the theology he taught as in the tradition of "Burkean conservatism," after the eighteenth-century reactionary philosopher's belief that change should be slow and come without the sort of "social leveling" that offends class hierarchy. Elites rule because they rule; tradition is its own justification, a tautology of power neither left nor right but circular.

Under Jones's mentorship, Clinton learned about theologians such as Reinhold Niebuhr and Paul Tillich. Liberals may consider Niebuhr their own, but the Niebuhr whom Hillary Rodham studied with Jones and later at Wellesley College was a Cold Warrior, dismissive of the progressive politics of his earlier writing. "He'd thought that once we were unionized, the kingdom of God would be ushered in," Jones says, explaining Niebuhr as he and Hillary came to see him. "But the effect of those two world wars and the violence that they produced shook [his] faith in liberal theology." The late Niebuhr replaced his devotion to messianic unionism with a darker view of humanity and replaced his emphasis on domestic social justice with a global realpolitik, easily hijacked by liberal hawks in rhetorical need of a justification for aggressive American power.

Tillich also enjoys a following among conservative Christian intellectuals for arguments on behalf of revising the once-radical Social Gospel to favor individual redemption, the heart of conservative evangelicalism. Hillary once said she regretted that her denomination, the Methodists, had focused too much on Social Gospel concerns—that is, the rights of the poor—"to the exclusion of personal faith and growth." Abram, once a Methodist himself, had made the very same observation a half century before. The spirit, conservative Christians believe, matters more than the flesh, and the salvation of the former should be a higher priority than that of the latter. In worldly terms, religious freedom trumps political freedom, moral values matter more than food on the table, and if might doesn't make right, it sure makes right, or wrong, easier. Taken together, Niebuhr and Tillich as Hillary encountered them represent the most reactionary elements of her "worldview": a militantly aggressive approach to foreign affairs and a domestic policy of narrow horizons. Under the spiritual tutelage of the Family, Hillary moved further rightward, drifting from traditional liberalism toward the kind of privatized social welfare the Family has favored ever since Abram reacted in horror to the New Deal.

The Reverend Rob Schenck's favorite example? Clinton's collaboration with Brownback on anti–sex trafficking legislation condemned by the very activists it should have helped. Brownback and Chuck Colson, one of the leading thinkers behind the law, were more interested in extracting pledges of purity than in helping the already fallen. That resulted in the de-funding of longtime federal partners that, for instance, provide health care for prostitutes, and increased funding for faith-based groups that simply preach Christ and abstinence to foreign sex slaves. And it's not just those who are trapped in involuntary sex work who are ill served by the switch; epidemics of sexually transmitted diseases, notoriously resistant to sermonizing, ripple out into the general population. It's bad law for everyone. But Clinton was willing to lend her name, and her fundamentalist friends noticed. "I welcome that," says Colson.

Hillary fights side-by-side with Brownback and others for legislation dedicated less to overturning the wall between church and state than to tunneling beneath it. Practically speaking, such work appeased evangelical elites without drawing the notice of liberals who thought Hillary stood for separation, but such tunnels genuinely undermine the foundations.

For instance, a law she backed to ensure "religious freedom" in the workplace that so distorts the meaning of the words that it makes even Republicans such as Senator Arlen Specter uneasy about its encroachments on First Amendment freedoms. It's a sort of Bartleby option for those "who prefer not to": pharmacists who refuse to fill birth-control prescriptions, nurses who refuse to treat gay or lesbian patients, police officers who refuse to guard abortion clinics. And then there was the passage, during Bill's presidency, of the International Religious Freedom Act, a move supported by Hillary. Like the workplace bill, it seemed sensible. Who's opposed to religious freedom? But in reality it shifted the monitoring of religion in other countries from the State Department to an independent, evangelical-dominated agency that drew much of its leadership from the Christian Legal Society, creating a platform for U.S. evangelicals to use religious freedom ratings as leverage for a sort of shadow foreign policy. Hillary's stance toward Iran, more hawkish than that of many Republicans, is just one example of a position long held by elite fundamentalists mainstreamed through the work of an ostensibly liberal ally.

Liberals, says Clinton's prayer partner Grace Nelson, are welcome in the Family as long as they submit to "the person of Jesus." Jesus, not ideology, "is what gives us power." But the Jesus preached by the Family is ideology personified. For all of the Family's talk of Jesus as a person, he remains oddly abstract in the teachings they derive from him, a mix of "free market" economics, aggressive American internationalism, and "leadership" as a fetishized term for power, a good in itself regardless of its ends. By eschewing the politics of the moment—party loyalties and culture wars—Family cells cultivate an ethos of elite unity that allows long-term political transformation, whereby political rivals aren't flipped but won over gradually through fellowship with former enemies, as in the case of former Representative Tony Hall.

Hall, one of the few Democrats appointed by Bush in his first term (he was made ambassador to the UN for hunger issues, a position he used to push the Monsanto corporation's genetically modified crops onto African nations) was brought into the Family in the 1980s by Jerry Regier, an ultra-right Reagan administration official in the Department of Health and Human Services who went on to work with James Dobson. Upon his conversion, Hall abandoned his liberal social views and became a vocal opponent of abortion and, eventually, same-sex marriage. He also championed a bill establishing a National Day of Prayer with an event at the White House organized by Dobson's wife, Shirley. But he didn't switch parties, and the Family would never ask him to. Hall isn't a Republican; he's a Democrat who called on his fellow party members to follow President Bush's example by injecting more religion into their rhetoric. Hillary did just that in 2007, boasting of the "prayer warriors" who carried her through Bill's infidelities, a bit of spiritual warfare jargon instantly recognizable to evangelicals who worried about her feminism.[3]

The Family wants to "transcend" left and right with a faith that consumes politics, replacing fundamental differences with the unity to be found in submission to religious authority. Conservatives sit pretty in prayer and wait for liberals looking for "common ground" to come to them in search of compromise. Hillary, Rob Schenck noted, became a regular visitor to the Family's C Street House in 2005. "She needs that nucleus of energy that the Coe camp produces." That summer, she appeared as part of a threesome that shocked old school fundamentalists: Bill, Hillary, and Billy, live in New York for Graham's last crusade. Before tens of thousands, the patriarch of Christian conservatism said Bill "ought to let his wife run the country." Bonhomie and cheap blessing, maybe, but it was the kind of endorsement that Bill never won, despite Graham's custom of speaking sweet nothings to power.

A Thing and Its Shadow

How much power can a movement have if it's sufficiently vague in its principles to encompass both Sam Brownback and Hillary Clinton? If measured only according to the advocates of domestic "moral values" who choose fights in part for the clarity of their "sides"—abortion, yes or no? homosexuality, yes or no?—it would seem like the Family doesn't have much influence at all. Neither abortion nor sex will be legislated away soon. But the fact that fundamentalism, a faith that by definition aims to address the totality of human experience, is measured according to a handful of issues decided by a yea or a nay is, itself, evidence of the broad success of Abram's Idea.

Following the Scopes trial of 1925, American fundamentalism split in two. One branch busied itself with the creation of new institutions, Bible colleges, and "parachurch" ministries, the foundation for a populist faith that could stand on its own in the face of secular ridicule—often enough, a real problem—and fight for control of the public sphere. The second, elite branch concerned itself with what believers saw as threats to the nation itself. That was a move that conflated the nation with the faith. This new civil religion was what enabled Cold Warriors, liberal as well as conservative, to project the shadow of American freedom around the globe.

But a thing and its shadow are not the same. Even as American power fueled nightmares in Vietnam, in Indonesia, in Haiti, in dozens of other nations whose histories disappeared into the blob of the Cold War, real freedom has endured and even prospered within the borders of the United States. It's the relatively bright prospects of domestic democracy—even at its most endangered moments—that have blinded us to the shadow it casts. "Freedom," more than one general has declared from the pulpit of the National Prayer Breakfast, comes at a cost. Liberals scoff at such an apparent oxymoron, but the lesson of elite fundamentalism is that it's true; for that matter, the last seventy years of history prove even the Christian doctrine of blood atonement. Only, the blood is not Christ's, and despite the very notable exception of tens of thousands of American soldiers killed overseas, it's not ours, either. It's the rest of the world that pays for American fundamentalism's sins, and for the failure of American liberalism to even recognize the fundamentalist faith with which it has all too often—in Vietnam, in Indonesia, in Haiti—made common cause.

We might quibble that point. We might ask, Which came first, American fundamentalism or the Cold War? Is American fundamentalism the essence of the economic policies by which we unraveled the New Deal, or is it simply a coincidental phenomenon of the Reagan Revolution and then "globalization"? Don't the good intentions with which America gives billions in foreign aid for food for the starving and medicine for the sick and, yes, weapons for governments that actually use them in defense mitigate—outweigh, even— the trillions spent on weapons for governments that put them to other ends, and the uncountable sums reaped by corporations dependent on the American global order? Then again, how different are such questions from that of Greg Unumb, the Family oilman who thought Doug Coe's culpability in the crimes of the killers for whom he served as a matchmaker depended entirely on whether they killed *before* or *during* their fellowship with Coe? Such a strange concern. As if one might be excused for giving a gun to a mass murderer because his first victims were already buried; as if Christ's injunction to forgive demanded also that we forget. That is, in fact, exactly what the Family believes, the complexities of "reconciliation" reduced to a gross equivalence of sins. The center slouches rightward, and the faithful forget that anyone ever dreamed otherwise.

Dick Halverson preached as much once during his tenure as Senate chaplain. He framed it as a story relayed to him by Coe and Senator

Harold Hughes after a visit to the Philippines, during which he, in turn, heard the story from the Philippines' Archbishop Jaime Cardinal Sin.[4] Archbishop Sin was a moderate with a mixed record in relation to the Marcos regime; at its end, he helped lead the "People Power" revolution, but for years before that he preached obedience to dictatorship. "He told Harold and Doug this true story," Halverson sermonized. One of Sin's nuns said to him that Jesus was coming to her bed at night. Sin decided to test the apparition. "Ask Him"— Halverson, the old actor, pretended to be the Filipino clergyman— "What sins did the archbishop commit before he became an archbishop?" The nun did so and reported back to Sin. Christ's answer? "I can't remember."

Did this suggest to Sin or Halverson that the nun had simply been dreaming? Just the opposite. Their Christ did not just forgive the sins of Archbishop Sin; he couldn't remember them. That, Halverson thought, was as it should be, Christ's mercy not a balance to justice but a gift for the powerful. The church loves the down and out, but who loves the up and out? Jesus of the Family, the Christ of Coe's "social order."

"Love," preached Halverson, "forgets. That's what God does with your sin and mine when it's under the Blood. He forgets all about it."

HERE'S ONE LAST Family story love forgot, from a country so blighted by misfortune and misrule that it's not really a country anymore. Somalia, lost in the shadow of American fundamentalism's freedom. Somalia—one of the last cases I found in the Family's archives before they began closing them—is, in the correspondence I retrieved, nothing more than a web of "facts" that I'm hard-pressed to make sense of. What they add up to is too bleak, too broken. The dead who haunt the name of Siad Barre, the dictator Coe called "brother," seem uncountable. All I can be sure about is the answer to the question Greg Unumb asked me when I told him about Coe's support for another dictator guilty of murder: *before* or *during*? Before, during, after. I will relate the facts as briefly as I can.[5]

Somalia, shaped like an upside-down musical note, wraps around the Horn of Africa, across from the Arabian Peninsula. Granted independence in 1960, it should have been a success story; its people were linguistically unified and, while poor, were heirs to a tradition of pastoral democracy that had survived colonialism roughly intact. Then General Siad Barre seized power in 1969, and the Soviet Union poured money into Siad's regime to make it a counterweight to Ethiopia, which under Emperor Selassie was the major beneficiary of American military aid in Africa. When a Marxist coup overthrew the Ethiopian emperor, Siad saw a chance to distract his own discontented people by seizing part of Ethiopia in its moment of weakness, using his Soviet-armed military. But the Soviets backed now-communist Ethiopia, deeming its new regime more useful than duplicitous Siad, who announced that he was in the market for a new patron. After the Iranian Revolution overthrew the Shah, the U.S. puppet just across the water from Somalia, the United States put its money on Siad and his ports, which would become essential if Ayatollah Khomeini cut off the oil supply. By late 1980, the United States and the USSR had switched proxies: once-red Somalia had become an American outpost, while Ethiopia had turned into a Soviet satellite.

It would have been absurd if it hadn't been so bloody. Siad, freed from even his veneer of socialism, devolved from an autocrat into the worst thing that had ever happened to Somalia. His heroes, he declared, were Kim Jong Il and the Romanian dictator Nicolae Ceau-şescu. He decided to allow American-style democracy, then killed his opposition as well as those he suspected of opposing him, and those who might grow up to be opponents. His secret police developed techniques to spy even on nomads. He sent his troops to machine-gun their herds. He poisoned their wells. For his urban enemies, he developed torture chambers he considered world-class, and his men concluded that rape proved especially productive of useful information.

To his neighbors, he preached the virtues of the United States, but his creed was "Koranic Marxism," illustrated by a triptych of portraits hung throughout the nation depicting Marx, Lenin, and Siad as the new Muhammad. His official portrait shows him as a young general in a khaki uniform and a mustache he seems to have copied from Hitler. He bombed more civilians than rebels, reduced an entire city to rubble, and directed his air force to strafe refugees. He turned his country into a garden of land mines that continue to blossom to this day.

Before Coe found Siad through a West German Bundestag member, Siad waged war on Ethiopia. *After* they met, he waged war on his own nation. For the past seventeen years, there has been no nation, only war. If Coe ever said a word about the killings, it was not recorded in the documents I found. "I don't wish to embarrass people," Coe said of his relationships with dictators in 2007. "I don't take positions. The only thing I do is bring people together."

In 1981, Family members made contact with Siad on behalf of his then-enemy, Kenyan dictator Daniel arap Moi—a brutal American ally—whom Siad agreed to meet. The Family took this news to General David Jones, chairman of the Joint Chiefs of Staff (and a Family member), who in thanks invited Siad to the Pentagon, a visit that resulted in a special breakfast in America for the dictator, with General Jones, members of congress, and Department of Defense officials. In 1983, Coe arranged for the dictator his own international prayer cell, which included the Bundestag member, Rudolf Decker; a defense contractor, William K. Brehm; and the outgoing chairman of the Joint Chiefs of Staff. A year later Coe strengthened Siad's hand by proposing Mogadishu as the site for a "fellowship meeting" with two other anti-Soviet dictators, arap Moi and Gaafar Nimeiry of Sudan.

From America, Coe sent Siad Senator Chuck Grassley, ultraright Iowa Republican (still serving as of 2008). But Coe was distracted; his twenty-seven-year-old son, Jonathan, was fighting lymphoma. He rallied, though—Doug, that is—when he put Christ's social order before his father, his mother, his brother, his sister, and even his own grief to use what must have been one of the saddest days of his life to reach out to the general: "You are much in my thoughts today," wrote

Coe. "Jonathan my son to whom you were so kind died this morning. You influenced his life for God and he never forgot you."

"I did not have the occasion to meet him," Siad wrote by way of condolences.

A document titled "Siad Barre's Somalia and the USA," prepared for the Family and marked "Very Confidential," is one of the rare Family documents to move beyond what Elgin Groseclose called "the facade of brotherhood." It is undated but appears to have been written near the beginning of the relationship. Siad, it begins, is the only head of state to have expelled the Soviets, and the only regional leader to offer "full military, air, and naval bases." He pledges, too, to provide for a pro-American successor, and to purge his government of all officials linked to Somalia's former patron, excepting himself, presumably. Then he notes that he has already supplied the Pentagon with a list of armaments he needed to fight the Cubans. Received.

In 1983, Somalia's minister of defense went to Washington at Coe's invitation to meet with the new chairman of the joint chiefs, General John J. Vessey. The United States nearly doubled military aid to the regime, pouring guns into a country that before the decade was out would achieve a moment of unity it has not seen since, when nearly everyone—politicians, warlords, children—united in opposition to Siad. He fled in 1991, taking refuge in Kenya with arap Moi. One of his last acts as Somalia's key man was to scorch as much of his enemy's land as he could, a biblical punishment for a nation that had resisted God's appointed authority. Three hundred thousand died in the famine that followed. It's considered Siad's legacy. It was also the Family's gift to Somalia.

ON ONE OF my last days at Ivanwald, a group of brothers returned from a trip to the movies. They'd gone to see *Black Hawk Down*, the story of nineteen American soldiers killed in 1993 in a battle with one of the Somali militias that have terrorized the country for most of the seventeen years since Siad's downfall. The movie had made such an impression on the brothers that Jeff C., one of the house leaders, decided to convene the boys to talk about the responsibilities of followers of Christ. Some of the men took a hard lesson from the film: you can't help savages. But Jeff C. corrected them. There was an international crew there at the time—men from Ecuador, Paraguay, the Czech Republic, Benin—but this, Jeff C. knew, was an American affair. "We help people," he said. "That's what we do. Even if they're, I don't know, 'savages.' We'll just keep loving on 'em."

Doug Coe did not pull any triggers in Somalia, did not poison any wells, and the Family was not one of the warring clans that obliterated what was left of the nation's infrastructure. For all the Family's talk of the "man-method," of "relationships," its members did not know Somalia very well. They treated it as a piece on a playing board. This Somalia wanted friends in Washington, so the Family became Somalia's friend. This Somalia wanted guns, so the Family helped it get guns. This Somalia wanted to be called "brother," so the Family called Siad Barre "brother." Families, as Coe would be the first to point out, are about love. Not accountability, ultimately, and there does not seem to have been any for Brother Siad.

Jesus plus nothing, remember, does not depend on scripture, its nuances, its hard lessons. Jesus plus nothing does not include, for instance, the ninth verse of the fourth chapter of the Book of Genesis. God asks Cain, who has just murdered Abel, where his brother is. "I do not know," replies Cain. "Am I my brother's keeper?" It's a genuinely difficult question. God never answers it directly, instead responding with what sounds like divine distress: "What have you done?" To Cain's existentialism, God answers with a demand for history. That's a more straightforward query, one I've attempted to answer with regard to the Family. But Cain's question, that one's too hard for me. To one who proclaims fellowship, as do the members of the Family, the answer is simple: "Yes, I am my brother's keeper." That was Jeff C.'s answer. But the Family has more often served as an accomplice, not a keeper. Where does that leave the rest of us? The

Family works through the men and women we put in power. Sam Brownback. Hillary Clinton. Pick your poison. In the calculus of party politics, these two do occupy distant coordinates, but in the geometry of power politics, the Family knows, they are on the same plane, and the distance between them is shrinking. They mean well, both of them, and I'm more partial to the views of one of them, but I can't help looking at that narrowing spectrum and thinking, This is an awful tight space into which to fit a democracy.

III.
THE POPULAR FRONT

INTERLUDE

Every revolutionary class must wage war on the cultural front.

—LEWIS COREY, *THE DECLINE OF AMERICAN CAPITALISM* (1934)

L EWIS COREY, A JOURNALIST and radical political theorist who
helped fight just such a battle, saw the shape, if not the tone, of
the future. I first learned about Corey in a history of the United
States' original *cultural front,* an alliance of radical workers, artists,
and intellectuals that briefly flourished in the 1930s, guided by Stalin's invisible hand, and then was thought to have disappeared. Or so
held conventional wisdom, until Yale scholar Michael Denning discovered that the cultural politics of those years were an unstable mix
of totalitarian influence and wild diversity that didn't dead-end with
the close of the decade. Rather, the cultural front of the 1930s flowed
into postwar American life in diluted but more widespread form.
The cultural front—the spirit of a more tightly defined "Popular
Front" of antifascist political parties, sects, and factions—transformed
class politics in America: it gave classes a sense of themselves as
struggling over not just wages but also ideas, aesthetics, rituals, cus-
toms, the imagination of things to come.[1]

The idea of "classes" disappeared from America following World
War II, absorbed into the great blob of the Cold War. And yet a cultural front survived. The evidence? The so-called culture war fought
to this day between fundamentalism and secularism.

That American fundamentalism contains within it a multitude of beliefs, impulses, traditions, politics—just a few of which have been explored here—must lead us to question the other side of the battle. Secularism, of course, conceives of itself as rational and thus open to all empirical data. And yet it, too, is subject to the broad brush with which it's easiest to paint social conditions. *Culture war* was a label created by conservative elites who wanted to demand of the public the old question of union battles: which side are you on? But the lesson of elite fundamentalism is that the sides are not just blurry; they're interwoven.

The Cold War liberalism that led to American wars and proxy wars, for example, ran parallel with elite fundamentalism's sense of its own divine universalism. The Family's Worldwide Spiritual Offensive infused America's global mission—the economic reconstruction of Western Europe and the militaristic destruction of Southeast Asia alike—and that imperial project in turn sparked the imaginations of elite fundamentalists, providing them with an alternative to traditional fundamentalist separatism. Domestically, the establishment practice of containing political argument within such narrow confines that most Americans could barely conceive of the radicalisms, left and right, that shape politics throughout the rest of the world sat comfortably with the desire of elite fundamentalists for a politics of no politics. The results include elections based on "character" rather than ideas, debates as rituals meant to result in reconciliation, the consensus of the powerful represented as a reasonable process in which everyone gets some small piece of the action. We call this "compromise," and consider our democracy healthy.

During the 1960s and early 1970s, it was the Left that recognized that American democracy was drifting toward empire, and that the democratic project had never been anywhere near complete to begin with. Since then, it has been the Right that discerned the cracks in democracy's veneer and the hollowness behind it. From that perception arose the conservative movement that declared culture war. Culture war as a slogan may be relatively new, but we can easily identify its antecedents on the San Francisco docks in 1934, or with Jonathan

Edwards sitting beside Abigail Hutchinson's bed in Northampton in 1735. In both cases—and now—culture war revolves around an implicit critique of what Abram called "materialism."

Edwards saw as his enemy the unwitting banality of the American business society, fools who did not realize that they dangled over an abyss. Harry Bridges and the men and women whom he fought beside in San Francisco were all too aware of the abyss; they saw as their enemy the economic system that held them precariously suspended above it. The populist fundamentalism that in the late 1970s marched into the public square railed against the same familiar enemy, but now defined entirely as *secularism*. What does secularism do, according to this fundamentalist front? It cheapens life, it sells sex, it puts a price tag on the human soul. It makes people into commodities. And who will oppose this godless deviltry? "Followers of Christ," a term that requires quotes to distinguish it from the much broader category of those who believe in or are born into one of the many Christian traditions no longer considered valid by the new fundamentalists. Followers of Christ—those who cleave to a unique American fundamentalism—define themselves more sharply. They are a class, a revolutionary one, no less, dedicated, in theory at least, to the transformation of American life and thus the world.

But they're vague on the details. They'd like to abolish abortion, and they'd like to pray in school and do away with pornography, and drive queer people back into the closet (or "cure" them, say the optimists among them). And then what? What about hunger, poverty, the greed and blindness that drives global warming? All important concerns, concede American fundamentalism's elites and populist champions. Would the steps they've proposed bring an end to the commodification of bodies, the pricing of souls, a culture in which dollars pass for ideas? Hardly. But the believers, the fundamentalists, those who would reshape society along lines of their idea of Christ's order, have no further solutions. They are a cultural front without a politics. Where once there was a critique of what some might call godlessness and others might call capitalism, there is a vacuum. And in that empty space, the status quo remains unthreatened. Secular democracy, such as it is, faces no serious challenge. Nor, for that matter, does the elite fundamentalism that for the last seventy years has coexisted alongside it, ensuring that the United States was never fully secular, nor democratic.

The story so far has been about how elite fundamentalism has shaped domestic and foreign politics, how a theocratic strand ran through the "American century" and remains taut in the new one. Now the story turns inward, into the lives of ordinary Americans, toward the cultural front of fundamentalism. It's this cultural front, converging with the political project of elite fundamentalism, that justifies the label of "Popular Front." In the United States in the twenty-first century, the Popular Front is that of fundamentalism, the faith that promises that you can be born again, that miracles still occur, that we might yet revive the nation. This Popular Front will no more rebuild the economic and structural foundations of America or its soft empire than did that of the 1930s, but it has already transformed the way we think, the way we live, the way we feel, the way we know ourselves and the world.

Culture war, then, is a misleading term for such a metamorphosis. What the elite and populist movements of American fundamentalism have together wrought is not a culture war but a cultural evolution, one that is adapting to the twenty-first century much faster than secularism. This religion isn't an opiate of the masses; it's the American Christ on methamphetamine.

11.

WHAT EVERYBODY WANTS

T HEY ARE DRAWN AS if by magnetic forces; they speak of Colorado Springs, home to the greatest concentration of fundamentalist activist groups in American history, both as a last stand and as a
kind of utopia in the making. They say it is new and unique and precious, embattled by enemies, and also that it is "traditional," a blueprint for what everybody wants, and envied by enemies. The city
itself is unspectacular, a grid of wide western avenues lined with
squat, gray and beige box buildings, only a handful of them taller
than a dozen stories. Local cynics point out that if you put Colorado
Springs on a truck and carted it to Nebraska, it would make Omaha
look lovely. But the architecture is not what draws Christians looking
for clean living. The mountains help, but there are other mountain
towns. What Colorado Springs offers, finally, is a story.

Lori Rose is from Minnesota and heard rumors about this holy
city when she lived on an air force base near Washington, D.C. Her
husband isn't a Christian, refuses Jesus, looks at things he shouldn't;
but she has found a church to attend without him. "I want a relationship like my relationship with God," she says. "It's almost like
an affair." Ron Poelstra came from Los Angeles. Now he volunteers
at his church, selling his pastor's books on "free-market theology"
after services. His two teenage boys stand behind him, display
models for the benefits of faith. They fold their hands in front of
themselves and both smile whenever Ron glances their way. L.A.,
Ron says, would have eaten them up: the gangs. Adam Taylor grew

up in Westchester County, an heir to the Bergdorf Goodman fortune, the son of artists and writers, a prince of the city. He lived the life of Augustine, and it nearly killed him. He came to Colorado Springs to learn the Bible the hard way, each word a nail pounded into sin. Now he's a pastor, and the Bible doesn't hurt anymore.[1]

The story they found in Colorado Springs is about newness: new houses, new roads, new stores. And about oldness, imagined: what is thought to be the traditional way of life, families as they were after the world wars, before the culture wars, which is to say, during the brief, Cold War moment when America was a nation of single-breadwinner nuclear families.

Crime, of course, looms over this story. Not the actual facts of it—the burglary rate in and around Colorado Springs exceeds that in New York City and Los Angeles—but the idea of it: a faith in the absence of crime. And of politics, too: Colorado Springs' fundamentalists believe they live in a politics-free zone, a carved-out space for civility and for like-minded dedication to commonsense principles. Even pollution plays a part: Christian conservatives there believe that they breathe cleaner air, despite the smog that collects against the foothills of the Rockies and the cyanide, from a century of mining, that is leaching into the aquifers and mountain streams.

But those are facts, and Colorado Springs is a city of faith. A shining city at the foot of a hill. No one there believes it is perfect. And no one is so self-centered as to claim the perfection of Colorado Springs as his or her ambition. The shared vision is more modest, and more grandiose. It is a city of people who have fled the cities, people who have fought a spiritual war for the ground they are on, for an interior frontier on which they have built new temples to the Lord. From these temples they will retake their forsaken promised lands, remake them in the likeness of a dream. They call the dream *Christian,* but in its particulars it is *American,* populated by cowboys and Indians, monsters and prayer warriors to slay them, and ladies to reward the warriors with chaste kisses. Colorado Springs is a city of moral fabulousness. It is a city of fables.

THE CITY'S MIGHTIEST megachurch crests silver and blue atop a gentle slope of pale yellow prairie grass on the outskirts of town. Silver and blue, as it happens, are the air force colors. New Life Church was built far north of town in part so it could be seen from the Air Force Academy. New Life wanted that kind of character in its congregation.[2]

Church is insufficient to describe the complex. There is a permanent structure called the Tent, which regularly fills with hundreds or thousands of teens and twentysomethings for New Life's various youth gatherings. Next to the Tent stands the old sanctuary, a gray box capable of seating 1,500; this juts out into the new sanctuary, capacity 7,500, already too small. At the complex's western edge is the World Prayer Center, which looks like a great iron wedge driven into the plains. The true architectural wonder of New Life, however, isn't a physical structure but the pyramid of authority into which it orders its roughly 12,000 members. At the base are 1,300 cell groups, whose leaders answer to section leaders, who answer to zone, who answer to district, who used to answer to Pastor Ted Haggard, New Life's founder.

In late 2006, Pastor Ted achieved a notoriety that surpassed the fame he had won as a preacher, when a middle-aged prostitute named Mike Jones played for the press answering machine messages from a regular client of his, "Art," whom Jones had just learned was Ted Haggard, one of the most powerful fundamentalist leaders in the country. That wasn't all. It turned out that Pastor Ted had been using methamphetamine—speed—as well. At first, Ted denied everything; but there was too much evidence, and he soon resigned. Since then, Ted, married and a father, has been "healed," according to a panel of fundamentalist leaders charged with his cure; he is now "100 percent heterosexual." But he is not back in his pulpit. And yet the

pulpit itself—the fundamentalist experiment known as New Life—
endures. Pastor Ted's ideas survive, even prosper, for Ted's downfall
was taken by many within his congregation as evidence of the great
works he had been doing. So great, that is, that the Enemy, Satan
himself, targeted Ted above all others. The two antigay initiatives on
the 2006 ballot, which Jones hoped to defeat by outing Ted's hypocrisy, passed with greater support than their backers—including
Ted—had imagined possible.

When I met him, Pastor Ted was a handsome forty-eight-year-
old Indianan transplanted to Colorado, a casual man most comfortable in denim. He insisted he was an ordinary man, in an ordinary
church, in an ordinary city. On the other hand, he also wanted me to
know that he talked to George W. Bush in a conference call every
Monday. He liked to say that his only disagreement with the president was automotive; Bush drove a Ford pickup, whereas Pastor Ted
loved his Chevy. At the time, Pastor Ted presided over the National
Association of Evangelicals, whose 45,000 churches and 30 million
believers make up the nation's most powerful religious lobbying
group. The NAE had come a long way since its creation in 1942,
when its leaders had to ask Abram for help in making contact with
U.S. government officials. Under Pastor Ted, the NAE was a force
unto itself, no longer in need of favors from anyone.

Under Ted, the NAE made its headquarters in Colorado Springs.
Some believers call the city the "Wheaton of the West," in honor of
Wheaton, Illinois, once the headquarters of a more genteel Christian
conservatism. Others call Colorado Springs the "evangelical Vatican," a nickname that says much both about the city and about the
easeful orthodoxy with which the movement now views itself. Certainly the gathering there has no parallel in this country, not in
Lynchburg, Virginia, nor Tulsa, nor Pasadena, nor Orlando, nor any
other city that has aspired to be the capital of evangelical America.
Fundamentalist activist groups and parachurch ministries in Colorado Springs number in the hundreds. Groups migrate there and
multiply. They produce missionary guides, "family resources," school
curricula, financial advice, athletic training programs, Bibles for

every occasion. The city is home to Young Life, to the Navigators, to Compassion International; to Every Home for Christ and Global Ethnic Missions (Youth Ablaze). Most prominent among the ministries is Dr. James Dobson's Focus on the Family, whose radio programs (the most extensive in the world, religious or secular), magazines, videos, and books reach more than 200 million people worldwide. It was Pastor Ted who persuaded Dobson to relocate from Pasadena to Colorado Springs, where his operation is so vast it earned its own zip code.

Whereas Dobson plays the part of national scold, promising to destroy politicians who defy the Bible, Pastor Ted quietly guided those politicians through the ritual of acquiescence required to save face. He didn't strut, like Dobson; he gushed. When Bush invited him to the Oval Office to discuss policy with seven other chieftains of the Christian Right in late 2003, Pastor Ted regaled his congregation with the story via e-mail. "Well, on Monday I was in the World Prayer Center"—New Life's high-tech, twenty-four-hour-a-day prayer chapel—"and my cell phone rang." It was a presidential aide. The president, said Pastor Ted, wanted him on hand for the signing of the Partial-Birth Abortion Ban Act. Pastor Ted was on a plane the next morning and in the president's office the following afternoon. "It was incredible," wrote Pastor Ted. He left it to the press to note that Dobson wasn't there.[3]

Moreover, it was Pastor Ted, not Dobson—a child psychologist with a Ph.D.—who proved most comfortable in the secular atmosphere of Washington politics, where he was as likely to lobby for his views on international trade negotiations as on sexual morality. In Ted, the populist and elite strands of American fundamentalism had merged. At the height of his power, no pastor in America held more sway over the political direction of fundamentalism than did Pastor Ted, and no church more than New Life. It was by no means the largest megachurch, but New Life was a crucible for the ideas that inspire the movement. Fundamentalism is as much an intellectual as an emotional movement; and what Pastor Ted built in Colorado Springs was not just a battalion of spiritual warriors but a factory for ideas to arm them.

New Life began with a prophecy. In November 1984, a missionary friend of Pastor Ted's named Danny Ost—known for his gifts of discernment—asked Ted to pull over on a bend of Highway 83 as they were driving, somewhat aimlessly, in the open spaces north of the city. Pastor Ted—then twenty-eight, married, father to Christy and Marcus, given to fasting and oddly pragmatic visions (he believes he foresaw Internet prayer networks before the Internet existed)— had been wondering why God had called him to this bleak city, then known as a "pastor's graveyard." Ost got out of the car and squinted. "This," said the missionary, "this will be your church. Build here."[4]

So Pastor Ted did. First, he started a church in his basement. The pulpit was three five-gallon buckets stacked one atop the other, and the pews were lawn chairs. A man who lived in a trailer came round if he remembered it was Sunday and played guitar. Another man got the Spirit and filled a five-gallon garden sprayer with cooking oil and began anointing nearby intersections, then streets and buildings all over town. Pastor Ted told his flock to focus their prayers on houses with For Sale signs so that more Christians would come and join them.

He was always on the lookout for spies. At the time, Colorado Springs was a small city split between the air force and the New Age, and the latter, Pastor Ted believed, worked for the devil. Pastor Ted soon began upsetting the devil's plans. He staked out gay bars, inviting men to come to his church;[5] his whole congregation pitched itself into invisible battles with demonic forces, sometimes in front of public buildings. One day, while Pastor Ted was working in his garage, a woman who said she'd been sent by a witches' coven tried to stab him with a five-inch knife she pulled from a leg sheath; Pastor Ted wrestled the blade out of her hand. He let that story get around. He called the evil forces that dominated Colorado Springs—and every other metropolitan area in the country—*Control.*

Sometimes, he says, Control would call him late on Saturday night, threatening to kill him. "Any more impertinence out of you, Ted Haggard," he claims Control once told him, "and there will be unrelenting pandemonium in this city." No kidding! Pastor Ted hadn't come to Colorado Springs for his health; he had come to wage "spiritual war."[6]

He moved the church to a strip mall. There was a bar, a liquor store, New Life Church, a massage parlor. His congregation spilled out and blocked the other businesses. He set up chairs in the alley. He strung up a banner: SIEGE THIS CITY FOR ME, signed JESUS.[7] He assigned everyone in the church names, taken from the phone book, they were to pray for. He sent teams to pray in front of the homes of supposed witches—in one month, ten out of fifteen of his targets put their houses on the market.[8] His congregation "prayer-walked" nearly every street of the city.

Population boomed, crime dipped; Pastor Ted believed that New Life helped chase the bad out of town. His church grew so fast there were times when no one knew how many members to claim. So they stopped talking about "members." There was just New Life. "Are you New Life?" a person might ask. New Life moved into some corporate office space. Soon it bought the land that had been prophesied, thirty-five acres, and began to build what Pastor Ted promised would be a new Jerusalem.

JERUSALEM, COLORADO. To the east is sky, empty land, Kansas. To the west, Pike's Peak, 14,110 feet above sea level, king of a jagged skyline of the lower forty-eight states' tallest mountains. The old city core of Colorado Springs withers into irrelevance thirteen miles south; New Life leads the charge north, toward fusion with Denver and Boulder and a future of one giant front-range suburb, a muddy wave of big-box stores and beige tract houses eddying along roads so new they had yet to be added to the gas-station map I bought. Sunday mornings, traffic backs up from the church half a mile in all four directions. When parents finally pull into a space amid the thousands of cars packed into a gray ocean of lot, their kids tumble out and dash toward the five silver pillars of the entrance to New Life, eager to slide across the expanse of tiled floor, run circles around *The Defender,* a massive bronze of a glowering angel, its muscular wings in full flex, and bound up the stairs to "Fort Victory," whose rooms are designed to look like an Old West cavalry outpost where soldiers once battled real live Indians, back when Colorado still had Indians to conquer and convert.

There were no kids in Fort Victory on my first Sunday at New Life, the first Sunday of the year. It was a special day, "Dedication," the spiritual anointing of the church's new sanctuary. Metallic and modern, laced with steel girders and catwalks, the sanctuary is built like two great satellite dishes clapped belly to belly. It was designed, I was told, to "beam" prayer across the land. (New Lifers always turn to metaphors to describe their church and their city, between which they make little distinction. It is like a "training camp" in that its young men and women go forth on "missions." It is like a "bomb" in that it "explodes," "gifting" the rest of us with its fallout: revival, which is to say, "values," which is to say, "the Word," which is to say, as so many there do, "a better way of life.")

At the heart of the sanctuary rises a four-sided stage, on either side of which are two giant cross-shaped swimming pools with mechanical covers. Above the stage a great assemblage of machinery hovers, wrapped in six massive video screens. A woman near me compared it to Ezekiel's vision of a metallic angel, circular and "full of eyes all around." When the lights went down and the screens buzzed to life, the sanctuary turned a soft, silvery blue. Then the six screens filled with faces of tribute, paying homage to New Life and Pastor Ted: a senator, a congressman, Colorado's lieutenant governor, the city's mayor, and Tony Perkins, Dobson's enforcer on Capitol Hill; denominational chieftains, such as Thomas E. Trask, "general superintendent" of the 51 million worldwide members of the Assemblies of God; and a succession of minor nobles from the nation's megachurches. These I know now by numbers: Church of the Highlands, in Alabama—pastored by a New Life alumnus—that has grown from 34 to 2,500 souls in the last four years; a New Life look-alike in Biddeford, Maine, that has multiplied to 5,000; Rocky Mountain Calvary, the New Life neighbor that has swelled in a decade from a handful to 6,000.

Kyle Fisk, then the executive administrator of the National Association of Evangelicals, had guided me to a seat in the front row, which meant I had to crane my neck back ninety degrees to follow the video screen above me. The worship band, dressed in black, goateed or soul-patched or shag-headed, lay flat on their backs, staring straight up. To my right sat a middle-aged woman in a floor-length flower-print dress with shades of orange and brown. Her hair was thick, chestnut, wavy, her face big-boned and raw and beautiful, her eyelids electric blue with eyeshadow when she closed them in prayer, her eyes dark and wide as she tilted her head back to watch the tributes roll past. Her mouth hung open.

The band stood. A skinny, chinless man with a big, tenor voice, Ross Parsley, directed the musicians and the crowd, leading us and them and the choir as the guitarists kicked on the fuzz and the drummer pounded the music toward arena-rock frenzy. Two fog machines on each side of the stage filled the sanctuary with white clouds. Pod-shaped projectors cast a light show across the ceiling, giant spinning white snowflakes and cartwheeling yellow flowers and a shimmering blue water-effect. "Prepare the way!" shouted Worship Pastor Ross. "Prepare the way! The King is coming!" A man in a suit in the eastern front row shuddered and shot his right foot forward and fell into a kickboxing match with the air, keeping time with the rhythm. Across the stage teens began leaping straight up, a dance that swept across the arena: kids hopped; old men hopped; middle-aged women hopped. Spinners wheeled out from the ranks and danced like dervishes around the stage. The dark-eyed woman next to me swayed, her hips filling one side of her dress, then the other, her hands waving like sea grass. The light pods dilated and blasted the sanctuary with red. Worship Pastor Ross roared, *Let the King of Glory enter in!* The woman beside me screamed, fell down to her knees, rocked back and forth until her arms slid out before her and her forehead tapped the carpeted floor. The guitars thickened the fuzz, and ushers rushed through the crowds throwing out rainbow glow strings, glow necklaces, glow crowns. The arena went dark, and 8,000 New Lifers danced with their glow strings, like a giant bowl of rainbow sorbet.

White light flared, blinding us, and then disappeared, leaving us in darkness again. Fog pumped out double-time. We would have been lost had it not been for the blue video glow of the six big screens. All heads tilted upward again. Watching the screens, we moved in slow motion through prairie grass. A voiceover announced, "The heart of God, beating in our hearts." Then the music and video quickened as the camera rose to meet the new sanctuary. The woman beside me gasped. Images spliced and jumped over one another: thousands of New Lifers holding candles, and dozens skydiving, and Pastor Ted, Bible in hand, blond head thrust forward above the Good Book, smiling, finger-shaking, singing, more smiling, filling half of his face with perfect white teeth. His nose is snubby and his brow overhung, lending him an impishness crucial to the smile's success; without that edge he would look not happy but stoned. Now Pastor Ted, wearing a puffy ski jacket in red, white, and blue, took us to the suburban ranch house where he stayed on his fateful visit to Colorado Springs; then on to another suburban ranch house, nearly indistinguishable, where he made plans for the church. Then to a long succession of one-story corporate office spaces and strip-mall storefronts, the "sanctuaries" Pastor Ted rented as his congregation grew, each identical to the last but for the greater floor space.

The lights came up. Pastor Ted, now before us in the flesh, introduced a guest speaker, one of his mentors, Jack Hayford, founding pastor of the ten-thousand-strong Church On The Way, in Van Nuys, California. Hayford is a legend among evangelicals, one of the men responsible for the revival that made *Bible-believing* churches—what the rest of the world refers to as *fundamentalist*—safe for suburbia. He is a white-haired, balding, eagle-beaked man, a preacher of the old school, which is to say that he delivers his sermons with an actual Bible in hand. (Pastor Ted uses a PalmPilot.) Pastor Hayford wanted to "wedge" an idea in our minds. The idea was "Order." The illustration was the Book of Revelation's description of four creatures surrounding Christ's throne. "The first . . . was like a lion, the second was like an ox, the third had a face like a man, the fourth was like a flying angel." Look! said Pastor Hayford, his voice sonorous and dignified. "All wonderful, all angels." The angels were merely different from one another. Just, he said, as we have different "ethnicities." And just as we have, in politics, a "hierarchy." And just as we have, in business, "different responsibilities," employer and employees. Angels, ethnicities, hierarchy, employers and employees—each category must follow a natural order.

Next came Pastor Larry Stockstill, from Ted's old church in Baton Rouge, presenting yet another variation of preacher. He took the stage with his wife, Melanie, who wore a pink pantsuit. Pastor Larry wore a brown pinstripe suit over a striped brown shirt and a golden tie. His voice was Louisiana; the word *pulpit* came out as *pull-peet.*

"There's a world," he preached, pacing across the stage. "I call it the Underworld." The Underworld, he explained, is similar to what he sees when he goes skin diving; only instead of strange fishes, there are strange people. Too many churches, he said, focus on the Overworld. "That's where the nice people are. The successful people. But the Lord said, 'I'm not sending you to the Overworld, I'm sending you to the *Underworld.*' Where the creatures are. The critters! The people who are out of it. People you see in Colorado Springs, even. You got an Underworld of people. The tattoo crowd, the people into drugs, the people into sex. You find 'em . . . in the Underworld."

AFTER CHURCH, I crossed the parking lot to the World Prayer Center, where I watched prayers scroll over two giant flat-screen televisions while a young man played piano. The Prayer Center—a joint effort of several fundamentalist organizations but located at and presided over by New Life—houses a bookstore as well as "corporate" prayer rooms, personal "prayer closets," hotel rooms, and the headquarters of Global Harvest, a ministry dedicated to "spiritual warfare." The atrium is a soaring hall adorned with the flags of the nations and guarded by another bronze warrior angel, a scowling, bearded type with massive biceps and, again, a sword. The angel's pedestal stands at the center of a great, eight-pointed compass laid out in muted red, white, and blue-black stone. Each point directs the eye to a contemporary painting, most depicting gorgeous, muscular men—one is a blacksmith, another is bound, fetish-style, in chains—in various states of undress. My favorite is *The Vessel*, by Thomas Blackshear, a major figure in the evangelical-art world. Here in the World Prayer Center is a print of *The Vessel*, a tall, vertical panel of two nude, ample-breasted, white female angels pouring an urn of honey onto the shaved head of a naked, olive-skinned man below. The honey drips down over his slablike pecs and his six-pack abs and overflows the eponymous vessel, which he holds in front of his crotch, oozing over the edges and spilling down yet another level, presumably onto our heads, drenching us in golden, godly love. Part of what makes Blackshear's work so compelling is precisely its unabashed eroticism; it aims to turn you on, and then to turn that passion toward Jesus.

In the chapel are several computer terminals, where one can sign on to the World Prayer Team and enter a prayer. Eventually one's words will scroll across the large flat screens, as well as across screens around the world, which as many as 70,000 other Prayer Team members are watching in their homes or churches at any moment. Prayers range from the mundane (real-estate deals and job situations demand frequent attention) to the urgent, such as this prayer request from "Rachel" of Colorado: *Danielle. 15 months old. Temperature just shy of 105 degrees. Lethargic. Won't eat.*

Or this one from "Lauralee" of Vermont: *If you never pray for anyone else, please choose this one! I'm in such pain I think I'm going to die; pray a healing MIRACLE for me for kidney problems (disease? failure?); I'm so alone; no insurance!*

One might be tempted to see an implicit class politics in that last point, but to join the Prayer Team one must promise to refrain from explicitly political prayer. That is reserved for the professionals. The Prayer Team screen, whether viewed at the center or on a monitor at home, is split between "Individual Focus Requests," such as the above, and "Worldwide Focus" requests, which are composed by the staff of the World Prayer Center. Sometimes these are domestic—*USA: Pray for the Arlington Group, pastors working with Whitehouse to renew Mar-*

riage Amendm. Pray for appts. of new justices. Pray for Pastor meetings with Amb. of Israel, and President Bush. Lord, let them speak only your words, represent YOU! Bless! But more often they are international—*N. KO-REA: Pray God will crush demonic stronghold and communist regime of Kim Jung Il.*

The Iraqis come up often, particularly with regard to their conversion: *Despite the efforts of the news media, believing soldiers and others testify to the effective preaching of the Gospel, and the openness of so many to hear of Jesus. Pray for continued success!*

Another prayer request puts numbers to that news: *900,000 Bibles in the Arabic language distributed by Christians in Iraq.* And one explicitly aligns the quest for democracy in Iraq with the quest for more Christians in Iraq: *May the people stand for their rights, and open to the idea of making choices, such as studying the Bible.*

The most common Iraq-related prayer requests, however, are strategic in the most worldly sense, such as this one: *Baghdad—God, press back the enemy.*

Behind the piano player in the main hall of the World Prayer Center, the front range of the Rocky Mountains stretched across a floor-to-ceiling, semicircular window with a 270-degree view. Above him, a globe fifteen feet in diameter rotated on a metal spindle. He played songs that sounded familiar but unnamable, the soundtrack to a sentimental movie I hadn't seen. When he took a break, I sat with him in the front row. His name was Jayson Tice, he was twenty-five, and he worked at Red Lobster. He wasn't from Colorado Springs, and he knew very few people who were. He'd grown up in San Diego, and once, he said, he'd been good enough to play Division I college basketball. But he broke his ankle, and because the marines promised him court time, he joined. There didn't turn out to be much basketball for him in the marines, just what he described as "making bombs and missiles," so he didn't re-up. Instead, he decided to start over in a new city. His mother had moved to Colorado Springs, so Jayson and his girlfriend did, too; his mother left after three months, but Jayson had already decided that God, not his mother, had called him to the mountains. He discovered that a lot of the people he knew, working as waiters or store clerks or at one of the air force bases, felt the same way.

"Colorado Springs," Jayson told me, "this particular city, this *one* city, is a battleground"—he paused—"between good and evil. This is spiritual Gettysburg." Why here? I asked. He thought about it and rephrased his answer. "This place is just a watering hole for Christians. For God's people. Something extra powerful's about to pour out of this city. I hope not to stay in Colorado Springs, because I want to spread what's going on here. I'm a warrior, dude. I'm a warrior for God. Colorado Springs is my training ground."

"THERE *WAS*," PASTOR Ted said one afternoon in his office, "a significant influence exerted on the [2004] election by Colorado Springs." He was meeting with me and another reporter, an Australian from a financial paper.

"You mean," the Australian asked, "almost like a force going out from Colorado Springs?"

A force—Pastor Ted liked that. He smiled and offered other examples. His favorite was the Ukraine, where, he claimed, a sister church to New Life had led the protests that helped sweep a pro-Western candidate into power. Kiev is, in fact, home to Europe's largest evangelical church, and over the last dozen years the Ukrainian evangelical population has grown more than tenfold, from 250,000 to 3 million. According to Ted, it was this army of Christian capitalists that took to the streets. "They're pro–free markets, they're pro–private property," he said. "That's what evangelical stands for."

In Pastor Ted's book *Dog Training, Fly Fishing, & Sharing Christ in the 21st Century*, he describes the church he thinks Christians want. "I want my finances in order, my kids trained, and my wife to love life. I want good friends who are a delight and who provide protection for my family and me should life become difficult someday . . . I don't want surprises, scandals, or secrets . . . I want stability and, at the same time, steady, forward movement. I want the church to help me live life well, not exhaust me with endless 'worthwhile' projects." By *worthwhile projects* Ted means new building funds and soup kitchens alike. It's not that he opposes these; it's just that he is sick of hearing about them and believes that other Christians are, too. He knows that for Christianity to prosper in the free market, it needs more than "moral values"; it needs customer value.[8]

New Lifers, Pastor Ted writes with evident pride, "like the benefits, risks, and maybe above all, the excitement of a free-market society." They like the stimulation of a new brand. "Have you ever switched your toothpaste brand, just for the fun of it?" Pastor Ted asks. Admit it, he insists. All the way home, you felt a "secret little thrill," as excited questions ran through your mind: "Will it make my teeth whiter? My breath fresher?" This is the sensation Ted wants pastors to bring to the Christian experience. He believes it is time "to harness the forces of free-market capitalism in our ministry." Once a pastor does that, his flock can start organizing itself according to each member's abilities and tastes.[9]

Which brings us back to "Order." Key to the growth of evangelicalism during the last twenty years has been a social structure of cell groups that allows churches to grow endlessly while maintaining orthodoxy in their ranks. Outsiders to evangelicalism often note the seemingly anonymous experience of the megachurch and conclude that such institutions prosper because they make so few demands, moral or intellectual, on their congregants. But a strong network of cells makes megachurch membership more all-encompassing than traditional Sunday congregations. That was why Abram developed the system for businessmen in 1935; he dreamed of a faith that would address every aspect of a believer's life, all the time. But Abram didn't imagine that such commitment could extend beyond his small circle of elites. Ordinary people, he thought, had too little power over the circumstances of their days—or too many distractions in the form of a consumer society's pleasures—to make such an intimate involvement feasible. He may have been correct at the time.[10]

Pastor Ted's insight was that the very growth of consumer society itself had conditioned ordinary Americans to perceive themselves as decision makers. "Free-market globalization" has made Americans so free, he concluded, that a populist cell-group system could function just like a market. One of Pastor Ted's favorite books is Thomas Friedman's *The Lexus and the Olive Tree*, which he made required reading for the hundreds of pastors under Ted's spiritual authority across the country. From Friedman, Pastor Ted says he learned that everything, including spirituality, can be understood as a commodity.

Friedman may have been the transmitter, but it was elite fundamentalism's belief that international capitalism is at the heart of the Gospel that migrated from Abram's cells into the seminaries and sermons of populist fundamentalism. Ted grew up in a faith that began and ended with moral control, but as he grew in power, so did the complexity of his beliefs. Unregulated trade, he concluded, was the key to achieving both worldly and spiritual freedom. His real challenge became one not of policing individual morality but of persuading his working- and middle-class congregation that the deregulated market that had driven so many of them to Colorado Springs in search of fresh starts was both biblical and in their interest. The former was the easier task, as the Family has long known; followers with an uneven knowledge of scripture but a reverence for authority are easily sold the idea of "biblical capitalism." That's all it takes for the Family, since such laissez-faire economics really are in the interest of its elite members, but Ted faced a more difficult challenge, since the economics of globalization have not so much increased competition and opportunity as squashed it, ushering in an age of unprecedented corporate consolidation. The cell-group system, which functions much like consumer capitalism—offering the semblance of "choice" even as it forecloses genuine alternatives—proved the perfect means of persuasion.

The irony of both Ted's and Abram's embrace of the cell group, an idea originally borrowed from communist revolutionaries, is that both settled on the "truth" of laissez-faire economics by obsessing over communism. In 1935, Abram saw communism as a menace within his city; forty years later, Ted had to go looking for it. His first job in professional Christendom was smuggling Bibles into Eastern

Europe—a project with which the Family had been involved since the 1950s. As it had been to Abram, it was important to Ted not to confuse America with Jesus, so instead of declaring the U.S. holier than other nations, he blended Jesus' teachings with American political aims and then convinced himself that the hybrid was objective truth, much like what Abram had once called the *universal inevitable,* much like Sam Brownback's conviction that free trade is foretold in the Bible. The process of economic globalization, Ted believed, is a vehicle for the spread of Christ's power.

By that, he meant Protestantism; Catholics, he believed, "constantly look back. And the nations dominated by Catholicism look back. They don't tend to create our greatest entrepreneurs, inventors, research and development. Typically, Catholic nations aren't shooting people into space. Protestantism, though, always looks to the future. A typical kid raised in Protestantism dreams about the future. A typical kid raised in Catholicism values and relishes the past, the saints, the history. That is one of the changes that is happening in America. In America the descendants of the Protestants, the Puritan descendants, we want to create a better future, and our speakers say that sort of thing."

For Ted, though, the battle boils down to evangelicals versus Islam. "My fear," he said, "is that my children will grow up in an Islamic state." That is why he believed spiritual war requires a virile, worldly counterpart. "I teach a strong ideology of the use of power," he said, "of military might as a public service." He was for preemptive war, because he believed the Bible's exhortations against sin set for us a preemptive paradigm, and he was for ferocious war, because "the Bible's bloody. There's a lot about blood."

LINDA BURTON, THE woman next to whom I'd sat at the dedication of New Life's sanctuary, told me she'd been "specifically called by God" to Colorado Springs seventeen years ago. Linda was not a Christian back then. She had married young and moved west from Buffalo so her husband could work for Martin Marietta, a defense

contractor. He wouldn't let her go to church because he was determined to forget his Baptist past, and she was a Catholic, which he
considered simply "Roman" and bad. That was fine with Linda.
Church didn't feel middle-class. Linda never did find out what
middle-class felt like, though, because her marriage fell apart. When
her husband left, he took their two daughters with him. After that
there were many men, and there was an abortion. With the man who
beat her she bore a son, whom she named Aaron Michael, the "strong
right hand of God." Linda took the baby and fled to Colorado Springs,
which she remembered from a vacation she and her ex-husband had
taken with their daughters. They'd ridden one of those Old West
trains almost to the top of Pike's Peak, a climb of more than two
miles. In her mind she drew a straight line from Buffalo to this point
high up in the Rockies, and there, for the first time, she had felt close
to God. Years later, when she had to run, she went where she remembered God had been.

At first, she and Aaron Michael lived in a shelter, and she got a
job at a Popeye's Fried Chicken. She worked every hour they gave
her, but the money she made was barely enough to eat on. She took
another job, waiting tables at the best hotel in town, and another at
Red Lobster. She was working seventy hours a week, and she was
still broke. A friend at the hotel invited her to New Life. She didn't
want to be around all these people weeping and babbling and shaking. But then Pastor Ted started talking, and he sounded so ordinary
he made Linda feel ordinary, too: middle-class.

One day, Pastor Ted preached that all she had to do was pray for
what she needed, as specifically as possible. She went right home and
got down on her knees in the kitchen and said, Lord, I need $2,500.
The next day, a check came. Her wages had been docked for child-
care payments to her ex-husband, but he had waived the payments
without telling her. The check was for $2,495. She wept.

Now Linda is an insurance agent, and she and Aaron Michael live
in a suburban home. Aaron Michael is sixteen. He wears his black
hair long, and his denim jacket is dirty. He likes violent movies—
"anything with blood," he tells me—and video games and fantasy

novels. But he's a good church boy: he loves most of all his youth cell, and reading the Bible, and talking with his mom about how to be a follower of Christ. His mom has grown strong in her faith. She hears voices, but they do not disturb her. "The Holy Spirit is a gentleman," she told me over a basket of cinnamon muffins she'd baked for my visit, still warm from the oven. Sitting across from me in her kitchen, she closed her big brown eyes and shushed herself. "I'm listening," she said quietly.

"To the TV?" I asked. In the next room, Aaron Michael was watching an action movie; the house was filled with the sound of explosions.

"No," said Linda. "To my Spirit." She opened her eyes and explained the process she had undergone to reach her refined state. She called it *spiritual restoration*. Anyone can do it, she promised, "even a gay activist." Linda had seen with her own eyes the sex demons that make homosexuals rebel against God, and she said they were gruesome; but she did not name them, for she would not "give demons glory." They are all the same, she said. "It's *radicalism*."

She reached across the table and touched my hand. "I have to tell you, the spiritual battle is very real." We are surrounded by demons, she explained, reciting the lessons she had learned in her small-group studies at New Life. The demons are cold; they need bodies; they long to come inside. People let them in in two different ways. One is to be sinned against. "Molested," suggested Linda. The other is to be in the wrong place at the wrong time. You could walk by a sin—a murder, a homosexual act—and a demon might leap onto your bones. Cities, therefore, are especially dangerous.

IT IS NOT so much the large populations, with their uneasy mix of sinner and saved, that make Christian conservatives leery of urban areas. Even downtown Colorado Springs, presumably as godly as any big town in America, struck the New Lifers I met as unclean. Whenever I asked where to eat, they would warn me away from downtown's neat little grid of cafés and ethnic joints. Stick to Academy, they'd tell me, referring to the vein of superstores and prepackaged eateries—P. F. Chang's, California Pizza Kitchen, Chili's—that bypasses the city. Downtown, they said, is "confusing."

Part of their antipathy is literally biblical: the Hebrew Bible is the scripture of a provincial desert people, suspicious of the cosmopolitan powers that threatened to destroy them, and fundamentalists read the New Testament as a catalog of urban ills: sophistication, cynicism, lust. But the anti-urban sentiments of modern fundamentalists are also more specific to the moment in which they find themselves.

In the 2002 election, fundamentalists swept Georgia's elected offices. They toppled an incumbent Democratic governor, a war-hero Democratic senator, the Speaker of the state house, the Democratic leader of the state senate, and his son, the Democratic candidate for Congress in a majority-black district that state Democrats had drawn up especially for him. The new Republican senator, Saxby Chambliss, and the new governor, Sonny Perdue, both conservatives and Christian, won not on "moral values" but on an exurban platform. The mastermind behind the coup was Ralph Reed, once of the Christian Coalition, who had been reborn as Georgia's Republican chairman. Reed remains a fundamentalist, the same man who once tested employees' commitment to "Christian values" by asking them if they supported the death penalty for adultery, but he was too canny to talk like that in public. The term *Christian,* he'd learned, is a "divider," not a "unifier," so he had left overt faith behind. He backed candidates who ran under the mantra of the exurbs: "Shorter commutes. More time with family. Lower mortgages."

This troika of exurban ambition worked on multiple levels. Just as Nixon used marijuana and heroin in the 1960s as code for hippies and blacks, Reed devised a platform that conflated ordinary personal goals with fundamentalist values. *Shorter commutes* is a ploy that any old-time ward heeler would recognize. It means "Let's move the good jobs out of the city." Atlanta, like Colorado Springs, has an urban core that conservatives would just as soon see wither. *More time with family* extends that promise of exurban jobs but also speaks in code to the fundamentalist preoccupation with "family"—that is, with defining it, with excluding not just gay couples but any combination not organized around "biblical" principles of "male headship."

As for *lower mortgages,* they are lower in exurbs because cities subsidize them. The city pays the taxes that build the sewers and the roads for the exurbs. The city provides the organization that makes them possible. Exurbs are parasites. And what else does *lower mortgages* mean? More land. More space between you and your neighbors. And this, too, is necessary for fundamentalism, which depends on the absence of conflict—the Family's *reconciliation*—as one of its main selling points. For all its talk of community, it is wary of community's main asset: the conflict, and the resulting cultural innovation, born of proximity. Such cultural innovation is death to today's populist fundamentalism, which tosses a gauzy veil of tradition over the big-box consumerism of its megachurches, much as the Family's elite fundamentalism once cast big-business conservatism as "first-century" Christianity.

As contemporary fundamentalism, populist and elite, has become an exurban movement, it has reframed the question of theodicy—if God is good, then why does He allow suffering?—as a matter of geography. Some places are simply more blessed than others. Cities equal more fallen souls equal more demons equal more temptation, which leads to more fallen souls. The threats that suffuse urban centers have forced Christian conservatives to flee—to Cobb County, Georgia, to Colorado Springs. Hounded by the sins they see as rampant in the cities (homosexuality, atheistic schoolteaching, ungodly imagery), they imagine themselves to be outcasts in their own land. They are the "persecuted church"—just as Jesus promised, and just as their cell-group leaders teach them.

This exurban exile is not an escape to easy living, to barbecue and lawn care. "We [Christians] have lost every major city in North America," Pastor Ted writes in his 1995 book *Primary Purpose,* but he believes they can be reclaimed through prayer—"violent, confrontive prayer."[11] He encourages believers to obtain maps of cities and to identify "power points" that "strengthen the demonic activities." He suggests especially popular bars, as well as "cult-type" churches. "Sometimes," he writes, "particular government buildings . . . are power points." The exurban position is one of strategic retreat, where believers are to "plant" their churches as strategic outposts encircling the enemy.

I RETURNED TO the World Prayer Center for a church staff meeting. More than one hundred employees began with "worship"—which means they started with a band, one of New Life's many "worship teams" of musicians. This one was composed of students in New Life's Worship and Praise School, a one-year college-credit program created to train and staff churches around the country. The students were all young and attractive, dressed in the kind of quality-cotton punk clothing one buys at the Gap. "Lift up your hands, open the door," crooned the lead singer, an inoffensive tenor. Male singers at New Life and other megachurches are almost always tenors, their voices clean and indistinguishable, R&B-inflected one moment, New Country the next, with a little bit of early 1990s grunge at the beginning and the end.

The worship style was a kind of musical correlate to Pastor Ted's free-market theology: designed for total accessibility, with the illusion of choice between strikingly similar brands. (Pastor Ted preferred the term *flavors* and often used Baskin-Robbins, the chain of ice cream stores, as a metaphor when explaining his views.) The drummers all stuck to soft cymbals and beats anyone could handle. Lyrics tended to be rhythmic and perfectly pronounced, the better to sing along with when the words were projected onto movie screens. There are no sad songs in a megachurch, and there are no angry songs. There are songs about desperation but none about despair; songs convey longing only if it has already been fulfilled.

The idea of applying market economics to church originated not within fundamentalism or evangelicalism, nor even in the petri dishes of the laissez-faire think tanks in D.C., but with a sociologist from the University of Washington named Rodney Stark, whose work has won a broad readership beyond his discipline. Stark (who now teaches at Baylor, a Baptist university in Texas) and various collaborators began interpreting religious-affiliation data through the lens of neoliberal market theory in the 1980s.[12] The very best sort of religious economy, insists Stark, is one unregulated by either the state or large denominations. Left to form, change, and die organically, Stark believes, churches will naturally come to meet the populace's diverse spiritual needs, which he divides into a spectrum of six "niches" akin to a left/right political scheme. He argues that the law of the market spurs new religious movements, which start out small, in "high tension" with the society around them, at the "ultraconservative" end of the spectrum. As these sects grow, their tension usually decreases—that is, writes Stark, they dilute the "seriousness" of their faith—until they eventually drift to the "ultraliberal" end. Implicit is that there is a natural and fairly steady demand for religion that needs only to find expression in a properly varied supply.[13]

Despite its academic prose, Stark's work has won a wide readership among local pastors, who have propagated his ideas through the cell-group structure. On the surface, at least, the evangelical enthusiasm for Stark's work might seem somewhat puzzling. Certainly Stark does celebrate the entrepreneurial, "ultraconservative" church as the engine of religious vigor. And yet he also seems to promise fundamentalists that their eventual fate will be moderation, or pluralistic irrelevance, or both.

In fact, the analogy with free-market economics holds up quite neatly. Stark is an economist of religion; his theory tells him that unfettered markets will lead to competition, diversity, pluralism. His fundamentalist adherents, by contrast, are like businessmen, who understand and approve of where the theory leads in practice: toward consolidation, control, manufacture of demand. What the most farsighted are doing is fostering something like Stark's spectrum of "niches," but all within the confines of their individual megachurches. They are building aisles and aisles in which everyone can find something, but behind it all a single corporate entity persists, and with it an ideology.

In devising New Life's small-group system (Pastor Ted preferred *small-group* to *cell*, but he considered the terms interchangeable), Ted asked himself and his staff a simple question: "Do you like your neighbors?" And, for that matter, "Do you even know your neighbors?" The answers he got—the golden rule to the contrary—were "Not really" and "No."[14] Okay, said Pastor Ted, so why would you want to be in a small group with them? Ted deduced a few "rules." One was, "I Want to Meet with People I Like." That is, he *didn't* want to be forced into fellowship with people who weren't his type. That wasn't un-Christian, he decided; it was biblical. God loves everyone, Ted decided, but God likes some people more than others. And so did he. Another rule was, "I Don't Want to Study Something I'm Not Interested In." Ted, for instance, got mad when he thought of all the dull Bible studies he'd sat through that had ignored his passion, free-market economics.[15] His point was that arbitrary small groups would make less sense than self-selected groups organized around common interests. Hence New Life members can choose among small groups dedicated to motorcycles, or rock climbing, or homeschooling, or protesting outside abortion clinics. There are even stealth small groups, such as a film club created to draw in people unaware that they've joined a Christian group, much less a New Life evangelical effort. The New Lifers involved simply "choose movies with subtle Christian themes [and] gently nudge the conversation toward spiritual themes." An ostensibly secular group created to help young couples with their finances teaches that the primary cause of poverty is divorce; from there it's a short leap to Christian "family values" such as male authority.[16]

Pastor Ted's true genius lay in his organizational hierarchy, which ensured ideological rigidity even as it allowed for individual expression. For all his talk about "free markets," Pastor Ted was oddly deterministic. Not just in his assumption that social networks should remain entrenched along class lines, but in his belief that social science provides the tools with which to quantify the condition of the soul and to direct it—some might say "engineer" it—accordingly. Absent the societal vetting of the elites gathered in the Family's prayer cells, the aspiring group leaders of populist fundamentalism must undergo a battery of personality and spiritual tests, as well as an official background check. Once chosen, they meet regularly with their own leaders in the chain of command, and members are encouraged to jump the chain and speak to a higher level if they think their leader is straying into "false teachings": moral relativism, ecumenism, or even "Satanism," in the form of New Age notions such as crystal healing.

Whether the system is common sense or heresy itself—the Body of Christ atomized—is beside the point; New Lifers found it powerfully persuasive. Pastor Ted instituted a semester system, so that no one needed to be locked into a group he or she didn't like for too long. And since New Life's cell groups didn't limit themselves to Bible study, they functioned as covert evangelizing engines. In return, what Pastor Ted gave his flock, and American fundamentalism, were lifestyle choices.

COMMANDER TOM PARKER and his family live a long way from New Life, far south in a neighborhood of postage-stamp yards and houses without foundations and streets without sidewalks. Not because they're suburban but because nobody bothered to pour concrete. Commander Tom used to make computer chips; his wife is a maid. Their living room set is comprised of two couches a leg-stretch apart, with Commander Tom's recliner between. An upright piano, painted red-and-white, is backed against one wall; a TV, no longer much used, squats against the other. When I visited, Commander Tom's wife stayed in the kitchen, but his son, Junior Commander TJ, joined us in the living room. The two men—TJ is only fifteen, but he's been bar mitzvahed, about which more in a moment—owe their officer's ranks to the Royal Rangers, a Christian alternative to the Boy Scouts.[17] The largest "outpost" of the Rangers in the country, 475 boys and men, rallies at New Life.

Royal Rangers wear khaki military uniforms and black ties. They study rope craft and smallbore shooting and "American

Cultures." There is a badge for "Atomic Energy," which boys can earn by making scale models of a nuclear reactor. Mainly, though, Rangers earn merit badges for reading the Bible. Most boys go book by book, which earns them a special vest stitched over entirely in badges, but truly dedicated Rangers take it all in one giant swallow, a feat of reading for which they earn a single Golden Achievement Badge. TJ, who traveled to Los Angeles last year to claim second place in the regional Ranger of the Year competition, has such a Golden Achievement Badge. He is a sturdy boy, with a swimmer's shoulders and an honest, rectangular face, baby fat all gone but for plump roses over his cheekbones. His blue eyes have more focus than that of most boys his age, and his smile is shy but sweet and wide. In another setting, he'd be a teen dream, but TJ doesn't meet many girls. He is homeschooled, and most of his out-of-the-house hours are dedicated to the Rangers, an all-male organization. TJ's purity ring, which he wears on a delicate silver chain, is a symbol of his commitment to virginity until marriage. It was given to him two years ago by Commander Tom on the occasion of TJ's bar mitzvah.

The bar mitzvah was Tom's idea. A heavier, darker-haired version of TJ plus glasses and a mustache, Tom decided his son deserved a ritual to mark his entrance into manhood, just like the Jewish people have. TJ took as his text not a portion of Torah but the song "Shine," by a Christian rock band called the Newsboys.

> *The Kind of Light*
> *That might persuade*
> *A strict dictator to retire*
> *Fire the army*
> *Teach the poor origami.*

TJ and Commander Tom are both members of an elite Ranger cadre known as the Frontier Christian Fellowship, in which boys and men regress to pioneer life in pursuit of ultimate Christian manhood.

Father and son are still Frontiersmen, which is the lowest level, but
they dream of becoming Buckskin Men. "The problem," said TJ, "is
that it takes time and money. Because you have to make an outfit.
And it has to be out of leather."

"If you're a Frontiersman, you can't wear regular clothes," Tom
explained.

"You don't have to catch the deer yourself," said TJ. "You can just
buy the leather at a store. But you gotta learn how to sew it."

"And you gotta make up something you can live off."

"A trade."

"Like making candles," said Tom.

You also have to choose a special name. TJ was thinking about
"White Flame," to follow up on his bar mitzvah theme of "Shine."
Tom had chosen "Rain Bolt." *Rain* came from his favorite contemporary Christian song. "Word of God speak," he sings gently, "Let it fall
down like rain, open my eyes to see His majesty." *Bolt*, he adds, "is
just the awesome power of God."

Tom thought that power was misunderstood, even by his fellow
Christians. It's about being *in* the Father, he said. *In* the sabbath,
too, but he couldn't really explain this in-ness. "At the end of Hebrews
4, it has this verse"—he looked to TJ, who recited from memory:
"The Word of God is living and active, sharper than any double-edged
sword, cutting until it divides soul from spirit, joints from marrow."

TJ is the kind of boy who always has a book with him. Dickens's
Old Curiosity Shop sat on the couch in case the conversation grew
boring, and on the coffee table between TJ and his father was a pile of
Christian thrillers Tom was reading on TJ's recommendation. Mostly,
Tom read the Bible, and *The Lord of the Rings*, over and over. He
would have liked to have joined the Riders of Rohan, a New Life cell
of suburban bikers that took its name from Tolkien's noble horsemen,
but he couldn't afford a motorcycle. He couldn't afford much of anything but religion itself. Tom's favorite book of the Bible is the Gospel
of John. "It's dying to yourself, so you can be with Jesus, going into

the throne of God. It says don't be ashamed, going into the throne of God. But how can you not be ashamed?"

One day the previous August, Tom had been at work, making computer chips, when for no apparent reason his mind said good-bye to his body and left it standing there with no power to move. He told it to turn, but it wouldn't turn. Blink, but it wouldn't blink. When he regained control, the first thing he did was take himself to the doctor for an MRI. But the moment the nurse turned on the machine, his eyeballs felt as if they were popping; his hands clenched into claws. All he could do was whisper, "Turn . . . it . . . off." Electronics seemed to exacerbate the condition. "I'm allergic," he said. He believed that years of working with powerful magnets have broken his "polars." His company moved him to a desk job, but the computer made his eyes wobble. He can't talk on a cell phone, and TV causes a meltdown. His company pays him a modest sum for disability. He wouldn't dream of suing. New Life helps out when his finances get close to nothing. "God keeps saying to me, 'Tom, this is not about you. It's about Me,'" he told me. "There's something going on. And God is just trying to get me ready."

In December, Tom received a vision. It is not unheard of for ordinary New Lifers to experience visions, but most are wary about their provenance; what a secularist would call *psychological* they call *satanic*. But Tom thought that this one was real. He told two New Life pastors about it, and he told his mother, because, he said, "it was so threatening to me." His voice trembled with the recollection, and grew quieter, shy and childish, and he seemed close to tears. This is what he had seen: "Complete darkness over all of America. But there was a light coming down to the center of America," that is, Colorado Springs. "And it was just a circle. And in it there were angels, and the angels were battling. And they were fighting hard as they could"— here Tom's voice broke—"but they couldn't hold back the dark, and the Lord said to me, 'America has to repent, or this hole will close.'"

Tom returned to the moment. "I'm not even saying I know what to do with it. It's just—that's what I see. And I pray. There's something going on here, and God's gonna explode it. There's gonna be an explosion from here bigger than anyone's ever seen."

New Life, he believed, would marshal the shock waves. "I think Pastor Ted is Gandalf," the wizard of *The Lord of the Rings*, he said. Tom had received a few minivisions, just glimpses really, and in them he saw a pastor kneeling, praying, in spiritual battle with a demon trying to pull him into a flaming abyss.

I grew up reading Tolkien, too. "Who's the Balrog?" I asked, referring to a demon that nearly kills Gandalf. I expected Commander Tom to reply with the usual enemies: "the culture" and the homosexuals and the humanists. But the Balrog, he said, is *inside* Pastor Ted, inside New Life, inside every follower of Christ.

ON ANY NIGHT of the week in Colorado Springs, if one knows where to look, one can join a conversation about God that will stretch late into the evening. Some of these are cell groups, spin-offs from New Life or from the city's other churches, but others are more free-form. On a Thursday, I joined one as the guest of a friend of a friend named Lisa Anderson. Lisa is an editor at the International Bible Society. A few nights earlier, after I bought her several rounds of mojitos, she had promised to send me *Our City, God's Word*, a glossy New Testament produced by the IBS and included not long before as an insert in the local paper. "Colorado Springs is a special place," declares the introduction. "The Bible is a special book."[18]

Lisa's Thursday-night group met in a town house owned by a young couple with two children, Alethea (Greek for Truth), age three, and Justus (Justice), age one and a half. The father is assistant to the president of the Navigators, a conservative parachurch ministry, and the mother works for Head Start. Also in attendance were two graduates of the Moody Bible Institute and Lisa's boyfriend, a graduate student and a writer for Summit Ministries, a parachurch organization that creates curricula on America's "Christian heritage" for homeschoolers and private academies. There was also a gourmet chef.

When I walked in, an hour late, they were talking about Chris-tian film criticism—whether such a thing could, or should, exist. Then they talked about the tsunami that had just hit South Asia and wondered with concern whether any of the city's preachers would try to score points off it. When I mentioned that Pastor Ted already had, they cringed. I told them that at the previous Sunday's full-immersion baptism service, Pastor Ted had noted that the waves hit the "number-one exporter of radical Islam," Indonesia. "That's not a judgment," he'd announced. "It's an opportunity." I told them of similar analyses from Pastor Ted's congregation: one man said that he wished he could "get in there" among the survivors, since their souls were "ripe," and another told me he was "psyched" about what God was "doing with His ocean."

"That's not funny," one woman said, and the room fell silent.

James, an aspiring film critic with oval glasses and a red goatee, spoke up from the floor, where he'd been sitting cross-legged. "You know that Bruce Springsteen song on *Nebraska*, about the highway cop?" he asked. He was referring to a song called "Highway Patrol-man," in which the patrolman's brother has left "a kid lyin' on the floor, lookin' bad," and the patrolman sets out to chase him down. Instead, he pulls over and watches his brother's "taillights disappear," thinking of "how nothin' feels better than blood on blood."

"He can't arrest his brother," James said, and quoted the song: "a man turns his back on family, well, he just ain't no good."

"I think that's how it is," James continued. "That's how I feel about Dobson, or Haggard. They're family. We have loyalties, even if we disagree."

I told James about a little man I had met in the hallway at New Life who, when I said I was from New York City, said, simply, "Ka-boom!" I told him also about Joseph Torrez, a New Lifer I had eaten dinner with, who, when describing the evangelical gathering under way in Colorado Springs, compared it to "Shaquille O'Neal driving the lane, dunking on *you*." Torrez had said, "It's time to choose sides," a refrain I had heard over and over again during my time in Colorado Springs.

"So which is it?" I asked. "Which side are you on? Theirs? Are you ready to declare war on me, on my city?"

"No—"

"Then choose."

"I—"

"We can't," Lisa interrupted, from the corner.

"We can," said John, another Bible Society editor. "We *do*. Just by being here."

12.

THE ROMANCE OF AMERICAN
FUNDAMENTALISM

AFTER NEW LIFE BANISHED Pastor Ted from his pulpit in late 2006, the press wondered if this glaring evidence of hypocrisy would spell the end of fundamentalism's broad appeal. The press had asked the same question many times during the televangelist sex scandals of the 1980s and '90s—Jimmy Swaggart's motel rendezvous, Jim Bakker's hush money for his secretary—and, long forgotten now, another decade earlier when *Time* reported that two students at the evangelist Billy James Hargis's American Christian College, married by Reverend Hargis himself, had discovered on their honeymoon that neither was a virgin; Hargis not only had married the pair but had deflowered both husband and wife.[1] Hargis's reputation never recovered, but his cause survived; so did the college vice president to whom the students confessed, David Noebel, who used Hargis's downfall to consolidate his own power. Today, Noebel is president of Summit Ministries, headquartered just west of New Life, where he oversees the education of 2,000 students a year and the distribution of fundamentalist homeschooling materials to thousands more. His most influential book is *The Homosexual Revolution*.

Scandal does not destroy American fundamentalism. Rather, like a natural fire that purges the forest of overgrowth, it makes the movement stronger. And fiercer. Such was the case in the aftermath of the Hargis affair, when Noebel managed to convince millions that Hargis's fall was not an occasion for a reconsideration of fundamentalism's concept of sexuality but rather a call to action. Noebel's subsequent antigay manifesto, *The Homosexual Revolution*, helped make sex one of the movement's most potent political causes.

Something similar happened after Ted Haggard's disgrace. The Reverend Mel White, a former ghostwriter for Jerry Falwell who has since come out and now leads Soulforce, a pro-gay evangelical ministry, told me that Ted's ordeal would serve only to drive more gay fundamentalists into the closet. Nobody would want to face the public shaming Ted endured, while the fact that fundamentalist leaders embraced Ted and promised to cure him would offer queer fundamentalists hope that they, too, could be made pure again by one of the many "ex-gay" ministries that have arisen in recent years.

Following the end of the Cold War, during which anticommunism was the organizing principle of American fundamentalism, sex provided a new battleground. No longer would fundamentalism present itself primarily as *against* an enemy, godless communism; after the fall of the Berlin Wall, fundamentalism looked to sex as the new frontier of its empire, and "purity" as the promise of its campaign. Sexual purity also lends to the movement a radical tenor that's thrilling to young believers eager to distance themselves from the clumsy politics of the old Christian Right. It is, one virgin told me, a rebellion against materialism, consumerism, and "the idea that anything can be bought and sold." It is a spiritual war against the world, against "sensuality." This elevation of sexual purity—especially for men—as a way of understanding yourself and your place in the world is new. It's also very old. First-century Christians took the idea so seriously that many left their wives for "house monasteries," threatening the very structure of the family. The early church responded by institutionalizing virginity through a priestly caste set apart from the world, a condition that continues to this day within Roman Catholicism. Now, though, the Protestants of American fundamentalism are reclaiming that system, making every young man and woman within their sphere of influence part of a new virgin army.

Real sex is no more endangered by such an ambition than the political corruption—or, for that matter, radicalism—that Abram once dreamed he could abolish through the patient construction of a voluntary theocracy. The chaste spiritual warriors of populist fundamentalism continue to experience all the same desires as the rest of us, a fact they readily admit. The sexual purity they're pursuing isn't so much a static condition as a perpetual transformation, Charles Finney's revival machine rebuilt within one's own soul. Purity lends to populist fundamentalism the intensity of Jonathan Edwards's Great Awakening, the intimacy of Abram's prayer cells. To be pure is to be elite, or so chaste believers, looking at a world suffused with sex, may easily tell themselves.

MATT DUNBAR WAS a short and ruddy-faced twenty-three-year-old, a little shy, a man who kept his hands in his pockets. He was also funny and smart and possessed of excellent conversational timing. He had grown a small brown soul patch beneath his lower lip, and his voice was smooth. When he talked to you, he held your eyes as if he trusted you, which he did; Dunbar, wary of the world since he was a boy, had decided to trust people. He studied religion through an anthropological lens as a graduate student at New York University, where his friends called him Mr. Dunbar. He said in a matter-of-fact manner that women liked him, and it was true. Mr. Dunbar was a gentleman.

He lived in Brooklyn with his childhood best friend, Robin Power. Sometimes Robin had a thick brown beard, and sometimes he shaved himself clean and dyed his hair black and spiked it up, like Johnny Rotten. He usually worked a gutterpunk look—a ratty, layered look of sweatshirts and buttons advertising obscure bands. Sometimes, he wore eyeliner. He taught ninth-grade English at Martin Luther King High, in Manhattan, and he liked the fact that some of his students thought he was gay.

Robin, like Dunbar, was a conservative Christian, but he wasn't allowed to talk about that at school. He was permitted to talk about "values," though, and to him, loving everyone, even gay men—his students called them "faggots," but he considered them sinners, and

to him this was the difference between secularism and Christianity—
was a value he wanted to share with his pupils. Once, he went to
school in drag to teach them a lesson, about judging a soul based on
appearances.

When I first met Dunbar and Robin at their church—"The Journey," a fundamentalist congregation of actors, dancers, and young
professionals who want to know actors and dancers—Robin got
most of the glances, the smiles, the cute little laughs that said, "Call
me." But Robin was engaged. Dunbar didn't do badly himself; the
women who knew Robin was taken gravitated toward him, and during the time I knew him, he met a church girl, an actress named
Anna, blonde, broad-faced, and beautiful, quiet like Dunbar. He
thought she was a godly woman. He had been "waiting" for a long
time—"saving himself," as an older generation might have said—and
now he had someone to wait for.

Dunbar and Robin grew up together in Visalia, California, a hard
little agricultural town far from the coast. They were not part of the
megachurch nation; Dunbar was raised by a single mother, who took
him to a traditional Episcopal church, and Robin's parents and siblings were all musicians. They had their own little recording studio,
and they rocked, more Ramones than Partridge Family. Dunbar always wanted to be in their band. He and Robin went to the same
conservative, Christian college and moved to Manhattan afterward
with two other childhood friends, also Christians. They came because one of the men had a girlfriend here—the two are now
engaged—but the city has proven to be a sort of calling. "New York,"
said Dunbar, "is a great town for virgins."

We were sitting on a bench after church, watching Sunday traffic
stream up and down Broadway. "Cleavage everywhere," noted Dunbar. He had learned to look without desire. Robin held up his right
hand. Wrapped around his wrist, in a figure eight, was a black plastic
bracelet. "This," he said, "is a 'masturband.'" One of their friends at
college came up with the idea. As long as you stayed pure—resisted
masturbating—you could wear your masturband. Give in, and off it
went, like a scarlet letter in reverse. No masturband? Then no one

wanted to shake your hand. "It started with just four of us," said Dunbar. "Then there were, like, twenty guys wearing them. And girls too. The more people that wore them, the more people knew, the more reason you had to refrain." Dunbar even told his mother. He lasted the longest. "Eight and a half months," he said. I notice he's not wearing one now. He wasn't embarrassed. Sexuality, he believed, is not a private matter.

The other night, he said, he's out drinking, with "secular friends." They were all a little drunk—Dunbar was fond of Bible verses about wine—and they're talking about sex.

"Dunbar," volunteers one of the secular guys, "is a virgin." The jerk is laughing. "*By choice*," he says.

Huge mistake. All female eyes leave the man who wants their attention and rotate Dunbar's way. "Four girls surround me. They want to know everything."

Is he embarrassed? ("I'd only be embarrassed if I was *trying* to get some.") Is oral okay? Anal? (He doesn't like to be "legalistic," caught up in rules, and he has friends who enjoyed anal sex and still called themselves virgins, but—no.) Has he always been a virgin? ("Uh, yeah. That's what 'virgin' means.") Why? (Jesus, "romance," it all blends together . . .)

One of Dunbar's roommates had recently found himself in the same situation: young man from the sticks in a big-city bar, surrounded by women who genuinely want to know if anything can tempt him. They were tempting him, of course, which was the point. He was in trouble. One woman gave him the kind of look usually used only by teen movie seductresses. "Sex," she said, "is just something I do." Lucifer himself could not have whispered more sweetly. And then—the material world ruined it all. Satan's angel took a chip off a plate of cheesy nachos. "Like eating," she said. "It's easy."

Dunbar's virgin comrade took a big breath of virtue and girded his loins for continuing chastity. "The whole sex/nacho thing?" Dunbar said. "It just doesn't make sense to a virgin."

Food, after all, belongs to the mundane realm. Sex, on the other hand, is supernatural. Dunbar read the biblical Song of Solomon—lovers rhapsodizing over each other, he obsessed with her breasts like "two fawns" and her "rounded thighs like jewels"; she with his legs like "alabaster columns" and his lips like lilies, "dripping sweet-smelling myrrh"—not as erotica but as a metaphor for the love between man and God. Sex that is just two bodies in motion struck him as empty, even if love was involved. Every encounter must be a kind of threesome: man, wife, and God. Without Him, it's just fucking.

"Suckers for romance," Leslee Unruh, the founder of Abstinence Clearinghouse, described men like Dunbar and Robin. She meant it as praise, since she considers them the vanguard of a desexed revolution. "We want authenticity," she told me. "We want what's real." It's "safe sex," she explained, that requires faith, since there is "no evidence" that safe sex "works." Unruh is a youthful-looking grandmother from South Dakota with a big mouth, literally—outlined in fire-engine red for public performances—and dyed blonde hair. Since her early days as one of the most fervent antiabortion crusaders of the 1980s, she's made over her politics, too. She still fights abortion—she was one of the activists behind South Dakota's ban on all abortions, revoked by referendum in 2006—but she's discovered that she can win more converts by going to the root cause, sex itself.

So, in 1997, she launched Abstinence Clearinghouse in Sioux Falls. She'd been a self-declared "chastity" educator since the early 1980s, but it wasn't until the Clinton years that American fundamentalism fully discovered sex as a weapon in the culture wars. In 1994, a Southern Baptist celibacy program, True Love Waits, brought 200,000 virginity pledge cards to Washington, D.C. In 2004, the group brought a million to the Olympics in Athens. Now, Abstinence Clearinghouse acts as a nexus for activists and as their voice in Washington, claiming as "friends" a slew of officials with unrecognizable names, abstinence crusaders in the Departments of Health and Human Services, Education, and even State. Family members like

Brownback and Representative Joe Pitts used their Value Action Teams to insert chastity into foreign affairs.

Uganda, which following the collapse of Siad Barre's Somalia became the focus of the Family's interests in the African Horn, has been the most tragic victim of this projection of American sexual anxieties. Following implementation of one of the continent's only successful anti-AIDS program, President Yoweri Museveni, the Family's key man in Africa, came under pressure from the United States to emphasize abstinence instead of condoms. Congressman Pitts wrote that pressure into law, redirecting millions of dollars from effective sex-ed programs to projects such as Unruh's. This pressure achieved the desired result: an evangelical revival in Uganda, and a stigmatization of condoms and those who use them so severe that some college campuses held condom bonfires. Meanwhile, Ugandan souls may be more "pure," but their bodies are suffering; following the American intervention, the Ugandan AIDS rate, once dropping, nearly doubled. This fact goes unmentioned by activists such as Unruh and politicians such as Pitts, who continue to promote Uganda as an abstinence success story.

The actual fate of Ugandan citizens was never their concern. Pitts, in the Family tradition, may have had geopolitics on the mind: with Ethiopia limping along following decades of civil war and dictatorship and Somalia veering toward a Taliban state, tiny, Anglophone Uganda has become an American wedge into Islamic Africa. But the American uses and abuses of Uganda are still more cynical: Christian Africa has been appropriated for a story with which American fundamentalists argue for domestic policy, a parable detached from African realities, preached for the benefit of Americans. In Unruh's telling, the ostensible "success" of Uganda's abstinence program justifies the miseducation of American schoolchildren.

Under the Bush administration, Abstinence Clearinghouse helped the federal Centers for Disease Control establish a "gold standard" for abstinence-only sex education programs. A student in one of these programs may hear that sex outside of marriage can lead to suicide; that condoms don't prevent AIDS; that abortion often results in sterility; and that men's and women's gender roles are biologically determined as "knights" and "princesses," which, if violated, cause depression. And the Clearinghouse continues to lobby for more, bringing politicians together with activists at conferences intended to win support not just for abstinence curricula but for the privatization of public schooling altogether: vouchers for Christian academies, "character" charter schools such as those promoted by the Family's Eileen Bakke (who has become a Family prayer partner of Janet Museveni, Uganda's first lady), and homeschooling. The Clearinghouse hosts "purity balls" and abstinence teas. It sponsors "power virgins" around the country, good-looking young men and women who work the fundamentalist lecture circuit spreading the no-sex gospel. It also operates as a one-stop shop for abstinence paraphernalia, much of it fundamentalist despite the group's allegedly secular orientation: 14-karat gold "What Would Jesus Do" rings; books such as *Single Christian Female*; ready-to-go abstinence PowerPoint presentations. There's abstinence chewing gum, abstinence stickers in batches of 1,000, abstinence balloons in batches of 5,000. There's even an abstinence pencil.

Unruh considered herself broad-minded enough for the demands of an ostensibly secular society. If religion is to be kept out of the schools, she said, "shame and conscience are important tools" in its place. But "romance," more than anything else, guided her understanding of sexuality. This is what she found romantic: a father who gives his teenage daughter a purity ring only to take it back on her wedding day and hand it over to his daughter's new husband, her virginity passed from man to man like a baton.

Therein lies the paradox of the purity movement. It's at once an attempt to transcend cultural influences through the timelessness of scripture, and a painfully specific response to the sexual revolution. Populist fundamentalism grew into a political force in almost direct proportion to the mainstreaming (and subsequent weakening) of various sexual liberation movements, and as it did so it led the elites of American fundamentalism, so closely aligned with the secular conservatives as to be nearly invisible, out of the establishment coalition. Absent the sexual revolution, populist fundamentalism might still thrive only in enclaves, and elite fundamentalism still coexist easily with secular politics, as it did during the early days of the Cold War.

But the sexual revolution hardly invented sex or the anxieties it results in when mixed with conservative Christianity. The complaints of today's purity crusaders echo those of Abram's men in the 1930s when they resolved to meet in all-male cells rather than submit to the authority of churches in which women comprised the clear majority, if not the leadership. "Christianity, as it currently exists, has done some terrible things to men," writes John Eldredge, the author of a best-selling manhood guide called *Wild at Heart*. He thinks that church life in America has made Christian men weak. Women who are frustrated with their girlie-man husbands and boyfriends seize power, and the men retreat to the safe haven of porn instead of whipping the ladies back into line. What women really want, he says, is to "be fought for." And men, he claims, are "hardwired" by God for battle; Jesus wants them to be warriors in the vein of *Braveheart* and *Gladiator*.

Wild at Heart and Eldredge's other best sellers, *The Journey of Desire* and *The Sacred Romance* (as well as "field manual" workbooks that can be purchased separately), address sexual "purity" as part of the fabric of Christian manliness. Other books, such as *God's Gift to Women: Discovering the Lost Greatness of Masculinity* and *Every Man's Battle*, by Stephen Arterburn and Fred Stoeker, make sex their central concern. *Every Man's Battle* has become almost a genre unto itself, with dozens of *Every Man* spin-off titles: *Every Young Man's Battle, Every Woman's Battle, Every Man's Challenge, Preparing Your Son For Every Man's Battle*, and on and on. The *Every Man* premise is that men are sexual beasts, so sinful by nature that, without God in their lives, they don't stand a chance of resisting temptation. But the temptation they most fear is not the age-old seduction of the flesh but the image of the flesh. They are not opposed to modernity, but to postmodernity and what they perceive as its free-floating symbols. The books are anti-media manifestos, warning that we are prey to any media we look at;

images, they preach, are forever. One author confesses to being plagued by a picture of the sitcom actress Suzanne Somers, nude in a "surging mountain stream," that he had seen twenty years earlier. For the authors, the solution is simply not to look, an anti-iconographic stance that belongs more to the Old Testament than the New.

I first heard about the Every Man books from a volunteer at Dunbar and Robin's church, a twenty-five-year-old man who said he'd slept with forty women before he "revirgined" with the help of the series. I was more surprised to learn that Robin had been reading *Every Man's Battle* in preparation for marriage, and planned to lead a Bible study for men in the fall using *Every Man* as exegetical reading. Robin seemed too smart for these books. But then, what he wanted from them was not subtle thinking but clarity, a law of black and white.

"You're sexually pure," write Arterburn and Stoeker, "when sexual gratification only comes from your wife . . . [and] sexual purity has the same definition whether you're married or single." To achieve this, they argue, men must go to a kind of war. "Your life is under a withering barrage of machine-gun sexuality that rakes the landscape mercilessly," they report in their volume for single men. They encourage making lists of "areas of weakness" and seem particularly concerned with shorts: "nubile sweat-soaked girls in tight nylon shorts," "female joggers in tight nylon shorts," "young mothers in shorts," and "volleyball shorts," which are apparently so erotic that they require no bodies to fill them. To avoid these temptations, men must train themselves to "bounce" their eyes off female curves. Older men can help, too; the coauthors urge young men to find mentors who will check in with them by phone about their masturbation fantasies. This may be embarrassing for a young Christian, so the authors suggest a code. Homosexuality is relegated to a short afterword in which they list the number of Exodus International, a ministry dedicated to "freeing" people from homosexual desires.

What's really strange about all this is that it works. Not in the sense of de-eroticizing the world but in the sense of reinvigorating American fundamentalism with a new generation of foot soldiers, men and women who respond to a hypersexual consumer culture by making sex, in its absence, a top priority of their religion. "Abstinence," Dunbar told me, "is countercultural," a kind of rebellion, he said, against materialism, consumerism, and "the idea that anything can be bought and sold."

Every Man operates a hotline, 1–800 NEW LIFE, for men who've "threatened" their relationships with women through their use of pornography. When I called to confess that reading about tight-shorted women in *Every Young Man's Battle* struck me as weirdly erotic, a professional masturbation counselor named Jason told me that I needed to be more like a woman. Women, he said, don't like porn. In fact, if I asked any woman I knew, she'd tell me that for her to "use" porn, she'd have to fall out of love. Women are just that pure.

What if I became so womanly that I developed a desire for men? I asked. Perfectly normal, he assured me; many men passed through that dark corridor on their way to purity. The end result, he promised, would be total manhood. To get there, Jason suggested I sign up for a five-day, $1,800 *Every Man's Battle* workshop (held monthly in hotels around the country), in which I would take classes on shame, "false intimacy," and "temptation cycles" and work with other "men of purity" toward "recovery."

Every Man's Battle also offered a two-day "outpatient program" for women, *Every Heart Restored*, to help them deal with their husbands' depravity, which is another one of the paradoxes of the purity movement. Men's sexuality, according to the movement, is on the one hand all-encompassing, capable of eroticizing nearly anything, and at the same time so simple and dumb that the best they can hope for is to adjust themselves to their wives' slow simmer. Women, meanwhile, are inherently purer than men and thus simpler, and yet their sexuality is complicated and subtle, a story in which husband and wife must play carefully scripted roles. Books such as *Wait For Me*, a tie-in to a Christian pop hit of the same name by the Christian singer Rebecca St. James, *What Every Woman Wants in a Man*, by Diana Hagee, and *When God Writes Your Love Story*, by Eric and Leslie Ludy—not to mention the numerous *Every Woman's Battle* titles and countless

Christian romance novels—peddle a soft-focus vision of female desire drawn not from scripture but from fairy tales. *Wait For Me* opens
with the claim that God has planted in every man and woman a
dream in which women long to be rescued by a "champion warrior"
with a "double-edged sword" from the towers in which they've been
imprisoned by the "Dark Lord." All women, writes Lisa Bevere in
Kissed the Girls and Made Them Cry: Why Women Lose *When They* Give
In, "long to be rescued by a knight in shining armor."

And yet *Kissed the Girls and Made Them Cry* goes deeper than chiv-
alrous clichés. Bevere's description of the love of Christ isn't filled
with the inadvertent innuendos that plague the men's guides ("true
manhood," promises one Christian manhood guide, gets "polished by
the hand of God") but rather an eroticism, studiously gentle and
mysterious, that is revealing of chastity's allure. Riffing on the scene
from the Gospel of John in which Jesus refuses to condemn an adul-
teress, Bevere writes, "At first, He is not willing to look at her or to
answer them. He bends down and writes in the dust. The finger of
God etches in dust letters that are not recorded for our knowledge."
Jesus, Bevere supposes, is thinking about man's first love, Eve. "Perhaps, in His memory He is seeing another who attempted to cover
her nakedness in a Garden long ago." She imagines every woman in
the crowd waiting to hear what Jesus will say; she hears in Christ's
rebuke to the men a secret message for women. "Let He who is without sin cast the first stone," Jesus preaches. For most people, the
story ends there, but Bevere lingers until the frustrated accusers have
left, and there is just Jesus and this naked woman, and finally "she
lifts her head and meets His gaze," and Jesus tells her He does not
condemn her, and tells her to go, and sin no more.

It's a beautiful scene, depicting Jesus as romantic hero. And it really is "countercultural," an alternative not just to the sexualized
world but also to the unforgiving fundamentalists of generations
past. But then Bevere writes—and this is really the crux of the
whole virginity movement—that the problem arose not because the
woman sinned, which goes without saying for Christian conservatives,
but because "a treacherous enemy has dragged the women of this

generation"—us, now—"naked and guilty before a holy God."
God forgives; that's why "revirgining" is always an option. "The
enemy" is the problem. Who is it? In the Gospel of John, the enemy,
as Bevere puts it, were Jews, those whom the gospel writer called
"the children of Satan"; but in the Gospel of Lisa Bevere, the enemy
is more abstract and more powerful. It's sex. Not "real sex," the kind
she enjoys with her husband, but everything else—every fantasy that
doesn't conform to wedded bliss, every thrill that doesn't belong in
church, the lust that spoils the romance of Christianity.

BEFORE ROBIN BECAME fully Christian—back when he cared as
much about his guitar as he did about God—he dated a non-Christian
girl. His voice grew husky as he remembered: "There were times,
when we were naked, and my tongue was inside her, and she's whispering for me to go further." Dunbar stared at him. He knew this
story, but he didn't mind hearing it again. It wasn't prurient for
them; it was bonding. "There were times," continued Robin, "when I
had to ask myself, 'What do I believe?' "
"But you weren't alone with her," Dunbar said.
"No."
Dunbar turned to me. "He had responsibility to us." His brothers.
But Robin kept letting them down. After high school, he stayed at
home for a year while Dunbar and the rest of his friends went on to
college. He joined a Christian punk band, Straight Forward. He
started slipping. At college, he continued to slide. He began dating a
woman only recently born again, still immature in her faith. She was
thrilled by Robin's attention; he was a man known to be on fire for
God. The girl—a "baby Christian," in the lingo—wanted to get closer
to that warmth. She did so the only way she knew how. "A blow job,"
said Robin.
It had been one thing to go down on his girlfriend when he wasn't
sure what he believed. It was another to let a girlfriend go down on
him after he'd committed himself to God. But then, he said, that's
how it works all too often when a man looks like he's devoted to

Jesus. "It becomes more about giving than receiving"—an implicit recognition of the sexism he knew permeated the best intentions. Even among Christians, the girls "will go down on you, but you don't have to go down on them." The experience, he said, broke his heart. What it did for the girl who sucked him off and got dumped for her impurity, he couldn't even imagine.

That summer, Robin and his fiancée were to marry back home in Visalia, where Dunbar would be his best man. Power felt like he had waited a long time. He didn't want to marry for sex, so he'd restrained himself from proposing until it did not even enter his mind. Soon he would experience his reward. A "sexual payoff," according to the authors of *Every Man's Battle*, that will "explode off any known scale."

Like the fundamentalists of old, today's Christian conservatives define themselves as apart from the world, and yet the modern movement aims to enjoy its fruits. To the biblical austerity of chastity, they add the promise of mind-blowing sex, using the very terms of the sexual revolution they rally against. And that's just the beginning. Sexual regulation is a means, not an end. To believers, the movement offers a vision grander even than the loveliness of a virgin: a fairy tale in which every man will be a spiritual warrior, a knight in the service of the king of kings, promised the hand and the heart and, yes, the sexual services of a "lady." That is the erotic dream of American fundamentalism: a restoration of chivalry, a cleansing of impurity, a nation without sin, an empire of the personal as political.

13.

UNSCHOOLING

W E KEEP TRYING TO explain away American fundamentalism. That is, those of us not engaged personally or emotionally in the biggest political and cultural movement of our times—those on the sidelines of history—keep trying to come up with theories to discredit the evident allure of this punishing yet oddly comforting idea of a deity, this strange god. His invisible hand is everywhere, say His citizen-theologians, caressing and fixing every outcome: Little League games, job searches, test scores, the spread of sexually transmitted diseases, the success or failure of terrorists, victory or defeat in battle, at the ballot box, in bed. Those unable to feel His soothing touch at moments such as these snort at the notion of a God with the patience or the prurience to monitor every tick and twitch of desire, a supreme being able to make a lion and a lamb cuddle but unable to abide two men kissing. A divine love that speaks through hurricanes. Who would worship such a god? His followers, we try to reassure ourselves, must be dupes, or saps, or fools, their faith illiterate, insane, or misinformed, their strength fleeting, hollow, an aberration.

We don't like to consider the possibility that they are not newcomers to power but returnees, that the revivals that have been sweeping the nation with generational regularity since its inception are not flare-ups but the natural temperature fluctuations of American empire. We can't accept the possibility that those we dismiss as dupes, or saps, or fools—the believers—have been with us from the very beginning, that their story about what America once was and

should be seems to some great portion of the population more compelling, more just, and more beautiful than the perfunctory processes of secular democracy. Thus we are at a loss to account for this
recurring American mood. The classic means of explaining it away—
class envy, sexual anxiety—do not suffice. We cannot, like H. L.
Mencken writing from the Scopes "monkey" trial of 1925, dismiss
the Christian Right as a carnival of backward buffoons resentful of
modernity's privileges. We cannot, like the *Washington Post* in 1993,
explain away the movement as "largely poor, uneducated, and easy to
command." We cannot, like the writer Theodor Adorno, a refugee
from Nazi Germany, attribute America's radical religion—nascent
fascism?—to Freudian yearning for a father figure.

No, God isn't dead; Freud and Marx are. The old theories have
failed. The new Christ, fifty years ago no more than a corollary to
American power, twenty-five years ago at its vanguard, is now at the
very center. His followers are not anxiously awaiting his return at the
rapture; he's here right now. They're not envious of the middle class,
they are the middle class. They're not looking for a hero to lead
them; they're building biblical households, every man endowed with
"headship" over his own family. They don't silence sex; they promise
sacred sex to those who couple properly—orgasms, according to a
bit of fundamentalist folklore passed between young singles, "600
percent" more intense for those who wait than those experienced by
secular lovers.

Intensity! That's what one finds within the ranks of the American believers. "This thing is real!" declare our nation's fundamentalist pastors. It's all coming together: the sacred and the profane,
God's time and straight time, what theologians and graduates of the
new fundamentalist prep schools might call *kairos* and *chronos*, the mystical and the mundane. American fundamentalism—not a political
party, not a denomination, not a uniform ideology but a manifold
movement—is moving in every direction all at once, claiming the
earth for God's kingdom, "in the world but not of it" and yet just
loving it to death, anyway. It feels fabulous, this faith, it tingles in all
the right places.

Those of us who find ourselves suddenly (or so it seems) at the dried-out margins keep telling ourselves that this country is still a democracy, and that democracy still means "moderation," private religion and a public square safe for "civil society." The fundamentalist Christ is not, we tell ourselves, the real Christ. He's an imposter, a faker, a fraud recently perpetrated on the good-hearted but gullible American masses by cynical men, manipulators, profiteers, a cabal of televangelists. Why? Greed. Anger. Fundamentalists are bitter, an eminent divine of academe opined at a gathering of worthies convened in 2005 by Boston's PBS affiliate, because they feel neglected by the Ivies. Perhaps more dialogue between Cambridge and Lynchburg, Virginia, home of Jerry Falwell's Liberty University, will heal us all.

Rationalism itself has been colonized by fundamentalism, remade in the image of the seductive but strict logic of a prime mover that sets things in motion, not just at the beginning but always. The cause behind every effect, says fundamentalist science, is God. Even the inexorable facts of math are subject to his decree, as explained in homeschooling texts such as *Mathematics: Is God Silent?* Two plus two is four because God says so. If he chose, it could just as easily be five.

It would be cliché to quote George Orwell here were it not for the fact that fundamentalist intellectuals do so with even greater frequency than those of the Left. At a rally to expose the "myth" of church/state separation in the spring of 2006, Orwell was quoted at me four times, most emphatically by William J. Federer, a compiler of quotations whose *America's God and Country*—a collection of seemingly theocratic bon mots distilled from the founders and other great men "for use in speeches, papers, [and] debates"—has sold half a million copies. "Those who control the past," Federer quoted Orwell's *1984*, "control the future."

Federer, a tall, lean, oaken-voiced man, loved talking about history as revelation, nodding along gently to his own lectures. He wore a gray suit, a red tie marred by a stain, and an American flag pin in his lapel. He looked like a congressman. He'd twice run for former

House minority leader Dick Gephardt's St. Louis seat. He lost both times, but the movement considers him a winner—in 2000, he faced Gephardt in the nation's third most expensive congressional race, forcing him to spend down his war chest and default on promises to fellow Democrats, a move that led to Gephardt's fall.

Federer and I were riding together in a white school bus full of Christians from around the country to pray at the site on which the Danbury, Connecticut, First Baptist Church once stood. It was in an 1802 letter to this church that Thomas Jefferson coined the phrase "wall of separation," three words upon which the battle over whether the United States is to be a Christian nation turns. Federer, leaning over the back of his seat as several pastors bent their ears toward his story, wanted me to understand that what Jefferson—notorious deist and author of the Virginia Statute for Religious Freedom—had really meant to promote was a "one-way wall," designed to protect the church from the state, not the other way around. Jefferson, Federer told me, was a believer; like all the Founders, he knew that there could be no government without God. Why hadn't I been taught this? Because I was a victim of godless public schools.

"Those who control the *present*," Federer continued darkly, "control the past." He paused and stared at me to make sure I understood the equation. "Orson Welles wrote that," he said.

Welles, Orwell, who cares? Federer wasn't talking tactics or, for that matter, even history; he was talking revolution, past, present, and future.

THE FIRST PILLAR of American fundamentalism is Jesus Christ; the second is history, and in the fundamentalist mind the two are converging. Fundamentalism considers itself a faith of basic truths unaltered (if not always acknowledged) since their transmission from heaven, first through the Bible and second through what they see as American scripture, divinely inspired, devoutly intended: the Declaration of Independence, the Constitution, and the often overlooked Northwest Ordinance of 1787, which declared "religion" necessary to "good government" and thus to be encouraged through schools. Well into the nineteenth century, most American schoolchildren learned their ABCs from *The New-England Primer*, which begins with "In Adam's Fall, we sinned all" and continues on to "Spiritual Milk for American Babes, Drawn out of the Breasts of Both Testaments." In 1836, *McGuffey's Eclectic Readers* began to displace the *Primer*, selling some 122 million copies of lessons such as "The Bible the Best of Classics" and "Religion the Only Basis of Society" during the following century.

It wasn't until the 1930s, the most irreligious decade in American history, that public education veered away from biblical indoctrination so thoroughly that within a few decades most Americans wrongly believed that nationalistic manifest destiny—itself thinly veiled Calvinism—rather than open piety was the American educational tradition. The fundamentalist movement sees that to reclaim America for God, it must first reclaim that tradition, and so it is producing a flood of educational texts with which to wash away the stains of secular history.

Such chronicles are written primarily for the homeschoolers and the fundamentalist academies that as of this writing together account for as much as 10 percent or more of the nation's children, an expanding population that buys a billion dollars' worth of educational materials annually. These pupils are known by many within the movement as "Generation Joshua," in honor of the biblical hero who marched seven times around Jericho before slaughtering "every living thing in it." The Home School Legal Defense Association has lately been attempting to organize Generation Joshua into "GenJ" political action clubs for teens modeled, claims the association, on a scheme for Christian governance conceived of by Alexander Hamilton shortly before Aaron Burr shot him dead in a duel. Set up by congressional district, the clubs study "America's Godly heritage," write letters to the editor, and register older siblings as voters. They adopt thrilling names such as Joshua's Arrows of Nashville, Tennessee, or Operation Impact of Los Gatos, California, or the GenJ Hot Rockin' Awesomes of Purcellville, Virginia.

"Who, knowing the facts of our history," asks the epigraph to the 2000 edition of *The American Republic for Christian Schools*, a junior high–level textbook, "can doubt that the United States of America has been a thought in the mind of God from all eternity?"[1] So that I would know the facts, I undertook my own course of home-schooling: in addition to *The American Republic*, I read the two-volume teacher's edition of *United States History for Christian Schools*, appropriate for eleventh-graders, and the accompanying *Economics for Christian Schools,** and I walked the streets of Brooklyn listening to an eighteen-tape lecture series on America up to 1865 created for a Christian college by the late Rousas John Rushdoony, the theologian who helped launch Christian homeschooling and revived the idea of reading American history through a providential lens.[†] I was down by the waterfront, pausing to scribble a note on Alexis de Tocqueville—Rushdoony argues that de Tocqueville was really a fundamentalist Christian disguised as a Frenchman—when a white and blue police van rolled up behind me and squawked its siren. There were four officers inside.

"What are you writing?" the driver asked. The other three leaned toward the window.

"Notes," I said, tapping my headphones.

"Okay. What are you listening to?"

I said I didn't think I had to tell him.

"This is a high-security area," he said. On the other side of a barbed-wire fence, he said, was a Coast Guard storage facility for deadly chemicals. "Somebody blow that up and boom, bye-bye Brooklyn." Note taking in the vicinity might be a problem. "So, I gotta ask again, what are you listening to?"

How to explain—to the cop who had just clued me in on the

---

*Sample lesson: "Above all, one must never come to see the propagation of the free market as an end in itself. The free market merely sets the stage for an unhindered propagation of the gospel of Jesus Christ."

†For instance: the "Protestant Wind" with which, according to an eleventh-grade text, God helped the British defeat the Spanish Armada so that the New World would not be overly settled by agents of the Vatican.

ripest terrorist target in Brooklyn—that I was listening to a Christian jihadi lecture on how democracy as practiced in America was defiance of God's intentions, how God gave to the United States the "irresistible blessings" of biblical capitalism unknown to Europe, and how we have vandalized this with vulgar regulations, how God loves the righteous who fight in His name?

Like this: "American history."

Providence would have been a better word. I was "unschooling" myself, Bill Apelian, the director of Bob Jones University Press, explained. What seemed to me a self-directed course of study was, in fact, the replacement of my secular assumptions with a curriculum guided by God. When BJU Press, one of the biggest fundamentalist educational publishers, started out thirty years ago, science was its most popular subject, and it could be summed up in one word: *created*. Now, American history is on the rise. "We call it Heritage Studies," Apelian said, and explained its growing centrality: "History *is* God's working in man."

My unschooling continued. I read Rushdoony's most influential contemporary, the late Francis Schaeffer, an American whose Swiss mountain retreat, L'Abri (The Shelter), served as a Christian madrassa at which a generation of fundamentalist intellectuals studied a reenchanted American past, "Christian at least in memory." And I read Schaeffer's disciples. Tim LaHaye, who besides coauthoring the hugely popular *Left Behind* series of novels has published an equally fantastical work of history called *Mind Siege*. ("The leading authorities of Secular Humanism may be pictured as a baseball team," writes LaHaye, with John Dewey as pitcher, Margaret Sanger in centerfield, Bertrand Russell at third, and Isaac Asimov at first). And David Barton, the president of a history ministry called WallBuilders (as in, to keep the heathen out); and Chuck Colson, who searches from the Greeks to the American founders to fellow Watergate felon G. Gordon Liddy for the essence of the Christian worldview, a vision of an American future so entirely Christ-filtered that beside it *theocracy*— the clumsy governance of priestly bureaucrats, disdained by Schaeffer and Colson—seems a modest ambition. *Theocentric* is the preferred term, Randall Terry, the Schaeffer disciple who went on to found Operation Rescue, one of the galvanizing forces of the anti-abortion movement, told me. "That means you view the world in His terms. Theocentrists, we don't believe man can create law. Man can only embrace or reject law." The study of history for fundamentalists is a process of divining that law, and to that end the theocentric world-view collapses the past into one great parable—Colson, for instance, studies the Roman Empire for insight into the expansion of America's—applicable at all stages of learning.

It is *character,* in the nineteenth-century, British Empire sense of the word, that drives American fundamentalism's engagement with the past. History matters not for its progression of "fact, fact, fact," Michael McHugh, one of the pioneers of modern funda-mentalist education told me, but for "key personalities." In Francis Schaeffer's telling of U.S. history, for instance, John Witherspoon—the only pastor to have signed the Declaration of Independence—looms as large as Thomas Jefferson, because it was Witherspoon who infused the founding with the idea of *Lex Rex,* "law is king" (divine law, that is), derived from the fiercest Protestant reformers of the seven-teenth century, men who considered John Calvin's Geneva too gentle for God. In the movement's history, key men are often those such as Witherspoon or Schaeffer himself, intellectuals and activists who shape ideas. But in the movement's telling of American history, key personalities are often soldiers, such as General Douglas MacArthur. After the war, McHugh explained, MacArthur ruled Japan "accord-ing to Christian principles" for five years. "To what end?" I asked. Ja-pan is hardly any more Christian for this divine intervention. "The Japanese people did capture a vision," McHugh said. Not the whole Christian deal but one of its essential foundations: "MacArthur set the stage for free enterprise," he explained. With Japan committed to capitalism, the United States was free to turn its attention toward the Soviet Union. The general's providential flanking maneuver, you might say, helped America win the Cold War.[2]

But one needn't be a flag officer to be used by God. Another favorite of Christian history is Sergeant Alvin York, a farmer from

Pall Mall, Tennessee, who in World War I turned his trigger finger over to God and became perhaps the greatest Christian sniper of the twentieth century.

"God uses ordinary people," McHugh explained. Anyone might be a key personality. The proper study of history includes the student as a main character, an approach he described as *relational*, a buzz-word in contemporary fundamentalism that denotes a sort of pulsing circuit of energy between, say, pleasant Betty Johnson, your churchy neighbor, and the awesome realm of supernatural events in which her real life occurs. There, Jesus is as real to Betty as she is to you, and so are Sergeant York, General MacArthur, and even George Washington, who, as "father of our nation," is almost a fourth member of the Holy Trinity, a mind bender made possible through God's math.

You may have seen his ghostly form, along with that of Abraham Lincoln, flanking an image of George W. Bush deep in prayer in a lithograph widely distributed by the Presidential Prayer Team, a five-year-old outfit that claims to have organized nearly 3 million prayer warriors on the president's behalf. The Prayer Team claims to transcend ideology because it will pray for the president whether he or she is a Republican or a Democrat. That is, it will always pray for authority. Its reverence built upon American fundamentalism's imagined history, the Prayer Team has neatly rewritten not only America's democratic tradition but also traditional Christianity, replacing both with an amalgamation of elite and populist fundamentalism. The legacy of Abram Vereide echoes in the Prayer Team's belief that the right relationship of citizen to leader is both spiritual and submissive, an idea it has dilated from the prayer cells of elites to its 3-million-strong "small group" approach to authoritarian religion. The populist twist is the promise that the citizen is not the victim of such disguised politics but, potentially, their star. In a similar image pasted onto five hundred billboards around the country, an ethereal Washington kneels in prayer with an anonymous soldier in desert fatigues—just another everyday hero. That could be you, the key man theory of fundamentalist history proposes. It's like the

Rapture, when the saved shall rise together, but it's happening right now: George Washington and Betty Johnson and you, floating up toward victory with arms entwined, key personalities in Christian history.

ONE AFTERNOON IN 2005, I found in my mail an unsolicited copy of the "Vision Forum Family Catalog," a glossy, handsomely produced, eighty-eight-page publication featuring an array of books, videos, and toys for "The Biblical Family Now and Forever." Considered the intellectual vanguard of the homeschooling movement by the other fundamentalist publishers with whom I'd spoken, Vision Forum is nonetheless just one of any number of providers for the fundamentalist lifestyle and hardly the largest. But its catalog is as perfect and polished a distillation as I've found of the romance of American fundamentalism, the almost sexual tension of its contradictions: its reverence for both rebellion and authority, democracy and theocracy, blood and innocence. The edition I received was titled "A Line in the Sand," in tribute to the Alamo. There, in 1836, faced with near-certain annihilation at the hands of the Mexican army, the Anglo rebel Lieutenant Colonel William Barret Travis rallied his doomed men by drawing said line with his sword and challenging them to cross it. All who did so, he said, would prove their preparedness "to give their lives in freedom's cause."

A boy of about eight enacts the scene on the catalog's cover. He is dark-eyed, big-eared, and dimple-chinned, and he's dressed in an idyllic costume only a romantic could imagine Colonel Travis wearing so close to his apocalyptic end: a white straw planter's hat, a Confederate gray, double-breasted shell jacket, a bow tie of black ribbon, a red sash, khaki jodhpurs, and shiny black fetish boots, spread wide. The young rebel seems to have been photoshopped in front of the Alamo at unlikely scale: he towers over a dark wooden door, as big as an eight-year-old boy's imagination.

Much of the catalog is given over to educational materials for Christian homeschoolers, but the back of the book is dedicated to equipping one's son with the sort of toys that will allow him to "rebuild a culture of courageous boyhood." Hats, for instance—leather Civil War kepis, coonskin caps, and a ninety-five-dollar life-size replica of a fifteenth-century knight's helmet among them. An eighteen-dollar video titled *Putting on the Whole Armor of God* asks, "Boys, are you ready for warfare?" Young Christian soldiers may choose from a variety of actual weapons, ranging from a scaled-down version of the blade wielded by William Wallace, of *Braveheart* fame (which at four and a quarter feet long is still a lot of knife for a kid) to a thirty-two-and-a-half-inch Confederate officer's saber. It is history at knifepoint; a theology of arms.

Not all of the toys are made for literal battle. For thirty dollars you can buy your boy an "Estwing Professional Rock Hammer," identical to those used by creationist paleontologists to prove that dinosaurs coexisted with Adam and Eve. For thirty-eight dollars you can acquire a "stellarscope" that functions as a pocket-sized planetarium for understanding God's heavens. I was tempted to buy my nephew an "Ancient Roman Coin Kit," which includes "ten genuine ancient Roman coins with accumulated dirt" and tools and instructions for cleaning and identifying them. "They will captivate you," "Line in the Sand" promises. "Were they held by a third-century Christian? A martyr?"

Martyrdom, real and metaphorical, is something of a family concern at Vision Forum. Founder Douglas W. Phillips's father, Howard, is a Harvard graduate, a veteran of the Nixon administration, and a Jewish convert to evangelicalism, all marks of a fine pedigree within elite Christian conservative culture. Moreover, Phillips was one of the small group that "discovered" Jerry Falwell, recruiting the Virginian to lead the Moral Majority in 1979. And yet Phillips's commitment to the intellectually dense ideas of Rousas John Rushdoony, considered too difficult and too extreme by many within the movement, led to internal exile within the populist front of American fundamentalism.

In the past few years, though, Phillips has regained a measure of his former influence. Ideas once considered too heady for a movement that defined itself through televangelists are now taught in elite colleges and universities such as Patrick Henry, Liberty, and Regent—institutions funded by the millions those TV preachers raised from the masses—as well as in the most august of Bible schools and Christian colleges, Wheaton, Westmont, Moody, and Biola, invigorated by a new generation of book-hungry homeschoolers. The anti-intellectualism that shaped the fundamentalism of the twentieth century has been replaced by a feverish thirst for intellectual legitimacy—to be achieved, however, not on terms set by secularism but by the Christian Right's very own eggheads, come in from the cold.

They've brought with them the anxiety of a besieged minority. They've lent to the angry mob ethos of the Moral Majority—now defunct, displaced by countless divisions and battalions, a united front in place of a single army—the cachet of an avant-garde, with all the attendant wounded pride of a misunderstood genius.

The chief candidate for that label within fundamentalism's intellectual revival is the late Rushdoony, whose eighteen-tape American history lectures I had obtained from Vision Forum. Rushdoony is best known as the founder of Christian Reconstructionism, a politically defunct but subtly influential school of thought that drifted so far to the right that it dropped off the edge of the world, disavowed as "scary" even by Jerry Falwell. Most notably, Rushdoony proposed the death penalty for an ever-expanding subset of sinners, starting with gay men and growing to include blasphemers and badly behaved children. Such sentiments have made him a bogeyman of the Left but also a convenient scapegoat for fundamentalist apologists. Ralph Reed, for instance, the former head of the Christian Coalition, made a great show of attacking the ideas of Reconstructionism as misguided, not to mention bad public relations. More recently, *First Things*, a journal for academically pedigreed Christian conservatives, published an oddly skeptical antimanifesto titled "Theocracy! Theocracy! Theocracy!" in which a young journalist, Ross Douthat, eyes rolling, dismisses the fears of the "antitheocrat" Left by propping up Rushdoony as a fringe lunatic only to knock him down along with the liberal critiques that focus on his angriest notions. (Douthat was evidently unaware of *First Things*'s lengthy tribute to Rushdoony upon his death in 2001.) That reading of Rushdoony—by liberal critics and conservative apologists—misses what matters about his revival of providential history.[3]

Rushdoony was a monster, but he wasn't insane. His most violent positions were the result of fundamentalism's requisite literalist reading of scripture, an approach that one senses rather bored him. A natural ideologue, he seemed drawn most emotionally not to the strict legal code of Leviticus but to the "strange fire" of its tenth chapter, the blasphemous tribute paid to God by priests lost in the aesthetics of devotion. Rushdoony would have had them killed for their presumption, which is exactly what God did. But I imagine Rushdoony sympathized with their misguided sentiments. His Reconstructionist movement fell apart when his son-in-law, an even more bloodthirsty theologian named Gary North, split with Rushdoony over what he saw as his father-in-law's romantic insistence that the Constitution was an entirely God-breathed document, perverted by politicians, no doubt, but purely of heaven at its inception. North, who may actually be a psychopath—he favors stoning as a method of execution because it would double as a "community project"—was right on this one occasion.

Rushdoony was to the study of history what a holy warrior is to jihad, submitting his mind completely to God. He derived from the past not just a quaint hero worship but also a deep knowledge of history's losers, forgotten Americans—minor political figures like John Witherspoon and major revivalists like Charles Grandison Finney and all the soldiers who fought first for God, *then* country, the rugged men of the past who carried the theocratic strand through from the beginning. The Christian conservatives of his day, Rushdoony believed, had let themselves be bound by secularism. They railed against its tyranny but addressed themselves only to issues set aside by secularism as "moral"; the best minds of a fundamentalist generation burned themselves to furious cinders battling nothing more than naughty movies and heavy petting. Rushdoony did not believe in such skirmishes. He wanted a war, and he summoned the spirits of history to the struggle at hand.

Two central Rushdoony ideas, disassociated from his name, have since been assimilated into the mainstream of Christian conservative thinking. One is Christian education: homeschooling and private Protestant academies, both of which he was among the first to advocate during the early 1960s. Among the chief champions of that educational movement today are John W. Whitehead, a constitutional lawyer who counts Rushdoony as one of his greatest influences, and the founders of two fundamentalist colleges, Patrick Henry and New St. Andrews, explicitly dedicated to training culture warriors according to the tenets of Rushdoony's other major contribution to postwar fundamentalism: the revival of the American providential history that had been rusting since the nineteenth century, when no less a hero of the secular past than Daniel Webster declared history "a study of secondary causes that God uses and permits in order to fulfill his inscrutable decree." During the intervening years, elite fundamentalists studied at elite universities (Rushdoony attended Berkeley), and the rest of the faithful went to public schools and perhaps a Bible college. Elites learned secular history; the rest rarely learned much history at all, a state of affairs that kept the movement divided. It was Rushdoony's disdain for all things secular that cleared the course for the convergence in the last few decades of the two streams of fundamentalist culture, united across classes behind a vision of a "God-led" society.

A strict Calvinist influenced by his upbringing in the Armenian Presbyterian Church, Rushdoony found his way to the turn-of-the-century Dutch theologian Abraham Kuyper and his idea of *presuppositionalism,* which maintains that (a) everybody approaches the world with assumptions, thus ruling out the possibility of neutrality and a classically liberal state; and (b) that since Christian presuppositions acknowledge themselves as such (unlike liberalism's, which are deliberately ahistorical), every aspect of governance should be conducted in the light of its revealed truths. "There is not a square inch in the whole domain of our human experience," declared Kuyper, "over which Christ, who is Sovereign over *all*, does not cry 'Mine!' "[4]

And yet Kuyper's Christ—more the product of nineteenth-century imperialism than of scripture—is, in a sense, an afterthought to Kuyper's first assertion, which anticipated postmodernism and its distrust of modernity's claim that we can know "facts" absent the interference of values. Kuyper turned instead to divine love as the foundation of what Rushdoony—and now the majority of the Christian conservative intellectuals—called a *biblical worldview,* a refinement of theology into political ideology.

Kuyper was both a democrat and a theologian who as Dutch prime minister tried to conform all aspects of his country to his vision of God. For much of the twentieth century, he was remembered fondly only by progressive Social Gospel Christians, who saw in his European project of state health care and free education and even a market conformed to biblical law, to the detriment of raw capitalism, a foreshadowing of the "city upon a hill" prophesied for America by John Winthrop in 1630.[5]

Rushdoony agreed, and he thought most Americans would as well, once they understood that scripture was the source of the nation's idealism. He spoke often of his fondness for John F. Kennedy's rhetoric, for instance, in which he heard echoes of America as a redeemer nation. "God's work must be our own," declared Kennedy, and Rushdoony smiled sadly. "They've lost the theology," Rushdoony would lecture ten years after Kennedy's death, "but they haven't lost the faith."

Restoring the former was a matter not of grace but of education. New generations would have to be raised up who understood the ancestry of language such as Kennedy's, who would seek to fulfill the vision not through social programs—unlike Kuyper, Rushdoony scorned governmental attempts to ameliorate suffering that he took to be God's "inscrutable decree"—but through the intellectual as well as spiritual embrace of true religion. Telling kids to stay clear of bad influences would not do the job. Bible camps and radio preachers and all the various campus crusades and college clubs for the mildest of young people—no redeemers, they—had failed. Rushdoony decided to start from the beginning, to claim the future by reclaiming the past.

AMID A PANTHEON now celebrated by fundamentalist historians, the most surprising hero is Stonewall Jackson of the Confederacy, perhaps the most brilliant general in American history and certainly the most pious. *United States History for Christian Schools* devotes more space to Jackson, "Soldier of the Cross," and the revivals he led among his troops in the midst of the Civil War, than to either Robert E. Lee or U. S. Grant; *Practical Homeschooling* magazine offers instructions for making Stonewall costumes out of gray sweatsuits with which to celebrate his birthday, declared a homeschooling "fun day." Fundamentalists even celebrate him as an early civil rights visionary, dedicated to teaching slaves to read so that they could learn their Bible lessons. For fundamentalist admirers, that is enough, as evidenced by the 2006 publication of *Stonewall Jackson: The Black Man's Friend*, by Richard G. Williams, a regular contributor to the conservative *Washington Times*.

Jackson's popularity with fundamentalists represents the triumph of the Christian history Rushdoony dreamed of when he discovered, during the early 1960s, a forgotten volume titled *The Life and Campaigns of Lieutenant General Thomas J. Stonewall Jackson*. Its author, Robert Lewis Dabney, had served under Jackson, but more important he was a Calvinist theologian who believed deeply in a God who worked through chosen individuals, and he wrote the general's life in biblical terms. To Rushdoony, the story transcended its Confederate origins, and he helped make it a founding text of the nascent homeschooling movement. It's not the Confederacy fundamentalists love but martyrdom. Jackson fought first for God and only second for Virginia, and, as every fundamentalist fan knows, no Yankee bullet could touch him. He was shot accidentally by his own men and nonetheless died happy on a Sunday, content that he had arrived at God's chosen hour.

Born in the mountains of what later became West Virginia, Jackson was orphaned by the time he was seven. His stepfather shipped the boy off to one uncle who beat him and then another who gambled and counterfeited and drank but also let him read. Against all expectations and two years later than most, he became a cadet at West Point. He began at the bottom of his class.[6]

Four years later, he had climbed close to the top, and without the help of charisma. His frame and his face had broadened, but his eyes, pale irises of cornflower ringed in dead-of-night blue, seemed distant. His nose was long, wavering, and it ended in what looked like a permanent drip. His bright red lips curled inward, as if hiding. Even as an army officer, he felt so out of place in "society" that he was deathly afraid of public speaking. Absent enemy fire, he did not know how to take a stand. Before the war he watched John Brown hang with his own eyes and marveled at the strength of the man's Christian conviction and wondered, perhaps, what he would have done had it been his neck in the noose. And yet when his own time to fight came, he proved just as ferociously devoted to his cause. In *All Things for the Good: The Steadfast Fidelity of Stonewall Jackson*, the fundamentalist historian J. Steven Wilkins opens a chapter on Jackson's belief in the "black flag" of no quarter for the enemy with a quotation of Jackson's view of mercy toward Union soldiers: "Shoot them all, I do not wish them to be brave."

Earlier, in the Mexican War, Lieutenant Jackson defied an order to retreat, fought the Mexican cavalry alone with one artillery piece, and won. General Winfield Scott, commander of the U.S. forces, commended him for "the way [he] slaughtered those poor Mexicans." Many of the poor Mexicans slaughtered by Jackson were civilians. His small victory helped clear the way for the American advance, and Jackson was ordered to turn his guns on Mexico City residents attempting to flee the oncoming U.S. Army. He did so without hesitation—mowing them down even as they sought to surrender.

What are we to make of this murder? Fundamentalists see in that willingness to kill innocents confirmation of Romans 13:1. This snippet of Paul's best-known epistle is a key verse for the Christian Right: "For there is no power but of God; the powers that be are ordained of God." Obeying one's superiors, according to this logic, is an act of devotion to the God above them.

But wait. Fundamentalists also praise the heroism that resulted from Jackson's defiance of orders to retreat, his rout of the Mexican cavalry so miraculous—it's said that a cannonball bounced between his legs as he stood fast—that it seems to fundamentalist biographers proof that he was anointed by God. Is this hypocrisy on the part of his fans? Not exactly.

Key men always obey orders, but they follow the command of the highest authority. Jackson's amazing victory is taken as evidence that God was with him—that God overrode the orders of his earthly commanders. The civilians dead as a result of Jackson's subsequent obedience to those same earthly commanders are also signs of God's guiding hand. The providential God sees everything; that such a tragedy was allowed to occur must therefore be evidence of a greater plan. One of fundamentalist history's favorite proofs comes not from scripture itself but from Ben Franklin's paraphrase at the Constitutional Convention: "If a sparrow cannot fall to the ground without His notice, is it probable that an empire can rise without his aid?"

Put in political terms, the contradictory legend of Stonewall Jackson—rebellion and reverence, rage and order—results in the synthesis of self-destructive patriotism embraced by contemporary fundamentalism. A striking example is a short video on faith and diplomacy made in the aftermath of September 11, 2001, by Christian Embassy, a behind-the-scenes ministry for government and military elites created in 1974 as a sister ministry to the Family, with which it coordinates its efforts.[7] Its founders, Bill Bright of Campus Crusade and Congressman John Conlan, considered themselves America's saviors. For Bright, the threat was always communism, but for Conlan, it was a Jewish congressional opponent who, lacking "a clear testimony for Jesus Christ," would not be able to fulfill his responsibilities.[8]

And yet, Christian Embassy's self-promotional video almost seems to endorse deliberate negligence of duty. Dan Cooper, then an under-secretary of defense, grins for the camera as he announces that his evangelizing activities are "more important than doing the job." Major General Jack Catton, testifying in uniform at the Pentagon—an apparent violation of military regulations intended to keep the armed forces neutral on religious questions—says he sees his position as an adviser to the Joint Chiefs of Staff as a "wonderful opportunity" to evangelize men and women setting defense policy. "My first priority is my faith," he tells them; God before country. "I think it's a huge impact," he says. "You have many men and women who are seeking God's counsel and wisdom as they advise the chairman [of the Joint Chiefs] and the secretary of defense." Christian Embassy also sends congressional delegations to Africa and Eastern Europe. "We were congressmen goin' over there to represent the Lord," says Representative John Carter of Texas. "We are here to tell you about Jesus . . . and that's it."

The Embassy encourages its prayer-cell members in the State Department to do the same; their first priority is not to explain U.S. positions but to send the diplomats home "with a personal relationship with the King of Kings, Jesus Christ."[9] Brigadier General Bob Caslen, promoted since the making of the video to commandant of West Point, puts it in sensual terms: "We are the aroma of Jesus." There's a joyous disregard for democracy in these sentiments, its demands and its compromises, that in its darkest manifestation becomes the overlooked piety at the heart of the old logic of Vietnam, lately applied to Iraq: in order to save the village, we must destroy it.[10]

But that story is older than Vietnam. Here's the village life, modest and hard but sustained by tender mercies, that Jackson wanted to save: Between the Mexican War and the Civil War, he moved to tiny Lexington, Virginia, to become a teacher. He married a minister's daughter, gardened, took long strolls, meditated often on peaceful portions of scripture. The bloody hero of the Mexican War disappeared, replaced by a shy, painfully polite man, obsessed with "taking the waters" for his frail constitution. When the minister's daughter died bearing their stillborn child, he married again, his "beloved esposa," Anna Jackson, who, after his death, revealed that whenever they were alone together the publicly awkward, nervous man would grab her, kiss her, and twirl her round. They danced secret polkas. He taught Sunday school.

This is the myth of the quiet man, a noble soul of no outward distinction. "When it came to learning," writes the Christian biographer J. Steven Wilkins, assessing his hero's visible assets in *All Things for the Good,* "everything was a challenge." Wilkins continues: "He did not have striking characteristics . . . He was gangly, uncoordinated, and spoke in a high-pitched voice . . . He did not have a great personality." Slow, homely, and squeaky; also, peculiar in his posture—he sat ramrod straight, he said, because he was afraid of squishing his organs—and known by what friends he had for smiling lamely when he guessed that someone was saying something funny. Then came the war.

Jackson didn't want it. Didn't want slavery (but accepted it as ordained of God and kept five slaves), didn't want secession (but accepted it as the will of Virginia, "to which [his] sword belongs"), didn't want anything but quiet in which to consider his diet (a source of deep fascination and increasing asceticism as the war grew closer) and Scripture (he wished he'd been called by God to the ministry). Instead, he was called to killing. "Draw the sword," he told his students, "and throw away the scabbard."

Anxious about praying aloud in front of others, in battle, Jackson would abandon the reins of his horse to lift up his hands toward heaven. In camp he led revivals and stumbled about as if blind, his eyes shut as he talked to God. Under fire he shouted his prayers, imploring God not for mercy but for the blood of his enemies. "He lives by the New Testament and fights by the Old," wrote a contemporary, a standard to which the movement now aspires. "He had none of the things held to be essential for leadership," writes biographer Wilkins. "All he had was a sincere fear of God."

This, too, is the American myth of the quiet man, transformed by crisis into a hero. This is the model for spiritual warfare American fundamentalism wants to implement in every household, each family and every living room Bible study group discovering within itself unexpected reserves of leadership and, as need arises, ferocity. Jackson's troops thought he was literally invulnerable. His presence among his men inspired them to fearlessness in battle. And yet Jackson was killed in 1863 by his own men, who mistook his return from an unannounced scouting sortie as a Union charge. This, too, is an old story: felled within the walls. Our heroes are too great to be killed by the enemy; only our own weaknesses can undo us. Southern dreamers say the Confederacy would have won, abolished slavery peacefully, and established a true Christian nation had Jackson, "the greatest Christian general in the history of this nation," lived to continue outflanking the Union army.

Of course, we would have won in Vietnam, too, if only we hadn't tied our own hands, and we'd win in Iraq, if only Democrats would stop whining. Most of all, we—the believers—could finally build that city upon a hill God promised the as-yet-unformed nation nearly four centuries ago, if only we could submit to God. Jackson, note his Christian biographers, saw this problem even before the war. "We call ourselves a Christian people," Jackson once wrote, but what he considered the "extreme" doctrine of separation prevented the United States from fulfilling its destiny.

Look at his wisdom! say his Christian biographers. "A gift from God," he would have demurred. Oh, the humility of this fallen hero, cries American fundamentalism, always deep in conversation with its mythic past, the model for a new struggle.

WHEN WILLIAM FEDERER and I reached the overgrown foundation stones of Danbury Baptist, which sit on a grassy hill sprinkled with pale violets, we gathered in a circle with an invitation-only crowd of pastors and activists from around the country. The event's organizer was Dave Daubenmire, a former high school football coach from Ohio who'd done battle with the ACLU over his insistence on praying with his players. Since then he'd launched a fundamentalist ministry called Minutemen United, with which he was climbing the ladder of the activist hierarchy.* Still a minor league outfit, the Minutemen had managed to wrangle some respectable B-list activists. Besides Federer, there was the Reverend Rob Schenck. Schenck brought greetings from the Library of Congress's chief of manuscripts, who, he said, had used "FBI classified technology" to discover previously unknown margin notes in Jefferson's 1802 letter proving his Christian intentions. There was the Patriot Pastor, a giant man from New Hampshire who travels the country in a tricorne hat, black vest, frilly shirt, and leggings, lecturing on the "Black Regiment," the fighting pastors of the Revolutionary War. "This is the manifest destiny of my life," he told me. There was the Reverend Flip Benham, head of Operation Save America, also known as Operation Rescue. He was the man who baptized Norma McCorvey—Jane Roe of *Roe v. Wade*—into fundamentalism. For the rally, he was wearing vintage white-and-brown wingtips, symbols of his commitment to pre-1947 America—1947 being the year when the Supreme Court ruled according to Jefferson's "wall of separation" for the first time, in a case concerning government funds for parochial schools.

Providential historians are divided on the question of whether it was this decision, *Everson v. Board of Education,* or FDR's socialistic New Deal that led God to withdraw his protection from the nation. Operation Save America's number two, Pastor Rusty Thomas of Waco, Texas, favors the less controversial New Deal school of thought. God, Rusty told me, "always gave us a left hook of judgment, then he gave us a right cross of revival." But when the left hook of the Great Depression came, goes the economic theory of fundamentalism, Americans turned to government as their savior instead of God. "So we got another left hook." Kennedy's assassination, he explained. Then another left hook: Vietnam. Still we didn't learn. So God kept throwing punches, said Rusty: crack, AIDS,

---

*The Minutemen United should not be confused with the anti-immigrant Minutemen militias. Coach Dave's outfit is every bit as militaristic in its rhetoric—one related ministry is called Polished Shaft—but educational in its operations, offering, for instance, instruction in America's "godly heritage" for schoolteachers.

global warming, September 11, thousands of flag-draped coffins shipped home from Iraq and more on the way.

Rusty began the day's preaching, pacing back and forth between Danbury Baptist's foundation stones. He looked like an exclamation point—tiny feet in thin-soled black leather shoes, almost dwarfish legs, and a powerful torso barely contained by a jacket of double-breasted gray houndstooth. But he had one of the most nuanced preaching voices I've ever heard, a soft rasp that seemed to come straight from a broken heart. "We are here to start a gentle revolution," he whispered, "to reclaim the godly heritage." He sounded sad, for his sin and mine. We were all guilty of turning our backs on the lessons of history. But then he growled up to a volume that made even the flaxen-haired pastor beside me literally blink before leaning forward into Rusty's thunder.

"And when you go to war in your land," Rusty recited from the Book of Numbers, "—and make no mistake about it, we are in a war—"

Amen! hollered Reverend Flip.

"And when you go to war in your land," continued Rusty, "against an adversary who *oppresses* you"—and here he interrupted himself: "How many besides me are *vexed* by what is happening in the United States of America today?"

The crowd, shedding jackets and coats beneath a wan but warm spring sun, murmured *amen.*

"Your soul is *vexed,*" Rusty moaned. Then he cried out, "We are under oppression!"

"AMEN!" responded the crowd, amping up to match Rusty's increased volume. The bill of grievances was hard: "Are we not in mourning?" Rusty asked, repeating the question and drawing it out as the women among us closed their eyes and said, plain and simple, *yes.* "Are we not in mournnnning?" he moaned. "As terrorism strikes us from without, corruptions from within?" *Yes,* said the women, the men seemingly shamed into silence. "How many know we're losing our children?" *Yes.* "Our marriages are failing!" *YES.*

Pastor Rusty, in fact, was a single father of ten, the youngest of whom is named Torah. Liz, his wife of twenty years, had died a year past from lymphoma, on the verge of what seemed like recovery. Reverend Flip had chronicled online her long fight, a roller coaster of remission and relapse, so that the family's prayer partners—activists and Christian radio listeners across the country—could help fight for her survival. "Good night for now, sweet sister," Flip wrote when they failed. "We'll see you in the morning."

Grief, not arrogance, translates the promise of salvation—"whosoever shall lose his life for my sake shall find it"—into a battle cry. For believers fortified by the providential past, all of history's lessons curdle into the tragedy of one's own awful losses, and the anguish that emerges is not singular but like that of a vast choir, a Christian nation punished for sin and yet promised ultimate victory. Later that afternoon, on the Danbury village green, Rusty would grip my arm and pull me close, tears streaming from jay-blue eyes as he confessed that he had betrayed God. He had neglected the twin sins fundamentalists believe to be the collective responsibility of the entire society in which they occur. "Child sacrifice"—by which he meant abortion—"and homosexual sodomy. Any nation that condoned those behaviors? That did not challenge them, that did not prevent them from happening? It will be reduced to rubble."

He shook his head, eyes squeezed shut. The church had allowed women to murder their children and men through sodomy to damn themselves and all their brothers. It was his fault more than theirs because he knew the "blueprint of God's Word." He had pored over the Bible and the Constitution and the Mayflower Compact, had memorized choice words from John Adams and John Witherspoon and Patrick Henry, Jeremiah and Nehemiah and John the Revelator. Scripture and American history are in agreement, he had found: beneath God, family, and church is the state, with only one simple responsibility: "The symbol of the state is a sword. Not a spoon, feeding the poor, not a teaching instrument to educate our young." Rusty stepped back, fists clenching. "And the sword is an instrument of death!" he yelled. He twitched his Italian loafers in a preacher two-step. He shook out his neck like a boxer. Then sorrow slumped his shoulders. He had failed to wield the sword. He had failed the widows and orphans. He had failed his brothers lost to sodomy. "There's nobody clean in this," he whispered.

There is a *mother church,* Rusty preaches, and a *father church,* separate but equal aspects of God. The mother church nurtures and holds a child when he's done wrong; the father church is the church of discipline. The mother church feeds the poor, comforts the dying, attempting to remind nations of righteous behavior. But to Rusty the lesson of American history, the lesson of Valley Forge and Shiloh, Khe Sanh and Baghdad, Dallas 1963, *Roe v. Wade* 1973, Manhattan 2001, is clear: this nation is too far gone to be redeemed by mercy alone. It is the father church's turn.

"Then shall you sound an alarm with a trumpet that you may be remembered before the Lord your God," he preached on the hill at Danbury, again quoting from the Book of Numbers, "and you SHOUT"—he replaced the future tense of the biblical *shall* with his own present-tense bellow—"to be saved from your enemy!" He turned to the man standing behind him, a wiry, goateed musician in a brown bomber jacket. "So, brother," Rusty called, his voice now joyful, "let it rip, potato chip!" At which the slender man blew his horn.

THE DAY'S APPOINTED born-again *ba'al tokea,* the "master of the blast," was named Lane Medcalf, and his instrument was a shofar, a Jewish trumpet, a three-foot-long spiral horn hewn from the head of a ram, boiled clean of cartilage, polished to a high gleam. Generally reserved for Rosh Hashanah and Yom Kippur, once upon a time its blast signaled Joshua's assault on Jericho, the first battle for the Promised Land.

Medcalf had borrowed his shofar from his boss's wife, also a Christian. He was an artificial flavor compounder, less than a chemist but more than a factory worker. He had been saved since he was a teenager, but lately he had become engrossed in Jewish history. He was slender and slight in the shoulders, cautious but earnest about his words. Except for his pale blue eyes, he could have passed for a rabbinical student on the lam from his studies, despite the fact that he was fifty-three. If he'd grown up in Brooklyn instead of Minnesota, he might have been called a *luftmensch*, Yiddish for a sweet soul who seems a little lost.

But Medcalf wasn't interested in Yiddish; he wanted to know Hebrew. And he wasn't contemplating conversion; he was simply going deeper into the past, in search of a truer Christianity, a faith more raw. "We've lost our Judeo side," he told me later. By this, he meant fighting spirit. "The shofar was for warfare," he explained. "You know, alarm, in a battle situation. It's still a weapon of warfare, but for fighting demonic influence." Medcalf's shofar blasts that day, for instance, were intended to travel through time and slay the invisible demons that had once surrounded Supreme Court justice Hugo Black, the author of the *Everson v. Board of Education* decision, in 1947.

"Hugo got a little skewed," he told me. Black himself had not been evil, Medcalf explained, just overwhelmed by Satan, who whispered in his ear. "I was told"—here Medcalf's voice dropped a note—"that he was a former Ku Klux Klan member." (This is true. He was also a Protestant, and his decision was in keeping with that period's fundamentalist animus toward Catholic schools.) Medcalf had also been told, he continued, that in the mid-1950s there had been another Supreme Court decision, he couldn't remember the name, that forced children to go to school where they didn't want to go. This also is technically true. Medcalf may have been referring to *Brown v. Board of Education,* the 1954 decision that overturned official school segregation, leading to busing and the formation of private, all-white evangelical academies.

It was *Brown*, along with two decisions in the early 1960s striking down school prayer, that led to fundamentalism's embrace of history as a redeeming creed. They had a right to educate their children religiously. Catholics already had a system for doing so. Fundamentalists began to build one, and the bricks of its construction were the proof-texts of an alternate Christian nation: the letters of John Jay, the first chief justice of the Supreme Court, on the biblical justifications for America's wars; President James Garfield's Gilded Age plea for more Christians in high offices; even, eventually, the speeches of Martin Luther King Jr., claimed now from megachurch pulpits across the country as a martyr of fundamentalism. "All it takes is a God-intoxicated people," they quote King, inaccurately and indifferent to context, "one generation, to alter the course of history from then on."[11]

Medcalf was part of the generation for whom King was a hero rather than a villain. When he was a kid, his older brother joined a Christian rock band, and when he played his guitar kids prayed out loud, free form, with their hands in the air and their whole bodies swaying, and girls flocked to him. "I had never seen Christianity like that before," Medcalf remembered. He wanted to join the band. He learned keyboards and the drums. "Suddenly, I could understand the Bible. The Holy Spirit got up on me. Man!" "Church" was no longer a place you went to; it was an experience you consumed, and you wanted as much as you could get. You wore your jeans to worship and grew your hair long. You called yourself a Jesus freak and you called Jesus a revolutionary. You listened to groups like The Way and Love Song and the All Saved Freak Band, and you read rags like *Right On!* and *The Fish* and *Hollywood Free Paper*. " 'Truckin' for Jesus,' " Medcalf remembered. "Solid stuff, man."

In 1972, he went to Dallas, for Campus Crusade's "Explo"— "Godstock" for the Jesus People.[12] Eighty-five thousand Jesus freaks packed the Cotton Bowl for a week straight of Christian rock and preaching. When Billy Graham took the stage, all he could do was smile with a hand outstretched in salute as the crowd screamed their love for ten minutes solid. "It was awesome," Medcalf said. "We knew what he had done for us. He gave us the pure gospel."

Medcalf suddenly looked sad. He blinked, as if holding back tears. What had gone wrong?

"We sold ourselves," he said, his voice nearly a whisper. He meant it literally: albums and t-shirts, "*bumper stickers*." Commercialism killed Christian rock n' roll. "We lost our teeth." One year after

Explo, the Supreme Court handed down *Roe v. Wade*. "It happened on our watch, man," Medcalf said. The Jesus freaks had failed. They had lived for today and forgotten tomorrow, and then it had slipped away from them. To get it back, Medcalf said, the movement must go backward. Not to the 1960s but to "before." It needs a foundation, he explained, eternal truths. These were to be found in two places: the Bible and the Constitution.

. While we were talking, Reverend Flip had begun to preach. He told the crowd about a recent victory he'd scored near Charlotte, North Carolina, where he'd led seven hundred prayer warriors to a school board meeting to protest the formation of a Gay-Straight Alliance club in a local high school. "The preachers preached, the singers sang, the pray-ers prayed, and the theology of the church became biography in the streets!" Flip said. The school board shut down the club—a deliberate bid, it had declared, to bring the issue before the courts and get gay-straight clubs outlawed everywhere. Flip said this was what Jesus wanted. He even did an impression: "Cry to me," he said in his best bass God voice; the prayers of the righteous will be answered.

Medcalf smiled and applauded gently. He told me how his prayers had changed when he started studying history and blowing the shofar. "I was praying for God to restore America back to its roots one day when I had what I guess you would call a supernatural experience. The Holy Spirit caused me to weep and cry, enabling me to have a broken heart. 'Please come back,' I prayed. It was just so intense." It worked: "Things have started changing." He said the appointments of Samuel Alito and John Roberts to the Supreme Court were probably the result of God's intervention. They may be the men God was waiting for, the right tools for the job of restoration. They may be under an anointing.

That's the secret of Christian history. It doesn't require great men—Medcalf considered Bush's 2000 election an "answer to prayer," but he was under no illusions about the president's natural abilities—only willing men, ready to be anointed. Bush was one; Medcalf was another. Medcalf submitted to Bush's authority according to

Romans 13—"the powers that be are ordained of God"—but both submitted equally to God's guiding hand. To Medcalf this resulted in a democracy more radical than any dreamed of in the 1960s. In the flow of secular time, Medcalf was a nebbish from Connecticut, mixing beakers full of artificial flavors. But in Christian time, he was a herald, blowing his shofar back to 1947, calling the key men of our Christian nation's history to battle.

AFTER THE RALLY in Danbury, I joined a group of about twenty pastors, activists, and a few wives for a victory dinner. It really had felt victorious; Pastor Rusty had worked the crowd into a high fever of *hallelujahs*, and then all the pastors had joined hands in a circle at the center for round robin prayer. The Reverend Jim Lilly, a white hip-hop Assemblies of God preacher from a nearby town, led the way, his neck heavy with cruciform bling and bobbing up and down to the beat of his own exhortations, his smooth tenor gone gravelly: "YES, LORD! PULL IT DOWN, LORD! PULL DOWN THAT LIE!" He meant history as told absent the anointing of God. "KING OF GLORY! COME IN! KING OF GLORY! MIGHTY IN BATTLE! MANIFEST YOURSELF ON THIS LAND!" A pastor from a Latino fundamentalist church in the Midwest grabbed the reins: "Lord God, we pray for the restoration of the land!" Reverend Lilly was overtaken by a fit of what's called *holy laughter,* a gift of the spirit that's like speaking in tongues. Medcalf got busy on his shofar, and the whole crowd decided to march seven times around the foundation, just like Jericho, singing in unison an old gospel hymn, "Power in the Blood," *There is pow'r, pow'r, wonder-workin' pow'r, in—the—prec—ious—blood—of—the—lamb!*

Everyone was feeling pretty high at the dinner later that evening. They dragged four long tables into a giant square on the second floor of the restaurant, an Italian joint that doubled as the kind of comedy club that brings in sidekicks from Howard Stern's radio show. I sat between the Patriot Pastor, still in costume, and Bill Federer, an accidental place of honor that seemed to make some of the event's local field organizers a little jealous. Across the table sat Pastor Rusty and Reverend Flip. Flip threw his tie over his shoulder and leaned back in his chair. The waitress, a handsome middle-aged woman named Anna, looked crushed when she learned that the whole group, out of respect for the nondrinkers among them, would be sticking to iced tea. Several of the men asked her where her accent was from. She said she was Polish-Russian, but when she came around to Flip, he said, "Hola, Señorita," and asked her where she was from. Anna rolled her eyes. We ordered, most of us the buffet. Anna came back to refill our iced tea. She tried to tally the orders, which the pastors kept changing. "You ordered the buffet?" she asked Flip.

Flip took a toothpick from his mouth, fixed her with a stare. He owned the room. "I think I already had a buffet," he said, pronouncing the word as *Buffy*. "Now I'd like to try an Anna."

Nobody missed a beat. The party went on.

I thought, Here's where it would be easiest to unravel the whole tapestry of fundamentalism. To dismiss it as rank hypocrisy, a bunch of bullies cloaking their lusts, for sex or money or power, in piety. But to do so would be to ignore the anointing. Flip doesn't command whatever small following he has in the movement because he's a good man but because he's God's chosen man. "God uses who he chooses," a North Carolina preacher once told me, the essence of John Calvin's dense theology of *election* boiled down to an advertising slogan. Flip obeyed orders, and that made him a key man.

"Obedience is my greatest weapon," Coach Dave told me after dinner. He took off the ball cap he'd had made, blue black with a red cross, and ran his hand through his white hair. In obedience, he said, he found strength. Coach Dave was built like an old can of beans, squat and solid with muscle except for a bulge in the middle. I imagined him lecturing his former football team. Obedience, he continued, was a gift from God; but you needed the Holy Spirit to open it. "The Holy Spirit is like the software," he said.

He tried to explain. "We may need another 9/11," he declared slowly, a teacher reciting a lesson, "to bring about a full spiritual revival." He must have seen my surprise. "Now, you don't get that, do you?" I admitted that I did not. Well, he continued, history's horrors are just like God spanking a child. "That's a perfect example of where you need the software to understand what I just said, or else you're gonna say, 'Coach, you mean he spanks us by killing people?' You need the software. What's the software? Well, it's history. You gotta understand what history is. It's collective. Are you getting the software? *Collective. History.*"

Now I got it. Fundamentalism blends the concept of a God involved in our daily affairs with the Enlightenment's rationalization of that deity as a broader, more vague "common good." The fundamentalist God is first and foremost all-powerful, his divinity defined by his authority; the "common good" is all-inclusive, its legitimacy established by democracy. Fundamentalism, as a theology, as a "worldview," wants both: the power and the legitimacy, divine will and democracy, one and the same. As theology, such confusion may be resolved with resort to miracles, but as politics, it is broken logic, a story that defeats itself. Why, then, does it prosper?

Secularists like to point out that many of the Founders were not, in fact, Christian but rather Deists or downright unbelievers. Fundamentalists respond by trotting out the Founders' most pious words, of which there are many (Franklin proposing prayer at the Constitutional Convention; Washington thanking God for His direct hand in revolutionary victories; etc., etc.). Secularists shoot back with the founders' Enlightenment writings and note their dependence on John Locke; fundamentalists respond that Locke helped South Carolina write a baldly theocratic constitution. Round and round it goes, a lucrative subgenre of popular history, "founder porn," that results in spasms of righteous ecstasy—secular as well as fundamentalist— over the mystical authority of origins.

But fundamentalist historians can also point, accurately, to the subsequent instances of overlooked religious influence in American history: not just Sergeant York's Christian trigger finger and Stonewall Jackson's tragic example, but also the religious roots of abolitionism, the divine justification used to convert or kill Native Americans, the violent pietism of presidents: not just Bush and

Reagan, but also Lincoln and McKinley and Wilson and even sweet Jimmy Carter, the first born-again president, led by God and Zbigniew Brzezinski to funnel anticommunist dollars to El Salvador, the most murderous regime in the hemisphere. Historians enmeshed in the assumptions of Enlightenment rationalism naturally seek rational explanations for events, and in so doing tend to deemphasize the religious beliefs of historical actors. Fundamentalist historians go straight to those beliefs; as a result, they really do see a history missed by most secular observers.

Fundamentalism embraces its mythic past; secular liberalism declares its own myth simply a matter of record. Liberalism proposes in place of nationalist epic a "demystified" state based on reason. And yet the imagination with which we, the levelheaded masses, view the "demigod" Founders and the Civil War, the Good Fight against Hitler, and the American tragedy of Vietnam (the tragedy is always ours alone) is almost as deeply mystical as that of fundamentalism's, thickened by "destiny," blind to all that which does not square with the story we tell ourselves about who we are as a nation. There are occasional attempts at recovering these near-invisible pieces, "people's history" and national apologies and HBO specials about embarrassing missteps in the march of progress, usually related to race and inevitably restored to forward motion by the courage of some "key man" of liberalism, Jackie Robinson at first base, 1947, Rosa Parks on the bus, 1955, Muhammad Ali refusing to fight in Vietnam, 1966. But such interventions are not so different from fundamentalism's addition of Martin Luther King to its pantheon; they are attempts to convince ourselves that the big *We* of nationalism was better than the little people of history actually were.

Likewise our attempts to shunt fundamentalists into the outer circle of kooks and haters and losers and left-behinds, undemocratic dimwits who do not understand the story the rest of us have agreed to live by. Our refusal to recognize the theocratic strand running throughout American history is as self-deceiving as fundamentalism's insistence that the United States was created a Christian nation.

The actual past no more serves the secular imagination than that of fundamentalism. While fundamentalism projects providence onto the past, secularism seeks to account for history with tools of rationalism. But history cannot be demystified; it is dependent as much on mystery—that which we recognize we cannot know about the past—as on the rationally understood. If we believe the aphorisms of literature—"The past isn't dead, it's not even past," and "The past is a foreign country"—then we believe in mystic history. We are not so secular after all. Fundamentalism knows this, and that is why, for now at least, those we've misunderstood as the dupes, the saps, and the fools—the believers—prefer its reenchanted past, alive to the dark magic with which all histories are constructed, to the demystified state's blind certainty that it is history's victor.

Most of us outside the influence of fundamentalism ask, when confronted with its burgeoning power, "What do these people want? What are they going to do?" But the more relevant question is, "What have they already done?" Consider the accomplishments of the movement, its populist and its elite branches combined: foreign policy on a near-constant footing of Manichean urgency for the last hundred years; "free markets" imprinted on the American mind as some sort of natural law; a manic-depressive sexuality that puzzles both prudes and libertines throughout the rest of the world; and a schizophrenic sense of democracy as founded on individual rights and yet indebted to a higher authority that trumps personal liberties.

Run that through Coach's software; look through a glass darkly. This, then, is what American fundamentalism understands democracy to mean, this is what it understands as "freedom of religion": the freedom to conform, to submit, to become one with the "biblical worldview," the "theocentric" parable, the story that swallows all others like a black hole. Within it time loops around, past becomes present, and the future is nothing but a matter of return. Not to the Garden but to the *Mayflower*, the Constitution, or Stonewall Jackson's last battle, moments of American purity, glimpses of the Camelot that haunts every nationalist imagination, fundamentalist or secular. History *is* God's love, its meanings revealed to his key men, presidents and generals, preachers and a schlemiel with a shofar. As for the rest of us, we are simply not part of the dream. Fundamentalism is writing us out of history.

"What is to be done?" the unbelievers ask. Oh, it's simple: think up a better story, a creation myth that is as rich as American fundamentalism's. We cannot just counter fundamentalism's key men with our own; nor can we simply switch out the celebratory model of history for an entirely grim chronicle of horrors. Rather, we must continue to revisit the history of American fundamentalism—which is to say, we must reconsider the story we speak of when we say "America."

14.

THIS IS NOT THE END

1. Suffering

She was as pretty as any nineteen-year-old girl thinned down to near nothing. Hair smooth and blonde, eyes big and blue, and her lips, pale red on white skin, were quivering. She stood between me and the door to the bar in which she'd just struck out at begging change from the last round of drinkers. She carried a piece of cardboard, the sum of her life to date scrawled with black marker in a hand too shaky to read. So she put it to a sort of song, a practiced routine she chanted with artificial sadness while something real inside actually broke down. "Mister, I just got to Portland, I got nowhere to go. They won't give me my TB card and, you know, so . . . I need money for a shelter, I slept under a bridge. Mister, I just got to Portland, I'm scared, I need somewhere to go."

I scrounged in my pocket and came up with a thin wad of twenties and small bills; I peeled off two singles and gave them to her.

"Thank you, Mister," she said.

I said, "Good luck." She began weeping. "Good luck," I said again.

"Thank you."

"I have to go," I said.

"Thank you." She turned and went out the door; as it swung shut behind her, she doubled over, sobbing.

I gave her a minute to gain some ground, and then I left, too. She was halfway up the block. I went to my rental car and took my bags out of the trunk. I was staying in a room above the bar, in Portland searching out the Family's early days in archives and at addresses long since given over to purposes other than Abram Vereide's or Doug Coe's. I hadn't found a trace. I was killing time.

The girl spotted me rolling my suitcase across the parking lot. She approached as if I might hit her. The yellow streetlight made her face look as if it had color; she was even prettier than she'd been inside. "Mister," she said, "I just got to Portland, I got nowhere to go . . ." Word for word the same song.

I stared at her. "I'm sorry. I just helped you inside."

"Oh," she said. "I'm sorry, too."

"I wish I could help more."

"Uh-huh."

"What's a TB card?"

"For a test," she said. "They got no reason not to give it to me."

She began crying again, her tears leaving trails of streetlight glimmer on her cheeks.

"Good luck," I said.

IF I WAS a believer, I would have said, "God bless you." If I wasn't a believer, I should have said, "God bless you." Either way, it would have cost me nothing and would have been so much less hopeless than wishing "good luck" to a woman who was not likely to have any. Such is the dilemma of the American city upon a hill with which I began this book, and the problem of fundamentalism's myths versus those of liberalism with which I closed the last chapter. Both are systems of knowing, of believing, of absorbing citizens into what Doug Coe calls the "social order." They are not means of "changing the world" but of reconciling us—the believers and the unbelievers—to its ordinary suffering.

If I was a believer, I might think my blessing would matter; if I wasn't, I'd know it would sound good and that it would not matter.

But I said, "Good luck," and the woman bent over crying again, and I left her like that, weeping on the street, and I went up to my room thinking of Christians and of "followers of Christ," of the Family's "heart for the poor." I was thinking, too, that I should go back and offer the woman a place to stay; of giving her a bed to sleep in, and how I wouldn't put any moves on her, and she would appreciate that, and she'd make me some kind of offer, and I'd decline, and I'd be a real hero. I was thinking, too, of tuberculosis, and of the cramped, airless rooms above the bar, and the germs swirling around me as I drifted off, her microscopic gratitude serving as a different kind of communion.

And I thought of the morning, of waking up with no money.

How would she get it? She couldn't sneak away without waking me. Maybe she had a knife. I imagined bringing her to the room and her big eyes turning mean and her lips and teeth snarling like she was a raccoon in a corner, her bone-and-skin hand swiping my money and her backing away with her knife ready for my gut should I make a wrong gesture.

That wouldn't have happened. There would have been no knife, and, for that matter, I'm guessing here, she would have said no if I'd offered to share my room with her. She needed something, but it wasn't a bed. I don't know what it was, whether it came in a pill or a pipe or a needle.

I asked myself, What would a believer do?

I was thinking about some believers whom I'd met earlier in the evening, a house church of a half dozen young families and a few single men and women who met every Sunday night in the living room of a couple named Adam and Christie Parent. I'd joined them because a false lead had suggested that theirs was a church that functions as a feeder to Ivanwald—I'd come across several around the country—but the connection turned out to be no deeper than one young man nobody knew well. Still, I stuck around, because what the Parents were doing—church in their living room, "small groups," discussions of "accountability" that denied personal responsibility— seemed to merge the methods of elite fundamentalism with the passions of the populists. I told them I was writing a book about religion in America; they welcomed me, I think, because they know they're its future.

Adam and Christie have three kids, two little boys and a girl, and they live in a handsome old box of a house with a real yard, in east Portland, just off the campus of Multnomah Bible College. Adam is starting his fourth year there. He is twenty-seven, tall, wide, and square in the shoulders. He grew up in San Diego and as a teenager wandered up to rural Washington, where he worked as a youth pastor until he decided to go back to school. He wears a small brown soul patch just beneath his lip and dresses like the frat boy he never was—loose plaid shirt, matching light blue ball cap—and he talks like a former surfer who has left the waves behind. He cracks smiles like they were flip tops on a six-pack, but he has developed a habit common to preachers and salesmen, of holding your eyes with his and transmitting sincerity. That it is real makes it no less disconcerting.

His wife, Christie, is short and strawberry blonde, all buttery cheeks and bouncy energy. But at twenty-nine she's one of the oldest in the group, and she talks with the authority befitting a young mother with more kids than any other couple in the "home community" has managed. When it came time to take all the children upstairs, Christie summoned a helper and herded them past Adam's golf clubs and his acoustic guitar, leaving the rest of us sitting on couches and cross-legged on the floor, in a big circle, waiting for Adam to tell us what we'll be discussing. First, a prayer: studded with *justs*: "I just want to thank You"; "I just, just really love You"; "I just pray and hope You show up tonight."

When I first heard the many justs of prayer at Ivanwald, I thought it was a southern thing. But here was a room of northwesterners and transplanted midwesterners and one Californian, and when I peeked during the prayer, I saw their heads nodding on the *just* like they were counting rhythm. Shirley Mullen, a religious historian and provost at Westmont College when I spoke with her in 2004, told me she had noticed the rise of *just* in evangelical prayer over the last twenty years. "It is a claim to innocence," she said. "A disqualifier."

Just is, in its ubiquity, a word central to the self-effacing desire for influence that has driven those evangelicals who stud their prayers with it out of their churches and into "the culture," a word they use to refer to something that is to be wrestled with and defeated. It's a word that hides its own hunger.

"Just use us, Lord, just use us, please," Adam concluded his prayer. They'd been brought together by a shared belief in the awesome power of God, "awesome" the way a skater might say it, "power" as an absolute, a totality. They wanted and believed they were called to be in the presence of that power, but to approach it in pride would be meaningless, and they were very keen on *meaning*. So they prefaced speculation about God and the nature of His power with *just*, as if by claiming their needs were simple they could slip beneath the radar God used to detect unseemly *want*. All they wanted, after all, was just to be *used*.

At Adam's direction, the group broke up into smaller groups of three and four and proceeded to work through a series of questions devised by Adam and the leaders of eleven other like-minded home churches, all part of something called the Imago Dei Community. Imago Dei is an odd mix of progressive evangelicalism and fundamentalism, a church that rejects the idea of "church"; its "vision" promises, instead, community and Jesus, stripped not so much of cultural accretion as of everything boring and less-than-intense about traditional church services. They do hold a Sunday morning service, but at the pulpit an artist, who paints or draws or sculpts the Gospel as directed by God, accompanies the preacher. They believe God is present, as in here, now. "Interventionist," as some theologians would describe their conception of the deity, is too wonky a word for the Jesus they believe is simultaneously sitting right next to them and possessing them, guiding every breath, every thought, every flicker of their eyes. They believe in sin but don't much care; they prefer love and discuss it often. *Love* is the word they use most frequently to evoke how completely in the control of Jesus they find themselves. Adam's home church group had instituted a collective prayer journal, a black hardcover notebook in which each member was to write, on one side of the page, his or her prayer requests; and, on the other, the date and time Jesus answered them. "We forget what God does in our lives," Adam explained. "We need to remind each other."

In the small groups, they planned to spend that evening reminding each other of what Truth is. The Truth they were talking about was the kind that comes with a capital *T*, and it was essential, Adam had written on the top of the worksheet, to "set us free from the destructive nature of life and the world."

Then followed the chief question: What is Truth?

I joined a group of three sitting on the carpet beside the stairs: Matt, a reedy Multnomah Bible philosophy student with presence greater than his age, who acted as group leader; Sara, a long-legged, long-armed, long-necked woman, given to elaborate stretching, who worked in standardized testing; and Ben, a resident at a nearby hospital. Ben lay down in front of the screen door. Across the street behind him an orange and blue sign grew in the garden of each yard, declaring: ONE MAN / ONE WOMAN. VOTE YES ON PROP 36—a state initiative to ban even the possibility of proposing gay marriage.

"What is Truth?" Matt asked.

Sara jumped right in. "A lot of people say there is no Truth, but my problem with that is that it's an absolute itself."

"Right," said Ben. "It's self-contradictory."

"But *we're* here," Sara continued. "So there has to be some Truth."

Matt volunteered that one of his Multnomah Bible professors had brought in a woman who didn't believe in Truth. The class had challenged her by demanding that she admit that the attacks of September 11 had been wrong. But she wouldn't give. Right and wrong, she said, weren't categories she found useful; she was more interested in learning about what she, we, anyone could do better. It was as concise a definition of liberalism's strengths—and central weaknesses—as she could have given them.

Sara put a hand over her right eye, holding her head and shaking it at the same time. "I wonder how her opinion would change if someone near to her was martyred. Or raped!"

Matt said he had heard such people believe in what they call "pragmatism," which means, he explained, that you believe whatever happens to be useful at the moment.

"But some things never change!" Sara said.

"I know," Matt agreed. "But they deny that." He had learned about pragmatism, he added, in an education class; pragmatism, he'd been told, was infecting public schools. Matt hadn't heard of John Dewey, the early twentieth-century reformer who'd introduced the philosophical school of pragmatism into American education in the form of an emphasis on critical thinking rather than memorization. But the ideas of Tim LaHaye, who writes that Dewey was part of a prideful conspiracy to undermine Truth, had infused his lessons at Multnomah Bible College.

Sara wove her fingers together and twisted her hands backward and stretched them out in front of her, then arched her back and leaned forward, her shirt riding up her spine; Ben and Matt, red-faced, averted their eyes. "What Truth does," Sara said, "is: Truth names things." She rose up out of her stretch and pointed between Matt and Ben. "Truth puts a value on things. The culture tries to portray a Truth, like with women." She didn't like the pressure put on women to be thin and beautiful, she explained. Either you are or you aren't, she felt, and the culture shouldn't tell you differently. "That's the culture trying to name us," she said. "We want *God* to name us."

"Yeah," agreed Ben. "Science"—it seemed to be his word for what Sara called "the culture"—"gives you at best fragmentary truth. It doesn't try to unify things."

They concluded the small group with a scripture study, looking for evidence of Truth, and then everyone reassembled in the living room, where Adam asked each group to announce their results. He reminded everyone to stay centered on Jesus and scripture. "Don't get too caught up in the huge concepts."

Truth did a lot of things, the groups had discovered: sets you free, protects you from lies, exposes deception, gives you a solid foundation. Truth's solidity was key to Adam's closing sermon. He sat in a chair in the corner and punctuated his remarks with both hands curled like commas and slicing downward.

"The postmodern culture, they lay aside Truth. It can be hard to interact with them. They say, 'I don't care about the Bible; it's just a book of words.'" Adam shook his head. "But I don't want a shifty foundation. God gave us His Word! I am so thankful I have that, because it's easy to get sucked in by the culture. We want a solid foundation. Christ is a solid foundation. I was looking at my Bible today. Christ says seventy-eight times, 'I tell you the Truth.' That is a lot of times. The culture then was similar to ours now; they were *questioning* the Truth." Adam didn't mean good questioning. "So Christ told them 'I tell you the Truth.' That's awesome. He did that for them so they'd know he wasn't just some guy. No way. He said, '*I* tell you the truth.' I was getting stoked looking at that because I have a solid foundation. I'm protected. Unbelievers think there is no absolute Truth. They trust feelings and experience. The power of Truth is lost to them. But we don't have to change our conception of Truth for the culture, because it's absolute. Its power is absolute."

I thought of a book by Art Lindsley, a fundamentalist writer who would stop in at Ivanwald from time to time to teach the young men about "character" and politics. A slim volume called *True Truth: Defending Absolute Truth in a Relativistic World* was Lindsley's most popular work among the brothers, who took its tautological butchery of language for a closed circuit of power and wisdom. This ultrarigid intellectualization of "Truth" is the doctrine that merges elite and populist fundamentalism. The elite fundamentalism of the Family preaches its unbending concept of "Truth" as a defense of privilege; populist fundamentalism embraces these philosophical underpinnings as a response to suffering. Many of the men and women in the Parents' living room, in fact, were employed as social workers or nurses; several were former activists, some of them even once radical leftists. They were good-hearted folk. They wanted to help the poor, the sick, the weak, and on small, everyday levels, they did so more than most do; and yet nothing seemed to get better. Their commitment to this stern Truth enabled them to let go of the feelings of powerlessness that often afflict those whose hearts are largest. Indeed, many of them had so let go of power that they'd lost their politics, too. Former liberals had stopped voting; conservatives trusted giant evangelical organizations to make the best use of their small donations, a form of "big government" by another name. Their Truth had proven itself relative, emboldening the powerful and tranquilizing the powerless.

Adam continued. They all knew, he said, that a couple of weeks ago the mentor of Imago Dei's pastor had been shot. The details didn't matter; he had been *shot*. "Well, if you don't believe in absolute Truth, what do you do with that? What's your foundation?" True Truth makes such losses bearable. It absolves you of the need to ask more questions. True Truth is God's will, Coe's "social order." It's the power and solace of submission.

We bowed our heads in prayer. We prayed for friends and relatives with cancer, just that they might know God, and that if God wanted to heal them that he would, but just, please God, let them know you. And we prayed for me, for my book, that it just be a good book, a True book, one by which I'd come to know what I had been created for.

And—just—amen.

LATER THAT NIGHT, I thought about Truth and the junkie, what she wanted and what she needed, and what a believer might have done. I couldn't come up with answers, and I knew it wouldn't help to ask Adam. Because even if there is a Truth, what we *would* have done in a given situation is always subjective. But I'm pretty sure Adam would have prayed for her salvation, and I wouldn't have been surprised if he had taken her by the arm and guided her to a shelter. Nor would I have been shocked if he had given her a blessing and a sad, half-mouthed smile and sent her packing. In either case, what would be the Truth of the matter?

I checked into my room, a tiny box with a window looking out on an air shaft and a skylight above the bed revealing the dark purple night. The room was stuffy, so I turned on its rotating table fan and lay on top of the covers. "Everything is connected," Ben the doctor had told me at the house church. "Everything is Jesus. It's like a web, and He's at the center"—where otherwise you'd find a spider.

2. SALVATION

In 2007, as this book neared completion, I met with a former special assistant to President Bush the younger named David Kuo, in a quiet office he'd rented outside of Washington to write his memoirs. He'd published a book called *Tempting Faith: The Inside Story of a Political Seduction*, in which he recounts his own journey from liberalism to fundamentalism and, after a fashion, back again. Kuo is a tall, big-boned man with spiky black hair and a pleasantly padded face given to loose smiles. His demeanor is naive, but by his own account he can be calculating; yet he doesn't seem to want to deceive.

As a student at Tufts University in the 1980s, Kuo found the Family. Or rather, they found him. He was bright, political, and moving rightward, from a girlfriend's abortion to antiabortion activism. A man named Kevin, who "worked with" student Christians on elite campuses, fed him books by conservative Christian writers and took him to go hear Chuck Colson speak. "I was dazzled," writes Kuo. "If I followed Jesus, helped others follow Jesus, and did it all publicly, I'd be fighting back against the secularizing forces that were sweeping God into the corner." Kuo has always been a service-minded soul. He wanted to help—as a young man, he didn't think too much about *what* he wanted to help—and he wanted to do so on a grand scale.

Before he graduated, Kevin gave him a "political gift": an invitation to the National Prayer Breakfast, where he'd be one of "150 student leaders" initiated into "the mysterious—some thought secretive—group behind the prayer breakfast." It was, he'd learn, "the most powerful group in Washington that nobody knows." At a session with Doug Coe after the official event, he learned that "Jesus the man" is more important than politics, that faith must be individual, that Jesus chose certain individuals to whom to reveal greater secrets. "The three within the twelve," Coe called them—Peter, James, and John, the three disciples who, according to Coe's teaching, Jesus took aside for "glimpses of his power" and "special instruction." That was a "model," Coe taught, "of intimate relationships" followed by only a few very clever leaders. "[Coe] pointed to Hitler, to Stalin, to Mao, to Castro." Evil men, said Coe, but wise. "Do you want to prove your worth?" Coe asked Kuo and the other students selected for special instruction. "Then pursue Jesus, pursue real relationships. Forget about power."

It was like the note Abram wrote to himself in 1935, his scribbled list of delegated authority for his new movement: To this man went responsibility for organization, to that one finances. And beside his own name, he'd written "power"—and then crossed himself out, erasing the evidence of his desire.

Kuo began to rise in politics. An intern for Ted Kennedy in college, he became a Republican, working in the orbit of Family men such as Jack Kemp and John Ashcroft. He tried to strike out on his own—and failed. Coe took him up as a project. "Without my realizing it, the Fellowship"—as he prefers to call the Family—"began subverting my ideas of power, and, more specifically, of Christian power." Coe took Kuo fishing in Montana, with Supreme Court Justice Sandra Day O'Connor. He introduced him to Billy Graham and Bill Bright of Campus Crusade, to Democrats and Republicans. Through the Family, he met former vice president Dan Quayle. In 1996, Quayle arranged for his conservative backers to support a non-profit Kuo had created to evaluate groups doing "effective" poverty work and channel more money their way—an experience Kuo would draw on when the grand experiment in "faith-based initiatives" to which he'd been contributing went federal in 2001.

In the first months of the new Bush administration, John DiIulio, the Democrat Bush had tapped to sell his faith-based program, called to invite Kuo to move into the West Wing. "Karen Hughes is on board, Karl Rove is on board," he told Kuo. "When can you start?" Faith-Based and Community Initiatives merged DiIulio's old-school urban politics, rooted in Catholic social justice teachings, with the ideas long championed by the Family. Its chief advocates in Congress during the late 1990s were two Family members, Senator Dan Coats of Indiana and Ashcroft, who as a senator from Missouri inserted the concept of "charitable choice"—allowing religious groups to win government funding without separating out their religious agenda—into the 1996 welfare-reform bill. The theory behind faith-based initiatives grew out of the work of scholars and theologians schooled in traditions that could hardly be considered fundamentalist, or even conservative. But its implementation was in many senses the logical result of the Family's decades of ministry to Washington's elite combined with the increasingly established power of populist fundamentalism: a mix of sophisticated policy maneuvers and the kind of sentimentalism that blinded many supporters to the fact that faith-based initiatives, no matter how well intended, are nothing less than "the privatization of welfare," as the faith-based theorist Marvin Olasky put it in a 1996 report commissioned by then-Governor Bush. Such an outcome satisfied elite fundamentalism's long-standing belief in the relationship between laissez-faire economics and God's invisible, interventionist hand, and populist fundamentalism's desire for public expressions of faith, preferably heartwarming ones. The goal, Senator Coats declared, was the "transfer of resources and authority . . . to those private and religious institutions that shape, direct, and reclaim individual lives."[1]

Coats, a bulb so dim he considers Dan Quayle a mentor, isn't much of a thinker on his own, but he couldn't have summed up Abram's original Idea any more succinctly. The Family's interests have always tended toward foreign affairs, but faith-based initiatives embody a core philosophy of governance fundamentalists have long sought on every front. During the 1980s, Attorney General Ed Meese and Gary Bauer, Reagan's domestic policy adviser, corresponded with Coe about creating a federal, faith-based response to poverty—a broad application of the methods Coe had experimented with a decade earlier by backing the Black Buffers as an alternative to black power. Meese's plans never came to fruition, but the outlines of compassionate conservatism, as Olasky would describe the trickle-down approach to helping the poor, began to cohere in those letters.

What is the cause of poverty? they asked themselves. Their answer was simple: "disobedience," according to a special report commissioned by the Family. At the right end of the Family spectrum, this was interpreted according to the logic of just deserts (Bauer, for instance, seemed to believe AIDS was a punishment from God) or plain denial (in 1983, Meese said he had a hard time believing there actually were any hungry children in the United States). But both those positions eroded as the Family's international realpolitik asserted itself domestically: the poor existed, and they had to be helped. Or *reconciled*, in the Family's words. The goal was not the eradication of poverty; it was the maintenance of a social order through the salvation of souls. That's always been the main agenda of populist fundamentalism; now, elite fundamentalism began to embrace it as well.

But that's not what Kuo cared about when he went to work in the West Wing. Kuo's religion was as infused with liberal Christianity as it was with the obedience-based theology of the Family. For that matter, faith-based initiatives are as liberal as they are fundamentalist, their privatization of social services an exercise of the unstated conviction of classical liberalism that the free market is absolute and yet requires government subsidy. They are to religion what Clinton-era "free trade" deals were to labor: a "rationalization" in the name of "efficiency." Both turn on a contradiction: a belief in a universal principle—faith, free markets—put into practice by denying the importance of universal principles. "That we hoped everyone would one day know Jesus was simply a private goal," writes Kuo, even as he insists that one's "worldview" informs one's every action.

That's why supporters of faith-based governance can't comprehend the critics who accuse them of theocratic inclinations. They think they're going in just the opposite direction, secularizing salvation, reconciling theology *into* law. Theocracy is a collective endeavor, they point out; American fundamentalism reveres the individual. So, too, the mystic liberalism of free markets, more similar to fundamentalism in function than secularists believe. Classical liberalism fetishizes the rational actor; fundamentalism savors the individual soul. Both deny possessing any ideology; both inevitably become vehicles for the kind of power that possesses and consumes the best intentions of true believers.

When Kuo discovered that Bush's faith-based rhetoric was for the most part just that—lost in the shadow of the Iraq War, the program never received anywhere near the $8 billion Bush had once spoken of—he resolved to prove its value to the money men. *Tempting Faith* is, most damningly, the story of how he and a few others transformed the Office of Faith-Based Initiatives into the very Republican vote-getting machine its critics had accused it of being from the beginning. "We laid out a plan whereby we would hold 'roundtable events' for threatened incumbents with faith and community leaders," he writes. In 2002, those roundtables contributed to nineteen out of twenty victories in targeted races. In 2004, the Office of Faith-Based Initiatives repeated the trick on the presidential scale. But by that time, Kuo was gone. He had quit. "We were good people forced to run a sad charade, to provide political cover to a White House that needed compassion and religion as political tools."

It was a startlingly honest admission. The media celebrated Kuo as a truth teller and his book as the first big crack in the Christian Right's alliance with the Republican Party. By 2007, the press was declaring the Christian Right dead and evangelicalism a waning force in American life, despite the fact that by Kuo's own confession, the machine he helped build will likely continue to lurch along after Bush is gone. Bush never provided it the funds he had promised in idealistic speeches aimed at evangelical voters, but he did something more significant: through administrative changes made by executive order, he transformed Clinton's 1996 welfare reforms into a wedge with which to drive irreparable cracks into the wall of separation between church and state. Suddenly, there were faith-based offices not just in the Department of Health and Human Services but also in the Department of Justice, not only in the Department of Education but also in the Department of Commerce. The Small Business Administration gained a faith-based office; so, too, did the Agency for International Development, through which the United States distributes its imperial largesse, the diplomacy of foreign aid. None of these offices had much money, but then, they didn't need to. Their budgets didn't matter so much as the budgets of the departments and agencies in which they were housed, huge portions of which could now be tapped for faith-based ends even if the money didn't flow directly through the faith-based office. The real achievement of faith-based initiatives was not to launch flashy programs or even to buy votes for Republicans; it was to open the door for religious groups to the whole treasure house of federal social-services funding, tens of billions of dollars.

But that, too, was only a means to an end: Abram's Idea written into the DNA of the government of a world power, Chuck Colson's "worldview" fused with constitutional tradition. The dream, hardening now not into politics but the very structures in which politics happen, is the sanctification and privatization of power as one and the same process, proclaimed as "service" by the powerful and accepted as God's will by the powerless.

This is no more nor less than a theological restatement of globalization—a transfer of wealth and power embraced by most Democrats as well as Republicans as a natural "fact," as if divinely ordained. The difference between the two parties, economically, theologically, is one of degrees, not principles. "The United States is also a one-party state," Julius Nyerere, the first president of Tanzania, once observed in defending his own one-party system. "But with typical American extravagance, they have two of them." That was a truth Abram grasped seven decades ago. The first law of the Family's elite fundamentalism is that power does not require partisanship. "True Truth," transcending traditional left and right, is a doctrine of obedience, not a bill of particulars.

Bush's mistake—the misapplication of power that cost him the loyalty of men such as Kuo and even John Ashcroft, who emerged as a late critic of the administration—was to bend the "True Truth" of American fundamentalism to the needs of the electoral cycle. The slow convergence of the elite and populist fundamentalism separated at the Scopes trial in 1925 doesn't promise the permanent victory of a political party but of a social order, served with greater or lesser devotion by Republicans *and* Democrats bound together in prayer cells.

After Kuo and I had been talking for several hours, I mentioned that I'd written about the Family for *Harper's*. Kuo seemed surprised. "I think I remember your article," he said. He tapped a couple of his keys on his computer. Not a Google search; a couple of keys. "This is how they pray," he began reading, and then shot me a goofy grin. Was I supposed to think he'd had the story on his screen before I arrived? "You should call Doug Coe," he said, and gave me a number. (I did, as I had before; no response.) Coe, he said, had entered semiretirement. Stepping up to replace him was a man named Dick Foth, a longtime adviser to John Ashcroft. I'd listened to a recorded sermon by Foth; it'd struck me as unremarkable stuff, platitudes and tautologies. Kuo wasn't offended. This, he said, is proof that the Family is not political. Politics are specific, Kuo said; the Family's faith is universal.

In a sense, this was true. The cell structure that defined Abram's movement in 1935 has since become the model for populist fundamentalism and more, one of the common denominators of evangelicalism. Both elite and populist cells look upward, their concept of faith drawn along the vertical axis. Elected elites look up to their greatest constituent, God; the people who elect them pray that their leaders listen to God. Both call this gaze "love," and in exchange both demand "salvation."

The popular front promises the salvation of individuals, a chance to buy into "purpose," "meaning," a movement: to feel like a part of the big picture. Elite fundamentalism pursues the literal salvation of that big picture: the preservation of power, even as those who serve it change churches, or parties, or particular political whims. Power is what remains. The popular front rises and falls in an ebb and tide of "revivals," spontaneous and cultivated, each, so far, stronger than the last, each surging just as secularism says that *this* time that bad old religion, the superstitious kind, the political kind, the powerful kind, is a thing of the past. The key men endure. Indeed, they prosper.

3. DELIVERANCE

The numbing authority of American fundamentalism resides in its language, "love" as an expression of obedience, "just" as a disclaimer for desire, "Jesus plus nothing" as a description not of a brilliant divine but of blunt authority. Such banalities do not disguise evil, as Hannah Arendt argued in her famous study of traditional fascism, but rather subvert what is essentially generous about fundamentalism, its dream of a community in which every member is free to approach the divine as he or she feels guided, its desire for a city upon a hill in which hunger and regret are unknown. At their roots, evangelicalism and its child, American fundamentalism—both driven by the democratic feeling of individual belief toward faith in authority—arise in response to the central dilemma of nearly all religion: suffering, from that of Abigail Hutchinson to that of lonesome immigrant Abram to that, even, of Ted Haggard. Fundamentalism wants to ease the pain, to banish fear, forget loneliness; to erase desire. Populist fundamentalism does so by offering certainty, a fixed story about the relationship between this world and the world to come; elite fundamentalism, certain in its entitlement, responds in this world with a politics of noblesse oblige, the missionary impulse married to military and economic power. The result is empire. Not the old imperialism of Rome or the Ottomans or the British navy, that of a central power forcing weaker groups to pay tribute. Rather, the soft empire of America that across the span of the twentieth century recruited fundamentalism to its cause even as it seduced liberalism to its service "presents itself," in the useful formulation of the political theorists Michael Hardt and Antonio Negri, "not as a historical regime originating in conquest, but rather as an order that effectively suspends history and thereby fixes the existing state of affairs for eternity."[2]

Eternity! There's a word that the subjects of this book understand better than Hardt and Negri and the entire establishment of political theorists, political scientists, policy wonks, and newspaper editorial boards. Eternity, says fundamentalism, is the only real response to the basic fact of suffering, the constant of human existence that compels us to seek knowledge, or understanding, or faith, or grace. Fundamentalism frames that response as a story with a neat beginning, middle, and, most of all, an end that can be known. The better story we—believers and unbelievers alike, all of us who love our neighbors more than we love power or empire or even the solace of certainty—must tell is not simply a different answer, secular myths opposed to fundamentalism's, but a question. Maybe it's about that city upon a hill. Maybe it's about how we get there, and what we must walk away from. Such a question isn't to be found in revelation, but in exodus, the act of stepping into the unknown. I suspect it has something to do with the difference between salvation, as imagined by fundamentalism, and deliverance. Salvation ends in heaven; deliverance begins in the desert. Salvation is the last word of a story; deliverance is the first. Salvation is the certainty of empire; deliverance is the hope of democracy. It's not humble, because hope isn't humble, it's impertinent. It's a question, always another question, always leaving Egypt behind.

ACKNOWLEDGMENTS

This book is the product of many years, during which I have been the beneficiary of the efforts and generosity of many friends and colleagues. First among them is my editor at *Harper's*, Bill Wasik, without whose early encouragement this book would not exist. I'm grateful, too, for the insights of several other magazine editors who helped me develop my ideas, sharpen my prose, and get my facts straight along the way, including but not limited to: Ben Austen, Naomi Kirsten, Lewis Lapham, Miriam Markowitz, and Ben Metcalf at *Harper's;* Will Dana, Sean Woods, Eric Bates, Eric Magnuson, and Coco MacPherson at *Rolling Stone*; Bob Moser at *The Nation*; and Monika Bauerlein at *Mother Jones*. Claire Wachtel at HarperCollins saw the whole thing through with patience, wit, and wisdom. Her assistant, Julia Novitch, shepherded it along with care, for which I'm grateful. Vicki Haire saved me from capitalizing heaven. Special thanks to Kathy Anderson, who helped me understand what this book should be, found the right publisher, and made sure I actually finished it. Giulia Melucci, vice president of public relations at *Harper's*, advised me on launching it.

My most critical and trustworthy readers were Julie Rabig, Robert Sharlet, JoAnn Wypijewski, Kathryn Joyce, and Peter Manseau. Thank you.

Kim Nauer and Joe Conason at The Nation Institute provided support, as did the incomparable MacDowell Colony, at which several of these chapters were written and revised during three visits.

I'm especially grateful for MacDowell's Michelle Aldredge, without whose account of her secondary education this book would not have its thirteenth chapter. Hampshire College, a strange and wonderful school unlike any other, is present in everything I write. I'm also grateful to the KGB Bar, which has given me a forum to test out much of this book piece by piece. The results are incalculably better than they would have been otherwise for the influence of New York University's Center for Religion and Media, where I have been an associate research scholar for the last four years—which is to say, a sponge soaking up the ideas and insights of some very smart people. I am particularly indebted to Angela Zito, Faye Ginsburg, Barbara Abrash, Adam H. Becker, and Omri Elisha. Scholars at other institutions to whom I'm indebted include Diane Winston, Michael Janson, Kenneth Osgood, Ron Enroth, and Jamie K. A. Smith.

I'm likewise indebted to a number of journalists and researchers who shared their knowledge of Christian conservatism with me, including Chip Berlet, Max Blumenthal, Frederick Clarkson, Doug Ireland, Scott McLemee, Suzanne Pharr, Michael Reynolds, and Bruce Wilson.

Several former members, associates, and neighbors of the Family, as well as a few current ones, spoke with me. Many of them preferred to remain on background; among those I'm able to thank publicly are Cliff Gosney, Ben Daniel, Carl von Bernewitz, Steve Bauer, Mary McCutcheon, and David Kuo. I'm also very grateful to the hundreds of evangelical conservatives and other Christians who've agreed to speak with me about their faith and their politics over the years, especially Matt Dunbar and Lisa Anderson. Several evangelical journalists have kept talking to me even when my work infuriated them, and it's the better for those conversations. Among them are Bob Smietana, Patton Dodd, Ted Olsen, and Tony Carnes.

Then there are the friends, family, and fellow travelers who provided the kind of crucial support—responding to chapters on short notice, providing me with housing, sharing ideas—without which the book would have fizzled. Which is to say, for better or worse, the accomplices. I've been working on this book for a long time, which means there are more than I can list, but among those who spent time on the front lines of this book's production were Gretchen Aguiar, Jeff Allred, Laura Brahm, Fiona Burde, Colleen Clancy, Stellar Kim, Michael Lesy, Victoria McKernan, Paul Morris, David Rabig, Don Rabig, Jude Rabig, Irina Reyn, Gwen Seznec, Jocelyn Sharlet, Darcey Steinke, Baki Tezcan, and Tom Windish. And the researchers: Martha Lincoln, Sherally Munshi, Meera Subramanian, Jaime Pensado, and Seonaid Valiant.

Most of all, Julie Rabig, wise as serpents and innocent as doves, and also as funny as a sea otter, brave as a buffalo, and more beautiful than a great blue heron. Thank you for enduring, provoking, and inspiring.

NOTES

1.   I was loaned a copy of "Thoughts on a Core Group" in 2002 by one of the men with whom I lived at Ivanwald. I cited this document in an article titled "Jesus Plus Nothing" in the March 2003 *Harper's*, the fact checkers of which gave Ivanwald full opportunity to respond. They have never publicly contested the document. You can now find a similar text on the Web site of a conservative evangelical named Glenn Murray. Murray has added some and subtracted some, including this peculiar reference, but he leaves the spirit intact: "The mafia," his "Thoughts" read, "operates like this," and so too should the community of believers. Accessed 2006 at http://www.glennmurray. nccn.net/thoughts_on_a_core_group.htm. The very ideological promiscuity of the document—Hitler, Lenin, and the mafia—proves that it is the principle of organization admired, not the essence of Hitler's or Lenin's beliefs. Cold comfort.

2.   Nancy T. Ammerman, "A Brief Introduction and Definition," in Martin E. Marty and Scott Appleby, *Fundamentalisms Observed* (University of Chicago Press, 1994), p. 2. This is one volume in the University of Chicago Press's comprehensive five-volume "Fundamentalism Project," in many ways the first and last word on fundamentalism. George M. Marsden's *Fundamentalism and American Culture: The Shaping of Twentieth-Century Evangelicalism* (Oxford University Press, 1980), updated in a new edition in 2006, is another authoritative text on Christian fundamentalism as a specific idea and movement in American history. "A fundamentalist is an evangelical who is angry about something," Marsden simplified his definition in a follow-up collection of essays, *Understanding*

Fundamentalism and Evangelicalism (William B. Eerdmans, 1991), a pithy summation from a scholar sympathetic to evangelicalism. It suffices so long as we
remember that anger takes many forms, and that the "something" a fundamentalist is opposed to is not, in his or her mind at least, necessarily modernity, but
sin, whether defined as sex outside of marriage or the disobedience to God
many fundamentalists believe is implicit in managed economies.

1. IVANWALD

1.   In this chapter, I use the full names of men who held leadership positions
at Ivanwald. Such men are activists, and some, such as Gannon Sims, built on
their Ivanwald experiences to develop careers in government. (Gannon became a spokesman for the Department of State's Office to Monitor and Combat Human Trafficking.) Men who were not in leadership or government
positions I identify only by their first names. "Zeke" is a pseudonym for a man
who I fear might face repercussions for his role in introducing me to the Family. In the years since then, several former members have contacted me with
accounts of ostracization and even retaliation for various actions, and while
I've no way of confirming these stories, there's no need to unduly expose
Zeke to the possibility of similar responses.

2.   A note on notes: In this chapter and throughout *The Family*, I use endnotes
to identify archival sources and to provide sources for historical events that
may not be well known. Chapters 4–9, which depend largely on historical
research, are extensively endnoted, but where I rely on personal experience
(chapters 1, 9, 14) or directly reference interviews (chapters 10–14), or on
publicly available sources identified within the text (chapters 12–14), I generally refrain from notes. As for this account of Ivanwald: like several of the
brothers, I openly kept a journal. When writing about a conversation that had
occurred earlier, I often asked individual brothers for their recollections. This
was not "undercover." Although I had no inkling of a book about the Family or
fundamentalism at the time, I told the brothers I was a writer, the publications
I'd written for, and that I was working on a book about unusual religious communities (*Killing the Buddha: A Heretic's Bible*, with Peter Manseau [Free Press,
2004]). A few documentary notes in chapters 4–10 identify the only general
collection in which the relevant documents can be found. I made my first,
brief archival research trip in late 2002, after I had decided to write about
Ivanwald but before I had even imagined this book. Since magazine fact checkers

are more interested in actual evidence than my assurances that memo *x* can be found in folder *y* in an archive, I made Xerox copies instead of notes for future researchers. When I returned to the main archive of the Family at the Billy Graham Center at Wheaton College with a book in mind, I made note of appropriate filing numbers. In total I or my research assistants reviewed well over 60,000 pages of primary-source documents, and made copies of around 5,000 pages; I lack folder numbers for a very few pages, and those I have copies of.

3.   Senator Brownback, Senator Pryor, and Representative Wolf told me of their involvement in interviews. I met Senator Ensign while he was living in the C Street House, a former convent maintained as a group home for congressmen by a Family-affiliated organization, and Senators Grassley and Nelson and Representative Pitts are well represented in the Family's archives. Senator Coburn told the reporter Tom Hess of his residence in C Street House and his participation in a Family cell for a feature in James Dobson's *Citizen* magazine, " 'There's No One I'm Afraid to Challenge,' " accessed at http://www.family.org/cforum/citizenmag/coverstory/a0012717.cfm on October 10, 2004. Senator Thune cited the Family's leader, Doug Coe, and a house the Family maintains on Capitol Hill in a *Christianity Today* interview with Collin Hansen (http://www.christianitytoday.com/ct/2005/februaryweb-only/42.0a.html, accessed January 7, 2007). Most of the rest of these men were spoken of as members by Ivanwalders and senior men in the Family—for instance, Steve South, former senior counsel for Senator Don Nickles, told me of Senator Domenici's involvement, confirmed in the Family's archives (file 15, box 354, collection 459, Papers of the Fellowship Foundation, Billy Graham Center Archives [hereafter cited as BGCA]). I've no reason to doubt these claims; members of the Family are scrupulous about distinguishing between *members,* those who have joined a prayer cell or made some other commitment to the work, and *friends,* those with whom they're comfortable working. Representative Eric Cantor, for instance, a Jewish Republican from Virginia, is just a friend. Representative McIntyre, who joined Representative Wolf's prayer cell, is a member. This is only a partial list. The Family believes in a concentric model of holiness, with a few key men close to Christ at the center (Representative Pitts, for instance), another circle of active supporters farther out (Senator Grassley), followed by one of casual allies (such as Senator Pryor) who are mostly unaware of the group's inner workings.

4   *Thurmond:* Interview, Cliford B. Gosney, former Family member. Thurmond's association was among the Family's most long-standing, stretching

across the decades. On October 30, 1987, Family leader Doug Coe sent to Representative Tony Hall, a Democrat from Ohio who moved rightward under the Family's guidance, a sermon preached by Thurmond to a meeting of the weekly Senate Prayer Breakfast. The subject was "integrity" and "the unraveling of the fabric of our society," to which Thurmond—a segregationist who refused to publicly acknowledge his African-American daughter—responded with four suggestions on becoming "men and women of integrity." Folder 3, box 166, collection 459, BGCA. *Talmadge and Robertson:* Annual Report of the Fellowship Foundation, 1962, folder 2, box 563, collection 459, BGCA. *Ford:* Paul Wilkes, "Prayer: The Search for a Spiritual Life in Washington and Elsewhere: A Country on Its Knees?" *New York Times*, December 22, 1974. Besides Laird and Ford, the other two members of the cell were Republican congressmen John Rhodes, a Barry Goldwater protégé from Arizona, and Al Quie of Minnesota, an early opponent of affirmative action. The four had been organized into a Family prayer group during the late 1960s. *Rehnquist:* Doug Coe to Panayiotis Touzmazis, April 24, 1974, folder 11, box 200, collection 459, BGCA. And then there are the jocks: Buffalo Bills legend and vice presidential candidate Jack Kemp; Seattle Seahawks NFL Hall of Famer Steve Largent, one of the fiercest ideologues of the Republican Revolution of 1994; and Oklahoma Sooners Orange Bowl champ J. C. Watts, the highest-ranking black Republican in congressional history. According to Bob Jones IV, Watts preferred Campus Crusade's related effort, Christian Embassy ("The Church Inside the State," *World*, October 12, 1996), but when I interviewed him in 2003, he told me he prayed with "the Prayer Breakfast people" as well.

5. *NCCL News Letter*, April 1948. *Christian Leadership News*, October 1950. Collection 459, BGCA.

6. On July 15, 1965, the Family's founder, Abraham Vereide, boasted in an address to a prayer meeting that in Generalissimo Franco's Spain, initially hostile to the Protestant Family, "there are secret cells, such as the American embassy, the Standard Oil office, allowing [our men] to move practically anywhere." No box number, collection 459, BGCA. *350:* D. Michael Lindsay, "Is the National Prayer Breakfast Surrounded by a 'Christian Mafia'? Religious Publicity and Secrecy Within the Corridors of Power," *Journal of the American Academy of Religion* 74, no. 2 (June 2006): 390–419.

7. Quoted in Stephen Scott, "Jesus' Name Has Drawing Power for Prayer Breakfast," *St. Paul Pioneer Press*, April 14, 2001.

8. The Fellowship Foundation's 2005 990 tax form showed official income of

nearly $17 million and program expenses of nearly $14 million. Among the expenses, $900,000 went to the National Prayer Breakfast, a Fellowship-produced event that appears to the world to be an official function of the federal government. (When I attended in 2003, I got my press credentials through the White House.) In 2005, the Fellowship actually turned a profit on the Breakfast, taking in $47,000 more than it cost. In "Showing Faith in Discretion," *Los Angeles Times*, September 27, 2002, the journalist Lisa Getter noted that the Family has paid for overseas congressional junkets and even loaned congressmen money.

9.   Bakke's deal is documented in Deepak Gopinath, "The Divine Power of Profit," *Institutional Investor*, March 1, 2001. Bakke isn't conservative in the conventional sense—he's a major Democratic donor—but he has made a career out of deregulation and anti-union management, and he's used his wealth to create the Harvey Fellows Program, which aims to train an "expanding beachhead of evangelicals in the American elite" and "the corridors of power" through funds for graduate students who agree to sign a statement of faith. D. Michael Lindsay, *Faith in the Halls of Power: How Evangelicals Joined the American Elite* (Oxford University Press, 2007), p. 80.

10.   Getter, "Showing Faith in Discretion."

11.   Lindsay, "Is the National Prayer Breakfast Surrounded by a 'Christian Mafia'?" Lindsay, a fellow at Princeton University's Department of Sociology during the period of this study and now on the faculty at Rice University, enjoyed tremendous access to what he refers to as the "backstage" of Family leadership of his study of the "Christian Mafia," in which he asserts that the Family is not secret but private. Secrecy, he notes, "often protects the interests of the powerful." Of course, so may privacy when maintained by elites who use it to shield networks of influence from public transparency. The difference between secrecy and privacy, Lindsay argues, is that those who are not in on secrets—especially secrets about power—resent them, whereas those excluded from a private association of elites don't mind, since such "privacy" appeals to traditions of deference to the elite. Thus, the "privacy" used by the Family to protect the privilege of its members, Lindsay argues, is "legitimated" by the public status of the Family's members. Such are the justifications for power by the ivory tower so often derided as too leftist by conservative pundits.

12.   Monday Associates Meeting, January 23, 1995, Burnett Thompson presiding.

13.   David Kuo, *Tempting Faith: An Inside Story of Political Seduction* (Free Press, 2006), pp. 21–24.

14. *Doug Coe and General Vessey*: Minutes of a luncheon held at the Cedars, the Family's Arlington, Virginia headquarters, October 19, 1983, collection 459, BGCA; no box number. The luncheon was organized by Aquilino E. Boyd, the Panamanian dictator Manuel Noriega's ambassador to the United States. Also in attendance was an inner-circle member of the Family named Herb Ellingwood, a longtime Reagan aide who had been responsible for "psychological warfare" against student protestors in California. In 1970, Ellingwood was one of the small circle of men who laid hands on Reagan and heard a voice, allegedly God's, promising Reagan the White House. Paul Kengor, *God and Ronald Reagan: A Spiritual Life* (Regan Books, 2004), pp. 135–36. When Reagan ascended to 1600 Pennsylvania Avenue, he took Ellingwood with him as a deputy counsel. Ellingwood's advice? "Economic salvation and spiritual salvation go side by side." John Micklethwait and Adrian Wooldridge, *The Right Nation: Conservative Power in America* (Penguin Press, 2004), pp. 331–32. *Lugar et al.*: Telegram to General Manual Antonio Noriega, January 25, 1984, collection 459, BGCA. *Casanova and Martinez*: Getter, "Showing Faith in Discretion." *Military aid to Honduras*: Elaine Sciolino, "U.S. Said to Link Latin Aid to Support for Contras," *New York Times*, May 18, 1987.

15. Quoted in Lindsay, *Faith in the Halls of Power*, p. 36.

16 Ibid., p. 35.

17. Paul N. Temple to James F. Bell, October 7, 1976, collection 459, BGCA; no box number. Phillips gave $30,000 toward the cost of the Cedars; Stone, a self-help author of get-rich-quick books who was also famous for having given $2 million to Nixon's 1968 and 1972 campaigns, donated $100,000. Temple, a former Standard Oil executive, gave $150,000, while the oilman Harold McClure gave $100,000. Other financing for the Cedars came from: William Loflin, $150,000; James Millen, $150,000; Mike Myers (not the actor), $150,000; Otto Zerbe, $100,000; the PGA pro Jim Hiskey, $100,000; and Ken Olsen, the founder of Digital, $83,000. The president of a local bank who was also a member of a Family prayer group arranged for a loan up to $400,000 (Temple to Bell, January. 6, 1977).

18. *Thomas*: Kuo, *Tempting Faith*, p. 92; *Durenberger*: Edward Walsh, "Senator Goes Public with Private Life," *Washington Post*, March 2, 1986, and Tony Bouza, *The Decline and Fall of the American Empire: Corruption, Decadence, and the American Dream* (Da Capo, 1996), p. 102; *Watt*: Lindsay, *Faith in the Halls of Power*, "Is the National Prayer Breakfast Surrounded by a 'Christian Mafia'?"

19. *New chosen* and *throwaway religion* are ordinary phrases in the daily vernacular of the Family, no more than variations on contemporary evangelical

rhetoric, but the *din of the vox populi*—the voice of the people—I found as far back as an account of the first National Prayer Breakfast (then known as the Presidential Prayer Breakfast) held shortly after Eisenhower's inauguration in 1953, by the then-Senate chaplain Dr. Frederick Brown Harris. Dr. Harris is quoted at length in a hagiography of the Family's founder by the Family evangelist Norman Grubb: *Modern Viking: The Story of Abraham Vereide, Pioneer in Christian Leadership* (Zondervan, 1961), p. 131. The existence of a published biography may seem like a paradox for a group so bent on invisibility, but the early Family leaders assumed a lack of public scrutiny as the due of their elite status. It wasn't until the antiestablishment revolt of the late 1960s that Vereide's successor, Coe, led the group "underground."

20.   Lynette Clemetson, "Meese's Influence Looms Large in Today's Judicial Wars," *New York Times,* August 17, 2005. Meese is credited with moving into the mainstream the idea of a *jurisprudence of original intention*—the basis for a conservative judicial philosophy that rejects worker protections, the right to privacy, women's reproductive rights, and queer rights.

21.   Ben Daniel, a minister in the Presbyterian Church (U.S.A.) and a former member of the Family, interviewed former residents of Potomac Point for a study of what he views as the Family's "spiritual abuse": "A former resident of Potomac Point told me about her nine months there. Having been encouraged to share her every thought and to expose her secrets and sins, she found her confessions and confidences used against her when she would ask questions or resist Fellowship authority. As the Fellowship exerted control over every aspect of her life she became angry and bitter. Something broke inside her. 'When I came to Potomac Point I struggled with self-esteem issues,' she told me. 'While I was there my low self-esteem moved from a personal to a spiritual level.' When, at last, she expressed a desire to leave, she was told that, without the teaching and company of the Fellowship, her well-being would disintegrate. She became terrified of life on the outside." The wife of a Fellowship member describes her role in the Family: "I'm always third. The Fellowship comes first in my husband's life. Then our children. Then me." "Dysfunction in the Fellowship Family," http://bendaniel.org/?p=110 accessed November 27, 2007.

22.   Congressmen who have lived there include former representatives Steve Largent (R., Oklahoma), Ed Bryant (R., Tennessee), and John Elias Baldacci (D., Maine). The house's eight congressman-tenants each paid $600 per month in rent for use of a town house that includes nine bathrooms and five living rooms. Lara Jakes Jordan, "Religious Group Helps Lawmakers With

Rent," Associated Press, April 20, 2003. When the *Los Angeles Times* asked then-resident Representative Bart Stupak, a pro-life Democrat from Michigan, about the property, he replied, "We sort of don't talk to the press about the house." Getter, "Showing Faith in Discretion."

23.   On October 29, 2007, a reporter for the Norwegian daily *Dagbladet*, Tore Gjerstad, who was following up on Norwegian conservatives' connections to the Family, managed to confront Coe with some of the language about Hitler I've quoted. Coe, Gjerstad told me, responded, "No one who really knows me would think I admire Lenin, Hitler, Stalin. They were evil men. But they were successful when it came to power . . . All power is with Jesus. You can choose to go against him, but you can never have more power than what he gives you."

24.   Carter's contacts with Doug Coe, whom he told the sociologist D. Michael Lindsay ("Is the National Prayer Breakfast Surrounded by a 'Christian Mafia'?") had been a "very important person" in his life, predated his presidency. In a 1972 briefing to the Family's leadership, Coe wrote that Carter was involved with the Family's mission to Brazil's dictatorial government. Folder 1, box 362, collection 459, BGCA. That same year, the Family's chief Central American associate, a Costa Rican lawyer named Juan Edgar Picado, hosted Carter in Costa Rica; in 1976, Picado boasted to his Central American allies that Carter would increase aid to the region, which he did. It was Carter, not Ronald Reagan, who began the United States' support for El Salvador's brutal regime. (Howard Siner, "Attorney Knows Carter as Smart, Kind Friend," *San Jose News*, March 4, 1977.) Nixon kept his personal distance from the Family until after his presidency, when, according to Lindsay, he "ministered" Reagan's national security adviser, Robert "Bud" McFarlane, into a Family prayer cell in the wake of McFarlane's disgrace as an Iran-Contra conspirator.

25.   Folder 1, box 166, collection 459, BGCA.

2. EXPERIMENTAL RELIGION

1.   Doug Coe, "The Person of Christ, Pt. 4," videotape of an address given to a conference of presidents of evangelical organizations, Navigators Great Hall Productions, January 15, 1989.

2.   There are many great biographies of Edwards, but my method of research for this account of his life was to rely primarily on original sources, which I tried to read through the filter of my own half-secular mind and as I imagine a Family man might, attuned to power and relationships. I depended on the two-volume

Works of Jonathan Edwards, with a Memoir by Sereno E. Dwight, ed. Edward Hickman (F. Westley and A. H. Davis, Stationers Court, 1834); *Works of Jonathan Edwards,* particularly vol. 2, *Religious Affections,* ed. John E. Smith (Yale University Press, 1959); vol. 7, *The Life of David Brainerd,* ed. Norman Pettit (ibid., 1985); and vol. 16, *Letters and Personal Writings,* ed. George S. Claghorn (ibid., 1998); Samuel Hopkins, *The Life and Character of the Late Reverend Mr. Jonathan Edwards,* first published in 1765 and collected—along with a useful portrait by Peter Gay, "Jonathan Edwards: An American Tragedy," and two fine poems about Edwards by Robert Lowell—in David Levin, ed., *Jonathan Edwards: A Profile* (Hill and Wang, 1969). For a full account by a sympathetic biographer, I recommend George Marsden's authoritative *Jonathan Edwards* (Yale University Press, 2003). I also found useful portions of Philip J. Gura's brief biography, *Jonathan Edwards: America's Evangelical* (Hill and Wang, 2005); Perry Miller's classic portrait of the Puritan mood, *The New England Mind: The Seventeenth Century* (Macmillan, 1939); Jon Butler's investigation of the eccentricities of American religion, *Awash In A Sea of Faith: Christianizing the American People* (Harvard University Press, 1990); Ann Taves's history of religious enthusiasm, *Fits, Trances, and Visions: Experiencing Religion and Explaining Experience from Wesley to James* (Princeton University Press, 1999); Nancy Carlisle, "Pursuing Refinement in Rural New England, 1750–1850: An Exhibition Review," *Winterthur Portfolio* 34, no. 4 (1999): 239–49; Ava Chamberlain, "Bad Books and Bad Boys: The Transformation of Gender in Eighteenth-Century Northampton, Massachusetts," *New England Quarterly* 75, no. 2 (2002): 179–203; Chamberlain, "The Immaculate Ovum: Jonathan Edwards and the Construction of the Female Body," *William and Mary Quarterly* 57, no. 2 (2000): 289–322; Sandra Gustafson, "Jonathan Edwards and the Reconstruction of 'Feminine' Speech," *American Literary History* 6, no. 2 (Summer 1994): 185–212; and "Jonathan Edwards in 2003," a special issue of *Theology Matters,* "A Publication of Presbyterians for Faith, Family, and Ministry" published in November/December of 2003 and edited by, among others, Richard Lovelace, a mentor of sorts to Doug Coe's son Jonathan, and the inspiration for Jonathan House, an Ivanwald-like residence for young men on Capitol Hill in Washington.

3. THE REVIVAL MACHINE

1.   Timothy L. Smith, *Revivalism and Social Reform: American Protestantism on the Eve of the Civil War* (Harper and Row, 1965), p. 79.

2.   Charles G., Finney, *The Original Memoirs of Charles G. Finney*, ed. Garth M. Rosell and Richard A. G. Dupuis (Zondervan, 1989), p. 66. The first edition of Finney's memoirs was published in 1876; the edition I rely on most is published by one of the biggest evangelical publishers of today but is a scholarly work in the sense that it reflects the text as Finney intended it, not as his nineteenth-century publishers presented it. Finney, who in his old age dictated these memoirs to a former student, is one of the great underappreciated memoirists of American letters. His memoirs are not high art, but they are storytelling in a distinct American vein, and I make extensive use of them in this chapter. Biographical details are taken from the memoirs unless otherwise indicated.

3.   Ibid., jacket blurb.

4.   William C. Cochran, "Charles Grandison Finney Memorial Address" (J. B. Lippincott, 1908).

5.   Richard Hofstadter, *Anti-Intellectualism in American Life* (Alfred A. Knopf, 1963), p. 92.

6.   Marianne Perciaccante, *Calling Down Fire: Charles Grandison Finney and Revivalism in Jefferson County, New York, 1800–1840* (State University of New York Press, 2003), p. 38.

7.   I don't mean to suggest that the arguments of Finney scholars such as William G. McLoughlin, Keith J. Hardman, Allen C. Guelzo, John L. Hammond, and others miss the point. Indeed, from their close readings of nineteenth-century theological disputes they derive great insights into the evolution of American religion and politics. (Of particular interest in the latter regard are Paul E. Johnson's *A Shopkeeper's Millennium: Society and Revivals in Rochester, New York, 1815–1837* [Hill and Wang, 1978], and "God and Mammon," chapter 7 of Charles Sellers's *The Market Revolution: Jacksonian America, 1815–1846* [Oxford University Press, 1991], both of which are among the rare works of academic specialization that are also splendid reading.) Rather, I mean to simply single out the strand of Finney's life that I believe is most relevant to the genealogy of American fundamentalism as it has appeared in recent times.

8.   For a discussion of the "machinery" of revival and its critics, see "The Businessmen's Revival," chapter 1 of John Corrigan's *Business of the Heart: Religion and Emotion in the Nineteenth Century* (University of California Press, 2002). Mark A. Noll provides a succinct description of Finney's "new measures" in *A History of Christianity in the United States and Canada* (William B. Eerdmans, 1992; reprint edition, 2003), pp. 176–77.

9.   Charles Chauncey, *Seasonable Thoughts on the State of Religion in New-England* (Rogers and Fowle, 1743), p. 218, cited in Eric Leigh Schmidt, *Hearing Things: Religion, Illusion, and the American Enlightenment* (Harvard University Press, 2000), p. 71.

10.   Finney, "Human Government," in *Finney's Systematic Theology* (Bethany House, 1994).

4. UNIT NUMBER ONE

1.   My account of Abram's early life is shaped by his own reminiscences in letters and notes for a biography, stored in collection 459 of the Billy Graham Center Archives, but the major details and quotations are for the most part from the two full-length, English-language biographies (there is a third, by an evangelical admirer, in Norwegian) written about Abram: *Modern Viking: The Story of Abraham Vereide, Pioneer in Christian Leadership* (Zondervan,1961), written by a revivalist named Norman Grubb mainly for private distribution to Abram's followers; and *Abraham, Abraham*, by Abram's son, Warren Vereide, and Claudia Minden Weisz, a privately published book (I received my copy from a former member of the Fellowship). The Abram story would be retold over the years in the literature produced by his various organizations; where I rely on such material in future chapters, I'll provide additional notes.

2.   James C. Hefley and Edward E. Plowman, *Washington: Christians in the Corridors of Power* (Tyndale House, 1975), p. 100.

3.   Mauritz A. Hallgren, "Panic in the Steel Towns," *The Nation*, March 30, 1932.

4.   Richard C. Berner, *Seattle in the 20th Century,* vol. 2, *Seattle, 1921–1940: From Boom to Bust* (Charles Press, 1992). For Seattle history, I rely on Abram's memoir, documents from the Washington State archives, and most of all the incomparable and epic multivolume *Seattle in the 20th Century*, by Richard C. Berner, who presents pieces of nearly every significant primary source on the city's politics and culture during the period he covers. In this chapter and in chapter 5, I draw especially on volume 2, *Seattle, 1921–1940: From Boom to Bust* (Philadelphia: Charles Press, 1992) and volume 3, *Seattle Transformed: World War II to the Cold War* (1999).

5.   Except where particular sources are indicated, my account of Abram's nightmare nemesis, Harry Bridges, the strike of 1934, and the factors that fed into it is based on the following: Charles P. Larrowe, *Harry Bridges: The Rise*

and Fall of Radical Labor in the United States (Lawrence Hill and Coe, 1972); David F. Selvin, *A Terrible Anger: The 1934 Waterfront and General Strikes in San Francisco* (Wayne State University Press, 1996); Mike Quin, *The Big Strike* (Olema, 1949); Paul Eliel, *The Waterfront and General Strikes, San Francisco, 1934* (Hooper, 1934); Warren Hinckle, *The Big Strike: A Pictorial History of the 1934 San Francisco General Strike* (Silver Dollar Books, 1985); J. Anthony Lukas, *Big Trouble: A Murder in a Small Western Town Sets Off a Struggle for the Soul of America* (Simon and Schuster, 1997), Louis Adamic, *Dynamite: The Story of Class Violence in America* (Viking, 1934).

6.   Tillie Lerner, "The Strike," *Partisan Review*, September–October, 1934.

7.   Abraham Vereide, notes prepared for Grubb, *Modern Viking*, from collection 459 of the BGCA, no box number.

8.   Evelyn Seeley, "Our Number One Fascists," *The Nation*, April 15, 1936.

5. THE *F* WORD

1.   Kissinger's graduate work was recently brought to public attention by the economist Paul Krugman in *The Great Unraveling: Losing Our Way in the New Century* (W. W. Norton, 2003). Unfortunately, Krugman reads Kissinger too literally, settling for the either/or dichotomy established at first glance and then translating it to the present political situation as *us* (the secular state) versus *them* (the "right-wing movement" as "revolutionary power"). Krugman falls for this intellectual trap despite the fact that he acknowledges that the right-wing movement controls much or most of the state (depending on the electoral moment). The us and the them, status quo and revolutionary power, are not so different after all. As Pogo famously put it, "We have met the enemy, and it is us."

2.   Alan Brinkley, *Voices of Protest: Huey Long, Father Coughlin, and the Great Depression* (Alfred A. Knopf, 1982), pp. 83–95.

3.   Robert O. Paxton writes on the fascist penchant for colored shirts and its relationship to the appearance of perfect unity in *The Anatomy of Fascism* (Alfred A. Knopf, 2004).

4.   "Cincinattus Drive Is Sped in Seattle," *New York Times*, March 1, 1936.

5.   Mary McCarthy, "Circus Politics in Washington State," *The Nation*, October 17, 1936.

6.   Richard L. Neuberger, "State of the Slapstick in Politics," *New York Times*, February 20, 1938.

7.   "Seattle Deals Radicals a Blow," *Los Angeles Times,* March 10, 1938.

8.   *Los Angeles Times*, March 9, 1938; *New York Times*, March 10, 1938.

9.   Michael Janson, "A Christian Century: Liberal Protestantism, the New Deal, and the Origins of Post-War American Politics" (dissertation, University of Pennsylvania, 2007), pp. 163–70.

10.   *Hart's involvement with ICL;* Edward Cabannis to Abram, July 24, 1951. Folder 6, box 166, collection 459, BGCA. *FBI on Hart and Lindbergh, and Hart on the Jews*: Max Wallace, *The American Axis: Henry Ford, Charles Lindbergh, and the Rise of the Third Reich* (St. Martin's Press, 2003), p. 252. *Robert H. Jackson on Hart:* "Democracy Under Fire," delivered to a meeting of the Law Society of Massachusetts, Boston City Club, Boston, Massachusetts, October 16, 1940.

11.   For biographical details in this sketch of Buchman, I am indebted to the popular press of the era, which found Buchman a subject for admiration or a source of amusement, and especially to Tom Driberg's *The Mystery of Moral Re-Armament: A Study of Frank Buchman and His Movement* (Alfred A. Knopf, 1965). Driberg was the first British journalist to investigate Buchman in the late 1920s. By the time he published his book-length study, however, he was a member of Parliament for Labour, and Buchmanites had long sought to discredit him as a communist and homosexual. Driberg had, indeed, joined the British Communist Party as a young man, but as his biographer Francis Wheen writes in *The Soul of Indiscretion: Tom Driberg—Poet, Philanderer, Legislator, and Outlaw* (Fourth Estate, 2002), he had been expelled when it was discovered that he was reporting to M15. His homosexuality was hardly a secret; he was famous for it, and in case there was any confusion he outed himself once again in *The Mystery of Moral Re-Armament*. He died a British peer, Baron Bradwell, in 1975 and was charged with having been a KGB spy in 1999 by the ex-KGB archivist Vasili Mitrokhin, who claimed that the Soviets blackmailed Driberg on threat of exposure of his sexuality. This seems a rather dubious assertion, given the fact that Driberg was out, and Driberg's defenders say that their man had once again played double agent. Such facts are hard to ascertain, but for certainty's sake in my reliance on his account of Buchman, I've used only information that Driberg clearly sourced; flamboyant in politics and romance, he was a moderate writer who made his case with care.

12.   Peter Howard, *Frank Buchman's Secret* (Heinemann, 1961), p. 28. Howard's short book is an exercise in distortion. The most egregious of its misrepresentations is Howard's celebration of the Moral Re-Armament men who fought for the Allies in World War II. While many MRA followers no

doubt did fight, MRA went to such ends in seeking to obtain exemptions for military service for British and American followers that Colonel Arthur V. McDermott, New York City's draft director, declared that MRA was "reeking with hypocrisy and bad faith." Quoted in Driberg, *The Mystery of Moral Re-Armament,* p. 75.

13.   Frank Buchman, "Guidance or Guns," speech delivered at Interlaken on September 6, 1938, in *Remaking the World: The Speeches of Frank Buchman* (Blandford Press, 1961), p. 63.

14.   This fact, and the following description of a typical Buchmanite house party, are derived from "Soul Surgeon," a profile of Buchman by Alva Johnson in the April 23, 1932, *New Yorker,* pp. 22–25.

15.   Buchman, *Remaking the World.*

16.   Grubb, *Modern Viking,* p. 51.

17.   Buchman, "Will God Control America?" broadcast from Philadelphia, June 19, 1936, in *Remaking the World,* p. 33.

18.   Buchman, "How to Listen," speech delivered in Birmingham, England, July 26, 1936, in *Remaking the World,* p. 35.

19.   William A. H. Birnie, "Hitler or Any Fascist Leader Controlled By God Could Cure All Ills of World, Buchman Believes," *New York World-Telegram,* August 26, 1936. Buchman's high opinion of Hitler so addled his senses, writes Driberg in *The Mystery of Moral Re-Armament* (pp. 66–67), that before a trip to Germany he had one of his followers, a U.S. assistant attorney general, request a meeting with FDR for Buchman on the grounds that "Herr Hitler" had himself requested a meeting with Buchman, and Buchman would be embarrassed to report to Hitler that his own president would not receive him. It's not known whether or not Buchman did, in fact, meet Hitler, but if so, he must have been red-faced; Roosevelt wanted no truck with Moral Re-Armament's gnome.

20.   Buchman, "Miracles in the North," speech delivered in New York City, November 20, 1935, in *Remaking the World,* pp. 19, 23.

21.   Sinclair Lewis, *It Can't Happen Here* (Doubleday, Doran, 1935), p. 21.

22.   Richard M. Fried, *The Man Everybody Knew: Bruce Barton and the Making of Modern America* (Ivan R. Dee, 2005), p. 97.

23.   *American* magazine, June 1930, p. 202, quoted in *Barton in Blunderland,* a 1937 campaign pamphlet for the American Labor Party.

24.   "Dollar's Eagle Is a Sparrow, Barton Finds," *Washington Post,* June 10, 1934.

25.   Bruce Barton, "Hard Times," *Wall Street Journal,* March 30, 1926.

26. *Finding the Better Way,* periodicals, collection 459, Records of the Fellowship Foundation, BGCA.

27. Grubb, *Modern Viking,* p. 66. Poling's relationship to the Philadelphia machine is discussed in "Ring Job Ordered," *Time,* August 6, 1951.

28. Richard C. Berner, *Seattle in the 20th Century,* volume 3, *Seattle Transformed: World War II to the Cold War* (Philadelphia: Charles Press, 1999), p. 52.

29. Ibid., p. 54.

30. "Barton Breaks a Lance," *Wall Street Journal,* October 26, 1937.

31. Herbert Marcuse, *One-Dimensional Man: Studies in the Ideology of Advanced Industrial Society,* 2nd edition (Beacon Press, 1991), p. 1.

6. THE MINISTRY OF PROPER ENLIGHTENMENT

1. "Nazi Envoy Silent on Agency Ouster," *New York Times,* January 17, 1941.

2. Quoted in "D.C. Trial Bares German Secrets," *Washington Post,* July 24, 1941.

3. *"It is of paramount . . .":* Hans Thomsen to Zapp, August 30, 1938, reproduced in full in "Excerpts from White Paper on Nazi Activities Here Released," *New York Times,* November 22, 1940. *"My task here . . .":* Zapp to Rudolf Leitner, then the German ambassador to South Africa, November 25, 1938, in ibid.

4. "You can easily recognize Manfred Zapp, the Nazi agent, his madcap girlfriend, and . . . John Edgar Hoover," Walter Winchell wrote in a blurb for *High Stakes* (G. P. Putnam's Sons, 1942), a thinly fictionalized account of the FBI's investigation of Zapp by the journalist Curt Riess, a German émigré considered an authority on Nazi espionage. For Zapp in Havana, see Willard Edwards, "Find 200 Agents in Havana Push Cause of Hitler," *Chicago Tribune,* July 27, 1940.

5. Zapp's antagonism toward Ryan was all the more remarkable for the fact that Ryan occasionally struck a friendly note for fascism, as in his 1937 defense of Generalissimo Franco's fascist rebellion in Spain. Wilson D. Miscamble, "The Limits of American Catholic Anti-Fascism: The Case of John A. Ryan," *Church History,* 59, no. 4 (December 1990): 523–38. *Zapp's rebuttal:* Winifred Mallon, "Asks Public to Rise on Neutrality Act," *New York Times,* July 14, 1939.

6. "Roosevelt's Attack Comes as G-Men Order Probe of Nazi Press Service," *Washington Post,* October 25, 1940.

7. Drew Pearson, "Merry-Go-Round," *Washington Post*, October 25, 1946.

8. "Huge Area Shaken, But City Escapes," *New York Times,* September 13, 1940.

9. "West Point Sails With Axis Agents Ousted from the U.S.," *New York Times*, July 16, 1941.

10. "German Newsmen Tour Army Bases," *Information Bulletin*, September 1951 (U.S. High Commissioner's Office), p. 72. University of Wisconsin Digital Collections, http://digital.library.wisc.edu/1711.dl/History.

11. Correspondence between Donald C. Stone and Hoffman, "Re attached report by Donald C. Stone: Implications of Mutual Security Act and Requirements for Action, October 4, 1951," correspondence, 1951, Economic Cooperation Administration File, Paul G. Hoffman Papers, Truman Presidential Museum and Library. *"My main use . . .":* Stone to Abram, undated, circa 1948, folder 21, box 474, collection 459, BGCA.

12. National Security Council directive 10/2, quoted in Kenneth Osgood, *Total Cold War: Eisenhower's Secret Propaganda Battle at Home and Abroad* (University of Kansas Press, 2006), p. 39.

13. Letter to Abram, from unknown correspondent, December 25, 1945, folder 4, box 168, collection 459, BGCA; and Grubb, *Modern Viking*, pp. 101–2.

14. Timothy George, "Inventing Evangelicalism," *Christianity Today*, March 2004.

15. *"I believe honestly . . .":* Dianne Kirby, "Harry Truman's Religious Legacy: The Holy Alliance, Containment and the Cold War," in *Religion and the Cold War,* ed. Diane Kirby (Palgrave, 2003), p. 86. *Truman and MRA.:* Driberg, *The Mystery of Moral Re-Armament*, p. 92. *Truman's meeting with Robertson:* Donald C. Stone to John R. Steelman, the first man to hold the office later known as White House chief of staff, January 23, 1948, folder 21, box 474, collection 459, BGCA.

16. *"Imperial interests":* Gregor Dallas, *1945: The War That Never Ended* (Yale University Press, 2005), p. 581. *Carlson:* The phrase had popped up in Fellowship correspondence the year previous, but it seems that Carlson debuted it publicly and may well have coined it. In an undated memo he wrote in apparent preparation for the conference, he declares Worldwide Spiritual Offensive as the "theme" that unites church and state into a force strong enough to confront the "Red Hordes." Worldwide Spiritual Offensive in his view was distinctly American, since only the "new race" of Americans, "conscious of its dependence on divine providence," could confront the "alien way of life" prac-

ticed by leftists and foreigners (memo and speech). Folder 1, box 505, collection 459, BGCA. *Broger:* "Moral Doctrine for Free World Global Planning" was a presentation Broger made to a Fellowship group on June 14, 1954. No box number, collection 459, BGCA. The doctrine consisted of a study of communism and Broger's plan for reforming society after a "global war" using Fellowship-style networking, using "indoctrinated personnel who will form nucleus groups" to implement "the highest concepts of freedom, whether socially acceptable or not."

17.   This brief account of the NAE is derived from (and with apologies to) Joel A. Carpenter's more sympathetic but very insightful account in "An Evangelical United Front," chapter 8 of his excellent *Revive Us Again: The Reawakening of American Fundamentalism* (Oxford University Press, 1997).

18.   Harriet French, "To Make Christians Leaders, and Leaders Christians," in unidentified newspaper, box 411, folder 4, collection 459, BGCA.

19.   An undated brochure produced by the Fellowship shows on its front page just such a conversation between two men walking down the stone steps of the mansion. The man on the right, dressed in light gray and a dark tie, seems to be trying to persuade his companion, an older fellow with gray hair and black brows and an impatient air. The persuader, we learn in the caption, is Commissioner Sigurd Anderson of the Federal Trade Commission; the skeptic, Howard Blanchard of Union Pacific Railroad—two men with more than Christ in common. "The Bible," declares the brochure, "contains inexhaustible resources for the businessman fighting the economic battle in a two-fisted business world," like a vein of coal or a pool of oil "deposited" by God, awaiting refinement into a spiritual offensive against "materialism."

20.   FDR has long been a problematic figure for American fundamentalism, and not just because of his impossible-to-ignore leadership in World War II. On one hand, the New Deal benefited too many in both the populist rank and file of fundamentalism and at the elite level of Dixiecrat politicians for the movement to condemn FDR altogether. On the other hand, the avant-garde of fundamentalism was born in 1935 in response to FDR's perceived godless socialism. What is to be done with this historical paradox? William J. Federer, an accountant-turned-historian who has become a best-selling fundamentalist historian, attempts to resolve the dilemma with *The Faith of F.D.R.* (Amerisearch, 2006), a compilation of every banal piety Roosevelt ever uttered. Federer hopes the book will cement FDR, war-president, into the fundamentalist pantheon.

21.   Grubb, *Modern Viking,* p. 105. *"Nominal membership":* Otto Fricke, J. W. E. Sommer, Georg Reichel, Professor Landon Bender, Paul Orlamunder, Friedreich Wunderlich, to Abram, August 26, 1946, folder 4, box 218, collection 459, BGCA.

22.   J. F. Byrnes, "Restatement of Policy on Germany, Stuttgart," September 6, 1946. http://usa.usembassy.de/etexts/ga4–460906.htm accessed August 20, 2006.

23.   *"You are God's man":* Abram to Fricke, August 29, 1947, folder 4, box 218, collection 459, BGCA.

24.   Michael H. Kater, *Different Drummers: Jazz in the Culture of Nazi Germany* (Oxford University Press, 1992), p. 49.

25.   Hans Spier, *From the Ashes of Disgrace: A Journal from Germany, 1945–1955* (Amherst: University of Massachusetts Press, 1985), pp. 31–32.

26.   Hans Kempe to Abram, February 5, 1948, folder 5, box 218, collection 459, BGCA.

27.   Peter Grose, *Operation Rollback: America's Secret War Behind the Iron Curtain* (Houghton Mifflin, 2000), pp. 2–6.

28.   "Meeting Agenda," in folders 46–50, box 585, collection 459, BGCA.

29.   Most of this money came in individual donations raised by Abram's prayer cells (see Gedat to Abram, January 14, 1951; Abram to Gedat, April 18, 1951, folder 7, box 218, collection 459, BGCA), but some apparently came from the Mellon Foundation, as well. Gedat to Abram, March 26, 1950, folder 5, box 218, collection 459, BGCA.

30.   In *The Holy Reich: Nazi Conceptions of Christianity, 1919–1945* (Cambridge University Press, 2003), the historian Richard Steigmann-Gall delivers conclusive evidence that settles the debate over whether or not Nazism conceived of itself as anti-Christian: not at all. In fact, much of the top leadership, Steigmann-Gall documents, considered the cross and the swastika two different symbols for one great idea.

31.   "Directive to Commander-in-Chief of United States Forces of Occupation Regarding the Military Government of Germany," April 1945 (JCS 1067). Available online from the U.S. Embassy to Germany at http://usa. usembassy.de/etexts/ga3–450426.pdf.

32.   *"Asiatic nihilism":* Dr. H. O. Ahrens to Abram, November 10, 1949, folder 5, box 218, collection 459, BGCA. Ahrens was a vocal and effective lobbyist for German industrialists determined to avoid the dismantling of factories used for military production. At the time of this letter, he was taking

one of Abram's American operatives, William Frary von Bromberg (who claimed the title of baron, perhaps falsely) on a tour of such properties.

33.   Abram to Fricke, September 21, 1949; Fricke to Abram, October 17, 1949; Abram to Fricke, November 2, 1949; folder 4, box 218, collection 459, BGCA. Gedat quoted in Inge Deutschkron, *Mein Leben nach dem Überleben* (Dtv, 2000), p. 130.

34.   The involvement of Abs, Schmelz, Rohrbach, and Speidel is reported in "The Highlights of the ICL Conference at Castle Mainau, Germany, June 14–17, 1951," an account by the ICL employee Wallace Haines, and an undated, untitled report on the same conference by a German ICL employee, Margarete Gärtner (herself a former prewar propagandist for German expansion), folders 10 and 11, respectively, of box 218, collection 459, BGCA.

35.   Hans von Eicken, a leader with Gedat and Fricke of the German division of the Fellowship, wrote to Abram on July 11, 1951, to tell Abram that the German Fellowship's advocacy on behalf of Pohl and another war criminal, Otto Ohlendorf—an influential economist who'd boasted at his trial of having overseen the murder of 90,000 Jews and other non-Aryans—had helped soothe the concerns of those in "important circles" who felt that the German Fellowship was the "cleverly engineered product of an American power group." Folder 7, box 218, collection 459, BGCA. On October 12, 1951, von Neurath's daughter had written Abram a letter begging for help with the case of her father. He'd been treated well by his American guards, she wrote, but persecuted by the Soviets who ran the prison in tandem with the United States. She was outraged that her father, one of the seven "Major War Criminals," suffered from bad dentistry. "It was difficult for him to talk," during her last visit to him in prison, "as his artificial set of teeth—put in about a year ago at Spandau—was fitting very badly." Abram opened a file on the case. "Can we do anything about this?" he wrote in a note to one of his aides. "Maybe [Congressman O. K.] Armstrong should see this." Von Neurath won his release as a medical parolee in 1953 (Arieh J. Kochavi, *Prelude to Nuremberg: Allied War Crimes Policy and the Question of Punishment* [University of North Carolina Press, 1998], p. 245), but besides this letter, the file Abram opened is lost, leaving us uncertain whether Abram's intervention played a part in von Neurath's good fortune. Winifred von Mackensen (née von Neurath) to Abram, folder 1, box 218, collection 459, BGCA.

36.   "Church Group Votes, Elects 17 from Congress," *Washington Post*, January 14, 17, 1945. *"Panty-waist diplomacy"*: Grose, *Operation Rollback*, p. 6.

37.   Lance Morrow, *The Best Year of their Lives: Kennedy, Nixon, and Johnson in 1948: Learning the Secrets of Power* (Basic Books, 2005), p. 128. Jack Powers, *South Bend Tribune*, February 24, 1991.

38.   Address to the United States Senate, February 5, 1946. One can find extensive excerpts from the speech on a number of Holocaust revisionist Web sites, including, as of 2006, http://www.sweetliberty.org/issues/wars/witness2history/21.html.

39.   Spier, *From the Ashes of Disgrace*, p. 27.

40.   Lecture to the Frankfurt chapter of International Christian Leadership, August 9, 1950, folder 11, box 218, collection 459, BGCA.

41.   Von Gienanth to Wallace Haines, ICL "Field Director for Europe," March 29, 1952, folder 1, box 218, collection 459, BGCA.

42.   Abram to Ropp, October 6, 1953, folder 3, box 218, collection 459, BGCA. Ropp was himself an admirer of Merwin K. Hart, the anti-Semitic American fascist whom Abram had welcomed into the Fellowship's inner circle. Ropp to Wallace Haines, August 12, 1952, folder 1, box 218, collection 459, BGCA.

43.   Frances Hepp, April 23, 1947, folder 4, box 218, collection 459, BGCA.

44.   Haines to Abram, June 23, 1951, folder 8, box 218, collection 459, BGCA.

45.   This account of the meeting at Mainau is drawn from K. C. Liddel, "Notes on Mainau Conference," June 28, 1951, folder 8, box 218, collection 459, BGCA; Wallace Haines, "The Highlights of ICL Conference at Castle Mainau, Germany," folder 10, box 218, collection 459; *Christian Leadership News*, September 1951, collection 459; Margarete Gärtner, "Newsletter," July 30, 1951, folder 10, box 218, collection 459; undated reports for Abram by Margarete Gärtner in folders 10 and 11, box 218, collection 459. Gärtner's past as a propagandist is referred to in John Hiden and Thomas Lane, eds., *The Baltic and the Outbreak of the Second World War* (Cambridge University Press, 1992), p. 126. The U-boat commander was Reinhard Hardegen. The fascist editor was Benno Mascher. Bishop Wurm's anti-Semitic remarks can be found in Wolfgang Erlich, *And the Witnesses Were Silent: The Confessing Church and the Persecution of the Jews* (University of Nebraska Press, 2000), p. 201.

46.   Tony Judt, *Postwar: A History of Europe Since 1945* (Penguin Press, 2005), p. 61.

47.   Dallas, *1945*, p. 615.

48.   Zapp to Abram, September 16, 1950, folder 6, box 218, collection 459, BGCA.

49.   Carpenter, *Revive Us Again*, p. 149.

7. THE BLOB

1.   Interview with Kate Phillips in Tom Weaver, *Science Fiction Confidential: Interviews With Monster Stars and Filmmakers* (McFarland, 2002), pp. 234–46.

2.   Joshua Muravchik, "Losing the Peace," *Commentary*, July 1992.

3.   Quoted in Richard Hofstadter's 1955 essay "The Pseudo-Conservative Revolt," in *The Radical Right* ed., Daniel Bell (Anchor Books, 1964), p. 76.

4.   A revealing statistic overlooked by conventional historians of the Cold War: between 1935, the year Abram and his fundamentalist elite came in from the cold of domestic exile, and 1980, the commencement of the Reagan era, the average number of American evangelical missionaries overseas grew from 5,000, many of them engaged in small projects close to home, to 32,000 spread all over the globe. Carpenter, *Revive Us Again*, p. 184. The anthropologist David Stoll explores the interconnections—ideological and actual— between the U.S. covert operations and the network of evangelical missionaries connected to what was then the largest missionary organization in the world in *Fishers of Men or Founders of Empire?: The Wycliffe Bible Translators in America* (Zed Press, 1982). Stoll takes pains to explain that such interconnections did not constitute a conspiracy, but rather, an overlapping worldview in which spiritual and imperial interests were not easily distinguished. As recently as 2006, when Venezuelan president Hugo Chavez expelled a group of evangelical missionaries he claimed were U.S. spies, *Christianity Today* felt compelled to condemn "The CIA Myth," apparently persuasive enough to seduce even some of the magazine's conservative evangelical readers. Deann Alford, January 2006.

5.   Quoted in Sara Diamond, *Roads to Dominion: Right-Wing Movements and Political Power in the United States* (Guilford Press, 1995), p. 101.

6.   "Our press," reads a memo in Abram's files on Cuba and the American media's ambivalence toward Castro, "is infested with crypto-Communists [and] intellectual prostitutes in their hire." Whether the Fellowship would extend that charge to even the evangelical press is unclear, but there can be no doubt on their position with regard to détente with Castro.

7.   Dwight D. Eisenhower, "Annual Message to Congress on the State of the Union," 1958. Eisenhower accused the Soviets of waging "total cold war," to which, he said, the United States must respond with "total peace" in which "every asset of our personal and national lives," particularly religion, would be dedicated to the fight. Ike also believed in "progress" as defined by the Atlas, Titan, Thor, Jupiter, and Polaris missile programs. The fact that such literally

totalitarian ambitions were considered calming is an indicator of the fear and loathing that infused the ostensibly bland 1950s.

8.   Kenneth Osgood, *Total Cold War: Eisenhower's Secret Propaganda Battle at Home and Abroad* (Kansas State University Press, 2006), pp. 270–75.

9.   Reverend John Collins, chairman of Christian Action, to Abram, September 8, 1950, folder 2, box 202, collection 459, BGCA.

10.   Osgood, *Total Cold War*, p. 40.

11.   "Government Curbs Scored," *New York Times*, May 11, 1949.

12.   Grubb to Abram, August 21, 1953, folder 2, box 202, collection 459, BGCA.

13.   Perhaps they carried with them reprints of a *Look* magazine article Abram had had made, his chief piece of literature that year. The lead story was by Norman Vincent Peale, Abram's colleague in the Twelve. Why was America experiencing a spiritual revival? Simple, said Peale: "for the first time in the country's history, we are filled with fear." Peale's solution: "It is now widely recognized that prayer is a skill, that it is an actual power." The demand of the hour, wrote Peale, was organizing such power into action, a "vital spiritual force." His inspiration? "The Vereide Organization," which inculcated "the country's lawmakers" in "the importance of divine guidance." Abram's reprint of Peale's May 22, 1951, *Look* article, "The Place of Prayer in America," was titled "These Scandalous Years in Washington," a reference to widespread suspicion that the Truman administration was riddled with red agents. Folder 51, box 585, collection 459, BGCA. *"Direct relationship . . ."*: Associated Press, "Wiley Trip Declared in U.S. Interest," *Washington Post*, May 21, 1952. Particularly controversial was Wiley's decision to bring his much younger new bride for a vacation, a practice that under Eisenhower would become unofficial policy, the chumminess of power couples meeting their peers used to cement "relationships" with foreign nations, as David F. Schmitz writes in *Thank God They're On Our Side: The United States & Right-Wing Dictatorships* (University of North Carolina Press, 1999), p. 183.

14.   Wilhelmina was at that point technically "princess," having passed her throne to her daughter, Juliana, but she was still referred to as queen, and both women were strong supporters of the Fellowship, though whether out of religious sentiment or other motives—the royal family was responsible for the interests of Royal Dutch-Shell Oil—is unclear in Abram's papers.

15. Robert C. Albright, "Ike Can't Find Titles for All His Talented Help," *Washington Post*, June 22, 1952.

16. "The June Brides," *Time*, June 23, 1952.

17. In *Phyllis Schlafly and Grassroots Conservatism: A Woman's Crusade* (Princeton University Press, 2005), the historian Donald T. Crichtlow argues that this sense of betrayal led to the formation of the New Right that would propel Barry Goldwater to the GOP nomination twelve years later. See pp. 46–47.

18. Drew Pearson, "Merry-Go-Round: Taft Talks Way Back to the Top," *Washington Post*, December 22, 1952.

19. Two of the Democratic candidates for the nomination, Senator Estes Kefauver of Tennessee and Senator Robert Kerr of Oklahoma, were Breakfast Groupers. The eventual nominee, Illinois governor Adlai Stevenson, was decidedly not, but his hawkish liberalism would lead him into even more militant expressions of faith. The "one supreme difference" between the United States and the USSR, Stevenson told a "Washington Pilgrimage" of Christian nationalists, "is that America and its leaders believe in God; the rulers of Russia have turned their back on God and deny His very existence." "Presidential Candidates Speak Out For Religion," *Washington Post*, May 3, 1952. Stevenson's surprising piety may be understood as a sign of the times; the 1952 election was, according to the *Washington Post*, the first time all presidential candidates had publicly paid tribute to America's ostensible religious—read, "Christian"—heritage.

20. Graham's account of his role can be found in "The General Who Became President," chapter 12 of his autobiography, *Just As I Am* (HarperSanFranciso/Zondervan, 1997), in which he says he met Abram during his Northwest Crusades. He does not mention the fact that Abram had been recruited by his own former Seattle cell—doubling as the sponsoring committee for the Graham Crusade's visit—to seek federal funds for a cover for the city's Memorial Stadium to ensure the Crusade's success. "Graham wants this," wrote Abram's Seattle lieutenant, a wealthy lawyer named Warren Dewar. "Langlie and Devin"—the governor and the mayor of Seattle, both men whose careers had been made by Breakfast Group connections—"want it too." Dewar suggests that $18,000, possibly federal funds, had already been directed toward Graham's appearance. Dewar to Abram, May 16, 1951, folder 7, box 168, collection 459, BGCA. Reference to *Oiltown U.S.A.* may be found in the BGEA's collection 214, the records of World Wide Pictures, Graham's film production company.

21.   Dr. Frederick Brown Harris, quoted in Grubb, *Modern Viking*, pp. 130–32.

22.   Nick Thimmesch, "Politicians and the Underground Prayer Movement," *Los Angeles Times*, January 13, 1974. Thimmesch, who admired the Fellowship, described it thusly: "They are secretive and guarded in discussing their experiences or activities . . . They genuinely avoid publicity. In fact, they shun it."

23.   *Ferguson:* Ferguson was a longtime inner circle member who regularly appeared in the Fellowship's brochures for new prospects. *Bennett:* Bennett's membership in ICL was reported in the July 1959 issue of *Moody Monthly*, the magazine of the fundamentalist Moody Institute in Chicago, in "Christians in Your Congress," by Donald H. Gill. Other members cited included Strom Thurmond, James B. Utt—the Orange County congressman who believed that the United Nations was training Africans to conquer the United States—and Representative Bruce Alger, the Dallas Republican who would lead a "mink coat mob" made up of his wealthy female supporters in a spitting attack on Ladybird Johnson. Bennett, a signer of the infamous Southern Manifesto, remained close to the Fellowship for decades. "I ask too much of you already," he wrote Doug Coe on January 27, 1987, "and therefore am not pressing for a particular appointment, but anytime that suits you I would certainly like to see you." Folder 4, box 166, collection 459, BGCA.

24.   Hefley and Plowman, *Washington: Christians in the Corridors of Power*, pp. 120–21.

25.   Associated Press, "Eisenhower Joins in a Breakfast Prayer Meeting," *New York Times*, February 5, 1954. Eisenhower didn't speak at the second breakfast, but Vice President Nixon did, initiating a tradition Nixon maintained for the rest of the decade. Personally indifferent to Abram's piety, he recognized the value of the Prayer Breakfast's pulpit and made it his own. *Guatemala*: Van Gosse, *Where the Boys Are: Cuba, Cold War America and the Making of a New Left* (Verso, 1993), pp. 26–29.

26.   Seth Jacobs, *America's Miracle Man in Vietnam: Ngo Dinh Diem, Religion, Race, and U.S. Intervention in Southeast Asia* (Duke University Press, 2005), pp. 60–62. "Wiley Would End Attack on Dulles," *New York Times*, July 25, 1954.

27.   "McCarthy to be Asked to Aid Ike," *Washington Post*, September 18, 1952. Ferdinand Kuhn, "McCarthy's Charges in Speech Stir Angry Denials, Protests," *Washington Post*, October 29, 1952.

28.   I. F. Stone, "The First Welts on Joe McCarthy," *I. F. Stone's Weekly*, March 15, 1954, reproduced in *The Best of I. F. Stone*, ed. Peter Osnos (Public Affairs, 2006).

29.   "For God and Country," *Vanguard University Magazine*, the alumni journal of the former Southern California Bible College, Spring 2002.

30.   Osgood, *Total Cold War*, p. 315.

31.   Drew Pearson, "The New JCS—and the Old," *Washington Post*, August 13, 1953.

32.   John Broger, "Moral Doctrine for Free World Global Planning," a presentation to Abram's ICL, June 14, 1954, folder 1, box 505, collection 459, BGCA.

33.   Marquis Childs, "A Strange Film Shown to Soldiers," *Washington Post*, January 27, 1961.

34.   "Militant Liberty Outline Plan," November 5, 1954, Operations Coordinating Board Central Files, box 70, OCB 091, from the collection of Kenneth Osgood, Florida Atlantic University.

35.   Wayne's USC football teammate Ward Bond joined forces with Broger as well, but although Bond appeared in some of the best movies Hollywood ever made, including *Gone With the Wind*, *It's a Wonderful Life*, and Ford's brilliant John Wayne vehicle, *The Searchers*, it wouldn't be fair to include him in the same category as those two tremendously talented reactionaries. Of course, Ford would have disagreed with me. Sort of: "Let's face it," he once said of Bond's anticommunist snitching, "Ward Bond is a shit. But he's our favorite shit." Frances Stonor Saunders, *The Cultural Cold War: The CIA and the World of Arts and Letters* (New Press, 2000), pp. 284–87.

36.   Broger, "Memorandum for the Secretary of Defense," July 26, 1957, no box number, collection 459, BGCA.

8. VIETNAMIZATION

1.   Clifton J. Robinson to Doug Coe, April 28, 1966, folder 2, box 372, collection 459, BGCA.

2.   "Carter Appoints 'Field Marshall' Sullivan Ambassador to Shah," *MERIP Report*, no. 59, August 1977, pp. 24–25. Sullivan went on to become the last American ambassador to Iran, an appointment of great controversy. Sullivan "is well-fitted to run secret presidential wars and lie to Congress about

them," editorialized *The Nation*, an assessment borne out in more admiring terms by a study conducted for the CIA: "The secret war in Laos, author Charles Stevenson has emphasized, was 'William Sullivan's war.' . . . Sullivan imposed two conditions upon his subordinates. First, the thin fiction of the Geneva accords had to be maintained . . . ; military operations, therefore, had to be carried out in relative secrecy. Second, no regular US ground troops were to become involved." Instead, Sullivan resorted to one of the most destructive bombing campaigns of the Vietnam War. William M. Leary, "CIA Air Operations in Laos, 1955–1974," *Studies in Intelligence* (published by the CIA), Winter 1999–2000.

3.   Abram, "Memorandum to the Board," circa 1966, folder 2, box 563, collection 459, BGCA.

4.   *Bold Satanic forces:* Ibid. *Cyclone:* Frank McLaughlin to Abram, December 15, 1966, folder 1, box 168, collection 459, BGCA. *"Ten steps . . .":* Coe to Jim Anderson of Young Life, November 18, 1981, folder 5, box 168, collection 459, BGCA.

5.   Robinson had won for the Fellowship's muscular Christ the ostensibly Ghandian Hindu A. M. Thomas, responsible for India's armed forces during some of the worst fighting with Pakistan. Robinson to Ford Mason, November 30, 1964, folder 2, box 232, collection 459, BGCA.

6.   Robinson to Halverson, April 13, 1963, ibid.

7.   Halverson to Robinson, May 22, 1963, ibid.

8.   *Cordle, Halverson:* Robinson to Mason, November 30, 1964, ibid.

9.   V. Raymond Edman, *They Found the Secret: Twenty Lives That Reveal A Touch of Eternity* (Zondervan, 1984), pp. 78–87.

10   Halverson's responsibility to a pluralistic nation did not mellow his religious convictions. Upon his death in 1995, Senator Dan Coats (R., Indiana) would eulogize him by expressing his admiration for a man who would preach thusly on the Senate floor: "God of our fathers, if we separate morality from politics, we imperil our Nation and threaten self-destruction. Imperial Rome was not defeated by an enemy from without; it was destroyed by moral decay from within. Mighty God, over and over again you warned your people, Israel, that righteousness is essential to national health." Halverson also preached in the Senate against investigative reporting. Cal Thomas, "The Most Powerful Man in Washington Retires," *York Daily Record*, November 9, 1994.

11.   Robert D. Foster, *The Navigator* (Challenge Books, 1983), p. 61.

12.   Doug Coe, "The Person of Christ," a videotaped address to the President's Meeting, a gathering of evangelical leaders, January 15, 1989.

13.   "Washington Welcomes Doug Coe," in *Christian Leadership*, October 1959, collection 459, BGCA.

14.   *"a woman so uncomplaining"*: Wallace Haines quoted in "A Key Man in Every Country," July 1973, folder 20, box 383, collection 459, BGCA. Sharpnack to Coe, December 28, 1959, folder 10, box 135, collection 459, BGCA.

15.   Cal Ludeman to Coe, April 27, 1960, folder 11, box 135, collection 459, BGCA.

16.   Kent Hotaling to Coe, January 18, 1960, folder 10, box 135, collection 459, BGCA.

17.   One of Coe's standard closings on letters written in 1960, folder 11, box 135, collection 459, BGCA.

18.   Haines is quoted back to himself in a letter from Coe to Haines dated December 27, 1967, folder 4, box 204, collection 459, BGCA. Coe to parents, November 4, 1959, folder 11, box 368, collection 459, BGCA.

19.   Frank Laubach, "A Pentagon of World Friendship," October 19, 1955, folder 1, box 505, collection 459, BGCA. Chuck Hull to Coe, January 15, 1960, folder 10, box 135, collection 459, BGCA.

20.   *Traveling on Fellowship behalf*: *Christian Leadership*, December 1959, collection 459, BGCA. "Capehart and Carlson Meet Duvalier; U.S. Senators Pledge Assistance to Haiti, *New Pittsburgh Courier*, December 5, 1959.

21.   Doug Barram to Coe, June 12, 1962, folder 5, box 168, collection 459, BGCA.

22.   "Finding the Better Way," January 15, 1942, pamphlet, collection 459, BGCA.

23.   March 1962 remarks to a prayer breakfast for the governor of Arizona, filed under "Thoughts on Prayer," file 16, box 449, collection 459, BGCA.

24.   "LBJ, Billy Graham Eloquent at Breakfast," *Washington Post*, February 18, 1966.

25.   March 8, 1962, folder 5, box 361, collection 459, BGCA.

26.   Carlson to José Joaquín Trejos Fernández, November 27, 1967, folder 17, box 365, collection 459, BGCA. Dorn was of no relation to the first W. J. Bryan, for whom he was named not in deference to Bryan's fundamentalism, ironically, but in honor of Bryan's anti-imperialism.

27.   Howard Siner, "Attorney Knows Carter as Smart, Kind Friend," *San Jose News*, March 4, 1977.

28.   Bill Green to Coe, August 4, 1960, folder 11, box 135, collection 459, BGCA.

29.   Savimbi, a black African leader who enjoyed support from the apartheid state as well as American Christian conservatives, is harder to pin down than Barre, who gambled his whole relationship with the United States on the Family. Interviews with and correspondence of Clif Gosney, a former Family liaison to the South African Zulu chief Mangosuthu Buthelezi, reveal that Savimbi was also within the Family's circle, his spiritual well-being tended by Gosney, a sincere Christian, and Piet Koornhof, a cabinet minister in the South African government of F. W. de Klerk.

30.   There are at least two nearly full boxes of documents at the Billy Graham Center Archives detailing the Family's relationship with Brazilian regimes. Boxes 184–85, collection 459, BGCA.

31.   Interview with Coe by Tore Gjerstad, October 29, 2007.

32.   Notes on reorganization folders 1–2, box 563, collection 459, BGCA.

33.   Abram to Admiral C. S. Freeman, November 23, 1949, folder 2, box 348, collection 459, BGCA. Abram never put an explicitly anti-Semitic word on record, and while Malik may have been holding out hope for a Christian Palestinian state to the south of Lebanon, he was likely motivated more by his understanding of scripture, which did not include anti-Semitism. Freeman, however, the point man on the project, was an old-fashioned Jew hater and a frequent collaborator with Merwin K. Hart, the American fascist organizer.

34. Quoted in the December 1959/January 1960 issue of *Christian Leadership*, a members-only newsletter of the International Christian Leadership—the Fellowship. Located in the periodicals section of collection 459 at the BGCA.

35.   June 28, 1963, "Thoughts on Prayer," folder 16, box 449, collection 459, BGCA.

36.   Bell made clear to the students that they'd been selected not for their good standing as Christians—some were not religious—or good grades, but solely for their status as big men on campus. February 5, 1970, "Young Men's Seminar," tape 107, collection 459, BGCA. "During the seminar, when I voiced my objection to the assumption that we were all devoted Christians," Joe Persico, the student body president of San Francisco State, had complained to Lyndon Johnson after a similar event in 1965, "we were told by Roger Staubach . . . from the U.S. Naval Academy, 'I feel sorry for all of you who are not Christians, because you have no chance of an after-life.' General Silverthorn"—one of Abram's chief aides, an ancient officer who'd held a

Kurtz-like post in the U.S. occupation of Haiti during the 1920s—"told us that, 'of course, Christ said a few oddball things, too, like the Sermon on the Mount.'" Andrew Kopkind, "The Power of Prayer," *New Republic*, March 6, 1965.

37. February 5, 1970, "Young Men's Seminar," tape 107, collection 459, BGCA.

38. Ibid.

39. For basic biographical details about Colson, I relied on his first two memoirs, *Born Again* (Spire, 1977) and *Life Sentence* (Chosen Books, 1979), and John Perry's admiring biography, *Charles Colson: A Story of Power, Corruption, and Redemption* (Broadman and Holman, 2003). Colson's output, augmented by numerous ghostwriters, is enormous. Texts I found particularly useful to understanding his thinking include *Against the Night: Living in the New Dark Ages* (Servant Publications, 1989); *How Now Shall We Live?* (Tyndale, 1999); and *Kingdoms in Conflict* (William Morrow, 1987).

40. Thimmesch, "Politicians and the Underground Prayer Movement," *Los Angeles Times*, January 13, 1974.

41. Hefley and Plowman, *Washington: Christians in the Corridors of Power*, pp. 38–55.

42. Paul Apostolidis, *Stations of the Cross*: Adorno and Christian Right Radio (Duke University Press, 2000), p. 151.

43. Kandy Stroud, "Chuck Colson: Reflections Before Prison," *Women's Wear Daily*, July 1, 1974.

44. Collection 275, BGCA.

45. Apostolidis, *Stations of the Cross*, p. 151.

46. Lindsay, *Faith in the Halls of Power*, p. 59.

47. Colson to Coe, November 20, 1980, folder 8, box 368, collection 459, BGCA.

48. Apostolidis, *Stations of the Cross*, p. 150.

49. Howard Gillette, Jr., *Between Beauty and Justice: Race, Planning and the Failure of Urban Policy in Washington, D.C.* (Johns Hopkins University Press, 1995), p. 153.

50. No signature to Coe, April 1, 1960, folder 10, box 135, collection 459, BGCA.

51. Julia Rabig, "'Black Buffers': Evangelical Entrepreneurship Meets Black Power on the Streets of Washington, D.C.," unpublished paper presented at the 2004 University of Pennsylvania Graduate Humanities Forum.

52. Ibid., p. 19.

53.   Interview with John Staggers, "How to Eat an Elephant," *HIS*, November 1981. *HIS* was a men's magazine published by the Inter-Varsity Christian Leadership.

54.   Flo Conway and Jim Siegelman, *Snapping: America's Epidemic of Sudden Personality Changes* (Stillpoint Press, 2005), p. 32.

9. *JESUS + 0 = X*

1.   Abram to Frank McLaughlin, February 14, 1968, folder 1, box 168, collection 459, BGCA.

2.   Kathy Kadane, "U.S. Officials' Lists Aided Indonesian Bloodbath in '60s," *Washington Post*, May 21, 1990.

3.   Wilkes, "Prayer," *New York Times*, December 22, 1974.

4.   Senator B. Everett Jordan, "Personal and Confidential Memo" to members of Congress on Family assets around the globe, April 1969, folder 2, box 363, collection 459, BGCA. Marpaung's contribution to the murderous crackdown is even celebrated by some evangelicals. "The story of Indonesian revival is an illustration of God's sovereignty," reads the subheading over an account of Marpaung's speech on an evangelical website, http://members.aol.com/the waycm/revival/asia.html, accessed July 20, 2007.

5.   Hatfield to Nixon, November 11, 1969, folder 5, box 584, collection 459, BGCA.

6.   Shortly after that meeting, Moorer, convinced that Nixon was soft on communism, began an espionage operation against the president's civilian advisers, "a hanging offense," in the words of the Pentagon investigator who uncovered the plot. "Don't tell Laird," Nixon instructed his attorney general as he considered prosecuting Moorer. James Rosen, "Nixon and the Chiefs," *Atlantic*, April 2002.

7.   Coe to Korry, October 10, 1970, folder 36, box 194, collection 459, BGCA. *Korry and the October 1970 Plot*: Gregory Palast, "A Marxist Threat to Cola Sales? Pepsi Demands a U.S. Coup. Goodbye Allende. Hello Pinochet," *Observer* (UK), November 8, 1998. Korry, to his very minor credit, opposed a military coup because he did not think it would work. The CIA-backed murder of Allende's defense minister that month seemed to bear out his point. The Chilean people rallied round Allende. But in 1973, Kissinger and General Pinochet, to Chile's lasting sorrow, proved him wrong. I could find no

record of Fellowship contact with Pinochet. They had long been allied with a right-wing civilian faction called the "Officialists," headed by Hector Valenzuela Valderrama, a conservative Catholic politician whom Coe and Korry shopped around in Washington in 1969 as an Allende alternative. "The Majority Leader of the Congress, with whom you visited, called me the other day," Coe wrote Valderrama. "He again expressed an interest in the ideas that you and he discussed. I think in the months to come such ideas can be pursued in private discussions and someday perhaps come to pass." Correspondence, Coe, Korry, and Valderrama, February–June 1969, folder 35, box 194, collection 459, BGCA. "The sun is just now beginning to shine again": Valderrama to Coe, December 21, 1973, box 194, BGCA.

8. Tape 109, January 4, 1971, titled "Family Night at Fellowship House during which "Sam Cram," Douglas Coe, and Clif Robinson gave reports on their recent trip to Japan, South Korea, South Vietnam, India, Hong Kong, Philippines, Thailand, Singapore, Indonesia, Turkey, and the Soviet Union to visit leaders in those countries," collection 459, BGCA.

9. B. Everett Jordan to members of the U.S. Senate and House of Representatives involved with the Presidential and Congressional Prayer Breakfasts, October 1970. "Mr. Howard Hardesty, Executive Vice President of Continental Oil company, recently traveled to Indonesia where he met for a day with men in the leadership groups there. He also had dinner with President Suharto and Members of the Indonesian Cabinet. The sense of spiritual relationship which was formed caused Mr. Hardesty to comment, 'This is one of the greatest days of my life.'" Folder 8, box 548, collection 459, BGCA.

10. *McClure:* Jordan to members of Congress involved with the Prayer Breakfasts, 1970, folder 2, box 362, collection 459, BGCA. *"Confidential" prayer:* Jordan to members of Congress, undated, in reference to 1970 National Prayer Breakfast, folder 5, box 584, collection 459, BGCA.

11. Elgin Groseclose to Clifton J. Robinson, November 28, 1972, folder 6, box 383, collection 459, BGCA.

12. Clifton J. Robinson to Elgin Groseclose, December 1, 1972, ibid.

13. From a 2005 interview with the Reverend Rob Schenck, president of Faith and Action, a small, Coe-style ministry with headquarters across from the U.S. Supreme Court.

14. Locke's remarks are found on p. 19 of "Trip to the [illegible] and Sermon by Doug Coe," circa 1988, National Prayer Breakfast, no box number, collection 459, BGCA.

10. INTERESTING BLOOD

1. Max Blumenthal, "God's Country," *Washington Monthly*, October 2003. Eyal Press's *Absolute Convictions: My Father, a City, and the Conflict that Divided America* (Henry Holt, 2006) is the definitive account of the Buffalo abortion wars and the murder of Barnett Slepian.

2. Hillary Clinton, *Living History* (Simon and Schuster, 2003), p. 168.

3. Interview with Tony Hall, August 30, 2006, by Meera Subramnian. Hall recently published a book (coauthored by Tom Price) with the evangelical publisher Thomas Nelson titled *Changing the Face of Hunger: One Man's Story of How Liberals, Conservatives, Democrats, Republicans, and People of Faith are Joining Forces to Help the Hungry, the Poor, the Oppressed* (2006). In it, Hall repeatedly refers to a figure who connects him with Republican members of the Family as "our mutual friend." Hall puts the connections to good effect, genuinely pursuing a foreign policy more oriented toward the problem of hunger. But his emphasis on religious freedom—and his disinterest in systemic economic critiques—persistently guides him toward worthy but sentimental projects of limited effect, or worse, actively depoliticizing local organizations.

4. As Marcos "disappeared" his opponents in the mid–1970s, the Family moved a full-time operative to Manila. In 1975, Marcos hosted his first Presidential Prayer Breakfast, with Coe and Senator Hughes as guests. The event's organizer, Bruce Sundberg, was blunt about his interest in the worst elements of Filipino politics: "that is where the wealth is," he wrote to his financial supporters in America. Sundberg didn't want it for himself, but he believed in a trickle-down fundamentalism. Win a "top man" for the faith, and the lesser people—those without money, those without power—will fall into line. Sundberg, general letter, October 17, 1975. Sundberg's salary was paid in part by such a top man, Filipino senator Gil Puyat, one of Marcos's financiers, who put $14,285 in a trust for Sundberg, according to a letter to Sundberg from Coe dated June 10, 1975, ibid. Puyat's financial support for the Marcos regime is documented in John T. Sidel's *Capital, Coercion and Crime: Bossism in the Philippines* (Stanford University Press, 1999), p. 74. Another top man cultivated by Sundberg was Butch Aquino, the son of Benigno Aquino, the opposition hero murdered by Marcos. The younger Aquino, Sundberg wrote to Coe on September 25, 1976, was "moving more and more to the 'left'" until Sundberg gave him a copy of Chuck Colson's *Born Again*, which persuaded him

not to join the anti-Marcos rebels. All Sundberg correspondence is located in folder 13, box 475, collection 459, BGCA.

5.   The Family's role in U.S.-Somali relations is documented in extensive correspondence in folders 18–24, box 254, collection 459, BGCA.

INTERLUDE

1.   Michael Denning, *The Cultural Front: The Laboring of American Culture in the Twentieth Century* (Verso, 1997).

11. WHAT EVERYBODY WANTS

1.   The stories of individual believers related in this chapter were gathered during two reporting trips to New Life Church, the first in January 2005, and the second in April 2005. Between these visits I corresponded with some of the members of the church. Where I draw from sources other than interviews conducted during this period, I'll provide additional notes.

2.   Pastor Ted Haggard, the former leader of New Life, has since disputed that the location of the Air Force Academy was a consideration, in contradiction of information provided me by church representatives.

3.   Cara Degette, "All the President's Men," *Colorado Springs Independent*, November 13, 2003.

4.   This account of Pastor Ted's founding of New Life is drawn from personal interviews and Pastor Ted's *Primary Purpose: Making It Hard for People to Go to Hell From Your City* (Charisma House, 1995). The missionary in question, Danny Ost, is the son of Joseph Ost, a longtime collaborator of the Fellowship's on African work. In 1965, Joseph Ost went to work full-time for the Fellowship "behind the scenes" in West Africa. Ost introduced Doug Coe and Gustav Adolf Gedat, then in the late stages of his West German political career, to senior Ivory Coast and Liberia government officials. (Coe to Vittoria Vaccari, December 1965, folder 1, box 362, collection 459, BGCA. Coe to Gedat, December 30, 1965, folder 11, box 219, collection 459.) Coe included short reports of Ost's involvement—including his meetings with African heads of state—in November/December 1965, and April/May 1966 "confidential" briefings he prepared for congressional members of the Fellowship.

(Folder 2, box 362, and folder 19, box 449, collection 459, BGCA.) This is, of course, not evidence of any organizational connection between Haggard and the Family; rather, it is simply an illustration of the small world of American fundamentalism's elites.

5.　In *Primary Purpose*, Haggard writes of confronting men outside a gay bar he'd discovered with one of his associate pastors. "Two days later, I had a meeting scheduled with one of the men in the church. On my way there, I had to go near the intersection where the bar was located and wondered how many cars would be in the parking lot of that bar in the middle of the day." After observing for a while, Ted spotted a member of his church. Ted jumped out of his car. "'Jesus sent me here to rescue you,'" he called. His friend got into Ted's car and cried while Ted ministered to him. See pp. 107–8.

6.　Ibid., p. 26.

7.　Ibid., p. 33.

8.　Ted Haggard, *Dog Training, Fly Fishing, and Sharing Christ in the 21st Century* (Nelson Books, 2002), p. 9.

9.　Ibid., p. 48.

10.　The first populist church to successfully adopt the cell structure was not American, but South Korean, the work of Pastor Paul Cho, who built a congregation of nearly eight hundred thousand, the largest single church in the world, using a cell-group structure that thrived under that nation's Cold War authoritarianism. Steve Brouwer, Paul Gifford, and Susan D. Rose, *Exporting the American Gospel: Global Christian Fundamentalism* (Routledge, 1996), p. 2.

11.　Haggard, *Primary Purpose*, p. 160. Pastor Ted is aware that his martial plans alarm some outsiders; in *Primary Purpose* he also writes that when he began his campaign for Colorado Springs, "spiritual warfare was not a popular subject . . . I didn't speak publicly about my own experiences" (p. 32). Even in his more mainstream position atop the NAE, Ted's belief in less than full disclosure persisted. When the evangelical journalist Ayelish McGarvey asked Pastor Ted in 2004 why President Bush, as a Christian, had not apologized for the false assertions used to justify the Iraq War, or for the dishonest smears marshaled on his campaign's behalf, Ted said: "I think if you asked the President these questions once he's out of office, he'd say, 'You're right. We shouldn't have done it.' But right now if he said something like that, well, the world would spin out of control! . . .

Listen, I think [we Christian believers] are responsible not to lie, but I don't think we're responsible to say everything we know." (McGarvey, "As God Is His Witness," *American Prospect* online edition, October 19, 2004, http://www.prospect.org/web/page.ww?section=root&name=ViewWeb &articleId=8790.

12.   William Sims Bainbridge and Rodney Stark, *A Theory of Religion* (Lang, 1987); Roger Finke and Rodney Stark, *The Churching of America, 1776–1990: Winners and Losers in Our Religious Economy* (Rutgers University Press, 1992); Rodney Stark and Roger Finke, *Acts of Faith: Explaining the Human Side of Religion* (University of California Press, 2000). Since I wrote this chapter, Stark has published a new book that signals his shift from scholarship into wholesale Christian triumphalism of a variety barely distinguishable from Pastor Ted's: *The Victory of Reason: How Christianity Led to Freedom, Capitalism, and Western Success* (Random House, 2005).

13.   Stark and Finke, Chapter 8, "A Theoretical Model of Religious Economies," in *Acts of Faith.*

14.   Haggard, *Dog Training*, p. 12.

15.   Ibid., pp. 35–39.

16.   Ibid., p. 24.

17.   Both organizations have their roots in the dubious late-nineteenth-century science of *boyology,* practiced by mostly Protestant, upper-class men concerned about the degenerative effects of "city rot," immigrants, and professional female educators on future generations of men. The Boy Scouts was the most militant of many groups that started up, but over the years, it grew soft—or maybe Christian fundamentalists grew harder in spirit. (Clifford Putney, *Muscular Christianity: Manhood and Sports in Protestant America, 1880– 1920* [Harvard University Press, 2001].) An Assemblies of God preacher named Johnny Barnes founded the Royal Rangers in 1962, blatantly copying the Scouts and adding an extra dose of scripture. It has since prospered on the conservative fringe. New Life's success with the program, though, has been a big factor in moving it toward the mainstream. The Scouts still offer a "God and Country Program," but that can't compare with the Rangers' emphasis on foreign missions, adventures that appeal to kids and fundamentalist parents alike. http://royalrangers.ag.org/.

18.   *Our City, God's Word* (International Bible Society, 2004). "Who is the 'Our' in 'Our City, God's Word' that the International Bible Society refers to?" asked Colorado Springs resident Susan Hindman in a letter published in

the November 7, 2004, *Colorado Springs Gazette*. The IBS proceeded to produce editions for two more cities, further confusing the issue.

12. THE ROMANCE OF AMERICAN FUNDAMENTALISM

1.   Anne Constable, Richard Walker, and Tom Carter, "The Sins of Billy James," *Time*, February 16, 1976.

13. UNSCHOOLING

1.   *The American Republic for Christian Schools*, second edition, by Rachel C. Larson, Pamela B. Creason, and Michael D. Matthews, is published by Bob Jones University Press (2000). Bob Jones University, perhaps the most traditional school in Christian higher education, is too elite to be representative of populist fundamentalism but too separatist and intolerant even within the faith to be part of elite fundamentalism. And yet its publishing arm, one of the biggest suppliers of evangelical textbooks, reaches far beyond the university's sphere of influence. I first learned of the press and its offerings in 2005 at Mac-Dowell, an artists' colony in New Hampshire, as a group of writers and artists were discussing the texts they'd read as schoolchildren. One, Michelle Aldredge, had us all beat, with quick recall of an impressive sample of eighteenth- and nineteenth-century American literature, from Jonathan Edwards to Walt Whitman. What kind of amazing school had she attended? An evangelical academy, where she'd studied Dr. Raymond St. John's two-volume *American Literature for Christian Schools*. I ordered Bob Jones University Press's 2003 teachers' edition of the text and soon realized that my secular public school education had failed to provide me an adequate grounding in American literature. Dr. St. John's text offered excerpts from writers I didn't encounter until college or behind. On the other hand, students were advised to ponder how much better the already-great Melville could have been had he not been a pagan.

2.   MacArthur did more than that, according to the historian Lawrence S. Wittnew: "Despite the official policy of religious freedom and separation of church and state in occupied Japan . . . General Douglas MacArthur openly and actively assisted the propagation of the Christian faith . . . Christianity

and democracy were closely tied in MacArthur's opinion, and during the Cold War period he looked to Christianity as a major weapon against Communism in Japan." That weapon took the form of a campaign to bring thousands of missionaries into Japan and distribute 10 million Bibles. Christianity didn't take, but it's possible that it did help blunt the powerful postwar appeal of Japanese leftism. "MacArthur and the Missionaries: God and Man in Occupied Japan," *Pacific Historical Review* 40, no. 1 (1971): 77–98.

3. Douthat's article, published to mild fanfare in the August/September 2006 issue of *First Things*, missed the lengthy and admiring obituary published by the magazine just five years previous, William Edgar's August/September 2001 tribute, "The Passing of R. J. Rushdoony," in which Edgar eulogized him as "a man of extraordinary brilliance possessing an almost encyclopedic knowledge of human affairs," and recalled with fondness his early study of Rushdoony at Francis Schaeffer's L'Abri. Schaeffer, we are told by the respectable Right, took only Rushdoony's most civilized ideas. Which is to say, he narrowed Rushdoony's rage down to abortionists, writing in the early 1970s of abortion as symbolic of all of secularism and thus the front line in a battle between good and evil that justified breaking laws. Some fans took action, burning and bombing hundreds of abortion clinics and shooting several doctors. See Press, *Absolute Convictions* (Henry Holt, 2006).

4. Quoted in John Bolt, *A Free Church, A Holy Nation: Abraham Kuyper's American Public Theology* (William B. Eerdmans, 2001), p. 21. Bolt, a fellow with the fundamentalist Family Research Council, is at the forefront of a broad attempt to claim Kuyper as a forebear of radical Christian conservatism, part of the long-term project of constructing an intellectual history for a religious tradition that has long eschewed intellectualism.

5. The historian James D. Bratt argues for the progressive interpretation of Kuyper in his edited *Abraham Kuyper: A Centennial Reader* (William B. Eerdmans, 1998). "Kuyper was and was not a Protestant 'fundamentalist,'" writes Bratt. "He *was* in a manner: a militant in all things, including his anti-Modernism . . . He did not try to eradicate history, but grow from it" (p. 3). In responding to an early draft of this chapter, Bratt noted that while Rushdoony and other contemporary fundamentalists—notably Chuck Colson—may have thought they were Kuyperians, their rejection of Kuyper's pluralism and socialist inclinations puts them directly at odds not only with Kuyper's writing, which is open to interpretation, but with the historical evidence, in the Dutch state, of Kuyper's intentions. Kuyper, he argues,

would have rejected the flattened perspective implied by a fundamentalist *biblical worldview.*

6.   James I. Robertson, Jr., *Stonewall Jackson: The Man, the Soldier, the Legend* (Macmillan, 1997), p. xiii. This is by far the best of the Stonewall biographies, of interest even if the reader has no Confederate sympathies. I used it as verification for the claims made by less responsible fundamentalist Stonewalliana.

7.   Like the Family, Christian Embassy prefers to keep a low profile, but on November 2, 2005, I obtained an interview with Christian Embassy's chief of staff, Sam McCullough. McCullough's main business is explaining the Bible's position on contemporary concerns to congressmen—Brownback among them, as well as Family members Senator James Inhofe and Senator John Thune; and former representative Tom DeLay, "about 80 members of Congress . . . in our rotation," McCullough told me. Christian Embassy also believes it has a special calling in the Pentagon, explaining the Bible's view on war, for example—it's "all throughout the Bible," points outs McCullough—to a group of forty senior officers.

8.   Diamond, *Roads to Dominion*, 1995, p. 173.

9.   It works: An elegant booklet that accompanies the DVD is filled not just with the testimonies of generals and congressmen, but also with those of foreign diplomats declaring Washington a sort of holy city. "The most important thing since coming to Washington from my communist-dominated society is that I have discovered God," writes a "European ambassador," thanking Christian Embassy. Fijian ambassador Pita Nacuva, reports the booklet, following his "years of spiritual training in Washington, D.C.," reconfigured his country's schools "on the model of Jesus Christ" using an American Christian curriculum designed for developing nations, currently exported to around forty countries.

10.   After I first wrote about Christian Embassy in 2006, Mikey Weinstein, a former air force lawyer and Reagan White House counsel, reviewed its video and saw not just bad theology but also a potential violation of military regulations regarding separation of church and state. Moreover, with his son—a recent graduate of the Air Force Academy—headed for Iraq, Weinstein worried that the video functioned as almost made-to-order Al Qaeda propaganda. After all, how hard would it be to convince a potential Al Qaeda recruit that the United States is fighting a Christian crusade when U.S. generals and Department of Defense officials say so in so many words? A similar concern

arose around one of the Christian witnesses in the video, Major General Peter U. Sutton at the Office of Defense Cooperation in Turkey. When news of his participation in the video hit the Turkish press following my article (one Turkish paper characterized Sutton as a member of a "radical fundamentalist sect"), his Turkish counterpart demanded to know why he had appeared in the video, undermining their trust in him.

Weinstein's organization, the Military Religious Freedom Foundation, pressed the Pentagon for an investigation, and on July 20, 2007, the Department of Defense Inspector General issued Report. H06L102270308, "Alleged Misconduct by DOD Officials Concerning Christian Embassy," which found that seven top officers had violated military ethics by participating in the video in uniform, that the Pentagon chaplain had obtained approval by "mischaracterizing the purpose and proponent of the video," and that his office had authorized contractor badge status to Christian Embassy employees, allowing them access to restricted areas. Most disturbing of all was the defense offered by one officer: Christian Embassy, he believed, was a "quasi-federal entity." The full text of the report is available at the Military Religious Freedom Foundation's website, http://militaryreligiousfreedom.org.

11.   Ted Haggard appropriated King's words at the August 14, 2005, "Justice Sunday II" televised forum organized by the fundamentalist Family Research Council. Haggard invoked King, alongside famed civil rights champions Tom DeLay and Phyllis Schlafly, as part of a call for the kind of right-wing judges who'd undo *Brown v. Board*. And in *Tempting Faith: An Inside Story of Political Seduction* (Free Press, 2007), former Bush faith-based official David Kuo tells of drawing on King as he wrote a pivotal speech for the former Christian Coalition leader Ralph Reed, in which Reed claimed that the Christian Right was a victim of discrimination. "I was fighting my own little civil rights battle," writes Kuo (p. 67).

12.   There are an increasing number of scholarly sources on the Jesus people movement, but far more entertaining and revealing are two memoirs by participants. Charles Marsh, a historian, contextualizes the Jesus people in the strife of southern race relations in *The Last Days: A Son's Story of Sin and Segregation in the New South* (Basic Books, 2001), while the music writer Mark Curtis Anderson evokes the strange mix of rock and roll and piety that thrilled him as a child in *Jesus Sound Explosion* (University of Georgia Press, 2003).

14. THIS IS NOT THE END

1.   Quoted in Lew Daly, *God and the Welfare State* (Boston Review/MIT Press, 2006), p. 33.

2.   Michael Hardt and Antonio Negri, *Empire* (Harvard University Press, 2000), p. xiv.

INDEX